WORLD OF CRICKET 1980

Edited by
TREVOR BAILEY

Compiled by
BILL FRINDALL

QUEEN ANNE PRESS
MACDONALD AND JANE'S, LONDON AND SYDNEY

Unless otherwise credited, all pictures were supplied by Patrick Eagar

Editing and design by Graeme Wright

Front cover: Captains victorious – Brian Rose of Somerset (left) and Keith Fletcher of Essex.
Back cover: West Indies have retained their world title, defeating England at Lord's by 92 runs, and Clive Lloyd holds aloft the Prudential Cup for their jubilant supporters.

© Queen Anne Press
Published by
Queen Anne Press, Macdonald and Jane's Publishing Group Limited,
Paulton House, 8 Shepherdess Walk, London N1 7LW
Photoset in Times by Woolaston Parker Ltd, Leicester
Printed and bound by Butler and Tanner, Frome

CONTENTS

FOREWORD FROM SCHWEPPES LIMITED

In a period of cricket turmoil, Trevor Bailey's *World of Cricket* continues its high tradition of excellence. Schweppes, as sponsors of the County Championship, are pleased to be associated with this prestigious publication for the third time.

The summer of 1980 should be an exciting season, with the arrival of the West Indies and Australia, one can only hope that the weather matches the quality of the cricket.

The prize-money for the Schweppes Championship has been increased, so that nearly 25 per cent of the total sponsorship money actually goes to the players. If we want to attract the best players, and ensure the prestige of the most important competition, then the prize-money must reflect this status.

We, with everyone, players, umpires, and spectators alike, look forward to another enjoyable season.

Wynn Price-Davies
Managing Director
Schweppes Limited

EDITORIAL

The 1979 season proved to be an exceptionally interesting one for both international and domestic cricket. The majority of the minor cricket-playing countries of the world came to England to take part in the first ICC Trophy competition, which gave a considerable boost to the game. Sri Lanka, who went on to win the Trophy as expected, qualified to take part in the Prudential World Cup, as did, rather surprisingly, Canada. Sri Lanka already have a number of first-class players, and if they possessed a stronger attack would not be all that far removed from Test match status.

West Indies, under Clive Lloyd, retained the Prudential World Cup by beating England in the final at Lord's before a capacity crowd. Pakistan went down to West Indies in a memorable semi-final which contained the best batting of the competition, and New Zealand came close to beating England in the other. A Packerless Australia were disappointing, while India's defeat by Sri Lanka showed that they have yet to come to terms with the needs of limited-overs cricket. In the four-Test series that followed, the insipid Indian attack failed to provide an adequate trial for the suspect England batting and Mike Brearley won the series. However, in the final Test at The Oval, Sunil Gavaskar played the innings of the season and almost steered the tourists to an impossible victory on the last day.

The Australian Board of Control, in serious financial difficulties, made peace with, or capitulated to, World Series Cricket. In doing so, they gave Kerry Packer what he has always wanted – cricket on his television channel and permission to market a cricket spectacular. The TCCB were asked to participate in an entirely new style of double tour which contained only three Anglo–Australian Tests, less first-class and up-country cricket than usual, and a limited-overs triangular tournament involving Australia and West Indies.

Although the itinerary for this new venture was badly put together, the TCCB, subject to certain reservations, agreed to send a full England team and cancelled their previous arrangements. In addition to helping the Australian Board, the tour also provided good financial rewards for the players, even if these were inevitably not as substantial as the participants would have liked. The TCCB also refused to put up the Ashes, which automatically led to adverse criticism from Australia. To make matters worse, the financial terms were not agreed until after the team had been selected and, quite incredibly, the England party found themselves quibbling over the playing conditions *after they had actually arrived in Australia.* This was utterly nonsensical. These should obviously have been agreed before.

In spite of the cessation of hostilities between WSC and the ICC, there were still plenty of problems, and there is no doubt that international cricket will never quite be the same again. The costs have risen alarmingly as a result of increased rewards for the players, but the money available for the betterment of the game has decreased, and the power of the ICC is greatly reduced.

The eventual outcome of the four domestic competitions can only be described as unique. Those two perpetual bridesmaids, Essex and Somerset, both 'came good' and carried off all the trophies between them; Essex winning the Schweppes Championship and the Benson and Hedges Cup, and Somerset capturing the Gillette Cup and the John Player League. Essex won in fine style and with a broad smile, while Somerset, after the disappointments of 1978, showed they were the best limited-overs team in the land.

Other counties with good reason to be well satisfied with the summer were Worcestershire, for whom Younis Ahmed proved an outstanding investment, Surrey, who would have done even better but for injuries, and Northamptonshire, whose fine batting largely camouflaged their fragile attack. However, they were not the only club with limited bowling resources, for the overall standard of bowling among the counties was lower than at any period since the forties. In these circumstances, it was frustrating that many of the young batting hopefuls failed to blossom forth. Yorkshire fielded splendidly and bowled well, but their young batsmen were disappointing.

The three clubs who will most want to forget 1979 were Glamorgan, for whom it was an almost continual disaster, Warwickshire, and Lancashire, who once again failed to play to their considerable potential. But Nottinghamshire gave evidence that they have improved, and barring injuries could well be a serious threat this summer.

Individually, the player of the season was John Lever, who was first to take 100 wickets and played such a major part in Essex's successes. Boycott, after his unhappy experiences in Australia, was back to his very best and finished with a batting average of over a hundred. Procter's performances for Gloucestershire showed that he is still a world-class all-rounder, and Garner, with his steep bounce, was generally reckoned to be the most difficult bowler to face.

In conclusion, I would like to thank Bill Frindall, the walking talking human cricket computer for the statistics, Patrick Eagar for the photographs, Alan Lee for his summary of domestic cricket, Wendy Wimbush for tidying up the loose ends, and Graeme Wright for retaining his sanity while the book was assembled. My grateful thanks are also due to our sponsors for their generosity.

T.E.B.

SUMMER OF '79

April

21   The 1979 first-class season opens at Lord's on a cold, dark, damp day, when MCC meet the reigning champions, Kent. Johnson and Knott, a useful seven and eight in a county batting line-up, rescue Kent from disaster; Knott's first appearance for Kent since he joined WSC. Meanwhile Essex, still never having won an honour, limber up at Fenner's in an effort to rectify this matter.

22   Although the seamers move the ball about, Gower, with 66, makes batting look easy for MCC.

24   The Australian Board of Control gives Kerry Packer the exclusive rights to televise official Tests on Channel 9. This should mark the end of the war, which has certainly harmed international cricket but has, conversely, benefited international players. Negotiations about what will happen to WSC in Australia now taking place, with Packer holding all the aces for the forthcoming winter. He is in a much stronger position than the Australian Board, who are in financial trouble and several light years behind in marketing terms.

26   Commercial Union Assurance announce a new £40,000 cricket sponsorship, which includes an Under 16 county championship and is designed to improve and encourage youth cricket. A medal and video-tape recorder are also to be given each month to the best Under 23 player in county cricket. There are now so many awards that the market is flooded. Awaited with interest is the award to the only county cricketer not to receive an award in the season; he could take some finding!

27   Glamorgan beat Oxford University to record their first victory under their surprise-choice new captain, Robin Hobbs, formerly with Essex and retired from the first-class game for several seasons.

28   The commencement of the Benson and Hedges Cup zonal action in November football weather. No play takes place in three matches but Minor Counties (North) annihilated by Kent, who dismiss them for 67 in 45.5 overs and knock off the runs in under 30 overs for the loss of one wicket.

29   The start of the John Player League. Northamptonshire beat Sussex, thanks largely to a splendid 75 not out from Willey. Essex in second gear still too much for an unimpressive Warwickshire. No play in three matches.

30   Northants follow yesterday's victory with another over Sussex and again chase a total; this time Lamb, with sensible support from Cook, is the main contributor. Derek Randall needs stitches in his hand during Notts' unfinished game with Middlesex.

May

1   Three days still not sufficient to complete the one-day match between Middlesex and Notts. The former declared the winner on a faster run-rate.

2   Snow, sleet and rain welcome the Schweppes Championship. Snow halts play at Middlesbrough, where Lumb scores first century of the season. No play is possible at Lord's, Hove, Trent Bridge and Derby.

A remarkable incident occurs at Worcester, where the roller's starting-handle was literally rolled into the pitch on a length. Although Turner is prepared to accept it as an unnatural hazard, Rose objects and a new wicket is cut.

3   The Tories top 300 to gain bonus points in a convincing defeat of Callaghan's team, despite a fine all-round personal performance by Labour's captain.

A 113-minute century by Turner takes Essex from 129–5 to 304–7 dec. in 90 overs to give the Championship runners-up the edge over Kent, the holders.

Cec Pepper, after 15 years as a first-class umpire, resigns as a protest against the TCCB's system of appointing officials for the big, and best paid, matches. He complained, with some justification: 'Umpiring at the top now is full of comedians and gimmicks.'

4   The most dramatic moment is when Essex lose 8 wickets for 26 in their second innings against Kent, to finish 49–9; but the best writing comes from John Mason in the next day's *Daily Telegraph* on Rowe: 'His innings began at 1.55 p.m. on Thursday; significantly, by the time Rowe – having steered Kent to 250–8 – trooped off late yesterday afternoon, the

Refreshing the parts that . . . Time out for umpires Constant and Meyer.

possible at Bradford and Southport; just three days' expenses for a one-day game.

8   Still no play at Bradford. Warwickshire declared the winners over Lancashire on the grounds of a 0.75 faster run-rate. Not enough overs had been bowled in the Yorkshire v Notts game to operate the faster scoring system, so both teams share a point.

The Benson and Hedges Cup competition began in 1972. About time the TCCB realised that cricket cannot afford to allocate three days for a one-day game in the zonal stages of this very untidy competition. It is also not essential; the John Player League manages. They might also have appreciated that the chances of bad weather are highest in April and early May! Rain harms all forms of cricket, but the limited-overs game with the two-day back-up is especially vulnerable. There are times when a limited-overs game is a disaster when it limps into a second or a third day.

9   The England captain scores 73, three runs more than his top score last summer. Boycott hits 151 not out against Derbyshire, Roope produces an outstanding innings for Surrey, and Briers, a name to watch, demonstrates that Gower is not the only good young prospect in Leicestershire.

Charlie Palmer, chairman of the ICC, and two other officials from England have met in Melbourne to discuss a proposed World Cup on Kerry Packer lines; and certainly on his television channel. This will mean rearranging what would have been a bitty tour to India, Australia and New Zealand, the only justifications of which were: (1) It helped Australia, reeling under the onslaught by WSC; (2) India already have enough Test cricket; (3) It would provide the England players with a large amount of money, thus ensuring they do not fall for the temptations of WSC.

10   No play in any of the county matches, apart from at Lord's, where there is a little.

11   Little or no play again the order of the day, but Somerset rout Northants, suggesting that they are Championship material. A splendid all-round performance from Somerset's all-rounder Marks – 76 not out and 6–32.

12   Benson and Hedges Cup: Middlesex recover from 12–2 and 60–5 to reach 178, then shoot out Kent for 73; Surrey beat Essex by seven runs, despite a splendid 72 from Fletcher; Lancashire score 244–4 to defeat Leicestershire, and Warwickshire thrash Hampshire.

13   John Player League: Greenidge makes 75, which is sufficient for Hampshire to beat Essex, for whom Gooch and Fletcher again bat well. Another impressive innings by Briers, but Gower yet to find his touch. Somerset beat

government had changed.' Hampshire's fast bowling replacement for Roberts, young West Indian Malcolm Marshall, takes seven wickets in the two Glamorgan innings to give his county their first Schweppes victory.

5   Gallant failure by Northants, batting second on a slow pitch, to make 230 against the Essex attack in the Benson and Hedges Cup. Derbyshire beat Leicestershire, suggesting that the former would still be improving, while the latter may be on the decline after those five years under Illingworth.

6   Kent and Essex, with comfortable victories over Warwickshire and Derbyshire, indicate they could both be contenders for the Sunday League title. The holders, Hampshire, go down bravely against Middlesex, but unless Greenidge clicks they have limitations.

7   An impressive 82 not out by Turner enables Worcestershire to reach 178–3 in 50 overs to beat Gloucestershire on the second day of the Benson and Hedges Cup matches. Somerset brush Glamorgan aside, but no play is

Warwickshire by four runs, with 80 from Vivian Richards, back again after injuries received during an iron-bar assault in the Caribbean.

14   A convincing seven-wicket win by Somerset over a Procterless Gloucestershire in the Benson and Hedges Cup points to them breaking their duck and capturing a title.

16   Gooch and Fletcher strike Championship centuries against Derbyshire. The Essex captain, in sparkling form and with an average in international cricket of over 40, could be pressing for a Test place if India were stronger and the Prudential Cup another type of operation. Tavaré, very much an England prospect, produces an impressive 73 for Kent against Middlesex, for whom that fine swing bowler, Selvey, captures five wickets. Botham picks up six wickets in a sustained bowl against Surrey, for whom Howarth, with 95, indicates that the Londoners are improving under new manager Micky Stewart.

17   Parker, another England prospect, completes an undefeated century before Sussex dismiss Lancashire twice on a lively pitch. Derbyshire collapse against Essex for 63 before rain ends the rout.

18   Lever makes sure there is no escape for Derbyshire, who go down by an innings and 171 runs. Northants, with their under-rated off-spinner, Willey, claiming five wickets, beat Warwickshire by an innings. Randall plays a majestic innings of 121 while his colleagues struggle unconvincingly against Leicestershire.

19   Essex register the highest-ever total (350) against Combined Universities, the largest win (214 runs), and the biggest opening partnership (223 runs) in the history of the Benson and Hedges Cup. Gooch and Lilley are the first pair of English batsmen to put on over 200 in this tournament. Yorkshire crush Kent with an impressive team display; Warwickshire complete an impressive zonal section of the competition with a thoroughly professional win over Derbyshire to claim maximum points from the four matches; the only side to achieve this feat.

20   A largely rain-ruined John Player League, but Gloucestershire win a 15-overs slosh in the slush, and Surrey scrape home in one of those unsatisfactory games decided by a faster run-rate after the number of overs was reduced.

22   The 14 associate members of the ICC plus Wales, deputising for Gibraltar, commence their competition (60 overs matches) on club grounds in the Midlands. The two most successful countries will make up the numbers

Paul Parker, with a century early in the summer, re-confirmed his class and further improved his England prospects with a not out hundred for MCC against the Indians in July.

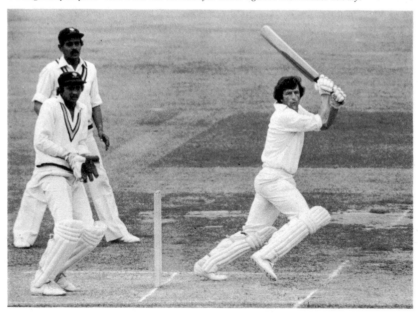

for the Prudential (World) Cup and also meet in their own final at Worcester.

23   Notts comfortably defeat Kent in the Benson and Hedges Cup but their hopes of further progress in the competition are ruined by bad weather earlier. Leicestershire go out with a flourish by beating Hampshire, and Essex win with surprising ease against Sussex. Another century opening partnership between Gooch and Lilley plays a not-inconsiderable part.

24   A black day for cricket. Rose declares the Somerset innings closed after one over, and Worcestershire knock off the run required to give them a 10-wicket victory. Although Somerset are already virtually assured of a place in the quarter-finals, this action makes absolutely sure, as it gives Worcestershire no chance of increasing their striking-rate. The statement by the Somerset captain that his action was justified – 'My first duty is to Somerset County Cricket Club' – shows a blindness which is frightening for any cricketer, let alone a skipper. He overlooks, or perhaps fails to realise, that he has several other duties. First, to cricket, and it is hardly cricket to lose deliberately. Second, to spectators, who come to see a game, not a 17-ball farce. One could say that, as a result of his action, the pre-match advertisements offend the Trade Descriptions Act. And there is a sneaking suspicion that he would not have done the same thing if the game had been played at Somerset with 4,000 people in the ground. Third, he has a duty to the other counties. By throwing the match, he displays a cynical disregard for Glamorgan, their players, and their supporters. Finally, he has a very real duty to Benson and Hedges, the sponsors.

Without them, and the other sponsors, he might not be captain of Somerset and there would not be any first-class cricket.

25   Glamorgan's match against Minor Counties (South) is abandoned, as a result of which the Welshmen fail to qualify for the Benson and Hedges quarter-finals. They would have done but for that Somerset declaration, and not surprisingly, are bitterly incensed. The Somerset president, Colin Atkinson, offers to play the match again, but fixtures make this impossible. Northants score 200, but fail by five runs to beat Surrey; a very brave try.

26   England beat Scotland 3–1 at Wembley on a sodden pitch, the Martini Golf Tournament is called off, and horse racing at Windsor is abandoned. It follows that cricketers spend most of the day in the pavilion.

27   All John Player League matches are determined on reduced overs, or by a faster scoring-rate, because of the continuing monsoon. That the present rules are unsatisfactory is underlined by the absurd finish to the Essex v Surrey game, in which Essex are deprived of victory by two balls, even though the 25 runs they scored in *9.4 overs* would have been sufficient in *10 completed overs.*

28   No play notices everywhere apart from Canterbury. The rain provides a damp welcome for the Australians, under Kim Hughes.

29   The Schweppes Championship Bank Holiday programme ends in an almost complete washout, with seven of the eight matches abandoned.

International incident in need of arbitration at Banbury during the ICC Trophy match between Papua–New Guinea and Argentina. Rain eventually stopped play and the match was drawn.

A damp greeting for the Indians, who, under the Holt Products sponsorship, are technically able to earn £100,000 if they win their 11 matches against the counties. The intention is to provide bite to these games with the tourists, which have declined in importance.

The bitter conflict between the Australian Board of Control and Kerry Packer, which sucked in all the members of the ICC, ends in Melbourne with the announcement that, in addition to securing an exclusive television contract for three years, another of Packer's companies will also promote the Board's cricket. Furthermore, the Australian players will wear the WSC badge in the limited-overs internationals. In return, Kerry Packer agrees to disband WSC and pay off his contracted players. The compromise by the Australian Board, giving Packer what he wanted, was inevitable. The Board were in serious financial trouble owing to poor receipts from the previous winter's series with England, increased costs of Test and state cricket, and the fact that the only other touring sides likely to draw large crowds in Australia – West Indies and Pakistan – had to rely on WSC players.

30 No play is again the order of the day, but at The Oval Larkins hits a memorable 93 out of a Northamptonshire total of 157 to press his claim for inclusion in England's Prudential Cup squad.

31 No play in any of the county games, and the match at Sheffield is abandoned.

June
1 Somerset are thrown out of the Benson and Hedges Cup by the TCCB by 17 votes to 1 – for bringing the game into disrepute. Somerset accept the decision and only Derbyshire vote against. They were due to meet Somerset and now take on the replacement, Glamorgan, which much increases their own chances of further advancement.

Essex go to the top of the Schweppes Championship by beating Glamorgan by nine wickets in a match restricted to one day. They claim 12 points; and McEwan finds his touch.

2 Mike Brearley hits 148 not out for Middlesex against Gloucestershire at Lord's, his first century in England since 1977. Essex race to 339–6 in only 92 overs; Hardie with a not out century and McEwan with a spectacular 88 in 116 minutes are the main contributors in a controlled demolition of a normally dependable Lancashire attack.

3 Victories by Yorkshire, Kent, Somerset and Worcestershire – and the manner in which they are obtained – suggest that the John Player title will go to one of this quartet. Gloucestershire, still up with the leaders, go down to Middlesex; unless Procter or Zaheer come off, they do not look championship material.

4 Essex take a sweet revenge on Lancashire, who had beaten them in the Sunday League the previous day, bowling them out twice and inflicting an innings defeat. Lever, strangely omitted from the England squad yet bowling better at this period than any other seamer in the country, takes 7–27. A splendid century by Wright for Derbyshire at Hove demonstrates the improvement of this New Zealander, and suggests that the Kiwis should do well in the Prudential Cup. Larkins celebrates his inclusion in the England squad with a sound 51 against Worcestershire.

5 Kent's Packer contingent – Underwood, Knott and Woolmer, all of whom were predictably ignored by the selectors – play a big part in their county's win over Leicestershire. If this attitude continues, Kent should be the side most likely to catch Essex, who have already established a large lead at the top of the table. Gifford declares at 146–6 – 148 runs behind Northants – overlooking that there was no play on Saturday and that the game was under two-day rules with a 100 runs follow-on figure. Northants promptly enforce the follow-on, but are unable to bowl Worcestershire out in 170 minutes.

6 The Benson and Hedges Cup quarter finals. Middlesex, put in on a lively green wicket at Lord's, stagger to 107 and Yorkshire, in slightly easier conditions, struggle home by four wickets. Derbyshire are too strong for Glamorgan, a Wright century helping them to a comfortable six-wicket win. Surrey, despite a fine century against them by their former player, Younis, beat Worcestershire by seven wickets in the 50th over. A brilliant 138 from Gooch, who sets the tempo, enables Essex to reach a match-winning 271, though Warwickshire, after losing their three best batsmen cheaply, do well to reach 227.

Sri Lanka, with a class batting line-up, beat Denmark, whom few expected to reach the ICC Trophy semi-finals, by 218 runs. Canada surprise all, except themselves, by fighting back with some aggressive batting from their middle order to defeat the strongly fancied Bermuda, and therefore qualify with Sri Lanka for the Prudential Cup.

9 The Prudential Cup, and four predictable results: West Indies crush India by nine wickets, Pakistan trounce Canada by eight wickets, New Zealand comfortably beat Sri Lanka by nine wickets, and England, aided by several suicidal run-outs, prove too strong for what must be the weakest Australian touring team in living memory.

Two former England players, Amiss and Denness, hit centuries, but the most impressive innings of the day was Rowe's 147 not out for Kent.

10   Kent take over the lead of the John Player League after a fine match with Northants, which they win by one run with a run-out off the last ball of the day. Somerset, clearly determined to make up for their disqualification from the Benson and Hedges Cup, sweep Gloucestershire aside. Warwickshire, like Notts, are still without a Sunday win.

11   The irrepressible Lever snaps up another six wickets, despite a masterly 72 by Davison.

12   Lever secures seven more wickets to finish with 13–117 in the match, his best-ever figures, and Essex win by 99 runs to increase their Championship lead. The only other victory is by Gloucestershire, who crush Worcestershire as a result of superb bowling from Procter, whose figures are 16.4–5–30–8.

13   The Prudential Cup is sabotaged by the weather: no play between England and Canada, and West Indies and Sri Lanka. New Zealand crush India, while Australia, confronted by a massive 286 from Pakistan, look doomed.

14   Canada are out for 45, the smallest ever total in the Prudential Cup and England just reach the target for the loss of two wickets before the rain comes down yet again. Australia are well beaten by Pakistan, and there is still no play at The Oval between West Indies and Sri Lanka. Lever grabs eight wickets, and

the headlines, against Warwickshire, and while most of the other county games are called off for the day, the sun smiles on Essex. McEwan hits 208 not out as they rattle up 393 in 97.4 overs. Reidy takes five wickets for Lancashire, who seem well placed to achieve their first Championship win.

15   Three days wasted for the West Indies v Sri Lanka game.

Essex top 100 points in the Championship to open up a 60 points gap. Leaver takes five further wickets, to finish with a career-best 13–87 against Warwickshire, and East finishes the job. While most counties have suffered from rain on waterlogged grounds. Essex – and especially Lever – have captalised on the sunshine that has followed them around and has allowed them to acquire 72 points from four matches. Lever has picked up 35 wickets in the tnonth. In the same period, no other club has won more than one match. Lancashire are still win-less as Worcestershire bring off a surprise victory after being outplayed for two days. Younis and acting-skipper Hemsley hammer 100 runs in 46 minutes, the former proving a fine investment for his new county.

16   England beat Pakistan in the Prudential Cup, thanks mainly to a magnificent spell by Hendrick on a pitch made for seam. Had Sarfraz been fit, the story might have been different. New Zealand make West Indies fight.

Underwood underlines that he still is the most effective left-arm spinner with his bowling against Gloucestershire. Reidy hits 131 not out for Lancashire, a county who possess so

Majid misreads Dymock's inswinger in the Australia v Pakistan Prudential Cup match at Trent Bridge. His dashing 61 helped set up his side's win by 89 runs.

many capable of playing a big innings yet lack consistency as a team.

17 Somerset crush Essex by nine wickets. Younis hits a rousing century in Worcestershire's five-run victory over Middlesex in a match undecided until the final ball.

18 Sri Lanka beat India in the Prudential Cup, another indication of just how ill-equipped India are for limited-overs cricket.

Kent in control against Gloucestershire; a century from Rowe, a total of 389, and six Gloucestershire second innings wickets, five of them to Underwood. A century reminder from Amiss that he is a very good batsman, though Warwickshire are clearly destined for a bad summer.

19 Somerset, starting the day with four wickets down and a lead of only 30, nearly beat Essex, thanks to a fine 90 from Marks, an unexpected 50 from Dredge, and hostile bowling from Moseley, who is able to play only when Richards or Garner is unavailable.

20 England scrape into the Prudential Cup final by nine runs against New Zealand, with two run-outs the turning factors. West Indies, with a massive 293, beat Pakistan, but not before a superb stand between Majid and Zaheer causes some panic.

Derbyshire recover from 53–6 against Essex to 258, but the England discard, Lever, picks up another five wickets. Foat, with 126, hits his first century of the season and the highest score of his career; the promising Richard Williams makes his maiden century for Northamptonshire.

21 Sri Lanka win the ICC Trophy, as expected, but Canada do well to make 264 runs. McEwan annihilates a fragile Derbyshire attack with an 85-minute century, the fastest of the summer to date, as he amasses a splendid 185, and Essex scamper to 435 in 99 overs. Centuries also from Alan Jones, Mike Harris, John Steele and Richard Lumb. Hampshire, shot out twice by the spin of Childs and Procter, lose by an innings and 42 runs.

22 Essex crush Derbyshire to set up a commanding 69 points' lead in the Championship. Lever finishes with 9–117 in the match, taking his tally of wickets for the month to more than 50. Nottinghamshire, second in the table, beat Northants in a run-chase: Harris hits his second hundred of the match; the South African, Lamb, follows up a 90 in the first innings with an undefeated hundred in the second for the losers.

23 West Indies win the Prudential Cup, defeating England in the 51st over by 92 runs. Richards and King bat brilliantly; England pay a price of 86 runs for going into the match

Collis King – West Indies' man for the moment in the Prudential Cup final.

with a non-existent fifth bowler! Confronted with a massive 286, Boycott and Brearley give the innings a sound start which lacks the required impetus. As a result, England find themselves needing to average 8 per over. The necessary charge promotes a collapse which is quicker and more dramatic than expected.

An elegant 150 by Tavaré puts Kent, the Championship pennant holders, on top against Essex, the current leaders. Yorkshire thrive at Worcester with 170 not out from Love, an 80 from Sharp, and a total of 393–4. Two Pakistanis celebrate their return to domestic cricket: Sadiq with a massive 165 against Northants and Imran with 154 not out against Hampshire.

24 In the John Player League Glamorgan enjoy a one run win over Surrey; Merry, a lively seamer, has an impressive début for Middlesex, who cruise home against Lancashire by 81 runs. Hadlee blasts out Leicestershire.

25 Imran follows up his undefeated century with 6–37 as Hampshire head for defeat. Hadlee hits Schepens in the Leicestershire–Notts Schweppes match and sends Cook to hospital; real pace unsettles even on a mild pitch.

Ian Greig, who captained Cambridge to victory over Oxford at Lord's in July.

26   Pocock produces career-best figures of 9–57 to give Surrey their first Championship win and further emphasise the number of good off-spinners in the county game. Lancashire also gain their first victory in a rain-reduced, three-declarations match. Yorkshire suffer their first defeat when Worcestershire successfully chase 329, racing home by five wickets with eight balls to spare, thanks largely to a splendidly paced 148 from Turner.

27   Lancashire follow their first Championship win by convincingly beating Essex in the Gillette Cup, recalling memories of those days when they were recognised as the one-day champions. Hampshire, without runs from Greenidge, rather surprisingly defeat Gloucesterrshire.
    Kapil Dev hits the fastest century of the season against Northants who, like Hants and Warwickshire, possess a bowling line-up with batting appeal. Somerset smash 392 in 100 overs off Worcestershire, and a Kallicharran century rescues Warwickshire.
    The ICC hear a report from the delegation that went to South Africa in the winter to report on multi-racial cricket. However favourable the report, the ICC will duck the main issue for political reasons.

28   Cook and the 21-year-old Williams hit centuries for Northamptonshire off the Indians. Butcher and Knight massacre the non-existent Warwickshire attack and race towards victory.

29   Somerset move majestically into second place on the Championship table after demolishing Worcestershire by 202 runs; Marks, an all-rounder to watch, picks up another five wickets. Warwickshire surrender tamely to Surrey as Hugh Wilson produces his best figures, 4–39, with a suggestion of real pace.
    The ICC hear the programme that the Australian Board of Control, as well as Kerry Packer and his·various companies, want next winter. As has been obvious from the moment that the Australian Board capitulated, they have given Packer what he has always wanted. They had to provide a formula with television appeal and likely to draw crowds. The obvious answer was a return of England, which provides the Australians, reinforced by their Packermen, with an excellent chance of inflicting a painful revenge. In addition, Australia will meet West Indies, most of whose players are under contract to WSC. Six Tests and a limited-overs knockout look a natural winner, and inevitably the ICC, with a few minor alterations, agree.
    If the TCCB, who certainly did not want to play three Tests in Australia during the winter, had said no, England could have been replaced by Pakistan, and would then face the problem of finding the money they were able to offer their players for the winter. Much of the power of the international boards is with the cricketers; just how much will be seen in Australia when the England, West Indian and Australian teams appreciate the extent and start exploiting the new situation.

30   India rattle up 305–3 against MCC on an easy pitch at Lord's.
    Davison continues to be the main Leicestershire run-maker, this time with 84 after an early collapse at The Oval. Another impressive century by Glenn Turner. Somerset show resilience and depth to reach 313 after being 77–5; Denning hits a century and Breakwell fifty.

July
1   Essex, who appear to have blown up in the John Player League, rout the leaders, Kent, by nine wickets. Graham Barlow supplies a timely reminder of his ability as an attacking lefthander with 114 off only 104 balls. Gloucestershire comfortably defeat Glamorgan in the televised match, which contains fine batting, excellent fielding and accomplished 'keeping. But much of the bowling can only be termed second-class – and that is being charitable!

2   MCC bat soundly. In the process Brearley, helmet encrusted which against the Indian pace attack seems rather farcical, retires mishooking a long-hop. Tavaré contributes a handsome 77; Parker, a possible future England captain, a most impressive undefeated century.

The opening partnership of 288 runs by Boycott and Lumb against Somerset is the highest since the 100 overs limitation was introduced. Wessels and Mendis plunder hundreds off Nottinghamshire, David Lloyd obtains a century for Lancashire, and the promising Holmes hits his first – but surely not his last – for Glamorgan.

David Steele resigns the Derbyshire captaincy, a strange appointment in the first place. Geoff Miller, who improved so much during the winter in Australia, takes over, but his absence on Test duty must be a handicap.

3   MCC collapse against spin in their second innings against the Indians, but hang on for a draw.

Lancashire beat Worcestershire, and David Lloyd records his second century of the match. Glenn Turner's century in this match means he has scored a hundred against all 17 first-class counties, having hit one against Worcestershire for the New Zealanders. Sadiq follows up his massive 171 in the first innings with 103 in the second against Glamorgan's limited attack.

4   Essex, fighting back after Yorkshire were 100 without loss, and Surrey, with some decisive fast bowling by Clarke, Jackman and Wilson, win through to the Benson and Hedges Cup final.

At Lord's, Surridge, a Hertfordshire player, and Ian Greig, brother of Tony, bowl Cambridge to a strong position in the 'Varsity Match as Oxford are dismissed for 97.

5   Pringle, a member of the Essex staff, hits a sparkling unbeaten 103 for Cambridge at Lord's.

6   Cambridge beat Oxford by an innings and 52 runs.

7   The day of the openers. Sadiq and Stovold both hit centuries for Gloucestershire at Southampton, Ormrod takes another off Notts, Boycott produces a typical 167 for Yorkshire against Derbyshire, Butcher scores a fine hundred and leads Surrey's recovery against Middlesex, and Denness presses for a place in the Benson and Hedges Cup final with a splendid 136 off Sussex on a lively pitch.

8   Butcher shows his partiality for the Middlesex attack with another hundred in the John Player League. Kent maintain their challenge with a convincing win over Lancashire, but Somerset stay in top spot on a faster scoring-rate against Glamorgan.

Leicestershire, shot out for 81 by the Indians, follow on and finish 42 runs behind with eight second innings wickets in hand.

9   Fine Leicestershire fight-back against the tourists to reach 372-7 declared, with Balderstone 122 not out.

Sussex struggle against Essex as Lever, strangely omitted from the England squad, captures three wickets in their first innings and a further four in the second when they follow on. He is called up as a replacement for the injured Old. Kallicharran makes 170 not out at Northampton in what has the hallmarks of a very high-scoring match. Glamorgan head for a big defeat by Somerset as Marks again impresses with his off-breaks.

10   Only three weeks ago Williams had never scored a first-class hundred, but against Warwickshire he hits his second of the match and his fourth in four games; a name to watch! Essex, with their 10-wicket victory over Sussex, stand 61 points clear at the top of the Schweppes table. Proctershire, with over 100 runs and eight wickets from him, prove too much for Hampshire. Somerset continue the chase by taking 20 points and inflicting an innings defeat on Glamorgan. Emburey makes his highest score and Radley hits a century as Middlesex force a draw against Surrey.

Mike Brearley's nose bears evidence that even helmet-encrusted batsmen suffer.

Hit me with your rhythm stick. Surrey 'keeper Jack Richards looks for help from the square leg umpire to end Graham Gooch's savage innings in the Benson and Hedges Cup Final.

11   Wessels leads a Sussex run-feast against a weakened Surrey at Hove. Essex in trouble against Nottinghamshire, thanks to Hadlee plus a competent reply by their batsmen, but the pitch is starting to take spin. Good off-break bowling by Hampshire's Cowley, who captures five wickets against Derbyshire, D'Oliveira emerges from the 2nd XI to hit a fine hundred against the Sri Lankans, and Middlesex top 400 against Yorkshire in 99 overs.

12   England meander to 318-3 in the first Test, Boycott predictably contributing an undefeated century.

Kent crash to an innings defeat against Leicestershire at Maidstone; Essex, finishing the day only 51 runs ahead of Notts with five wickets standing, could be heading for their first defeat.

13   England reach 633-5 with an undefeated double century from Gower and snatch two Indian wickets to suggest a comfortable victory in the offing.

Essex display balance, beating Nottinghamshire by 46 runs, thanks to a resolute tail and the spin of East and Acfield. Somerset, with a convincing win over Warwickshire, maintain the chase. Lumb is first to 1,000 runs in the drawn game with Middlesex. Glamorgan, despite an Ontong century, are still seeking a win.

14   India follow on.

Hampshire recover from a bad start against Yorkshire and finish the day on top. Wood and Clive Lloyd hit hundreds in a big Lancashire total against Derbyshire; centuries from the promising Briers and the bustling Tolchard upset the Championship hopes of Somerset.

15   Somerset suffer their first defeat in the Sunday League at the hands of the unpredictable Leicestershire and Kent, with an easy nine-wicket win over Surrey, go to the top. Rather surprisingly, as Greenidge fails, Hampshire beat Yorkshire, a blow to their title hopes, but Worcestershire maintain theirs with a difficult win over Sussex.

16   India lose by an innings and 83 runs, which suggests it is possible to pick at least three England teams capable of beating the tourists.

Clinton takes a hundred off his former county, Kent, for Surrey, and Howarth also reaches three figures. Nottinghamshire head for an innings win over Gloucestershire and, in this form and injury free, look like finishing in the first three.

17   Counties preach loyalty to their players, but do not always practise it themselves. Nottinghamshire replace Smedley as captain with Rice because they 'needed a different type of personality'. Why did they take quite so long to realise this? Smedley has been with the club, both as captain and player, for many years. Last summer they appointed, quite logically, Rice as skipper, then panicked when informed he had signed for WSC, promptly sacked him, and put Smedley in charge again. Fortunately, for the Nottinghamshire committee, Rice took legal action against them and was reinstated. Why did they not make Rice captain at the start of this summer, or has being a WSC player suddenly become respectable? Sacking your captain in mid-season is a strange reward for someone who has given fine service for nearly two decades.

18   The second round of the Gillette Cup. Middlesex scrape home by two wickets with seven balls to spare, despite a wonderful one-legged 87 from Greenidge. Boycott's 92 guides Yorkshire home against game Durham. With a century from Todd and Hadlee operating effectively, though injured, Nottinghamshire prove too strong for anaemic Warwickshire. Leicestershire kill Worcestershire, and the match, by making 326. Sussex struggle hard against Suffolk. Somerset with Rose again in fine form destroy Derbyshire, and Northamptonshire are too good for injury-hit Surrey.

19   Despite a remarkable hundred from Wood, who had retired injured at 24 – a result of catching Rowe on the previous day, when Kent rattled up 278-7 – Lancashire fall 19 runs short of their formidable target. The cynical not too impressed by Wood's gallantry; better theatre than cricket.

20   Lovely weather, yet no first-class cricket; and with the Benson and Hedges final on the morrow there will be little during a beautiful July week. Greig denies Brearley's revelations about him trying to sign up the whole England team last winter, though he admits having discussed the matter!

21   Essex break their duck and take the Benson and Hedges Cup. Gloucestershire in trouble against the tourists. Glamorgan batsmen gain confidence and runs at the expense of that Warwickshire attack.

22   Woolmer's 6–9 overcomes Derbyshire. and keeps Kent top of the John Player League. Another splendidly pugnacious run-chasing innings from Rose helps his side to an emphatic victory over Northamptonshire.

At one point in danger of following on against the Indians, Gloucestershire make a splendid recovery, thanks largely to the batting of Bainbridge and fiery opening spell from Procter and Brain.

Le Roux, the South African who flew to England to sign for Worcestershire, announces that he intends to join – wait for it – Sussex, whose talent for upsetting other counties is outstanding, though Lancashire run them close on occasions.

23   The Indians go down by seven wickets to Procter and Co. as the South African takes 7–13 and they slide to 117 all out.

An impressive return by Brown to Warwickshire after injury, capturing 5–23 against Glamorgan. But both teams are plainly destined for an undistinguished summer.

25   Lever's 7–40, plus an aggressive knock from Gooch, send Hampshire towards heavy defeat. Worcestershire batsmen prosper as they rattle up 413 against Surrey; a hundred from Turner while Younis again reminds his former employers of his ability with an undefeated 99. The dismissal of Middlesex for 97 at Leicester is another illustration of their strange decline. Larkins hits an impressive century against Kent at Northampton, surely the best batting pitch in the country.

26   The Indians in sight of their first victory as Bedi's spin baffles Glamorgan.

A masterful demonstration from Boycott of how to bat on a difficult pitch, making 91 not out (out of 175-5) as Yorkshire follow on. A spectacular 146 not out by Hardie underlines the all-round strength of Essex, and they surge towards another victory. Cumbes takes eight wickets for 62 on a day when Worcestershire force Surrey to follow on. A century from Roland Butcher rescues Middlesex from a two-day innings defeat.

27   Acfield and East spin Essex to a handsome victory over Hampshire. Boycott's undefeated 175 is not enough to prevent a Nottinghamshire victory. Middlesex, at one stage in danger of losing by an innings, dismiss

That man Botham strikes again: Reddy is caught behind by Bairstow. With 20 wickets against the Indians, the England all-rounder took his tally to 107 wickets in 21 Tests.

Leicestershire for 109 in their second innings to secure a famous victory by two runs – and make a nonsense of their lowly Championship position.

28   Cook, the consistent, hits a century against Sussex on that friendly Northampton pitch, but it is a different story at Colchester, where 21 wickets tumble. Essex dismiss Gloucestershire for 92, and then lose six for 36 before a rescue act from the tail takes them to the respectability of 170. After a disappointing total of 161, Kent come back to capture three cheap Nottinghamshire wickets.

29   Hampshire win by one run, largely through a record 163 by Greenidge, against Warwickshire, still without a win in the John Player League.

30   Essex make it four in a row by beating Gloucestershire in two days and take an 82 points' lead over second-placed Notts. A great day for left-armers at Folkestone, where Underwood takes 6–18 and Bore 8–89. Worcestershire, with the aid of a typical Turner century, acquire 380–7 against Leicestershire. Boycott continues to satisfy his hunger for runs with 76 against Middlesex. Williams samples the ups and downs of cricket, following a career best 5–57 by being struck for four sixes in an over by Imran Khan.

31   Northamptonshire defeat Sussex by one wicket; Underwood, with 7–35, bowls Kent to a comfortable win over Nottinghamshire. Yorkshire accept the Middlesex challenge, scoring 217 for the loss of only four wickets, and Hampshire make short work of a depleted and disheartened Warwickshire.

August
1   Neale hits a career-best 163 not out against Nottinghamshire to assist Worcestershire to a first innings total of 400–2 in 100 overs. Daniel grabs 6–38 as Essex collapse. Derbyshire fail to take advantage of a double-century opening partnership by Hill and Wright.

2   India crumple, 96 all out at Lord's with Botham and Hendrick the principal executioners.
    Yorkshire destroy Warwickshire, who follow on after being removed for a miserable 35. Although showing improvement at the second attempt, they finish the day with the opposition requiring only two runs with all their wickets in hand; Stevenson captures 6–14, a reminder of just how well he can bowl. Essex, despite an improbable five wickets by Fletcher, face their first defeat in the Schweppes Championship. Jackman routs Kent, who are destined for a heavy defeat; Sadiq and Procter take a heavy toll of the Leicestershire attack;

Imran Khan displays fine all-round form against Glamorgan who, as usual, are struggling.

3   After Boycott and Gooch go cheaply, the heavens open at Lord's.

Middlesex crush Essex; Surrey acquire their third win by 10 wickets, against Kent; Northamptonshire enjoy a comfortable victory over Derbyshire. Procter follows up his century of yesterday with 7–26, including the hat-trick, as Leicestershire are overwhelmed.

4   England take command of the second Test as they progress to 357-7, the highlight being a breathtaking 82 from Gower.

Impressive batting by Worcestershire against the leaders, Essex, includes a century from Ormrod. Warwickshire enjoy one of their few good days against Derbyshire; Larkins reminds the selectors with a century against Middlesex; Butcher and Clinton score hundreds for Surrey against Nottinghamshire, who are minus Hadlee and Rice.

5   Somerset's hopes of winning the John Player League receive a serious setback when they come badly unstuck against the unpredictable Lancashire. Meanwhile Kent go further ahead with a reasonably easy win over Sussex with that prince of 'brake' bowlers, Underwood, again showing his value. Worcestershire stay in the race with a clear-cut win over Hampshire; Warwickshire break their duck, but remain at the bottom.

6   Botham secures his 100th Test wicket in the fastest time, but India dig in. For the first time in the current series this match resembles a genuine international, with bowlers trying to dismiss good batsmen on an easy-paced pitch.

Essex catch 'timiditis' and are in danger of an innings defeat by Worcestershire. Somerset, after their setback on the previous day, gain revenge on Lancashire and assume control.

7   Centuries by Viswanath and Vengsarkar save India from defeat, and suggest that the England attack has limitations.

Essex suffer their second successive innings defeat as Worcestershire move into second place.

8   Gillette Cup quarter-finals: Garner and Botham tumble out Kent for 60 at Taunton to put Somerset through; solid Sussex overhaul Notts at Hove; Larkings hits an unbeaten 92 as Northants eliminate Leicestershire. At Lord's, Yorkshire, chasing Middlesex's 216, are in trouble at 78-3 – including Boycott run out.

9   More run outs, bad light, Edmonds and Emburey manipulate the downfall of Yorkshire.

10   Indian all-rounder Amarnath gains some useful batting practice, scoring his first century of the tour against Derbyshire in a match which died.

11   A career-best 141 not out by Edmonds rescues Middlesex from Glamorgan. Pocock

Monsoon Friday at St John's Wood makes Lord's look like a tributary of the Grand Union Canal. Next day, to the groundstaff's credit, the second Test resumed.

captures 8–61 against Hampshire, and Essex kindly provide the Indians with a pitch favouring spin. They are dismissed for 146, despite a fine innings from Fletcher, but hit back in the final session.

12   Kent suffer a setback at home to Worcestershire, who beat them by 13 runs and move to third place in the table; Somerset, in second place, keep up the pressure with an easy, Richards-inspired, win over Sussex. Larkins and Willey enjoy a double-hundred opening partnership against Leicestershire, but fail to impress the selectors sufficiently. With 100 per cent reliance on the previous winter's tourists for the third Test, the England team has that closed-shop look.

13   Younis Ahmed – what a great season he is enjoying – hits a masterly 170 to steer Worcestershire into a winning position against Kent. Selvey's swerve proves too much for Glamorgan, who are forced to follow on at Lord's.

14   A defiant 251 runs partnership between Ealham and Tavaré – both score centuries – stops Worcestershire and illustrates that their

Hard-hit hundreds and hat-tricks were a feature of Mike Procter's summer.

attack lacks the penetration to catch Essex, who are 64 points ahead with five matches to go. Somerset snatch the unlikeliest of victories with three balls to spare, although 75 minutes are lost through a wet pitch and they seemingly kill the contest by batting on into the afternoon. Sussex collapse unexpectedly to Garner for 64 and Somerset, between the showers, slog their way home. Notts, who needed 27 to win in six overs against Derbyshire, are robbed by rain and the umpires, who correctly come off but fail to reappear after the rain stops. This hardly pleases Nottinghamshire's supporters.

15   After Middlesex collapse against Hampshire's seamers, Greenidge makes batting look easy with an undefeated century out of 149–3 in reply. Dudleston and Steele amass a record opening stand of 390 for Leicestershire, against a passive Derbyshire attack without Miller and Hendrick. Woolmer and Tavaré plunder Yorkshire, while Sadiq with the bat and Procter with the ball upset Worcestershire's Championship hopes.

16   At Headingley, England slump to 80–4 against India before rain suspends play.
   A maiden century from Nick Pocock helps Hampshire to 403 against Middlesex. Alec Bedser and Ken Barrington appointed Manager and Assistant-Manager for the winter's Australian tour. As they are founder members of the present England team, such news is logical, if not especially exciting.

18   Again no play in the Headingley Test, but this time there could, and should, have been some.
   Essex, almost home, are held up by a splendid century from Peter Willey, and Glamorgan, anchored firmly at the bottom by lack of ability, are rolled over for 59 by Leicestershire.

19   Somerset shoot to the top of the Sunday League with the aid of their spinners, who are largely responsible for dismissing Middlesex for 82. Worcestershire are rather surprisingly beaten by Derbyshire, Kirsten's undefeated 91 being the decisive factor.

20   Botham blasts the Indian bowling for a spectacular hundred for England.
   At Lord's, the Middlesex attack is taken apart by a superb 156 from Vivian Richards; at Cheltenham Sadiq rattles up his seventh century of the season, against Surrey.

21   Essex beat Northants by seven wickets, bringing them 17 points. After six o'clock they know that nobody can catch them and that after 103 years, they are the champion county. A splendid finish at Cheltenham, where Surrey win off the last ball with nine wickets down. Earlier Procter had hit 5 sixes and 15 fours, scoring 102 in 76 minutes. Worcestershire, having bowled Derbyshire out in the 19th over of the last hour, find themselves requiring 25 runs in 10 minutes. The umpires inform Gifford he has four overs in which to complete the task and then, following instructions from Lord's, obtained by courtesy of Derbyshire, walk off after two overs with Worcestershire 17-1. Gifford, to put it mildly, is aggrieved.

22   Somerset beat Middlesex and Northamptonshire win a fine match against Sussex in the semi-finals of the Gillette Cup. The decisive factors are the pitch at Lord's and the batting of Lamb and Willey at Hove.

25   Boycott takes 4–14 against Lancashire, sufficient grounds for every self-respecting seamer to go out on strike. Lamb hits a spectacular 178 against Leicestershire.

26   Kent outplay Somerset to go top of the Sunday League at Taunton, where a policeman's jaw is broken and seven arrests are made in ugly, uncricket-like scenes. Glamorgan are bowled out for 42 by Derbyshire. Willey, Butcher and Bairstow come into the England squad for the fourth Test at The Oval.

27   Nottinghamshire, on a beautifully prepared 'green-top', beat the Indians by six wickets, and so share some Holt Products prize-money. No run shortage at Worcester where Younis and Kallicharran both hit undefeated centuries.

28   Essex, having been bowled out for 101, come back like true champions to dismiss Surrey for 99 and win by 15 runs. In the process Lever becomes the first bowler to capture 100 wickets in 1979. Underwood, with 8–28, destroys Hampshire; Yorkshire win a splendid Roses Match, which seemed destined for a draw, by scoring 107 in 14 overs with only three deliveries to spare.

29   Mike Brearley appointed captain for Australia with the selectors ignoring his batting record in international cricket and settling for his captaincy record, albeit against sub-standard opposition.

Warwickshire enjoy one of their rare good days; newcomer Andy Lloyd hits a maiden century, Amiss scores 130, and then the seamers snatch three Nottinghamshire wickets cheaply. The tall quickie, Robin Herkes, takes 6–60 for Middlesex on his début against Worcestershire at Lord's.

30   At The Oval, Gooch and Willey ensure a respectable England total and Botham completes the fastest-ever 'double' in Test cricket. Gifford wrecks Middlesex with 5–12 and Essex again demonstrate their recovery powers, coming within reach of the Northamptonshire total through the efforts of their rearguard and then snatching eight wickets and the initiative.

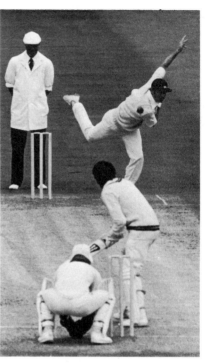

The becapped Boycott amused and bemused with his deceptive swing in 1979.

31   Botham gives a perfect reply to adverse comments from Australia's Jeff Thomson, hardly noted for knowledge, judgement or intellectual sophistication; he takes two Indian wickets and two fine slip catches.

Essex achieve their 13th Championship win of the season; Worcestershire's comfortable victory over Middlesex increases their chances of being runners-up.

September
1   England, with seven wickets still standing, extend their first innings lead to 280, without undue haste and little difficulty.

At Cardiff, Underwood gobbles up eight Glamorgan batsmen in a long, deadly spell. The swing of Lancashire's new Australian import, Malone, proves too much for Notts and brings him seven victims.

2   Warwickshire win only their second Sunday League game of the season, thanks largely to a 150 runs opening stand by Amiss and Kallicharran. Despite another Younis masterpiece, Essex beat Worcestershire with their last pair adding seven in the final over. Kent and Somerset both have emphatic victories to remain first and second respectively in the John Player League table.

3   England accumulate steadily before declaring but are unable to make any impression on the Indian opening pair.

Glamorgan sunk in two days by Kent, and the bowling of Underwood.

4   India, thanks to a masterly double-century from Gavaskar, almost make the 438 needed for victory.

The four county matches being played end as draws.

5   Hignell and Broad hit impressive centuries for Gloucestershire. Randall takes a double-hundred off Middlesex and Greenidge makes his third century of the season.

6   Sussex, inspired by a Wessels' hundred, reach 419–8 against Somerset, and Warwickshire score heavily against Kent, whose batting this year, despite Tavaré and Woolmer, has not been as fruitful as expected. Procter, after several earlier attempts, hammers the fastest century of the season in 57 minutes against Northamptonshire with two sixes and 15 fours.

7   Warwickshire crush Kent by an innings and 174 runs and Willis captures five wickets – more than he has taken in the rest of the season for his county! Yorkshire win a splendid match against Essex by one wicket. Worcestershire prove too strong for doomed Glamorgan and Sussex thrash Somerset, who are already thinking about the Gillette Cup final.

8   The batting of Richards and the bowling of Garner prove too much for Northamptonshire in the Gillette Cup final, despite an innings of class from Allan Lamb.

9   Another big celebration for Somerset and their supporters; they follow up their triumph in the Gillette Cup by beating Nottinghamshire. Roebuck's fifty plays a large part in a victory which proves sufficient to give Somerset the John Player League title when Kent fail rather miserably against Middlesex before their own supporters at Canterbury. Warwickshire go down again, this time to Yorkshire, but Glamorgan, against the odds, beat Essex at Chelmsford.

Test Match, Prudential Cup, and other Cup Final Attendances and Receipts 1979

Match		Venue	Paying Attendance	Total Attendance including Members	Gross Receipts
England v India	1st Test	Birmingham	19,414	25,000	53,000
	2nd Test	Lord's	55,361	62,086	166,057
	3rd Test	Leeds	10,835	15,382	65,794
	4th Test	Oval	32,616	36,297	97,154
	TEST MATCH TOTALS		118,226	138,765	£382,005
Prudential Cup					
England v Australia		Lord's	21,560	25,560	75,313
England v Canada		Manchester	1,268	2,268	2,330
England v Pakistan		Leeds	10,032	16,032	32,990
Other Group Matches (8)		Various	14,888	28,908	47,229
England v New Zealand	(S-F)	Manchester	12,000	20,000	45,000
Pakistan v West Indies	(S-F)	Oval	11,000	14,000	40,000
Prudential Cup Final		Lord's	21,500	26,000	117,000
	PRUDENTIAL CUP TOTALS		92,248	132,768	£359,862
Benson and Hedges Cup Final	Lord's		21,672	26,672	112,452
Gillette Cup Final		Lord's	21,741	26,741	112,072
TOTALS			253,887	324,946	£966,391

Right: As he did four years earlier, in 1975, Clive Lloyd led his formidable West Indians to victory in the 1979 Prudential Cup final.

PRUDENTIAL CUP 1979

*Left: Majid Khan cuts
Holding superbly during
his innings of 81 in the
Prudential Cup semi-final
at The Oval.
Below: A brilliant caught
and bowled by Gary
Cosier dismissed Zaheer
Abbas in the Group B
match between Australia
and Pakistan at Trent
Bridge.*

PRUDENTIAL CUP 1979

The second Prudential World Cup proved to be another outstanding success, even though the eventual outcome of West Indies winning the title for the second time, and without undue difficulty, was fairly predictable. Leaving the last two places in the two groups to be decided by the ICC Trophy was a pleasant touch and allowed Canada the opportunity of meeting the best teams in the world. The one obvious improvement would have been to seed the entire competition so that the strongest countries avoided each other in the group stage, therefore automatically increasing the chances of the best four sides meeting in the semi-finals.

On this occasion one from England, Australia and Pakistan had to be eliminated, whereas from the other group New Zealand, along with West Indies, were virtually guaranteed a semi-final spot because India were ill-equipped for limited-overs cricket, as was shown when Sri Lanka defeated them. If the ICC, or the TCCB, are afraid that they will offend countries by their seeding, all they need do is appoint an independent panel. It is not a difficult job, considerably easier than seeding for the soccer World Cup or Wimbledon, for at the moment there are only six Test-playing countries and two make-weights. The object of the organisers and the sponsors should be to reduce the likelihood of the weakest teams reaching the semi-finals, as could have been the case in 1979 if Group A had contained Australia, New Zealand and India and Group B England, Pakistan and West Indies. This line-up would have meant one of the best teams going out too soon. A fair order of merit for the Prudential teams of 1979 was West Indies, Pakistan, England, New Zealand, Australia, India, Sri Lanka, Canada.

ENGLAND IN THE PRUDENTIAL CUP

England had reason to be well satisfied with their overall performance, reaching the final and losing only one match, especially when, purely in terms of limited-overs cricket, the chosen squad could not seriously be considered the best available. One assumes that the selectors decided to reward the players who brought back the Ashes; otherwise it is hard to justify the inclusion of both Boycott and Brearley in an international batting line-up when the pace of the run-getting is vital. There was also much to be said for the inclusion of a fast-scoring wicket-keeper-batsman in a 60 overs contest rather than the admirable Bob Taylor. The omission of Lever, who has such a fine record in one-day cricket, and with 50 wickets in June did suggest reasonable form, plus the inclusion of Gatting in the squad did not make sense.

England v Australia, Lord's

England beat Australia very comfortably by six wickets with plenty of overs to spare. But the visitors contributed heavily to their own downfall by second-class batting and suicidal running between the wickets.

Having won the toss, Mike Brearley invited the Australians to take strike on a pitch which gave the seamers some assistance in the early stages. Although only 14 runs came in the first 10 overs, the bowlers did not gain any rewards until the 11th. However, the Australians, with 90 on the board for the loss of Darling, had reason to feel well satisfied with the way things were going until the introduction of England's new secret weapon, Geoff Boycott. With very gentle inswingers, the Yorkshireman proceeded to pick up two useful wickets in rather helpful conditions.

A veil is best drawn over the Australian batting and running during the afternoon when three players were run out, six wickets tumbled for 22 runs, and the team lumbered awkwardly to 159 for nine in 60 overs. This was plainly not enough, even against a team with such a frail batting line-up as England's. The usual collapse occurred – two wickets fell for five runs – but then Brearley, soundly, and Gooch, rather more eloquently, took the score to 113 before both departed in two overs to Laughlin, who had appeared the most innocuous of Australia's five bowlers. Gower and Botham then hurried towards the inevitable victory with a rush of strokes and the occasional unintentional edge.

Rodney Hogg, scourge of England's batsmen in Australia the previous winter, in action against England at Lord's. Botham, who saw England to victory, backs up.

ENGLAND v AUSTRALIA
Played at Lord's, London, 9 June
Toss: England   Result: **England** won by 6 wickets   Man of the Match: G. A. Gooch

AUSTRALIA		Runs	Mins	Balls	6s	4s
A. M. J. Hilditch	*b* Boycott	47	136	108	—	2
W. M. Darling	*lbw b* Willis	25	81	61	—	3
A. R. Border	*c* Taylor *b* Edmonds	34	96	74	—	4
K. J. Hughes*	*c* Hendrick *b* Boycott	6	12	13	—	1
G. N. Yallop	*run out (Randall)*	10	21	20	—	1
G. J. Cosier	*run out (Gower/Taylor)*	6	19	20	—	—
T. J. Laughlin	*run out (Botham/Taylor)*	8	40	22	—	—
K. J. Wright†	*lbw b* Old	6	18	15	—	—
G. Dymock	*not out*	4	22	12	—	—
R. M. Hogg	*run out (Brearley/Taylor)*	0	3	5	—	—
A. G. Hurst	*not out*	3	11	10	—	—
Extras	(*b* 4, *lb* 5, *w* 1)	10				
TOTAL	(9 wickets – 60 overs)	**159**				

ENGLAND		Runs	Mins	Balls	6s	4s
J. M. Brearley*	*c* Wright *b* Laughlin	44	169	147	—	2
G. Boycott	*lbw b* Hogg	1	11	5	—	—
D. W. Randall	*c* Wright *b* Hurst	1	4	3	—	—
G. A. Gooch	*lbw b* Laughlin	53	162	96	—	6
D. I. Gower	*not out*	22	42	30	—	2
I. T. Botham	*not out*	18	29	14	—	2
P. H. Edmonds						
R. W. Taylor†						
C. M. Old	*did not bat*					
M. Hendrick						
R. G. D. Willis						
Extras	(*lb* 10, *w* 1, *nb* 10)	**21**				
TOTAL	(4 wickets – 47.1 overs)	**160**				

ENGLAND	O	M	R	W		FALL OF WICKETS		
Willis	11	2	20	1				
Hendrick	12	2	24	0		Wkt	A	E
Old	12	2	33	1		1st	56	4
Botham	8	0	32	0		2nd	97	5
Edmonds	11	1	25	1		3rd	111	113
Boycott	6	0	15	2		4th	131	124
						5th	132	—
AUSTRALIA	O	M	R	W		6th	137	—
Hogg	9	1	25	1		7th	150	—
Hurst	10	3	33	1		8th	153	—
Dymock	11	2	19	0		9th	153	—
Cosier	8	1	24	0		10th	—	—
Laughlin	9.1	0	38	2				

Umpires: D. J. Constant and B. J. Meyer   *Captain   †Wicket-keeper

England v Canada, Old Trafford

Canada, who did so well to qualify for the Prudential Cup by their performances in the ICC Trophy competition, proved as expected no match for England. Heavy rain unfortunately dragged what was a non-event into the second, and very nearly the third, day. There was no play at all on the scheduled Wednesday.

Canada began batting on Thursday morning on a pitch giving seam bowlers some help and were bowled out for 45 in 40.3 overs. Dennis, who by his approach had obviously learned his cricket in the Caribbean, was top scorer with 21 and the only Canadian to reach double figures. He produced several aggressive strokes and was eventually out hit wicket, trying unsuccessfully to negotiate a short ball from Willis.

After further delay through rain, England began their innings at seven o'clock and again managed a collapse – 11 for two – but Gooch ensured that proceedings would not be continued on the morrow by producing several spectacular blows.

ENGLAND v CANADA

Played at Old Trafford, Manchester, 13 *(no play)*, 14 June
Toss: Canada   Result: **England** won by 8 wickets   Man of the Match: C. M. Old

CANADA		Runs	Mins	Balls	6s	4s
G. R. Sealy	*c* Botham *b* Hendrick	3	13	9	—	—
C. J. D. Chappell	*lbw b* Botham	5	36	31	—	—
F. A. Dennis	*hit wkt b* Willis	21	116	99	—	2
Tariq Javed	*lbw b* Old	4	46	40	—	—
J. C. B. Vaughan	*b* Old	1	9	10	—	—
C. A. Marshall	*b* Old	2	11	7	—	—
B. M. Mauricette*†	*b* Willis	0	10	8	—	—
M. P. Stead	*b* Old	0	14	12	—	—
J. M. Patel	*b* Willis	1	23	14	—	—
R. G. Callender	*b* Willis	0	2	3	—	—
J. N. Valentine	*not out*	3	14	11	—	—
Extras	(*lb* 4, *nb* 1)	5				
TOTAL	(40.3 overs)	**45**				

ENGLAND		Runs	Mins	Balls	6s	4s
J. M. Brearley*	*lbw b* Valentine	0	10	10	—	—
G. Boycott	*not out*	14	58	36	—	—
D. W. Randall	*b* Callender	5	17	11	—	1
G. A. Gooch	*not out*	21	27	31	1	2
D. I. Gower						
I. T. Botham						
G. Miller						
R. W. Taylor†	*did not bat*					
C. M. Old						
R. G. D. Willis						
M. Hendrick						
Extras	(*w* 3, *nb* 3)	6				
TOTAL	(2 wickets – 14 overs)	**46**				

ENGLAND	O	M	R	W
Willis	10.3	3	11	4
Hendrick	8	4	5	1
Botham	9	5	12	1
Miller	2	1	1	0
Boycott	1	0	3	0
Old	10	5	8	4

CANADA	O	M	R	W
Valentine	7	2	20	1
Callender	6	1	14	1
Stead	1	0	6	0

Umpires: J. G. Langridge and B. J. Meyer

FALL OF WICKETS

Wkt	C	E
1st	5	3
2nd	13	11
3rd	25	—
4th	29	
5th	37	—
6th	38	—
7th	41	—
8th	41	—
9th	42	—
10th	45	—

*Captain   †Wicket-keeper

Bob Willis, too fast and accurate for the Canadians at Old Trafford, was injured against the New Zealanders on the same ground and failed to recover for the final.

England v Pakistan, Headingley

The England-Pakistan game at Headingley was a genuine thriller with fortunes constantly swaying backwards and forwards throughout an absorbing contest. The end saw Boycott and Gooch sharing the attack against the visitors' last pair because, apart from Willis with one over left, the other front-line pacemen had used up their permitted number of overs.

The match was essentially a battle between the powerful Pakistan batting – which, with Imran Khan at number 9, possessed greater class and depth than any other team in the competition – and the England attack, splendidly supported in the field. Fortunately for England the match was fought on a seam-bowling paradise, and their opponents were unfortunate to be without Sarfraz, easily their best pace bowler.

England, put in to bat in conditions in which the ball moved both in the air and off the wicket, began with their usual disaster, Brearley departing in the first over and Randall in the second. Boycott and Gooch proceeded to take the score past 50 before the former was lbw to Majid, who was not only inexpensive but also secured three key wickets on a pitch tailor-made for pace, not slow, bowling.

Gower and Botham resumed after lunch with 25 overs remaining and 98 for four on the board. Both were mystifyingly bowled by Majid; Edmonds and Old promised little and achieved nothing; and when Willis joined Taylor, England were on the floor at 118 for eight. This pair then added 43 for the ninth wicket and so gave the England bowlers something to bowl at.

Majid and Sadiq began confidently and, when they were 27 without loss, it began to look as if the devil had departed from the pitch. However, within a very short time Hendrick and Botham changed all that with a deadly spell. Disaster after disaster befell the Pakistan batsmen; the early happiness was replaced by the gloom of 34 for six. England were very much back on top, which meant that they should win the game and so avoid meeting West

Mike Hendrick – England's Man of the Match against Pakistan.

Indies in the semi-finals. The scene seemed set for the ideal final at Lord's.
Asif, with a splendidly improvised innings – easily the best of the match – had other ideas. His 51, with useful contributions from Wasim Raja, Imran Khan and Wasim Bari, took his team ever closer to that 165. Moreover, Brearley, who had quite rightly gambled everything on Hendrick snatching one more wicket, was running short of mainline bowlers and had to call on Boycott, who responded before his own crowd with five overs for 14 runs and two wickets. The England captain handled his resources with great skill, but Pakistan will think back with regret.

ENGLAND v PAKISTAN
Played at Headingley, Leeds, 16 June
Toss: Pakistan   Result: **England** won by 14 runs   Man of the Match: M. Hendrick

ENGLAND		Runs	Mins	Balls	6s	4s
J. M. Brearley*	c Wasim Bari b Imran	0	1	2	—	—
G. Boycott	lbw b Majid	18	85	54	—	2
D. W. Randall	c Wasim Bari b Sikander	1	6	5	—	—
G. A. Gooch	c Sadiq b Sikander	33	97	90	—	5
D. I. Gower	b Majid	27	51	40	—	3
I. T. Botham	b Majid	22	58	48	1	1
P. H. Edmonds	c Wasim Raja b Asif	2	25	23	—	—
R. W. Taylor†	not out	20	61	59	—	1
C. M. Old	c and b Asif	2	4	7	—	—
R. G. D. Willis	b Sikander	24	50	37	—	3
M. Hendrick	not out	1	1	1	—	—
Extras	(lb 3, w 7, nb 5)	15				
TOTAL	(9 wickets – 60 overs)	**165**				

PAKISTAN		Runs	Mins	Balls	6s	4s
Majid Khan	c Botham b Hendrick	7	29	20	—	1
Sadiq Mohammad	b Hendrick	18	38	27	—	4
Mudassar Nazar	lbw b Hendrick	0	1	2	—	—
Zaheer Abbas	c Taylor b Botham	3	23	19	—	—
Haroon Rashid	c Brearley b Hendrick	1	2	2	—	—
Javed Miandad	lbw b Botham	0	5	4	—	—
Asif Iqbal*	c Brearley b Willis	51	109	104	—	5
Wasim Raja	lbw b Old	21	51	25	—	4
Imran Khan	not out	21	113	82	—	1
Wasim Bari†	c Taylor b Boycott	17	37	33	—	2
Sikander Bakht	c Hendrick b Boycott	2	23	19	—	—
Extras	(lb 8, w 1, nb 1)	10				
TOTAL	(56 overs)	**151**				

PAKISTAN	O	M	R	W
Imran	12	3	24	1
Sikander	12	3	32	3
Mudassar	12	4	30	0
Asif	12	3	37	2
Majid	12	2	27	3

ENGLAND	O	M	R	W
Willis	11	2	37	1
Hendrick	12	6	15	4
Botham	12	3	38	2
Old	12	2	28	1
Edmonds	3	0	8	0
Boycott	5	0	14	2
Gooch	1	0	1	0

FALL OF WICKETS

Wkt	E	P
1st	0	27
2nd	4	27
3rd	51	28
4th	70	30
5th	99	31
6th	115	34
7th	115	86
8th	118	115
9th	161	145
10th	—	151

Umpires: W. L. Budd and D. G. L. Evans   *Captain   †Wicket-keeper

PRUDENTIAL CUP GROUP MATCH RESULTS

†Batted first

Group A

June	Venue		Score		Score	Winners	Man of the Match
9	Edgbaston	West Indies	194-1	†India	190	West Indies	C. G. Greenidge
9	Trent Bridge	New Zealand	190-1	†Sri Lanka	189	New Zealand	G. P. Howarth
13	Headingley	New Zealand	183-2	†India	182	New Zealand	B. A. Edgar
13–15	The Oval	West Indies	—	Sri Lanka	—	No result	
16	Trent Bridge	†West Indies	244-7	New Zealand	212-9	West Indies	C. H. Lloyd
16, 18	Old Trafford	India	191	†Sri Lanka	238-5	Sri Lanka	R. D. Mendis

	P	W	L	NR	Points
West Indies	3	2	0	1	10
New Zealand	3	2	1	0	8
Sri Lanka	3	1	1	1	6
India	3	0	3	0	0

Hundreds

Name	Score
C. G. Greenidge (WI v I)	106*

Four or more wickets

Name	Analysis
M. A. Holding (WI v I)	4–33

Group B

June	Venue		Score		Score	Winners	Man of the Match
9	Lord's	England	160-4	†Australia	159-9	England	G. A. Gooch
9	Headingley	Pakistan	140-2	†Canada	139-9	Pakistan	Sadiq Mohammad
13, 14	Trent Bridge	Australia	197	†Pakistan	286-7	Pakistan	Asif Iqbal
13, 14	Old Trafford	England	46-2	†Canada	45	England	C. M. Old
16	Headingley	†England	165-9	Pakistan	151	England	M. Hendrick
16	Edgbaston	Australia	106-3	†Canada	105	Australia	A. G. Hurst

	P	W	L	NR	Points
England	3	3	0	0	12
Pakistan	3	2	1	0	8
Australia	3	1	2	0	4
Canada	3	0	3	0	0

Four or more wickets

Name	Analysis
C. M. Old (E v C)	4–8
R. G. D. Willis (E v C)	4–11
M. Hendrick (E v P)	4–15
A. G. Hurst (A v C)	5–21

Right: A dashing captain's innings of 61 by Asif Iqbal helped Pakistan build a winning total against Australia at Trent Bridge and won him the Man of the Match award.

SEMI–FINAL

West Indies v Pakistan, The Oval

Although a good case can be made for inserting the opposition in a limited-overs game on an easy pitch – the side batting second knows exactly what their target is – it does come unstuck when the inserted capitalise on their good fortune by running up a really big score. This happened at The Oval where West Indies amassed 293 for the loss of six wickets in 60 overs.

Greenidge and Haynes, helped by some wayward bowling from both Sarfraz and Imran Khan, positively charged into the attack with a wealth of punishing strokes that brought up the hundred partnership at well over four runs an over. Not only were the Pakistan seamers summarily dispatched to all parts of the ground, but the fielding started to wilt under the assault. Asif became understandably worried, until he introduced the slow off-breaks of Majid Khan. Majid sent down 12 overs for only 26 runs and was the main reason why West Indies were never able to maximise fully on their rampaging start. Asif also put in a tidy and productive spell, capturing the wickets of Greenidge, brilliantly caught behind, Haynes, Richards, never at his best, and Lloyd; not a bad haul for the fifth or sixth bowler. However, the final total left Pakistan with an enormous task, certainly one far beyond the capabilities of any other team in the competition, and they have reason to be proud that, for a while, they came almost within touch.

Their beginning was anything but impressive. Sadiq was out for two, and Majid should have followed him to the pavilion when Greenidge dropped him off Holding shortly afterwards. Gradually, and with ever-increasing confidence and momentum, Zaheer and Majid began to find gaps in the field. The West Indian pacemen also began to lose their effectiveness, so that Lloyd had to turn to the flat non-turning off-breaks of Richards. Although

Desmond Haynes produced a punishing display in The Oval semi-final, sharing a century opening stand with Greenidge to set West Indies on the way to their second World Cup final.

12 runs came off his first over, this move proved successful and underlined, as in a different way Majid's spell had done earlier in the day, that slow bowling can play a vital part in one-day cricket.

The dreams of a truly historic Pakistan victory were ended by Croft, who in the space of 11 runs removed Majid, Zaheer and Javed Miandad. Asif and Haroon tried unsuccessfully to regain the initiative, but now West Indies were firmly in control and the batsmen were running short of overs. Roberts, who had looked far from international class at the start of the innings, came back to finish it off still 43 runs short of the highest score ever made in a Prudential Cup match.

WEST INDIES v PAKISTAN
Played at The Oval, London, 20 June
Toss: Pakistan   Result: **West Indies** won by 43 runs   Man of the Match: C. G. Greenidge

WEST INDIES		Runs	Mins	Balls	6s	4s
C. G. Greenidge	c Wasim Bari b Asif	73	122	107	1	5
D. L. Haynes	c and b Asif	65	155	114	—	4
I. V. A. Richards	b Asif	42	91	58	—	1
C. H. Lloyd*	c Mudassar b Asif	37	53	41	—	3
C. L. King	c sub (*Raja*) b Sarfraz	34	37	27	—	3
A. I. Kallicharran	b Imran	11	31	12	—	—
A. M. E. Roberts	*not out*	7	6	4	—	—
J. Garner	*not out*	1	4	1	—	—
D. L. Murray†						
M. A. Holding	*did not bat*					
C. E. H. Croft						
Extras	(*b* 1, *lb* 17, *w* 1, *nb* 4)	23				
TOTAL	(6 wickets – 60 overs)	**293**				

PAKISTAN		Runs	Mins	Balls	6s	4s
Majid Khan	c Kallicharran b Croft	81	175	70	—	8
Sadiq Mohammad	C Murray b Holding	2	15	8	—	—
Zaheer Abbas	c Murray b Croft	93	143	123	1	8
Haroon Rashid	*run out*	15	40	24	—	—
Javed Miandad	*lbw* b Croft	0	1	1	—	—
Asif Iqbal*	c Holding b Richards	17	15	17	—	1
Mudassar Nazar	c Kallicharran b Richards	2	10	8	—	—
Imran Khan	c and b Richards	6	9	4	—	1
Sarfraz Nawaz	c Haynes b Roberts	12	16	11	—	—
Wasim Bari†	c Murray b Roberts	9	13	12	—	—
Sikander Bakht	*not out*	1	3	4	—	—
Extras	(*lb* 9, *w* 2, *nb* 1)	12				
TOTAL	(56.2 overs)	**250**				

PAKISTAN	O	M	R	W
Imran	9	1	43	1
Sarfraz	12	1	71	1
Sikander	6	1	24	0
Mudassar	10	0	50	0
Majid	12	2	26	0
Asif	11	0	56	4

WEST INDIES	O	M	R	W
Roberts	9.2	2	41	2
Holding	9	1	28	1
Croft	11	0	29	3
Garner	12	1	47	0
King	7	0	41	0
Richards	8	0	52	3

FALL OF WICKETS

Wkt	WI	P
1st	132	10
2nd	165	176
3rd	233	187
4th	236	187
5th	285	208
6th	285	220
7th		221
8ph	—	228
9th	—	246
10th	—	250

Umpires: W. L. Budd and D. J. Constant   *Captain   †Wicket-keeper

SEMI-FINAL

England v New Zealand, Old Trafford

Although the semi-final between England and New Zealand proved to be an intensely dramatic limited-overs match, with the home side eventually winning by the narrow margin of nine runs, it must also be admitted that much of the cricket was undistinguished. With three overs to go the Kiwis needed 25 runs. Lees and Cairns were at the crease, Hendrick and Botham were bowling with deep-set defensive fields; it was a possible but somewhat unlikely target. When the final over started, 14 were still required and not surprisingly this proved well beyond McKechnie and Troup. England were through to the final, but not before the players, and their supporters, had experienced many anxious moments.

Put in to bat, Brearley's team reached a respectable but far from an unbeatable 221. Although Boycott and Larkins went cheaply – that usual bad start – Brearley and Gooch put on 54 before the captain departed for a very useful 53. The arrival of Botham to join Gooch saw an increase in the tempo, the former making a flamboyant 21 and the latter a splendid 71. Randall, who had been out of form, was dropped down the order and, with support from the tail, batted sensibly, steering the team past 200 and ending up 42 not out at the end of the 60th over.

New Zealand, on a very good pitch, were asked to make 222 at 3.7 runs per over against a seam quartet, plus 12 overs from Boycott and Gooch. They began well and after 16 overs were 47 for 0, but then they lost three wickets cheaply, all lbw; Howarth simply missed a straight full-toss from the delighted Boycott. Wright and Turner, who has an outstanding record in limited-overs games, had taken New Zealand to less than a hundred off their target when the former was brilliantly run out by Randall. This probably settled the outcome of the match. As long as Turner remained, the Kiwis

Randall looks back to see Cairns' throw beat Taylor's desperate lunge.

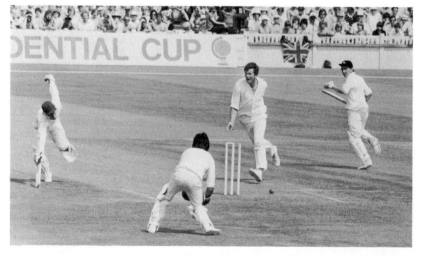

were in with a good chance, but when he was leg before to Willis for 30 and both Burgess and Hadlee were back in the pavilion, one felt the initiative had passed back to England. The Kiwis were running out of overs and recognised batsmen.

A few agricultural blows from Cairns and Lees raised the visitors' hopes briefly, but not for long. England finished winners rather more easily than a gap of nine runs might suggest. Nevertheless, if Howarth had not missed that gentle full-toss, or two players had not been run out, it might have been an entirely different story. As it was, it represented a fine performance by New Zealand, whom England should expect to beat in limited-overs cricket.

ENGLAND v NEW ZEALAND
Played at Old Trafford, Manchester, 20 June
Toss: New Zealand   Result: **England** won by 9 runs   Man of the Match: G. A. Gooch

ENGLAND		Runs	Mins	Balls	6s	4s
J. M. Brearley*	c Lees b Coney	53	114	115	—	3
G. Boycott	c Howarth b Hadlee	2	30	14	—	—
W. Larkins	c Coney b McKechnie	7	40	37	—	—
G. A. Gooch	b McKechnie	71	105	84	1	3
D. I. Gower	run out (Cairns/Coney)	1	2	1	—	—
I. T. Botham	lbw b Cairns	21	31	30	—	2
D. W. Randall	not out	42	66	50	1	1
C. M. Old	c Lees b Troup	0	2	2	—	—
R. W. Taylor†	run out (Cairns)	12	30	25	—	1
R. G. D. Willis	not out	1	1	2	—	—
M. Hendrick	did not bat					
Extras	(lb 8, w 3)	11				
TOTAL	(8 wickets – 60 overs)	**221**				

NEW ZEALAND		Runs	Mins	Balls	6s	4s
J. G. Wright	run out (Randall/Willis)	69	142	137	—	9
B. A. Edgar	lbw b Old	17	58	38	—	1
G. P. Howarth	lbw b Boycott	7	13	12	—	1
J. V. Coney	lbw b Hendrick	11	56	39	—	—
G. M. Turner	lbw b Willis	30	67	51	—	2
M. G. Burgess*	run out (Randall/Taylor)	10	28	13	—	—
R. J. Hadlee	b Botham	15	44	32	—	—
W. K. Lees†	b Hendrick	23	33	20	1	—
B. L. Cairns	c Brearley b Hendrick	14	5	6	1	1
B. J. McKechnie	not out	4	13	9	—	—
G. B. Troup	not out	3	2	3	—	—
Extras	(lb 5, w 4)	9				
TOTAL	(9 wickets – 60 overs)	**212**				

NEW ZEALAND	O	M	R	W
Hadlee	12	4	32	1
Troup	12	1	38	1
Cairns	12	2	47	1
Coney	12	0	47	1
McKechnie	12	1	46	2

ENGLAND	O	M	R	W
Botham	12	3	42	1
Hendrick	12	0	55	3
Willis	12	1	41	1
Old	12	1	33	1
Boycott	9	1	24	1
Gooch	3	1	8	0

FALL OF WICKETS

Wkt	E	NZ
1st	13	47
2nd	38	58
3rd	96	104
4th	98	112
5th	145	132
6th	177	162
7th	178	180
8th	219	195
9th	—	208
10th	—	—

Umpires: J. G. Langridge and K. E. Palmer   *Captain   †Wicket-keeper

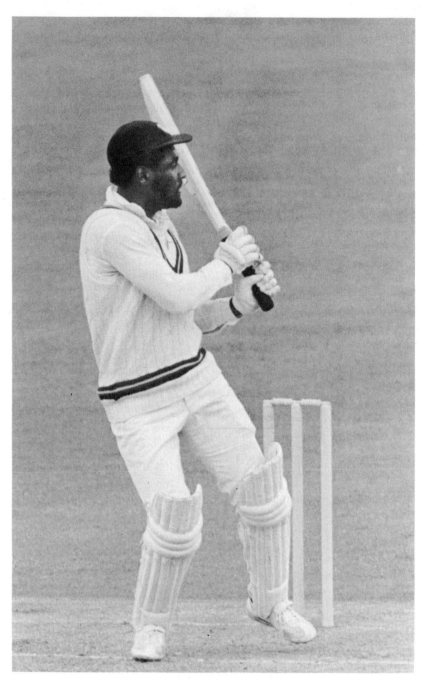

Vivian Richards, with an innings of initial patience, increasing tempo and final onslaught, graced the Prudential Cup final with batsmanship of supreme class.

PRUDENTIAL CUP FINAL 1979

England v West Indies, Lord's
As had always seemed probable, West Indies, who won the first Prudential Cup in an epic encounter against Australia in 1975, proved too strong for England in the final at Lord's. Yet this entertaining match, which ended in a 92 runs victory for the West Indians – a very large margin by one-day standards – was, in fact, wide open until Richards and King proceeded to savage England's apology for a fifth bowler after lunch. England were handicapped by the absence in their attack of Willis, who had injured his knee in the semi-final against New Zealand and failed to pass a late fitness test.

Confronted by the near-impossible task of making 287 to win in 60 overs against a formidable pace quartet, England might have gone rather closer had Boycott and Brearley scored a little faster at the start. In normal circumstances, 100 for no wicket represents a fine opening stand. But when the overall asking-rate is 4.8 per over, reaching three figures after 32 overs means that the later batsmen are required to score at seven and eight per over. Against an attack of West Indies' calibre, that is not on for much of the time. Inevitably England failed, but the abruptness with which eight wickets tumbled in the space of only 26 balls, with Garner the main destroyer, came both as a surprise and as a big anticlimax.

Having won the toss, and knowing that the pitch was more likely to give the pace bowlers some assistance in the early stages, Mike Brearley correctly decided on what could be termed both an offensive and a defensive insertion. Although his new-ball bowlers were not as successful as he hoped, the England captain had every reason to feel well satisfied with the position at lunch. Greenidge was brilliantly run out by Randall, Haynes and Lloyd were victims of Old – Lloyd to a magnificent caught and bowled – and Kallicharran was bowled round his legs by the ever-dangerous Hendrick. However, Richards, not in that session at his most convincing, was still there and King, from the moment he arrived at the crease, had introduced Caribbean flair to the proceedings. None the less, at 99 for four West Indies were in serious trouble, for they had a long tail.

Brearley decided against gambling on his main attacking bowlers immediately after the interval, and the two West Indians immediately began taking a heavy toll off Edmonds and the three batsmen who, between them, were intended to hide the missing fifth bowler. Understandably, Mike did not want to expose this trio to the slog which occurs in the last few overs, but it turned out to be a tactical error. Richards, who had now found his true form, and the majestic King hammered 86 runs from 12 Boycott, Gooch and

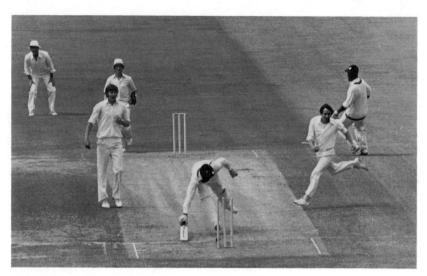

The end of Greenidge, run out by the exuberant Randall (right).

Larkins overs. In the process they took the total from 99 to a match-winning 238 before King departed, well held by Randall, who fielded throughout so well that it could be justifiably said that he was worth his place for his fielding alone.

Richards improvised several nigh-improbable strokes, including a six between fine and square leg off a good-length delivery from Hendrick, using what is perhaps best described as a front-foot straight-drive executed at right angles. Even though the long West Indian tail heaved hard and ineffectively, with three of them collecting ducks, Richards kept the score moving along. Such was his genius that, despite the deep-set fields with everyone back to stop the boundary, he managed to build an unassailable target and finished imperiously by hitting the last ball of the 60th over for six.

The West Indians' total of 286, which until the collapse of the last four wickets had promised to be in excess of 300, virtually assured them of victory. It also underlined the fact that the England captain would have been wiser to stake everything on breaking the Richards-King partnership by using his main strike bowler; if not right at the start, then certainly after lunch. However, the real mistake was in the selection of the side, trying to fiddle through 12 overs from non-recognised bowlers. A five-man attack is an essential, not a luxury, against international strokemakers on a good pitch.

The opening stand by Brearley and Boycott put on 129 runs and the former has seldom batted better for England. It would have been a wonderful start for a Test, but it never came to grips with the considerable problem of matching the required run-rate. The openers also permitted Richards to send down 10 overs for a mere 35 runs, which was suicidal in those particular circumstances. For a brief period, after both departed trying to increase the tempo rather too late in the proceedings, Gooch, large and powerful, and Randall, perky and skittish, provided the type of impetus required. But the asking-rate was too high against fast bowling directed at the stumps and supported by defensive fields.

It could not, and did not, last. Randall, essaying an optimistic hoick in the general direction of cow-shot corner, was bowled; Gooch, who had hit several memorable shots, was yorked by the massive Garner. From that moment the England innings developed into a rapid procession to and from the pavilion. Garner, with five wickets, was chiefly responsible, while Holding, yards faster than any other bowler, and Roberts still had plenty of overs in hand just in case things had gone wrong.

ENGLAND v WEST INDIES
Played at Lord's, London, 23 June
Toss: England   Result: **West Indies** won by 92 runs   Man of the Match: I. V. A. Richards

WEST INDIES		Runs	Mins	Balls	6s	4s
C. G. Greenidge	*run out (Randall)*	9	31	31	—	—
D. L. Haynes	c Hendrick b Old	20	49	27	—	3
I. V. A. Richards	*not out*	138	207	157	3	11
A. I. Kallicharran	b Hendrick	4	19	17	—	—
C. H. Lloyd*	c and b Old	13	42	33	—	2
C. L. King	c Randall b Edmonds	86	77	66	3	10
D. L. Murray†	c Gower b Edmonds	5	12	9	—	1
A. M. E. Roberts	c Brearley b Hendrick	0	8	7	—	—
J. Garner	c Taylor b Botham	0	4	5	—	—
M. A. Holding	b Botham	0	7	6	—	—
C. E. H. Croft	*not out*	0	6	2	—	—
Extras	(*b* 1, *lb* 10)	11				
TOTAL	(9 wickets – 60 overs)	**286**				

ENGLAND		Runs	Mins	Balls	6s	4s
J. M. Brearley*	c King b Holding	64	130	130	—	7
G. Boycott	c Kallicharran b Holding	57	137	105	—	3
D. W. Randall	b Croft	15	36	22	—	—
G. A. Gooch	b Garner	32	31	28	—	4
D. I. Gower	b Garner	0	6	4	—	—
I. T. Botham	c Richards b Croft	4	7	3	—	—
W. Larkins	b Garner	0	1	1	—	—
P. H. Edmonds	*not out*	5	14	8	—	—
C. M. Old	b Garner	0	4	2	—	—
R. W. Taylor†	c Murray b Garner	0	1	1	—	—
M. Hendrick	b Croft	0	4	5	—	—
Extras	(*lb* 12, *w* 2, *nb* 3)	17				
TOTAL	(51 overs)	**194**				

ENGLAND	O	M	R	W
Botham	12	2	44	2
Hendrick	12	2	50	2
Old	12	0	55	2
Boycott	6	0	38	0
Edmonds	12	2	40	2
Gooch	4	0	27	0
Larkins	2	0	21	0

WEST INDIES	O	M	R	W
Roberts	9	2	33	0
Holding	8	1	16	2
Croft	10	1	42	3
Garner	11	0	38	5
Richards	10	0	35	0
King	3	0	13	0

Umpires: H. D. Bird and B. J. Meyer

FALL OF WICKETS

Wkt	WI	E
1st	22	129
2nd	36	135
3rd	55	183
4th	99	183
5th	238	186
6th	252	186
7th	258	188
8th	260	192
9th	272	192
10th	—	194

*Captain   †Wicket-keeper

PRUDENTIAL CUP RECORDS

Highest Total	334–4 England v India, Lord's	1975
Highest Total Batting Second	276–4 Sri Lanka v Australia, Oval	1975
Lowest Total	45 Canada v England, Manchester	1979
Highest Match Aggregate	604 Australia (328–5) v Sri Lanka (276–4), Oval	1975
Lowest Match Aggregate	91 Canada (45) v England (46–1), Manchester	1979
Biggest Victories	10 wkts India beat East Africa, Leeds	1975
	202 runs England beat India, Lord's	1975
Narrowest Victories	1 wkt West Indies beat Pakistan, Birmingham	
	(*with 2 balls to spare*)	1975
	9 runs England beat New Zealand, Manchester	1979
Highest Individual Score	171* G. M. Turner, New Zealand v East Africa, Birmingham	1975
Hundred before Lunch	A. Turner (101), Australia v West Indies, Oval	1975
Highest Batting Aggregate	333 (av 166.50) G. M. Turner, New Zealand	1975

Highest Partnership for Each Wicket

1st	182	R. B. McCosker, A. Turner: Australia v Sri Lanka, Oval	1975
2nd	176	D. L. Amiss, K. W. R. Fletcher: England v India, Lord's	1975
3rd	149	G. M. Turner, J. M. Parker: New Zealand v East Africa, Birmingham	1975
4th	149	R. B. Kanhai, C. H. Lloyd: West Indies v Australia, Lord's	1975
5th	139	I. V. A. Richards, C. L. King: West Indies v England, Lord's	1979
6th	99	R. Edwards, R. W. Marsh: Australia v West Indies, Oval	1975
7th	55*	K. D. Walters, G. J. Gilmour: Australia v England, Leeds	1975
8th	48	D. R. Hadlee, B. J. McKechnie: New Zealand v England, Nottingham	1975
9th	60	S. Abid Ali, S. Venkataraghavan: India v New Zealand, Manchester	1975
10th	64*	D. L. Murray, A. M. E. Roberts: West Indies v Pakistan, Birmingham	1975

Best Bowling	6–14 G. J. Gilmour: Australia v England, Leeds	1975
Highest Bowling		
Aggregate	11 (av 5.63) G. J. Gilmour, Australia	1975
Most Economical		
Bowling	12–8 – 6–1 B. S. Bedi: India v East Africa, Leeds	1975
Most Expensive		
Bowling	11–1 – 83–0 K. D. Ghavri: India v England, Lord's	1975
Wicket-keeping –		
Most Dismissals	4 D. L. Murray: West Indies v Sri Lanka, Manchester	1975
Field –		
Most Catches	3 C. H. Lloyd: West Indies v Sri Lanka, Manchester	1975

Right: A moment of irony at Lord's, if not appreciated by Bob Taylor, felled by an Indian bouncer. Venkataraghavan, the Indian captain, Viswanath and wicket-keeper Reddy show their concern.

THE 1979 INDIANS

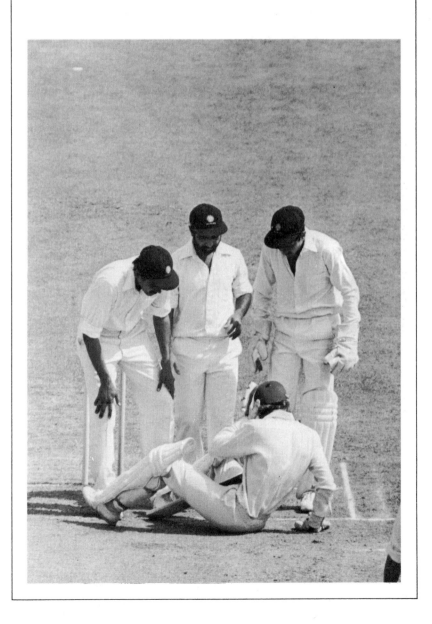

Sunil Gavaskar, the 'little master', sweeps on towards his double-century at The Oval.
England 'keeper Bairstow can only admire the quality of his stroke-play.

A MATTER OF CLASS

The England-Indian series was unexceptional and, until the last day of the final Test when Gavaskar produced an innings of genuine majesty, could be largely written off as predictable, mundane and short of class. There were various reasons why the four Cornhill Test matches failed to catch the imagination. First, after the excitement and the glamour of the Prudential Cup they came as something of an anticlimax. Secondly, the Indian team was simply not good enough to beat whatever side, or sides, the England selectors chose for a four-Test campaign in English conditions. This was the real snag; under our conditions, they were simply not sufficiently strong to provide England with the serious challenge required after two years against sub-standard opposition.

It is improbable these days that any touring team can win a series in this country with spin and without high-class seamers. For those who point to India in 1971, when the tourists won the three-match series one-nil, it must be pointed out that spin proved decisive only in the closing stages of the last match. The Indians would not have achieved their success had rain not prevented England winning the first two Tests. Although it was feasible last summer for the weather and the Indian batsmen to produce three draws, and then for their spinners to have won the deciding Test, the odds were unlikely. Furthermore, Chandra and Bedi were no longer such great bowlers as they had been in 1971 and Venkat was not as deadly as Prasanna.

The simple fact was that the Indian attack was not up to international standards. The seam section was considerably weaker than that of most counties, and lacked adequate cover. The Indian batting, apart from Gavaskar and Viswanath – both world-class players – lacked experience and was bound to have problems dealing with seam on pitches which favoured this type of bowling. The tourists could win only one county match, against unhappy Glamorgan, and Sri Lanka's victory over them in the Prudential Cup put everything into its true perspective.

New Zealand would certainly have fancied their chances against India over here, and as England experienced few problems against the Kiwis in 1978, it made them odds-on favourites. They duly won the series, and but for the vagaries of the weather the margin would have been greater. Yet at summer's end nobody was any nearer knowing whether Mike Brearley's men were an outstanding international eleven, or whether those fine results of the past two years were the result of second-class opposition.

Although the Indian players had their limitations on the field, their behaviour, both on and off it, was exemplary, and they will go down as one of the most polite and pleasant touring parties to visit this country. Their batting, though it had problems when the ball moved about, was good and at times brilliant. Gavaskar and Viswanath confirmed their high class; Vengsarkar, Yashpal Sharma and Yajurvindra Singh were three good, and improving, batsmen; and Chauhan showed himself to be a dependable opening bat with plenty of character. But neither Gaekwad nor Amarnath did himself justice.

The three main Indian spinners, Bedi, Chandrasekhar and Venkataraghavan, bowled well on occasions without ever looking as penetrating or as threatening as they have in the past. The bowler who made the biggest impression was Kapil Dev, probably the best fast-bowling prospect India have produced since the last world war. He has a good action, moves the ball, tackles his task with heart, and might become quicker. In addition he is a fine fieldsman and a spectacular, hard-hitting batsman, though he needs to tighten his defence. The big danger is that in the next few years he will be overworked, and it is hard to see this being avoided.

The Indian fielding was usually good, sometimes brilliant, but occasionally suffered from erratic spells. Reddy was not an international-class 'keeper, but Yajurvindra was superb in the bat-pad position with remarkable reflexes and very brave. However, it can be only a matter of time before he is seriously injured and loses the confidence needed to stand in a suicidal spot.

For England, Boycott batted with conviction in his own way and at his own tempo; Gower, as one would expect for a player of his style, tended to mix a big spectacular innings with small scores; and Gooch impressed without being able to break the three-figure barrier. But Brearley had another ineffectual series and Randall was below his best. Fortunately the Indian attack lacked penetration or, one feels, there would have been an acute shortage of runs.

Ian Botham deflects Bedi in the first innings of the fourth Test to bring up his 1,000th run in Test cricket and accomplish the fastest-ever Test 'double'.

Bat-pad specialist Yajurvindra Singh ends Alan Butcher's first innings hopes at The Oval.

The attack was far more impressive. Hendrick bowled with all his customary skill and accuracy, and Willis, though he did not have a happy season with the ball, caused problems with his pace and lift. The three spinners, Miller, Willey and Edmonds, were less impressive. Miller, who had bowled so well in Australia, was given few chances, almost ignored on occasions, but he did play some useful knocks. Willey was economical throughout some lengthy spells in his only Test, without ever suggesting he was a potential match-winning off-spinner at that level, and Edmonds, who had plenty of opportunities and bowled very well on occasions, was not as successful as had been hoped. There are times when it pays a slow left-armer to go over the wicket because the different line is a useful occasional ploy; but the Middlesex spinner probably overdid this method.

The England fielding and close catching was seldom less than brilliant. The accuracy of the returns by Randall and Gower was outstanding, both regularly hitting a single stump. As the overall standard was so high it is perhaps unfair to single out, for special praise, Hendrick, Edmonds, Botham, and one gulley catch by Miller. Behind the stumps, Taylor, after an uncharacteristic shaky start in the Prudential Cup, was back to near perfection in the Tests. The gap dividing the great from the competent certainly showed up clearly when Bairstow replaced him at The Oval.

Apart from the batting of Gavaskar, who is in an altogether different class from any other player on either side – given health, he must go on to shatter record after record – the outstanding feature of the series was the magnificent all-round form of Botham, the leading wicket-taker, third highest aggregate with the bat (though he did not come in until number 6), and holder of the highest number of catches.

THE ANNIHILATION

A scenario in four acts. Setting: a cricket ground in Birmingham.

Act I. The Foundation
Scene I. The Morning Meander
Having won the toss on the most benign of pitches, Boycott and Brearley take a leisurely stroll against an insipid attack. Without the help of extras, who frequently threaten to outscore both batsmen, England make fewer than 50 in a best-forgotten two hours before lunch. Brearley crawls quicker than his more accomplished partner before being caught behind off Kapil Dev, whose funeral march back to his mark is in keeping with the proceedings.

Scene II. The Afternoon Assault
After Randall brings life to affairs and then departs, Gooch takes command. Giving Boycott 25 runs and two and a half hours start, he overtakes him with a lofted drive and goes on to reach his half-century in a mere 82 minutes. The Gooch onslaught destroys the opposition, while Boycott finds runs easier to come by at the other end, taking the liberty of three successive fours off loose deliveries from Chandrasekhar.

Scene III. An Evening of Inevitability
Although Gooch is Kapil Dev's third victim, for a majestic 83, Boycott reaches a century, which seemed inevitable from the moment his occupation of the crease commenced. The only question was when: 5 runs in the first hour, 15 in the second, 17 in the third and 28 in the fourth. The longer he stays the easier batting appears, and when the curtain comes down England are already an almost invulnerable 318 for three.

Act II. Massacre in the Sun
Scene I. The Golden Oldie and the Golden Kid
Boycott and Gower plunder the Indian bowling with ease and charm. Indeed, it is something of a shock when the former is lbw to the tireless, and game, Kapil Dev for 155.

Scene II. Bowling for a Declaration
As Gower dispatches the ball to all quarters of the Edgbaston ground, in company with Botham during a boisterous interlude and then with the more restrained Miller, it looks as if the Indians are bowling for a declaration. This fails to materialise as numerous statistical records are broken. Finally, Gower reaches a glittering double-century and England mercifully declare.

Scene III. The Start of the Climb
India begin their long climb to avoid defeat. Nothing else is left, as only two

Geoffrey Boycott, having played his role so many times, strolled the Edgbaston stage regardless of time (and sometimes of motion).

results remain – a draw or defeat. The loss of two wickets makes the latter more probable.

Act III. The Up-Hill Fight

Scene I. The Brothers-in-Law
The brothers-in-law, the minute Gavaskar and the even smaller Viswanath, experience few problems, even though Brearley switches his bowlers around. They suggest permanency until Gavaskar runs himself out, choosing, of all people, Randall as the executioner.

Scene II. The Fall of Vishy
As long as Viswanath remains in charge at one end and gives succour and advice to his colleagues, hope remains. But after tea, and shortly before the second new ball is due, the little man is well caught bat-and-pad by Botham off Edmonds for 78.

Scene III. The Fold-Up
Gaekwad is caught from a wide off-volley with the old ball before the new ball winds up the innings, despite bold blows from Amarnath who relishes a diet of juicy Botham bouncers. There is an entertaining stand between numbers 9 and 10 before India follow on 336 behind.

Act IV. Operation 'Winkle'

Scene I. The Openers' Morning
Gavaskar and Chauhan negotiate the morning session without mishap. On this placid pitch it is necessary to 'winkle out' a determined player and this pair refuse to oblige. They are still together at lunch.

Scene II. A 'Winkling' Afternoon
England continue 'winkling' throughout the afternoon and acquire four victims, including Gavaskar who is unlucky to receive a virtually unplayable delivery from Hendrick. Taylor, not at his best, misses two stumping chances off Edmonds, who bowls impressively, but India, with Vishy still battling bravely, seem set to carry their resistance into the final day.

Scene III. The Botham Burst

A typical Botham burst sends India tumbling to a massive defeat by an innings and 83 runs. The last six wickets fall in 11 overs for 26 miserable runs as the Somerset all-rounder swings the second new ball and remembers to keep it up to the bat. This proves too much for the opposition and he picks up four for 10 in five overs.

ENGLAND v INDIA 1979 – 1st Test
Played at Edgbaston, Birmingham, 12, 13, 14, 16 July
Toss: England   Result: **England** won by an innings and 83 runs
Débuts: India – B. Reddy   Man of the Match: D. I. Gower

ENGLAND

J. M. Brearley*	c Reddy b Kapil Dev	24
G. Boycott	lbw b Kapil Dev	155
D. W. Randall	c Reddy b Kapil Dev	15
G. A. Gooch	c Reddy b Kapil Dev	83
D. I. Gower	not out	200
I. T. Botham	b Kapil Dev	33
G. Miller	not out	63
P. H. Edmonds		
R. W. Taylor†	did not bat	
R. G. D. Willis		
M. Hendrick		
Extras	(b 4, lb 27, w 11, nb 18)	60
TOTAL	(5 wickets declared)	**633**

INDIA

S. M. Gavaskar	run out (Randall/Taylor)	61	c Gooch b Hendrick	68
C. P. S. Chauhan	c Gooch b Botham	4	c Randall b Willis	56
D. B. Vengsarkar	c Gooch b Edmonds	22	c Edmonds b Hendrick	7
G. R. Viswanath	c Botham b Edmonds	78	c Taylor b Botham	51
A. D. Gaekwad	c Botham b Willis	25	c Gooch b Botham	15
M. Amarnath	b Willis	31	lbw b Botham	10
Kapil Dev	lbw b Botham	1	c Hendrick b Botham	21
K. D. Ghavri	c Brearley b Willis	6	c Randall b Hendrick	4
B. Reddy†	b Hendrick	21	lbw b Hendrick	0
S. Venkataraghavan*	c Botham b Hendrick	28	lbw b Botham	0
B. S. Chandrasekhar	not out	0	not out	0
Extras	(b 1, lb 4, w 3, nb 12)	20	(b 7, lb 12, nb 2)	21
TOTAL		**297**		**253**

INDIA	O	M	R	W			
Kapil Dev	48	15	146	5			
Ghavri	38	5	129	0			
Amarnath	13.2	2	47	0			
Chandrasekhar	29	1	113	0			
Venkataraghavan	31	4	107	0			
Gaekwad	3	0	12	0			
Chauhan	3	0	19	0			

ENGLAND	O	M	R	W	O	M	R	W
Willis	24	9	69	3	14	3	45	1
Botham	26	4	86	2	29	8	70	5
Hendrick	24.1	9	36	2	20.4	8	45	4
Edmonds	26	11	60	2	17	6	37	0
Boycott	5	1	8	0				
Miller	11	3	18	0	9	1	27	0
Gooch					6	3	8	0

FALL OF WICKETS

	E	I	I
Wkt	1st	1st	2nd
1st	66	15	124
2nd	90	59	136
3rd	235	129	136
4th	426	205	182
5th	468	209	227
6th	—	210	240
7th	—	229	249
8th	—	251	250
9th	—	294	251
10th	—	297	253

*Captain   †Wicket-keeper

Umpires: D. J. Constant and B. J. Meyer
Attendance: 25,000 (19,414 paid). Receipts: £53,000

A LORDLY RECOVERY

A scenario in five acts. Setting: a cricket ground in St John's Wood, London.

Act I. Indian Nightmare
Scene I. The Rout

The start is pure pantomime. Both captains are under the impression they have won the toss, but no unpleasantness ensues as India want to bat and England to field. The Indians get it wrong, and their innings of a mere 96 proves to be a sorry procession on a far from difficult pitch, though there is a slight unevenness of bounce. Only Gavaskar, a rather surprising Gooch victim, and Viswanath suggest permanence. Hendrick is the most dangerous bowler, but has to settle for two wickets. The irrepressible, and less accurate, Botham joyfully gobbles up another five. The fielding is excellent; Taylor keeps beautifully and Miller makes the catch of his life to remove Kapil Dev.

Scene II. The Steady Start

Boycott settles immediately, and with Brearley makes batting look comparatively easy until the latter fails to cope with a nasty lifting ball which his partner would almost certainly have negotiated successfully. Gooch, coming in at number 3, is calm and plays straight with time to spare.

Act II. The Deluge
Scene I. The Morning of the Question Mark

The question mark against the real strength of the England batting, which had been flattered by the weakness of the Indian attack at Edgbaston, remains. Boycott follows a ball wide of his off stump, Gooch hits across a near half-volley from the promising Kapil Dev, and Gower is perilously close to lbw. There is also a question mark against the overcast weather, which favours swing and seam.

Scene II. The Heavens Open

The expected rain commences, but the groundstaff perform such a splendid mopping-up operation that play seems probable during the afternoon. Then the heavens open and Lord's resembles one gigantic lake. This not only ends play for the day, but casts doubts about the morrow. In the meantime, some playgoers from the pit amuse themselves by playing in the puddles.

Act III. England Take Control
Scene I. Gower and Glory

After a delayed start Gower strokes his elegant way to a fine fifty. Randall sensibly bides his time, knowing that the Indian bowling quartet will find life increasingly difficult as the day wears on. The young left-hander greets the afternoon with a rattle of fours, some brilliant, some lucky, but all spectacular. When 82, he oddly leaves alone a straight ball and pays the penalty. The entertainment continues with Randall, batting with ever-increasing freedom, and the powerful Botham. Both appear more at home with the bowling than each other's calling, so it is no surprise when Randall, having put together a competent 57, is run out.

Scene II. Quietly Pressing Home the Advantage
After tea Brearley has two options. He can go for quick runs and declare, hoping for several wickets before close, or he can quietly press home his considerable advantage. To the chant of 'boring' from the more mellow supporters inside, and outside, the Tavern, he predictably chooses the second course. Miller and Taylor advance circumspectly and comfortably against bowling which has long since lost its bite. They are still together at stumps and England are in complete control.

Act IV. India Dig In
Scene I. The Run Scamper
Taylor and Miller plunder some quick runs from the Indian bowlers and Brearley declares at 419 for nine. Taylor is particularly severe on Venkat, who unwisely introduces himself into the attack in circumstances not dissimilar to the last few overs in a limited-overs match.

Scene II. Indian Fight-Back (part 1)
For the first time in the series the game resembles a real Test match, with good bowlers having to battle for wickets on an easy pitch against class batting. For once the England fielding is less than perfect, and early on Chauhan is dropped by Brearley off the unlucky Lever. He is eventually lbw to Edmonds, who shuts up one end between lunch and tea. Botham secures his 100th Test wicket during an eventful over in which Gavaskar plays three over-adventurous strokes, is put down twice, and finally is beautifully taken by Brearley at slip. Botham completes this feat in just over two years, faster than anyone, and in fewer Tests than any English cricketer.

Scene III. Indian Fight-Back (part 2)
Vengsarkar, after a certain amount of unease at the start, settles in to bat soundly and sensibly. He finds the ideal partner in the correct and diminutive Viswanath. At close they are still together at 196 for two. If they can see off the new ball tomorrow, India can save a match; an outcome which, at the start of the day, had seemed, if not impossible, at least most improbable.

Act V. An Historic Stand
Scene I. Overcoming the New Ball
England take the new ball in the second over, but are unable to make much impression on Vengsarkar and Viswanath. There is a slight air of unreality about the whole proceedings, which are not helped by a noticeable lack of urgency to remove the covers after a slight fall of rain, and the small crowd. Another 45 minutes are lost through light rain at lunch. Both batsmen have few problems, though Viswanath is dropped shortly before the first interval off Hendrick, whose introduction into the attack seems rather belated.

Scene II. The Centurians

Vengsarkar and Viswanath complete memorable centuries and stay together until 20 minutes after tea. Their stand of 210 lasts for just under five and a half hours and contains many fine strokes. Vengsarkar is especially impressive off his legs and also plays several resounding hooks; the angled driving and cutting of Viswanath are moments to cherish. When the two centurians depart, their successors are immediately in difficulties, under-lining the importance of this match-saving partnership.

ENGLAND v INDIA 1979 – 2nd Test
Played at Lord's, London, 2, 3, 4, 6, 7 August
Toss: India   Result: **Match drawn**
Débuts: India – Yashpal Sharma   Man of the Match: G. R. Viswanath

INDIA

S. M. Gavaskar	c Taylor b Gooch	42	c Brearley b Botham	59
C. P. S. Chauhan	c Randall b Botham	2	c Randall l b Edmonds	31
D. B. Vengsarkar	c Botham b Hendrick	0	c Boycott b Edmonds	103
G. R. Viswanath	c Brearley b Hendrick	21	c Gower b Lever	113
A. D. Gaekwad	c Taylor b Botham	13	not out	1
Yashpal Sharma	c Taylor b Botham	11	not out	5
Kapil Dev	c Miller b Botham	4		
K. D. Ghavri	not out	3		
B. Reddy†	lbw b Botham	0		
S. Venkataraghavan*	run out (Gower)	0		
B. S. Bedi	b Lever	0		
Extras		0	(b 2, lb 2, w 1, nb 1)	6
TOTAL		**96**	(4 wickets)	**318**

ENGLAND

J. M. Brearley*	c Reddy b Kapil Dev	12
G. Boycott	c Gavaskar b Ghavri	32
G. A. Gooch	b Kapil Dev	10
D. I. Gower	b Ghavri	82
D. W. Randall	run out (Gavaskar/Bedi)	57
I. T. Botham	b Venkataraghavan	36
G. Miller	st Reddy b Bedi	62
P. H. Edmonds	c Reddy b Kapil Dev	20
R. W. Taylor†	c Vengsarkar b Bedi	64
J. K. Lever	not out	6
M. Hendrick	did not bat	
Extras	(b 11, lb 21, w 2, nb 4)	38
TOTAL	(9 wickets declared)	**419**

ENGLAND	O	M	R	W	O	M	R	W
Lever	9.5	3	29	1	24	7	69	1
Botham	19	9	35	5	35	13	80	1
Hendrick	15	7	15	2	25	12	56	0
Edmonds	2	1	1	0	45	18	62	2
Gooch	10	5	16	1	2	0	8	0
Miller					17	6	37	0

INDIA	O	M	R	W
Kapil Dev	38	11	93	3
Ghavri	31	2	122	2
Bedi	38.5	13	87	2
Venkataraghavan	22	2	79	1

FALL OF WICKETS

	I	E	I
Wkt	1st	1st	2nd
1st	12	21	79
2nd	23	60	99
3rd	51	71	309
4th	75	185	312
5th	79	226	—
6th	89	253	—
7th	96	291	—
8th	96	394	—
9th	96	419	—
10th	96	—	—

Umpires: H. D. Bird and K. E. Palmer   *Captain   †Wicket-keeper
Attendance: 62,086 (55,361 paid). Receipts: £166,057

In conditions stage-managed for seamers, Kapil Dev lifted Indian hopes and hearts at Headingley by removing Boycott, Gooch and Gower in an inspired spell.

THE HEADINGLEY HOMILY

A scenario in four acts. Setting: a cricket ground in Leeds.

Act I. Even Stevens

Scene I. The Passive Start

England make a passive start on what appears to be a passive pitch as our two grafters ply their chosen trade. Boycott is far more impressive than Brearley, who is lucky to be put down at short leg early on. The local hero seems set for a major innings with runs coming easily from his broad, straight bat. However, with the score 53, Yorkshire's maestro, to everyone's surprise, hits a wide long-hop off his back foot and is caught in the gulley executing his favourite shot, the square drive.

Scene II. The Unexpected Collapse

The Indian bowlers take heart at this unexpected reward. The sun retires behind the clouds, the ball starts to move, and England collapse in a manner which indicates their serious batting limitations. Driving firm-footed, Gooch is caught in the slips. At the same total, 57, Brearley edges a straight ball outside his off stump, and a run later Gower is lbw to a fine inswinger from Kapil Dev. England stagger uncertainly into lunch at 61 for four. After the interval Randall and Botham, without great conviction but with plenty of common sense and application, steady the sinking ship. Their rescue act is in progress when the rains come and the curtain comes down on the first act with England 80 for four.

Act II. The Deluge

Scene I. Summer in Leeds

A few hardy optimists arrive in raincoats, though there is never the slightest hope of any action. There are also doubts about Saturday.

Scene II. How to Lose Friends

The outfield is very wet and soggy after the deluge, but the pitch and square are perfect. The umpires inspect at two o'clock on a fine Saturday and at 2.30 suspend activities for the day. Not surprisingly, this fails to please the spectators. They know cricket is possible, and to make matters even more irritating, it is taking place on all the adjacent grounds.

Is there not a strong case for an independent adjudicator at Test match grounds whose responsibility is more to the spectators and the sponsors than to the players? He is likely to be less fussy about what is playable, as distinct from what is ideal for play, than the umpires, whose livelihood depends upon captains' reports. Unless it suits them, players tend to favour the delights of the pavilion and it was ever thus.

Botham chooses to run a few for his memorable 137, 94 of which came from boundary strokes.

Act III. Smash, Bash, Crash
Scene I. King Botham
Botham smashes his way to a spectacular century, containing five massive sixes and 16 fours. Altogether, 99 runs flow from his rumbustious bat before lunch and his final score, 137, leaves him only three short of the fastest 'double' in international cricket. This is an innings to treasure, with the power of his strokes leaving everybody, including the Indian fieldsmen, gasping. His sixes, one of them a truly remarkable sweep, fly high into the crowd. It is the most spectacular batting by an Englishman in a Test for a very long time.

Making this *tour de force* even more remarkable is the fact that the conditions favour the seamers for the first 90 minutes and that the other England players, apart from a workmanlike 27 from Miller, do not impress. A ball, pitching well outside the leg stump, removes Randall's unguarded leg stump.

Scene II. Early Uncertainty
The pace and bounce of Willis prove too much for Chauhan and Amarnath, but England's apparent gallop towards victory ends at 3.38 with another downpour.

Act IV. The Stalemate
Scene I. The Last Chance
As so much time has been lost, the only chance of a win by England is to shoot out India for 70 and enforce the follow-on. But it is clearly a slim one. Although Viswanath goes quickly, the little master, Gavaskar, has no problems and Yashpal provides admirable support.

Scene II. Time to Go Home

India save the follow-on and the game loses its meaning. Gavaskar scores a disciplined 78 and Vengsarkar, coming in at number 6 because of a damaged finger, contributes an undefeated 65. Gooch supplies a touch of farce to the last rites with some amusing imitations of the bowling actions of various cricketers.

ENGLAND v INDIA 1979 – 3rd Test
Played at Headingley, Leeds, 16, 17 (*no play*), 18 (*no play*), 20, 21 August
Toss: England   Result: **Match drawn**
Man of the Match: I. T. Botham

ENGLAND

G. Boycott	*c* Viswanath *b* Kapil Dev	31
J. M. Brearley*	*c* Viswanath *b* Amarnath	15
G. A. Gooch	*c* Vengsarkar *b* Kapil Dev	4
D. I. Gower	*lbw b* Kapil Dev	0
D. W. Randall	*b* Ghavri	11
I. T. Botham	*c* Ghavri *b* Venkat	137
G. Miller	*c* Reddy *b* Amarnath	27
P. H. Edmonds	*run out (Yashpal/Bedi/ Reddy)*	18
R. W. Taylor†	*c* Chauhan *b* Bedi	1
R. G. D. Willis	*not out*	4
M. Hendrick	*c* sub *(Yajurvindra) b* Bedi	0
Extras	(*b* 4, *lb* 6, *w* 4, *nb* 8)	22
TOTAL		**270**

INDIA

S. M. Gavaskar	*b* Edmonds	78
C. P. S. Chauhan	*c* Botham *b* Willis	0
M. Amarnath	*c* Taylor *b* Willis	0
G. R. Viswanath	*c* Brearley *b* Hendrick	1
Yashpal Sharma	*c* Botham *b* Miller	40
D. B. Vengsarkar	*not out*	65
Kapil Dev	*c* Gooch *b* Miller	3
K. D. Ghavri	*not out*	20
B. Reddy†		
S. Venkataraghavan*	*did not bat*	
B. S. Bedi		
Extras	(*b* 11, *lb* 4, *nb* 1)	16
TOTAL	(6 wickets)	**223**

INDIA	O	M	R	W
Kapil Dev	27	7	84	3
Ghavri	18	4	60	1
Amarnath	20	7	53	2
Bedi	8.5	2	26	2
Venkataraghavan	7	2	25	1

ENGLAND	O	M	R	W
Willis	18	5	42	2
Hendrick	14	6	13	1
Botham	13	3	39	0
Edmonds	28	8	59	1
Miller	32	13	52	2
Gooch	3	1	2	0
Boycott	2	2	0	0

FALL OF WICKETS

Wkt	E 1st	I 1st
1st	53	1
2nd	57	9
3rd	57	12
4th	58	106
5th	89	156
6th	176	160
7th	264	—
8th	264	—
9th	266	—
10th	270	—

*Captain †Wicket-keeper

Umpires: H. D. Bird and B. J. Meyer
Attendance: 15,382 (10,835 paid). Receipts: £65,794

THE INDIAN ROPE-TRICK

A scenario in five acts. Setting: a cricket ground in south London.

Act I. A Gooch-Inspired Recovery
Scene I. An Indifferent Introduction
Boycott and Butcher move along very slowly against a far from menacing attack. The former is confident but the latter, even taking into account it is his Test début, makes such heavy weather of the situation that it is hard to imagine he is the same left-hander who has scored so positively for Surrey. His dismissal five minutes from lunch for 14 runs totally lacking in conviction comes as something of a relief. Boycott, however, looks set for another big innings.

Scene II. An Afternoon of Changing Fortunes
At 51 Kapil Dev traps Boycott lbw with an excellent swinging delivery and, without addition, Gower goes in the same fashion. Willey, receiving sensible support from Gooch, brings normality to the scene with an uninhibited fifty.

Scene III. England Consolidate
Willey appears less secure against spin and it is no great surprise when he falls victim to his former county colleague, Bedi. The arrival of Botham sees him complete his Test match 'double' in only 21 matches, and he plays with his accustomed power until stumped. Gooch continues safely towards what could be his first international century and at stumps, with 245 on the board, England are soundly placed.

Act II. Batting Deficiencies Camouflaged by Bowling Strength
Scene I. A Sub-standard Session
Gooch fails to add to his overnight score of 79. That maiden Test hundred is proving elusive. The rest of the England innings is undistinguished as the last five limp unconvincingly to 305 all out. In the process Bedi captures his 265th Test wicket.

Scene II. India Succumb to Pace
Once again the England pace bowlers prove too much for the Indian batsmen, despite a brave stand between Viswanath, who makes 62, and Yashpal Sharma. Fortunately for India, bad light stops play early, when they are 137 for five; 168 behind. Willis, with his extra pace and bounce, takes three wickets and Botham again demonstrates his all-round worth with two wickets – Gavaskar and Viswanath, notable scalps – and two catches.

Act III. Saturday, Bloody Saturday
Scene I. The Gentle Surrender
It is strange, but Saturday is so often the worst day of a Test. Certainly many at The Oval would gladly, and with reason, have preferred to be elsewhere. The last five Indian wickets fall regularly to the English seamers as they slump to 202 all out, even before the new ball is due. Yajurvindra Singh, who earlier had fielded so well and bravely in the closest of bat-pad positions, defends stoutly, but finds runs hard to acquire. Not surprisingly he runs out of partners for an undefeated 43, and Willis, Botham and Hendrick share the wickets.

Scene II. A Steady, Unspectacular Advance
Without urgency, and with no real excitement, England advance steadily to a position of complete control by extending their lead of 103 to 280 for three by stumps. Their tactics and method, predictable and effective, are not designed to make spectators vow to be present on the next Saturday of an Oval Test.

Butcher bats better than in the first innings without suggesting himself as a serious candidate for Australia; Gooch gets out when well set; Gower pays the price of cutting at Bedi without getting his left foot far enough over; and Boycott pursues that well-trod path towards another hundred with judgement, vigilance and the occasional handsome stroke, usually off the back foot. At the close he is 83 not out, while Willey, who earlier sent down some tidy overs of off-spin, is undefeated on 26 and has clearly improved his chances of making the Australian trip.

Act IV. England Take Control
Scene I. Grinding Down the Opposition
England are well placed and at some time will declare. The only question of real interest is when. Their position requires as many runs as possible in the shortest possible time, but they proceed fairly quietly along their way to that eventual declaration. Boycott completes another century, his 18th in Tests, though slightly handicapped by injury, and Bairstow contributes a competent fifty. Brearley declares at 334 for eight, leaving the Indians to make 438 for victory in 500 minutes. Everyone wonders just when and by how many England will win.

Scene II. The Start of the Fight-Back
Gavaskar, without undue worry, and Chauhan negotiate the rest of the day. They both suggest that, on this very good pitch with an even bounce, dismissing the Indians will be far from easy. This turns out to be a gross underestimation of the tourists' batting capabilities.

Act V The Impossible Almost Becomes Reality
Scene I. The Masterful Comeback
Gavaskar, with the highly competent assistance of Chauhan, stages a wonderful comeback and provides the most exhilarating day's play of the season; indeed, the most remarkable for many years. At the commencement few think India can survive, let alone come close to snatching what would be one of the greatest victories in the whole of cricket history. One exception is

the incredible Gavaskar, a magnificent batsman with a wonderful defence, intense powers of concentration, and a wide range of brilliant scoring strokes. A record-breaking first-wicket partnership of 213 makes the impossible a real possibility, and then Vengsarkar provides the diminutive Gavaskar, who is playing an innings which justifies the word genius, with more sensible support. Gavaskar reaches 100, 150 and 200 before he is finally caught off the irrepressible Botham for 221. He has steered his team from what looked like certain defeat to the edge of an incredible victory.

Scene II. The Heroic Failure

When Vengsarkar departs for a splendid 52, India, with eight wickets in hand, require 73 runs in 12.5 overs. Such a target is on, especially as Hendrick, the meanest and most dependable member of the England attack, is unable to bowl because of a damaged shoulder. This is where the Indians' lack of experience of chasing runs against the clock, with bowlers seeking only to contain and the field set to save runs, shows. Their big mistake is to change their order. Instead of sending in their second finest batsman, Viswanath, they settle for the hard-hitting of Kapil Dev and the move fails to work. Gavaskar and Viswanath together could have stroked India home against Edmonds and Willey, hardly the most frightening combination in those circumstances.

Tumbling acrobatics give pleasure to Bairstow but do nothing for India's supporters at The Oval. Venkat is run out as the Indians just fail to achieve an historic victory.

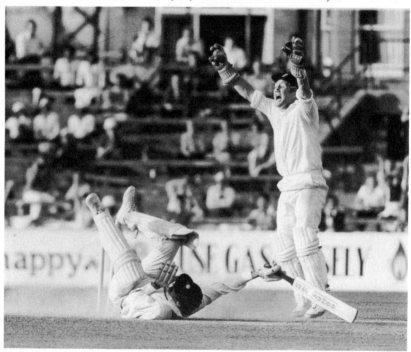

Wickets start to tumble as the overs run out. When the final curtain falls, India are 429 for eight, only nine runs away from a real Indian rope-trick. Predictably that great competitor Botham has a part in five of the last six wickets to fall, but the outstanding feature has been the performance of Sunny Gavaskar. It deserved Oscars for delivery, timing and grace, for the little man truly bestrode the Oval stage like a colossus.

ENGLAND v INDIA 1979 – 4th Test
Played at Kennington Oval, London, 30, 31 August, 1, 3, 4 September
Toss: England   Result: **Match drawn**
Débuts: England – D. L. Bairstow, A. R. Butcher   Man of the Match: S. M. Gavaskar

ENGLAND

G. Boycott	*lbw b* Kapil Dev	35	*b* Ghavri		125
A. R. Butcher	*c* Yajurvindra *b* Venkat	14	*c* Venkat *b* Ghavri		20
G. A. Gooch	*c* Viswanath *b* Ghavri	79	*lbw b* Kapil Dev		31
D. I. Gower	*lbw b* Kapil Dev	0	*c* Reddy *b* Bedi		7
P. Willey	*c* Yajurvindra *b* Bedi	52	*c* Reddy *b* Ghavri		31
I. T. Botham	*st* Reddy *b* Venkat	38	*run out (Bedi/Reddy)*		0
J. M. Brearley*	*b* Ghavri	34	*b* Venkat		11
D. L. Bairstow†	*c* Reddy *b* Kapil Dev	9	*c* Gavaskar *b* Kapil Dev		59
P. H. Edmonds	*c* Kapil Dev *b* Venkat	16	*not out*		27
R. G. D. Willis	*not out*	10			
M. Hendrick	*c* Gavaskar *b* Bedi	0			
Extras	(*lb* 9, *w* 4, *nb* 5)	18	(*lb* 14, *w* 2, *nb* 7)		23
TOTAL		**305**	(8 wickets declared)		**334**

INDIA

S. M. Gavaskar	*c* Bairstow *b* Botham	13		*c* Gower *b* Botham	221
C. P. S. Chauhan	*c* Botham *b* Willis	6		*c* Botham *b* Willis	80
D. B. Vengsarkar	*c* Botham *b* Willis	0		*c* Botham *b* Edmonds	52
G. R. Viswanath	*c* Brearley *b* Botham	62	(6)	*c* Brearley *b* Willey	15
Yashpal Sharma	*lbw b* Willis	27		*lbw b* Botham	19
Yajurvindra Singh	*not out*	43	(7)	*lbw b* Botham	1
Kapil Dev	*b* Hendrick	16	(4)	*c* Gooch *b* Willey	0
K. D. Ghavri	*c* Bairstow *b* Botham	7	(9)	*not out*	3
B. Reddy†	*c* Bairstow *b* Botham	12	(10)	*not out*	5
S. Venkataraghavan*	*c and b* Hendrick	2	(8)	*run out (Botham/Bairstow)*	6
B. S. Bedi	*c* Brearley *b* Hendrick	1			
Extras	(*b* 2, *lb* 3, *w* 5, *nb* 3)	13		(*b* 11, *lb* 15, *w* 1)	27
TOTAL		**202**		(8 wickets)	**429**

INDIA	O	M	R	W	O	M	R	W
Kapil Dev	32	12	83	3	28.5	4	89	2
Ghavri	26	8	61	2	34	11	76	3
Bedi	29.5	4	69	2	26	4	67	1
Yajurvindra	8	2	15	0	2	0	4	0
Venkataraghavan	29	9	59	3	26	4	75	1

ENGLAND	O	M	R	W	O	M	R	W
Willis	18	2	53	3	28	4	89	1
Botham	28	7	65	4	29	5	97	3
Hendrick	22.3	7	38	3	8	2	15	0
Willey	4	1	10	0	43.5	15	96	2
Gooch	2	0	6	0	2	0	9	0
Edmonds	5	1	17	0	38	11	87	1
Butcher					2	0	9	0

FALL OF WICKETS

	E	I	E	I
Wkt	1st	1st	2nd	2nd
1st	45	9	43	213
2nd	51	9	107	366
3rd	51	47	125	367
4th	148	91	192	389
5th	203	130	194	410
6th	245	161	215	411
7th	272	172	291	419
8th	275	192	334	423
9th	304	200	—	—
10th	305	202	—	—

Umpires: D. J. Constant and K. E. Palmer.
Attendance: 36,297 (32, 616 paid). Receipts: £97,154   *Captain   †Wicket-keeper

STATISTICAL SURVEY OF THE SERIES

*Not out

ENGLAND – BATTING AND FIELDING

	Tests	I	NO	HS	Runs	Av	Mins	Balls	Runs/100b	100s	50s	6s	4s	Ct
G. Miller	3	3	1	63*	152	76.00	415	329	46	—	2	—	12	1
G. Boycott	4	5	0	155	378	75.60	1,187	883	43	2	1	—	29	1
D. I. Gower	4	5	1	200*	289	72.25	526	407	71	1	1	2	34	2
I. T. Botham	4	5	0	137	244	48.80	364	312	78	1	—	7	27	10
P. Willey	1	2	0	52	83	41.50	212	175	47	—	—	—	12	—
G. A. Gooch	4	5	0	83	207	41.40	520	442	47	—	2	2	24	6
D. L. Bairstow	1	2	0	59	68	34.00	194	148	46	—	1	—	8	3
R. W. Taylor	3	3	0	64	65	32.50	133	127	51	—	—	—	9	5
D. W. Randall	3	3	0	57	83	27.66	255	223	37	—	1	—	11	4
P. H. Edmonds	4	4	1	27*	81	27.00	187	174	47	—	—	1	12	1
J. M. Brearley	4	5	0	34	96	19.20	400	315	30	—	—	—	8	7
A. R. Butcher	1	2	0	20	34	17.00	192	156	22	—	—	—	3	—
R. G. D. Willis	3	2	2	10*	14	—	54	39	36	—	—	—	2	1
J. K. Lever	1	1	1	6*	6	—	12	8	75	—	—	—	1	—
M. Hendrick	4	2	0	0	0	0.00	12	17	0	—	—	—	—	2
TOTALS	44	48	6	(200*)	1,800	42.85	4,663	3,755	48	4	9	12	192	42

INDIA – BATTING AND FIELDING

‡Plus one 'five'   †Plus one by a substitute

	Tests	I	NO	HS	Runs	Av	Mins	Balls	Runs/100b	100s	50s	6s	4s	Ct/St
S. M. Gavaskar	4	7	0	221	542	77.42	1,401	1,199	45	1	4	—	55	3
G. R. Viswanath	4	7	0	113	341	48.71	944	853	40	1	3	—	39‡	3
Yajurvindra Singh	1	2	1	43*	44	44.00	178	122	36	—	—	—	1	2
D. B. Vengsarkar	4	7	1	103	249	41.50	794	713	35	1	2	—	28	2
C. P. S. Chauhan	4	7	0	80	179	25.57	647	543	33	—	2	—	21	1
Yashpal Sharma	3	5	1	40	102	25.50	315	277	37	—	—	—	7	—
A. D. Gaekwad	2	4	0	25	54	18.00	316	280	19	—	—	—	7	—
K. D. Ghavri	4	6	3	20*	43	14.33	221	184	23	—	—	—	2	1
M. Amarnath	2	3	0	31	41	13.66	158	134	31	—	—	—	7	—
B. Reddy	4	5	1	21	38	9.50	131	100	38	—	—	—	6	9/2
Kapil Dev	4	6	0	21	45	7.50	94	80	56	—	—	2	6	—
S. Venkataraghavan	4	5	0	28	36	7.20	74	63	57	—	—	—	3	1
B. S. Bedi	3	2	0	1	1	0.50	7	9	11	—	—	—	—	—
B. S. Chandrasekhar	1	2	2	0*	0	—	8	3	0	—	—	—	—	—
TOTALS	44	68	10	(221)	1,715	29.56	5,288	4,560	38	3	11	2	182‡	23†/2

COMPARATIVE SCORING RATES
ENGLAND 52.2 runs per 100 balls (1,961 runs, including 161 extras, off 3,755 balls)
INDIA 39.9 runs per 100 balls (1,818 runs, including 103 extras, off 4,560 balls)

ENGLAND – BOWLING

	O	M	R	W	Av	BB	5wI	Balls/Wkt	Runs/100b	NB	Wides
M. Hendrick	129.2	51	218	12	18.16	4-45	—	65	28	4	1
I. T. Botham	179	49	472	20	23.60	5-35	2	54	44	2	4
R. G. D. Willis	102	23	298	10	29.80	3-53	—	61	49	18	4
J. K. Lever	33.5	10	98	2	49.00	1-29	—	102	48	—	1
G. A. Gooch	25	9	49	1	49.00	1-16	—	150	33	—	—
P. Willey	47.5	16	106	2	53.00	2-96	—	144	37	—	—
P. H. Edmonds	161	56	323	6	53.83	2-60	—	161	33	—	—
G. Miller	69	23	134	2	67.00	2-52	—	207	32	—	—
G. Boycott	7	3	8	0	—	—	—	—	19	—	—
A. R. Butcher	2	0	9	0	—	—	—	—	75	—	—
TOTALS	756	240	1,715	55	31.18	(5-35)	2	82	38	24	10

INDIA – BOWLING

	O	M	R	W	Av	BB	5wI	Balls/Wkt	Runs/100b	NB	Wides
Kapil Dev	173.5	49	495	16	30.93	5-146	1	65	47	13	6
B. S. Bedi	103.3	23	249	7	35.57	2-26	—	89	40	—	1
M. Amarnath	33.2	9	100	2	50.00	2-53	—	100	50	13	—
K. D. Ghavri	147	30	448	8	56.00	3-76	—	110	51	23	11
S. Venkataraghavan	115	21	345	6	57.50	3-59	—	115	50	—	—
Yajurvindra Singh	10	2	19	0	—	—	—	—	32	—	1
B. S. Chandrasekhar	29	1	113	0	—	—	—	—	65	—	4
A. D. Gaekwad	3	0	12	0	—	—	—	—	67	—	—
C. P. S. Chauhan	3	0	19	0	—	—	—	—	106	—	—
TOTALS	617.4	135	1,800	39	46.15	(5-146)	1	95	49	49	23

COMPARATIVE BOWLING RATES
ENGLAND 16 overs 5 balls per hour (756 overs in 2,697 minutes)
INDIA 15 overs 4 balls per hour (617.4 overs in 2,368 minutes)

TIME LOST DURING SERIES Unfit playing conditions: 27 hours 28 minutes

Bharath Reddy, India's wicket-keeper, looks back on the price paid for missing a Hendrick delivery in the first Test at Edgbaston.

TOURISTS' FIRST-CLASS MATCHES AND AVERAGES

RESULTS
Played 16   Won 1   Drew 12   Lost 3

NORTHAMPTONSHIRE at Northampton, 27, 28, 29 June. Match drawn. Indians 380–7d (Kapil Dev 102 including a century in 74 minutes, G. R. Viswanath 53) and 259 (D. B. Vengsarkar 63). Northamptonshire 336–3d (R. G. Williams 120, G. Cook 109, W. Larkins 51) and 151–1 (A. J. Lamb 100*).
Kapil Dev became the fourth Indian after S. Wazir Ali (1932), A. A. Baig (1959) and B. P. Patel (1974) to score a hundred in his first first-class match in Britain.

MCC at Lord's, 30 June, 2, 3 July. Match drawn. Indians 305–3d (G. R. Viswanath 105*, C. P. S. Chauhan 82, Yashpal 59*) and 206–5d (Yashpal 59*). MCC 248–3d (P. W. G. Parker 100*, C. J. Tavaré 77) and 117–8.

HAMPSHIRE at Southampton, 4, 5, 6 July. Match drawn. Indians 369–3d (S. M. Gavaskar 166, D. B. Vengsarkar 107) and 235–4d (A. D. Gaekwad 105, Yajurvindra Singh 59). Hampshire 315–9d (J. M. Rice 69, T. E. Jesty 62, D. J. Rock 59) and 145–7 (S. Venkataraghavan 5–33).

LEICESTERSHIRE at Leicester, 7, 8, 9 July. Match drawn. Indians 282 (M. Amarnath 73) and 53–3. Leicestershire 81 (K. D. Ghavri 5–23) and 372–7d (J. C. Balderstone 122*, B. Dudleston 58).

ENGLAND (1st Test) at Birmingham, 12, 13, 14, 16 July. England won by an innings and 83 runs. (See match report for full scorecard.)

MINOR COUNTIES at Orleton Park, Telford, Shropshire, 18, 19, 20 July. Match drawn. Minor Counties 355–4d (J. S. Johnson 146*, R. V. Lewis 88, D. Bailey 67) and 270–9d (D. Bailey 95). Indians 315–4d (D. B. Vengsarkar 138 and C. P. S. Chauhan 108 added 254 for the second wicket) and 205–2 (Yashpal 110*, A. D. Gaekwad 73*).

GLOUCESTERSHIRE at Bristol, 21, 22, 23 July. Gloucestershire won by 7 wickets. Indians 337–5d (S. M. Gavaskar 116, D. B. Vengsarkar 96, Yashpal 64*) and 117 (M. J. Procter 7–13 in 15.3 overs). Gloucestershire 254–7d (P. Bainbridge 81*, M. D. Partridge 65, Zaheer Abbas 59, Yajurvindra Singh 5–75) and 203–3 (Zaheer Abbas 53*).

GLAMORGAN at Swansea, 25, 26, 27 July. Indians won by 7 wickets. Indians 332–4d (G. R. Viswanath 112, A. D. Gaekwad 109) and 110–3. Glamorgan 122 (J. A. Hopkins 55, B. S. Bedi 6— 28) and 317 (P. D. Swart 60, A. Jones 55, B. S. Bedi 6–83).

SOMERSET at Taunton, 28, 29, 30 July. Match drawn. Somerset 298–9d (T. Gard 51*) and 185–7 (P. M. Roebuck 85*). Indians 289 (Yashpal 111).

ENGLAND (2nd Test) at Lord's, 2, 3, 4, 6, 7 August. Match drawn. (See match report for full scorecard.)

DERBYSHIRE at Derby, 8, 9 *(no play)*, 10 August. Match drawn. Derbyshire 253–4d (D. S. Steele 127*, J. G. Wright 55) and 55–0. Indians 329–8d (M. Amarnath 123, S. M. Gavaskar 65).

ESSEX at Chelmsford, 11, 12, 13 August. Match drawn. Essex 146 (K. W. R. Fletcher 64) and 295–6d (K. S. McEwan 68, N. Smith 65, M. H. Denness 58). Indians 215–8d (Yashpal 111, M. Amarnath 55) and 132–2.

ENGLAND (3rd Test) at Leeds, 16, 17 *(no play)*, 18 *(no play)*, 20, 21 August. Match drawn. (See match report for full scorecard.)

LANCASHIRE at Manchester, 22 *(no play)*, 23, 24 August. Match drawn. Indians 96–3d. Lancashire 1–0.

NOTTINGHAMSHIRE at Nottingham, 25, 26, 27 August. Nottinghamshire won by 6 wickets. Indians 149 and 161 (M. Amarnath 59). Nottinghamshire 199 (D. W. Randall 50, S. Venkataraghavan 4–4) and 113–4.

ENGLAND (4th Test) at The Oval, 30, 31 August, 1, 3, 4 September. Match drawn. (See match report for full scorecard.)

Matches between the counties and the Indian touring team were sponsored by Lloyds Industries. Gloucestershire were awarded the Holts Products Trophy and £3,250 for their victory, and Nottinghamshire received £2,750 as runners-up. The Indians won £500 for their win against Glamorgan. Individual awards of £500 went to J. C. Balderstone of Leicestershire (highest score – 122*), M. J. Procter of Gloucestershire (best bowling analysis – 7–13), and G. Sharp of Northamptonshire (most wicket-keeping dismissals – 4), for the best performances against the touring team.

BATTING AND FIELDING

†Plus 6 by substitutes   *Not out

	M	I	NO	HS	Runs	Av	100s	50s	Ct	St
Yashpal Sharma	12	21	6	111	884	58.93	3	3	6	1
S. M. Gavaskar	13	20	1	221	1,062	55.89	3	5	15	—
G. R. Viswanath	13	17	2	113	757	50.46	3	4	4	—
M. Amarnath	11	16	3	123	592	45.53	1	3	2	—
D. B. Vengsarkar	12	19	1	138	751	41.72	3	4	12	—
Yajurvindra Singh	9	14	6	59	293	36.62	—	1	10	—
A. D. Gaekwad	12	20	2	109	574	31.88	2	1	4	—
C. P. S. Chauhan	13	22	2	108	561	28.05	1	3	4	—
B. P. Patel	7	10	4	36*	137	22.83	—	—	1	—
K. D. Ghavri	12	12	5	33*	143	20.42	—	—	1	—
Kapil Dev	13	15	0	102	287	19.13	1	—	4	—
S. Khanna	6	4	1	20	41	13.66	—	—	6	4
B. Reddy	10	12	2	23	101	10.10	—	—	21	2
S. Venkataraghavan	13	10	0	28	101	10.10	—	—	3	—
B. S. Bedi	11	7	4	20	28	9.33	—	—	5	—
B. S. Chandrasekhar	9	5	3	1*	2	1.00	—	—	—	—
TOTALS	176	224	42(221)		6,314	34.69	17	24	98†	7

BOWLING

	O	M	R	W	Av	BB	5wI	10wM	Balls/ wkt	Runs/ 100b
B. S. Bedi	377.5	113	847	33	25.66	6–28	2	1	69	37
Yajurvindra Singh	138	26	437	15	29.13	5–75	1	—	55	53
S. Venkataraghavan	391.5	96	1,065	34	31.32	5–33	1	—	69	45
C. P. S. Chauhan	38.3	5	132	4	33.00	1–7	—	—	58	57
M. Amarnath	194.5	47	533	14	38.07	4–88	—	—	84	46
Yashpal Sharma	31.1	3	123	3	41.00	1–13	—	—	62	66
K. D. Ghavri	345.5	68	1,122	27	41.55	5–23	1	—	77	54
Kapil Dev	422	96	1,327	31	42.80	5–146	1	—	82	52
B. S. Chandrasekhar	204.2	32	655	14	46.78	4–30	—	—	88	53
A. D. Gaekwad	13	4	55	1	55.00	1–10	—	—	78	71
S. M. Gavaskar	8	1	23	0	—	—	—	—	—	48
TOTALS	2,165.2	491	6,319	176	35.90	(6–28)	6	1	74	49

SRI LANKAN TOUR 1979

RESULTS IN FIRST-CLASS MATCHES
Played 9   Won 1   Drew 7   Lost 1

NOTTINGHAMSHIRE at Nottingham, 12, 14, 15 May. Nottinghamshire won by 10 wickets. Sri Lankans 286 (S. R. de S. Wettimuny 83, R. D. Mendis 73, B. Warnapura 52) and 129 (S. A. Jayasinghe 55*, C. E. B. Rice 5–29). Nottinghamshire 408–9d (P. A. Todd 176, C. E. B. Rice 68, H. T. Tunnicliffe 50*) and 10–0.
Sri Lanka's first first-class match in Britain

OXFORD UNIVERSITY at Guildford, 24, 25 June. Sri Lankans won by an innings and 86 runs in two days. Oxford U. 63 (G. R. A. de Silva 6–30, D. S. de Silva 4–13) and 146 (D. S. de Silva 8–46). Sri Lankans 295–8d (R. L. Dias 84*, B. Warnapura 73, A. P. B. Tennekoon 63).

DERBYSHIRE at Derby, 27, 28, 29 June. Match drawn. Derbyshire 264–7d (A. Hill 63, K. J. Barnett 61*) and 250 (A. Hill 75*). Sri Lankans 300 (R. S. Madugalle 86, S. A. Jayasinghe 64).

KENT at Canterbury, 30 June, 2, 3 July. Match drawn. Kent 261–6d (N. Taylor 110 on début, R. A. Woolmer 60) and 201–7 (R. A. Woolmer 101*). Sri Lankans 400–9d (A. P. B. Tennekoon 112, R. S. Madugalle 88, D. S. de Silva 76).
A. P. B. Tennekoon scored Sri Lanka's first first-class hundred in Britain. Neil Taylor, aged 19 years 344 days, became the fifth Kent player to score a hundred on first-class début and the first since 1947 when P. Hearn scored 124 v Warwickshire at Gillingham.

Bandula Warnapura, who captained Sri Lanka to their Prudential Cup win over India, bats against the United States during their ICC Trophy match.

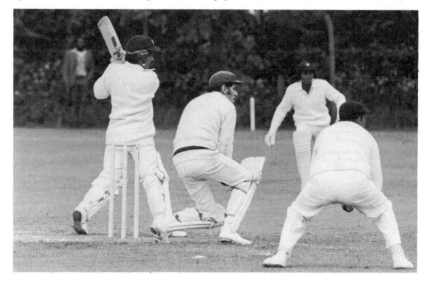

IRELAND at Eglinton, 7, 8, 9 July. Match drawn. Ireland 186–5d (I. J. Anderson 110) and 155–2 (J. F. Short 56). Sri Lankans 288–6d (S. P. Pasqual 101*, R. D. Mendis 82).

WORCESTERSHIRE at Worcester, 11, 12, 13 July. Match drawn. Worcestershire 317–6d (B. L. D'Oliveira 112, D. J. Humphries 68) and 226–5d (D. N. Patel 118*). Sri Lankans 264 (B. Warnapura 68) and 166–1 (R. S. A. Jayasekera 79*, A. P. B. Tennekoon 77*).
Basil D'Oliveira scored the last of his 43 first-class hundreds in his penultimate first-class match.

GLAMORGAN at Swansea, 14, 15, 16 July. Match drawn. Sri Lankans 309–9d (D. S. de Silva 76*) and 260–6d (R. D. Mendis 57, R. S. A. Jayasekera 55). Glamorgan 272–8d (C. L. Smith 67, P. D. Swart 54) and 145–3 (J. A. Hopkins 64).

SCOTLAND at Shawholm, 18, 19 *(no play)*, 20 July. Match drawn. Scotland 120 and 73–3. Sri Lankans 114 (F. Robertson 5–35).

SUSSEX at Horsham, 25, 26, 27 July. Match drawn. Sussex 180 (D. S. de Silva 5–57) and 283–8d (J. R. T. Barclay 102*, K. C. Wessels 66, D. S. de Silva 5–131). Sri Lankans 248 (R. L. Dias 51, J. R. T. Barclay 6–61) and 106–2 (A. P. B. Tennekoon 50).

BATTING AND FIELDING   *Not out

	M	I	NO	HS	Runs	Av	100s	50s	Ct	St
A. P. B. Tennekoon	7	11	1	112	491	49.10	1	3	5	—
D. S. de Silva	6	7	1	76*	291	48.50	—	2	3	—
B. Warnapura	5	7	1	73	232	38.66	—	3	1	—
R. S. A. Jayasekera	5	7	1	79*	230	38.33	—	2	5	2
R. L. Dias	8	10	2	84*	306	38.25	—	2	2	—
R. D. Mendis	7	10	1	82	329	36.55	—	3	2	—
S. P. Pasqual	7	9	2	101*	250	35.71	1	—	3	—
S. A. Jayasinghe	6	7	1	64	183	30.50	—	2	10	4
R. S. Madugalle	7	8	0	88	242	30.25	—	2	8	—
R. G. C. E. Wijesuriya	5	4	2	25	38	19.00	—	—	6	—
S. R. de S. Wettimuny	7	11	0	83	182	16.54	—	1	8	—
A. R. M. Opatha	7	8	1	24	101	14.42	—	—	5	—
F. R. M. de S. Goonetilleke	6	5	1	24*	41	10.25	—	—	—	—
G. R. A. de Silva	7	5	1	16	23	5.75	—	—	2	—
D. L. S. de Silva	4	3	1	7	11	5.50	—	—	2	—
S. Jeganathan	5	6	1	8	21	4.20	—	—	2	—
TOTALS	99	118	17	(112)	2,971	29.41	2	20	64	6

BOWLING

	O	M	R	W	Av	BB	5wI	10wM	Balls/ wkt	Runs/ 100b
D. S. de Silva	298.1	89	781	35	22.31	8–46	3	2	51	44
G. R. de Silva	291.3	85	699	30	23.30	6–30	1	—	58	40
D. L. S. de Silva	79	23	199	6	33.16	2–28	—	—	79	42
A. R. M. Opatha	141	32	443	12	36.91	3–27	—	—	71	52
R. G. C. E. Wijesuriya	153	41	377	10	37.70	3–13	—	—	92	41
S. Jeganathan	87	25	265	7	37.85	4–92	—	—	75	51
F. R. M. de S. Goonetilleke	125	34	360	7	51.42	3–32	—	—	107	48
Also bowled:										
R. L. Dias	1	0	3	0	—	0–3	—	—	—	50
R. S. Madugalle	9	0	32	0	—	0–7	—	—	—	59
S. P. Pasqual	42.1	12	144	2	72.00	1–22	—	—	127	57
B. Warnapura	20.5	6	54	2	27.00	1–12	—	—	63	43
S. R. de S. Wettimuny	1.3	0	10	1	10.00	1–10	—	—	9	111
TOTALS	1,249.1	347	3,367	112	30.06	(8–46)	4	2	67	45

Right: Ray East, the joker in a winning Essex pack.

THE 1979 DOMESTIC SEASON

SCHWEPPES CHAMPIONSHIP 1979

Alan Lee

Rarely, in recent times, has the destiny of the County Championship pennant seemed a foregone conclusion quite as early in the season as it did in 1979. The dominance achieved by Essex was such that, by the end of June, the bookmakers of Ladbrokes were prepared to offer the potential punter only 13 to 8 *on* Keith Fletcher's side winning the title for the first time in their 103-year history. By that time, Essex led by 60 points. They eventually triumphed by 77 as even the plucky few who dared mount a token challenge limped meekly away at the tail-end of the summer.

The success of Essex, however, was not only overwhelmingly convincing but universally popular. It was good to see this band of cheerful, talented jokers, who have long played cricket in the fashion of cavaliers, finally win reward for their enterprise. If John Lever, that remarkably consistent left-arm seamer, was the spearhead of so much of their best cricket, Essex were anything but a one-man team. Their squad, always one of the smallest in first-class cricket, scarcely contained a weak link – and it was that, not the alleged kindness of weather, which won them the Schweppes Championship.

Elsewhere, it must be confessed, suffering at the hands of the rains was acute. Ray Illingworth, experiencing mixed fortunes in his first year as Yorkshire's manager, reckons that they lost 60 per cent of first-class cricket to the weather in the first half of the so-called summer. They were not alone, and the comparative heatwaves of September and October once more prompted the popular chorus for a later start and a later finish. This time, there are distinct signs that action is under way.

Worcestershire, who stepped 13 places up the table from their 1978 poverty and finished runners-up, were perhaps the surprise package of the year. Shrewdly led by Norman Gifford, they relied extensively on the seemingly endless supplies of runs from such as Glenn Turner and Younis Ahmed. Surrey, the club Younis had left behind, prospered too, matching Worcestershire's advance and taking third place.

There were indications that Sussex, who rose to fourth, could be a powerful threat in coming years, but Yorkshire and Kent – that mighty duo from opposite ends of England – both disappointed. Somerset, who won two limited-overs awards and thus became the last county to break a trophy duck, will remember the year fondly . . . but at least three clubs will not. Warwickshire, Derbyshire and Glamorgan, who propped up the table, will be hoping that the cycle which has, in the past, brought all of them honours, turns again pretty sharply to arrest their current unhappy decline.

Left: With 99 wickets, John Lever spearheaded Essex to their first Championship title.

SCHWEPPES COUNTY CHAMPIONSHIP 1979 – FINAL TABLE

		P	W	L	D	Bonus Points Batting	Bowling	Total Points
1	**ESSEX** (2)	21	13	4	4	56	69	281
2	Worcestershire (15)	21	7	4	10	58	62	204
3	Surrey (16)	21	6	3	12	50	70	192
4	Sussex (9)	20	6	4	10	47	65	184
5	Kent (1)	22	6	3	13	49	60	181
6	Leicestershire (6)	21	4	5	12	60	68	176
7	Yorkshire (4)	21	5	3	13	52	63	175
8	Somerset (5)	21	5	1	15	56	55	171
9	Nottinghamshire (7)	19	6	4	9	43	54	169
10	Gloucestershire (10)	20	5	4	11	53	54	167
11	Northamptonshire (17)	21	3	6	12	59	58	153
12	Hampshire (8)	21	3	9	9	39	66	141
13 {	Lancashire (12)	22	4	4	14	37	55	140
	Middlesex (3)	20	3	3	14	44	60	140
15	Warwickshire (11)	21	3	7	11	46	51	133
16	Derbyshire (14)	21	1	6	14	46	60	118
17	Glamorgan (13)	21	0	10	11	35	58	93

Figures in brackets show the 1978 positions.
Ten matches were abandoned without a ball being bowled and are excluded from the above table: Sussex v Gloucestershire at Hove on May 2, 3, 4; Derbyshire v Nottinghamshire at Derby, Gloucestershire v Somerset at Bristol, Middlesex v Sussex at Lord's, Northamptonshire v Glamorgan at Northampton, Surrey v Essex at The Oval, Warwickshire v Worcestershire at Birmingham on May 26, 28, 29; Leicestershire v Hampshire at Leicester, Yorkshire v Nottinghamshire at Sheffield on May 30, 31, June 1; Middlesex v Nottinghamshire at Lord's on June 13, 14, 15.

RESULTS
Figures in brackets after each county in the result line show the total number of points gained from that match, followed by a breakdown of bonus points, e.g. Surrey (19:3/4) shows that Surrey gained 19 points from the match: 12 for winning, plus 3 batting bonus points, plus 4 bowling bonus points. Bonus points are awarded as follows during the first 100 overs of each first innings:

BATTING	POINTS	BOWLING
150—199 runs	*1*	*3 or 4 wickets taken*
200—249 runs	*2*	*5 or 6 wickets taken*
250—299 runs	*3*	*7 or 8 wickets taken*
300 runs and over	*4*	*9 or 10 wickets taken*

*Denotes a not out innings or unbroken partnership.

2, 3, 4 May
DERBYSHIRE (2:0/2) drew with LEICESTERSHIRE (2:1/1) at Derby. No play possible on first day. Leicestershire 160–5d (B. F. Davison 77) and 145–6d. Derbyshire 126–3d (D. S. Steele 74*).

ESSEX (6:4/2) drew with KENT (5:2/3) at Chelmsford. Essex 305–7d (S. Turner 102 in 113 minutes with 5 sixes and 9 fours) and 43–9 (G. W. Johnson 5–12). Kent 250–8 closed (110 overs) (C. J. C. Rowe 108*).
Stuart Turner reached his hundred in 107 minutes before lunch on the second day. Kent's total after 100 overs was 224–6.

HAMPSHIRE (18:2/4) beat GLAMORGAN (4:0/4) by 116 runs with three balls to spare at Southampton. Hampshire 237 (C. G. Greenidge 81, T. E. Jesty 54, A. H. Wilkins 6–79) and

117–6d. Glamorgan 138 (K. Stevenson 5–30) and 100.

MIDDLESEX (0) drew with WARWICKSHIRE (0) at Lord's. No play possible on first or second days. Single-innings match begun with fewer than eight hours remaining. Middlesex 183–3d (M. J. Smith 100*). Warwickshire 76–7.

NOTTINGHAMSHIRE (0) drew with LANCASHIRE (0) at Nottingham. No play possible on first and third days. Nottinghamshire 53–2.

SUSSEX (0) v GLOUCESTERSHIRE (0) at Hove. Match abandoned without a ball being bowled.

WORCESTERSHIRE (7:4/3) drew with SOMERSET (7:4/3) at Worcester. Worcestershire 300–7d (D. N. Patel 68, G. M. Turner 57, Younis

Ahmed 52, B. L. D'Oliveira 51*, J. Garner 6–80). Somerset 330–8d (V. J. Marks 85*, B. C. Rose 84).

Ninety minutes' play was lost on the first day when the pitch had to be moved 2 feet after a motor-roller handle was rolled into it.

YORKSHIRE (8:4/4) drew with NORTHAMPTON- SHIRE (6:3/3) at Middlesbrough. Yorkshire 322–8 closed (100 overs) (R. G. Lumb 113, J. H. Hampshire 55, G. Boycott 53) and 18–1. Northamptonshire 251–9 closed (100 overs) (T. J. Yardley 66*, R. G. Williams 59).

9, 10, 11 May

GLAMORGAN (4:4/0) drew with WORCESTER- SHIRE (2:0/2) at Swansea. No play possible on second and third days. Glamorgan 322–6d (P. D. Swart 122, M. J. Llewellyn 106*). Worcestershire 31–2.

GLOUCESTERSHIRE (4:4/0) drew with SUSSEX (2:0/2) at Bristol. No play possible on second and third days. Gloucestershire 336–6 closed (100 overs) (Sadiq Mohammad 78, A. W. Stovold 62, M. J. Procter 52, J. C. Foat 51). Sussex 29–0.

LANCASHIRE (4:0/4) drew with SURREY (2:2/0) at Manchester. No play possible on second and third days. Surrey 228 (G. R. J. Roope 114, R. M. Ratcliffe 5–63). Lancashire 9–2.

MIDDLESEX (6:3/3) drew with ESSEX (4:2/2) at Lord's. No play possible on third day. Middlesex 265–6d (J. M. Brearley 73). Essex 224–7 (K. S. McEwan 66).

SOMERSET (19:3/4) beat NORTHAMPTONSHIRE (1:0/1) at Taunton. No play possible on second day. Northamptonshire 129 and 122 (V. J. Marks 6–33). Somerset 251–7d (V. J. Marks 76*, P. W. Denning 56, Sarfaz Nawaz 5–79) and 1–0.

WARWICKSHIRE (2:0/2) drew with LEICESTER- SHIRE (5:4/1) at Birmingham. No play possible on second and third days. Leicestershire 301–6 closed (100 overs) (N. E. Briers 119, J. F. Steele 62, C. C. Clifford 5–102). Warwickshire 47–4.

YORKSHIRE (5:3/2) drew with DERBYSHIRE (5:2/3) at Leeds. No play possible on second day. Yorkshire 299–7 closed (100 overs) (G. Boycott 151*, R. G. Lumb 69). Derbyshire 200–6d (P. N. Kirsten 86).

16, 17, 18 May

ESSEX (20:4/4) beat DERBYSHIRE (1:0/1) by an innings and 171 runs at Chesterfield. Essex 335–4 closed (100 overs) (K. W. R. Fletcher 140*, G. A. Gooch 109). Derbyshire 63 (N. Phillip 5–23) and 101 (J. K. Lever 6–52).

Somerset all-rounder Vic Marks began his season in great form with 85 not out in the 'roller handle' match at Worcester and 76 not out and 6–33 against Northamptonshire at Taunton.

Glamorgan all-rounder Rodney Ontong.

GLAMORGAN (3:0/3) drew with YORKSHIRE (4:2/2) at Cardiff. No play possible on second day. Yorkshire 200–8d (G. Boycott 58). Glamorgan 87–6 (R. C. Ontong 52*).

MIDDLESEX (7:3/4) drew with KENT (6:2/4) at Lord's. Kent 242 (C. J. Tavaré 73, M. W. W. Selvey 5–78) and 248–9d (J. N. Shepherd 86). Middlesex 287 (I. J. Gould 89, P. H. Edmonds 61, G. R. Dilley 6–66) and 54–0.

NOTTINGHAMSHIRE (5:1/4) drew with LEICESTERSHIRE (5:1/4) at Nottingham. Nottinghamshire 184 and 215–6d (D. W. Randall 121, M. J. Harris 62). Leicestershire 153 and 68–3.
D. W. Randall scored 113 (1* to 114*) out of 160 in 135 minutes before lunch on the third day.*

SOMERSET (4:1/3) drew with SURREY (7:4/3) at Taunton. Surrey 301–8d (G. P. Howarth 95, D. M. Smith 69*, I. T. Botham 6–81). Somerset 171–7 (P. W. Denning 74).

SUSSEX (20:4/4) beat LANCASHIRE (1:0/1) by an innings and 47 runs in 2 days at Hove. Sussex 302–4d (P. W. G. Parker 100*, K. C. Wessels 95, Imran Khan 53). Lancashire 122 (G. G. Arnold 5–40) and 133.

NORTHAMPTONSHIRE (20:4/4) beat WARWICKSHIRE (1:0/1) by an innings and 70 runs at Birmingham. Northamptonshire 331–4 closed (100 overs) (G. Cook 130, W. Larkins 72, A. J. Lamb 55*). Warwickshire 122 and 139 (P. Willey 5–46).

WORCESTERSHIRE (4:3/1) drew with HAMPSHIRE (6:2/4) at Worcester. Worcestershire 254 (Younis Ahmed 78, J. A. Ormrod 56) and 145–8d. Hampshire 202–4d (J. M. Rice 84*) and 90–4.

26, 27, 28 May
KENT (1:0/1) drew with HAMPSHIRE (8:4/4) at Canterbury. No play possible on first day. Hampshire 309–3 closed (100 overs) (D. R. Turner 73*, T. E. Jesty 73, C. G. Greenidge 68). Kent 126 (K. Stevenson 5–40) and 22–1.

LANCASHIRE (0) drew with YORKSHIRE (0) at Manchester. No play possible on second and third days. Lancashire 29–0.

DERBYSHIRE · (0) v NOTTINGHAMSHIRE (0) at Derby. Match abandoned without a ball being bowled.

GLOUCESTERSHIRE (0) v SOMERSET (0) at Bristol. Match abandoned without a ball being bowled.

MIDDLESEX (0) v SUSSEX (0) at Lord's. Match abandoned without a ball being bowled.

NORTHAMPTONSHIRE (0) v GLAMORGAN (0) at Northampton. Match abandoned without a ball being bowled.

SURREY (0) v ESSEX (0) at The Oval. Match abandoned without a ball being bowled.

WARWICKSHIRE (0) v WORCESTERSHIRE (0) at Birmingham. Match abandoned without a ball being bowled.

30, 31 May, 1 June
ESSEX (12:0/0) beat GLAMORGAN (0) by 9 wickets at Ilford. No play possible on first and second days. Single-innings match begun with fewer than eight hours remaining. Glamorgan 184–7d (R. C. Ontong 86). Essex 185–1 (G. A. Gooch 93*, K. S. McEwan 67*).

LANCASHIRE (1:0/1) drew with GLOUCESTERSHIRE (0) at Manchester. No play possible on second and third days. Gloucestershire 121–4.

LEICESTERSHIRE (0) v HAMPSHIRE (0) at Leicester. Match abandoned without a ball being bowled.

SURREY (4:0/4) drew with NORTHAMPTONSHIRE (1:1/0) at The Oval. No play possible on second day. Northamptonshire 157 (W. Larkins 93, S. T. Clarke 5–55) and 119–4d. Surrey 60–2d and 213–6 (G. S. Clinton 75, A. R. Butcher 61).

WARWICKSHIRE (0) drew with SOMERSET (0) at Birmingham. No play possible on first and second days. Single-innings match begun with less than 8 hours remaining. Somerset 214–7d (P. M. Roebuck 72*, A. M. Ferreira 5–66). Warwickshire 89–2.

YORKSHIRE (0) v NOTTINGHAMSHIRE (0) at Sheffield. Match abandoned without a ball being bowled.

2, 4, 5 June
ESSEX (20:4/4) beat LANCASHIRE (2:0/2) by an innings and 132 runs in 2 days at Ilford. Essex 339–6d (B. R. Hardie 100*, K. S. McEwan 88). Lancashire 84 (J. K. Lever 7–27) and 123.

KENT (16:2/2) beat LEICESTERSHIRE (7:3/4) by 8 wickets at Leicester. Leicestershire 252–6d (R. W. Tolchard 61, D. I. Gower 56) and 195 (D. I. Gower 56, J. C. Balderstone 51, D. L. Underwood 5–38). Kent 245 (A. G. E. Ealham 64, C. S. Cowdrey 53, G. W. Johnson 53, K. Higgs 5–37) and 206–2 (R. A. Woolmer 88*).

MIDDLESEX (8:4/4) drew with GLOUCESTER-SHIRE (2:2/0) at Lord's. Middlesex 300–2d (J. M. Brearley 148*, M. J. Smith 72) and 167–2d (C. T. Radley 65*). Gloucestershire 211 (D. R. Shepherd 70, A. W. Stovold 55) and 116–6.

NOTTINGHAMSHIRE (18:3/3) beat GLAMORGAN (6:2/4) by 6 wickets at Nottingham. Glamorgan 220–8 closed (100 overs) (R. C. Ontong 68, A. Jones 61) and 141 (P. D. Swart 74, R. J. Hadlee 7–28). Nottinghamshire 250–9d (H. T. Tunnicliffe 97) and 112–4.

SOMERSET (6:2/4) drew with HAMPSHIRE (4:2/2) at Taunton. No play possible on first day. Somerset 200–5d (B. C. Rose 51) and 201–6 (B. C. Rose 59). Hampshire 236 (C. G. Greenidge 104, T. E. Jesty 66).

DERBYSHIRE (19:3/4) beat SUSSEX (5:1/4) by 7 wickets with 8 balls to spare at Hove. Sussex 197 (J. R. T. Barclay 70) and 262 (K. C. Wessels 113, P. W. G. Parker 53, G. Miller 5–84). Derbyshire 280 (J. G. Wright 115) and 180–3 (J. G. Wright 61).

WORCESTERSHIRE (4:0/4) drew with NORTH-AMPTONSHIRE (5:3/2) at Worcester. No play possible on first day. Northamptonshire 294 (W. Larkins 51, G. Sharp 51). Worcestershire 146–6d and 129–1 (J. A. Ormrod 51*).
Worcestershire were asked to follow on after N. Gifford had declared without realising that the follow-on margin in a match reduced to two days is 100 runs.

YORKSHIRE (5:1/4) drew with SURREY (5:1/4) at Bradford. Yorkshire 162 (G. Boycott 52, P. Carrick 50, R. D. Jackman 5–59) and 191–6d (J. H. Hampshire 64). Surrey 161 (A. R. Butcher 69) and 181–5 (G. P. Howarth 58).

9, 11, 12 June
DERBYSHIRE (6:3/3) drew with MIDDLESEX (4:1/3) at Derby. Middlesex 194 (R. O. Butcher 56) and 289–4d (C. T. Radley 103, R. O. Butcher 67, G. D. Barlow 55*). Derbyshire 269–9 closed (120 overs) (A. J. Borrington 64) and 107–1 (D. S. Steele 66*).

ESSEX (20:4/4) beat LEICESTERSHIRE (6:2/4) by 99 runs at Chelmsford. Essex 303–9 closed (100 overs) (M. H. Denness 122, N. Smith 90*, K. Higgs 5–72) and 181 (L. B. Taylor 6–61). Leicestershire 232 (B. F. Davison 72, J. K. Lever 6–76) and 153 (B. F. Davison 67, J. K. Lever 7–41).

WARWICKSHIRE (20:4/4) beat GLAMORGAN (2:0/2) by 3 wickets at Swansea. Warwickshire 339–5 (D. L. Amiss 162, K. D. Smith 60) and 133–7. Glamorgan 86 (S. P. Perryman 5–30, C. C. Clifford 5–37) and 385 (E. W. Jones 108, A. Jones 84, J. A. Hopkins 66, S. P. Perryman 5–73).

HAMPSHIRE (6:2/4) drew with NORTHAMPTON-SHIRE (4:1/3) at Portsmouth. Hampshire 212–8 closed (100 overs) (T. E. Jesty 76, P. Willey 5–63) and 142–9d. Northamptonshire 170 and 44–0.

Alan Butcher's sound early-season form was rewarded with a first England cap.

KENT (5:4/1) drew with SUSSEX (5:2/3) at Canterbury. No play possible on second day. Kent 302–7d (C. J. C. Rowe 147*) and 67–5. Sussex 202–4d (K. C. Wessels 70).

SURREY (4:0/4) drew with LANCASHIRE (5:1/4) at The Oval. Lancashire 192 (R. D. Jackman 8–64) and 143–6d (F. C. Hayes 65*). Surrey 117 and 31–1.

GLOUCESTERSHIRE (18:2/4) beat WORCESTER-SHIRE (4:0/4) at Worcester. Gloucestershire 249 (J. D. Inchmore 5–61) and 184 (M. D. Partridge 59*). Worcestershire 149 (M. D. Partridge 5–29) and 119 (M. J. Procter 8–30).

13, 14, 15 June

KENT (1:0/1) drew with SOMERSET (0:0/0) at Dartford. No play possible on first day. Somerset 128–4d and 87–2 (P. A. Slocombe 59*). Kent 31–0d.

MIDDLESEX V NOTTINGHAMSHIRE at Lord's. Match abandoned without a ball being bowled.

NORTHAMPTONSHIRE (0) drew with DERBYSHIRE (0) at Northampton. Play restricted to 12 minutes (first day). Derbyshire 1–0.

ESSEX (20:4/4) beat WARWICKSHIRE (4:1/3) by an innings and 75 runs at Birmingham. Warwickshire 185 (D. L. Amiss 56, J. K. Lever 8–49) and 134 (J. K. Lever 5–38). Essex 394–7d (K. S. McEwan 208*, K. W. R. Fletcher 64).

WORCESTERSHIRE (15:1/2) beat LANCASHIRE (7:3/4) by 6 wickets at Worcester. Lancashire 270–5 closed (100 overs) (J. Simmons 74*, J. Abrahams 60) and 145–8d. Worcestershire 166 (J. A. Ormond 69*, B. W. Reidy 5–61) and 250–4 (Younis Ahmed 79*, E. J. O. Hemsley 68*).

16, 17, 18 June

DERBYSHIRE (7:4/3) drew with LANCASHIRE (6:3/3) at Chesterfield. Lancashire 253–8 closed (100 overs) (B. W. Reidy 131*, D. Lloyd 50) and 268 (G. E. Trim 91, D. S. Steele 5–40). Derbyshire 314–8d (K. J. Barnett 96, H. Cartwright 72) and 135–4 (A. Hill 58).

16, 18, 19 June

KENT (20:4/4) beat GLOUCESTERSHIRE (3:1/2) by an innings and 158 runs at Gloucester. Gloucestershire 154 (D. M. Partridge 56) and 77 (D. L. Underwood 6–24). Kent 389 (116 overs) (C. J. C. Rowe 102, A. G. E. Ealham 87, A. P. E. Knott 63, J. H. Childs 5–118).

NOTTINGHAMSHIRE (20:4/4) beat HAMPSHIRE (3:1/2) by 6 wickets at Bournemouth. Nottinghamshire 325–5 closed (100 overs) (E. E. Hemmings 85*, C. E. B. Rice 81, H. T. Tunnicliffe 58*) and 126–4. Hampshire 156 (T. E. Jesty 50, C. E. B. Rice 6–49) and 292 (D. R.

Turner 129, N. G. Cowley 85).

LEICESTERSHIRE (5:1/4) drew with GLAMORGAN (5:1/4) at Leicester. Leicestershire 194 (B. F. Davison 74, J. C. Balderstone 56, A. E. Cordle 6–49) and 326–7d (J. F. Steele 93, M. Schepens 57, P. B. Clift 56*). Glamorgan 199 (R. C. Ontong 65, P. B. Clift 5–57) and 199–6 (R. C. Ontong 110*).

MIDDLESEX (5:2/3) drew with SURREY (1:1/0) at Lord's. No play possible on first day. Middlesex 212–1d (M. J. Smith 106*, C. T. Radley 88*) and 140–8d (C. T. Radley 50). Surrey 152–8d (A. R. Butcher 83) and 133–6 (G. S. Clinton 52).

NORTHAMPTONSHIRE (7:3/4) drew with YORK-SHIRE (2:1/1) at Northampton. Yorkshire 181–9d and 289–5d (R. G. Lumb 129*, K. Sharp 50). Northamptonshire 250–4d (A. J. Lamb 92) and 59–0.

SOMERSET (6:3/3) drew with ESSEX (8:4/4) at Bath. Somerset 277–9 closed (100 overs) (V. J. Marks 70*, P. M. Roebuck 50) and 284–7d (V. J. Marks 93, C. H. Dredge 55, D. Breakwell 54*). Essex 302–8 closed (100 overs) (K. S. McEwan 71, R. E. East 70, B. R. Hardie 54) and 87–7 (H. R. Moseley 5–18).

SUSSEX (4:4/0) drew with WARWICKSHIRE (7:4/3) at Hove. Sussex 300–8d (J. R. T. Barclay 104*) and 229–6d (K. C. Wessels 66). Warwickshire 300–2d (D. L. Amiss 133, K. D. Smith 71, J. Whitehouse 61*) and 138–5 (D. L. Amiss 53).

20, 21, 22 June

ESSEX (20:4/4) beat DERBYSHIRE (7:3/4) by an innings and 40 runs at Chelmsford. Derbyshire 258 (C. J. Tunnicliffe 57, J. Walters 54, F. W. Swarbrook 52, J. K. Lever 5–72) and 137. Essex 435–9d (K. S. McEwan 185, K. R. Pont 77).

K. S. McEwan scored 100 in 85 minutes and took his overnight score of 0 past 100 before lunch on the second day.*

GLOUCESTERSHIRE (20:4/4) beat HAMPSHIRE (2:0/2) by an innings and 42 runs in 2 days at Gloucester. Gloucestershire 303–6 closed (100 overs) (J. C. Foat 126, A. J. Hignell 60). Hampshire 125 (M. J. Procter 6–67) and 136.

KENT (6:2/4) drew with MIDDLESEX (7:3/4) at Tunbridge Wells. Middlesex 267–9 closed (100 overs) (G. D. Barlow 55, C. T. Radley 52) and 167. Kent 242 (R. A. Woolmer 56, C. J. C. Rowe 56, W. W. Daniel 5–52) and 41–0.

LEICESTERSHIRE (7:3/4) drew with SUSSEX (5:4/1) at Leicester. Sussex 300–9 closed (100 overs) (K. C. Wessels 80, G. G. Arnold 51) and 154–9d. Leicestershire 254–4d (J. F. Steele 155*) and 131–7.

Graham Barlow scored 1,000 runs in the Championship for Middlesex, whose lowly position in the final table was one of the surprises of the 1979 county campaign.

NOTTINGHAMSHIRE (18:3/3) beat NORTH-AMPTONSHIRE (5:3/2) by 7 wickets with 3 balls to spare at Northampton. Northamptonshire 296–8 closed (100 overs) (R. G. Williams 103*, A. J. Lamb 94) and 214–3d (A. J. Lamb 118*, G. Cook 77). Nottinghamshire 255–6 closed (100 overs) (M. J. Harris 133*, C. E. B. Rice 63) and 258–3 (M. J. Harris 132, C. E. B. Rice 53, P. A. Todd 51).

SOMERSET (6:4/2) drew with GLAMORGAN (5:4/1) at Bath. Somerset 302–3 closed (100 overs) (P. A. Slocombe 92, P. W. Denning 88, B. C. Rose 56, P. M. Roebuck 52*) and 248–7d. Glamorgan 303–5 closed (100 overs) (A. Jones 115, M. J. Llewellyn 88) and 185–9 (J. A. Hopkins 90).

WARWICKSHIRE (7:4/3) drew with YORKSHIRE (8:4/4) at Birmingham. Warwickshire 302–9 closed (100 overs) (P. R. Oliver 83, A. M. Ferreira 57) and 253–5 (D. L. Amiss 119). Yorkshire 303–7 closed (100 overs) (R. G. Lumb 118, J. H. Hampshire 73).

23, 25, 26 June
SURREY (19:3/4) beat GLAMORGAN (5:1/4) by 5 wickets at Cardiff. Glamorgan 175 (S. T. Clarke 6–61) and 140 (P. I. Pocock 9–57). Surrey 279 (G. R. J. Roope 97*, G. S. Clinton 65) and 37–5.

KENT (4:4/0) drew with ESSEX (3:0/3) at Tunbridge Wells. No play possible on second and third days. Kent 316–8d (C. J. Tavaré 150*, C. S. Cowdrey 51). Essex 20–1.

LANCASHIRE (15:1/3) beat MIDDLESEX (3:2/1) by 6 wickets with 9 balls to spare at Manchester. Middlesex 200–6d (I. J. Gould 65) and 153–9d (J. Simmons 7–86). Lancashire 150–4d (B. Wood 88*) and 204–4 (B. Wood 74).

LEICESTERSHIRE (19:3/4) beat NOTTINGHAM-SHIRE (5:2/3) by 3 wickets with 3 overs to spare at Leicester. Nottinghamshire 243 (P. A. Todd 80, J. D. Birch 59) and 179. Leicestershire 270–8d (108.5 overs) (R. W. Tolchard 85) and 156–7.

NORTHAMPTONSHIRE (6:3/3) drew with GLOU-CESTERSHIRE (7:4/3) at Northampton. Gloucestershire 325–7 closed (100 overs) (Sadiq Mohammad 165, A. W. Stovold 85) and 266–4d (Zaheer Abbas 92), M. J. Procter 76*, Sadiq Mohammad 70). Northamptonshire 261–8 closed (100 overs) and 275–6 (A. J. Lamb 89).

SUSSEX (20:4/4) beat HAMPSHIRE (2:0/2) by an innings and 80 runs, 10 minutes before lunch at

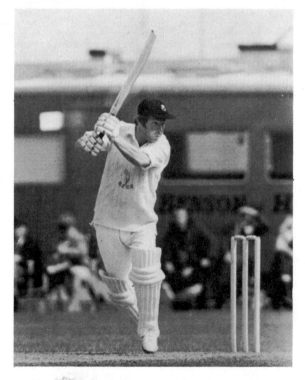

As his team-mates struggled for form, Alan Jones of Glamorgan steadily compiled 1,000 runs for the nineteenth season of his career.

Hove. Sussex 358–5 closed (100 overs) (Imran Khan 154*, K. C. Wessels 65). Hampshire 141 (Imran Khan 6–37) and 137 (T. E. Jesty 52, J. Spencer 6–42).
G. G. Arnold took his 1,000th first-class wicket when he bowled J. M. Rice (first innings).

WORCESTERSHIRE (16:3/1) beat YORKSHIRE (8:4/4) by 5 wickets with 8 balls to spare at Worcester. Yorkshire 393–4 closed (100 overs) (J. D. Love 170*, K. Sharp 80, D. L. Bairstow 52*) and 195–5d (C. W. J. Athey 79*). Worcestershire 260–9 closed (100 overs) (J. A. Ormrod 56) and 329–5 (G. M. Turner 148*).

27, 28, 29 June
SOMERSET (20:4/4) beat WORCESTERSHIRE (5: 2/3) by 208 runs at Taunton. Somerset 392–8 closed (100 overs) (B. C. Rose 93, P. M. Roebuck 78, I. T. Botham 70, J. Cumbes 6–103) and 228–3d (P. M. Roebuck 55*). Worcestershire 217 (Younis Ahmed 85, P. A. Neale 72, J. Garner 5–40) and 195 (V. J. Marks 5–63).

SURREY (20:4/4) beat WARWICKSHIRE (3:2/1) by an innings and 76 runs at The Oval. Warwickshire 221 (A. I. Kallicharran 100) and 128. Surrey 425–6d (125 overs) (A. R. Butcher 169, R. D. V. Knight 100*).

30 June, 2, 3 July
GLOUCESTERSHIRE (7:3/4) drew with GLAMORGAN (8:4/4) at Bristol. Gloucestershire 299 closed (100 overs) Sadiq Mohammad 171) and 288–4d (Sadiq Mohammad 103). Glamorgan 327 (G. C. Holmes 100*, P. D. Swart 75) and 134–3 (R. C. Ontong 50).

LANCASHIRE (20:4/4) beat WORCESTERSHIRE (7:4/3) by 8 wickets at Southport. Worcestershire 342–9 closed (100 overs) (G. M. Turner 109, E. J. O. Hemsley 63, Younis Ahmed 50) and 148 (P. J. W. Allott 5–39). Lancashire 303–7 closed (100 overs) (D. Lloyd 116, J. Abrahams 73) and 191–2 (D. Lloyd 104*, C. H. Lloyd 57*).

NOTTINGHAMSHIRE (3:1/2) drew with SUSSEX (7:3/4) at Nottingham. Nottinghamshire 163 (M. J. Harris 76) and 362–5d (P. A. Todd 174, M. J. Harris 61). Sussex 307–9d (123.2 overs) (G. D. Mendis 118, K. C. Wessels 100) and 64–9 (R. J. Hadlee 7–23).

SURREY (7:3/4) drew with LEICESTERSHIRE (7:4/3) at The Oval. Leicestershire 304 closed (100 overs) (B. F. Davison 84, P. B. Clift 64, J. C. Balderstone 60, R. D. Jackman 6–66) and 252–4d (D. I. Gower 75*, J. F. Steele 65). Surrey 261–8 closed (100 overs) (R. D. V. Knight 71, G. S. Clinton 50) and 168–5 (G. P. Howarth 85).

YORKSHIRE (8:4/4) drew with SOMERSET (4:4/0) at Harrogate. Somerset 313 (P. W. Denning 100, J. Garner 53, D. Breakwell 50*, C. M. Old 5–72) and 308–6d (I. V. A. Richards 116, P. A. Slocombe 51). Yorkshire 305–1d (R. G. Lumb 159, G. Boycott 130*) and 230–5 (J. H. Hampshire 96, C. W. J. Athey 50).
Lumb and Boycott shared the highest opening partnership (288) since the 100 overs limitation was introduced.

7, 9, 10 July
YORKSHIRE (20:4/4) beat DERBYSHIRE (5:2/3) by 9 wickets at Chesterfield. Yorkshire 366–7d (G. Boycott 167) and 113–1 (G. Boycott 57*). Derbyshire 203 (P. N. Kirsten 52) and 272 (G. Miller 82).

ESSEX (20:4/4) beat SUSSEX (2:0/2) by 10 wickets at Southend. Essex 338–5d (M. H. Denness 136, G. A. Gooch 86, K. W. R. Fletcher 52*) and 12–0. Sussex 143 and 204.

SOMERSET (20:4/4) beat GLAMORGAN (5:1/4) by an innings and 8 runs at Swansea. Somerset 340–9d (I. T. Botham 120, P. W. Denning 59, R. C. Ontong 5–78). Glamorgan 152 (J. A. Hopkins 55, V. J. Marks 5–62) and 180 (D. A. Francis 56*, D. Breakwell 6–41).

GLOUCESTERSHIRE (20:4/4) beat HAMPSHIRE (6:2/4) by 130 runs at Southampton. Gloucestershire 337 (A. W. Stovold 156, Sadiq Mohammad 100, M. N. S. Taylor 5–33) and 198–7d (M. J. Procter 74, M. D. Marshall 5–56). Hampshire 219 (J. M. Rice 63) and 186.

KENT (8:4/4) drew with LANCASHIRE (6:2/4) at Maidstone. Kent 301–9d (C. J. Tavaré 87, G. W. Johnson 62*, A. G. E. Ealham 54) and 189–4d (C. J. C Rowe 83*). Lancashire 241 (D. Lloyd 69, D. P. Hughes 60*) and 245–8 (J. Abrahams 79).

NORTHAMPTONSHIRE (5:4/1) drew with WARWICKSHIRE (5:4/1) at Northampton. Northamptonshire 356–3 closed (100 overs) (R. G. Williams 109, G. Cook 90, A. J. Lamb 72*) and 302–4d (R. G. Williams 151*, A. J. Lamb 93). Warwickshire 311–3 closed (100 overs) (A. I. Kallicharran 170*, J. Whitehouse 98) and 86–5.
R. G. Williams (109 and 151) completed a run of three successive hundreds and was capped at the crease on 10 July.*

WORCESTERSHIRE (18:4/2) beat NOTTINGHAMSHIRE (5:3/2) by 49 runs at Nottingham. Worcestershire 386–6 closed (100 overs) (Younis Ahmed 221*, J. A. Ormrod 107) and 227–5d (J. A. Ormrod 71, G. M. Turner 60). Nottinghamshire 287–6 closed (100 overs) (M. J. Harris 94, C. E. B. Rice 59) and 277 (C. E. B. Rice 78, D. W. Randall 75).
Ormrod and Younis Ahmed set a new Worcester-

David Acfield, with Ray East, spun Essex to victory over Notts at Southend.

shire fourth-wicket record with their partnership of 281.

SURREY (7:3/4) drew with MIDDLESEX (4:0/4) at The Oval. Surrey 267–9 closed (100 overs) (A. R. Butcher 108, R. D. Jackman 82) and 205–5d (D. M. Smith 60*, A. R. Butcher 51). Middlesex 147 (C. T. Radley 50, R. D. Jackman 6–41) and 271–6 (C. T. Radley 118*, J. E. Emburey 91*).
Radley and Emburey added 179* in 50 overs for the seventh wicket.

11, 12, 13 July
ESSEX (17:2/3) beat NOTTINGHAMSHIRE (7:3/4) by 46 runs at Southend. Essex 240 (M. H. Denness 65) and 229 (S. Turner 68*, M. K. Bore 5–79). Nottinghamshire 300 (111.5 overs) (C. E. B. Rice 86, H. T. Tunnicliffe 56) and 123 (R. E. East 5–56, D. L. Acfield 5–28).

GLAMORGAN (6:2/4) drew with GLOUCESTERSHIRE (6:2/4) at Cardiff. Glamorgan 239 (R. C. Ontong 56, A. Jones 55, D. A. Graveney 5–69) and 308–5d (R. C. Ontong 104, A. Jones 86). Gloucestershire 244 (Zaheer Abbas 101, A. W. Stovold 55, R. C. Ontong 5–40) and 232–9 (A. J. Hignell 81, D. A. Graveney 56*).

HAMPSHIRE (20:4/4) beat DERBYSHIRE (5:2/3) by 6 wickets at Basingstoke. Derbyshire 209 (C. J. Tunnicliffe 54, D. S. Steele 52, P. N. Kirsten 50. N. G. Cowley 5–44) and 275 (P. N. Kirsten 51, J. W. Southern 6–81). Hampshire 328 (102.1 overs) (M. N. S. Taylor 75, C. G. Greenidge 57, D. S. Steele 6–91) and 158–4 (T. E. Jesty 68*).

LEICESTERSHIRE (20:4/4) beat KENT (3:0/3) by an innings and 39 runs in 2 days at Maidstone. Leicestershire 301–7 closed (100 overs) (J. F. Steele 88, B. F. Davison 66, J. C. Balderstone 65). Kent 111 (L. B. Taylor 5–25) and 151.

MIDDLESEX (7:4/3) drew with YORKSHIRE (5: 3/2) at Lord's. Middlesex 438–5d (M. J. Smith 137, G. D. Barlow 97, N. G. Featherstone 59*) and 161–4d. Yorkshire 289–8 closed (101 overs) (R. G. Lumb 93) and 188–7.
R. G. Lumb became the first batsman to score 1,000 first-class runs in the 1979 season when he reached 30* at 2.58 pm on 13 July.

LANCASHIRE (19:3/4) beat NORTHAMPTONSHIRE (5:2/3) by 72 runs at Northampton. Lancashire 278–8 closed (100 overs) (D Lloyd 70, J. Abrahams 65) and 218–4d (C. H. Lloyd 102, B. Wood 94*). Northamptonshire 214 (P. Willey 68*) and 210 (T. J. Yardley 63, G. Cook 50, D. Lloyd 6–60).

SOMERSET (18:2/4) beat WARWICKSHIRE (5:1/4) by 153 runs at Taunton. Somerset 237 (P. M. Roebuck 89, B. C. Rose 68, D. C. Hopkins 6–67) and 285–4d (P. M. Roebuck 79*, I. V. A.

Richards 60, P. A. Slocomb 54). Warwickshire 169 and 200 (D. L. Amiss 79, V. J. Marks 5–77).

SUSSEX (20:4/4) beat SURREY (5:2/3) by 165 runs at Hove. Sussex 345–8 closed (100 overs) (K. C. Wessels 136, P. W. G. Parker 59, P. J. Graves 59) and 191–4d (G. D. Mendis 80). Surrey 222 (A. R. Butcher 59) and 149 (Imran Khan 5–33).

14, 16, 17 July
LANCASHIRE (5:4/1) drew with DERBYSHIRE (5:4/1) at Liverpool. Lancashire 406–4 (B. Wood 126, C. H. Lloyd 104*, F. C. Hayes 62) and 231–1d (D. Lloyd 135*). Derbyshire 300–4 closed (100 overs) (J. G. Wright 117, D. S. Steele 79) and 260–7 (D. S. Steele 72, J. G. Wright 63, A. J. Borrington 58).

LEICESTERSHIRE (7:4/3) drew with SOMERSET (7:4/3) at Leicester. Leicestershire 307–7 closed (100 overs) (N. E. Briers 109, R. W. Tolchard 109, J. Garner 5–62) and 303–6d (B. Dudleston 142, J. C. Balderstone 51). Somerset 320–7 closed (100 overs) (I. V. A. Richards 106, P. A. Slocombe 66) and 139–3 (B. C. Rose 72*).
Dudleston scored 100 before lunch on the third day (34 overnight).*

NOTTINGHAMSHIRE (20:4/4) beat GLOUCESTERSHIRE (4:0/4) by 8 wickets at Nottingham. Nottinghamshire 368–9 (C. E. B. Rice 129, M. J. Procter 6–81) and 67–2. Gloucestershire 116 (C. E. B. Rice 5–44) and 317 (Zaheer Abbas 96, M. D. Partridge 90).

SURREY (8:4/4) drew with KENT (5:4/1) at The Oval. Kent 303–9 closed (100 overs) (G. W. Johnson 70*, C. S. Cowdrey 65, C. J. C. Rowe 64) and 288–4d (R. A. Woolmer 64, C. J. Tavaré 51). Surrey 370–4 closed (100 overs) (G. S. Clinton 134, G. P. Howarth 109) and 38–0.

WORCESTERSHIRE (7:4/3) drew with SUSSEX (7:4/3) at Worcester. Sussex 300–8 closed (100 overs) (P. W. G. Parker 81*, K. C. Wessels 76, J. R. T. Barclay 56) and 274–8d (Imran Khan 81, J. R. T. Barclay 77, K. C. Wessels 54). Worcestershire 320–8 closed (100 overs) (G. M. Turner 118, P. A. Neale 108, J. R. T. Barclay 6–101) and 113–8.

YORKSHIRE (5:1/4) drew with HAMPSHIRE (6: 3/3) at Bradford. Hampshire 297 (C. G. Greenidge 90, J. W. Southern 61*, N. G. Cowley 50) and 158–4d (T. E. Jesty 68*). Yorkshire 171–7d and 59–4.

21, 23, 24 July
KENT (19:4/3) beat DERBYSHIRE (7:3/4) by 8 wickets at Chesterfield. Derbyshire 252–8 closed (100 overs) (K. J. Barnett 62) and 223 (D. S. Steele 58, D. L. Underwood 6–36). Kent

Mike Procter – hat-tricks against Leicestershire and Yorkshire in 1979.

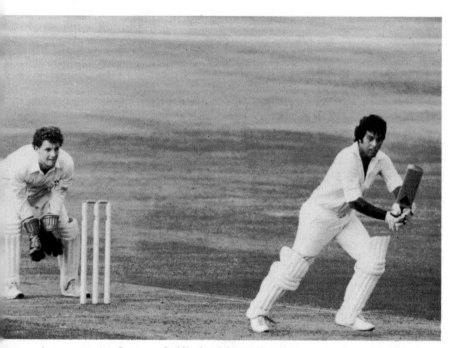

A century against Surrey at Guildford in July was Younis Ahmed's reply to his former employers. Superb throughout, he scored 1,508 Championship runs for Worcestershire.

381–9d (R. A. Woolmer 117, C. S. Cowdrey 83) and 95–2.

WARWICKSHIRE (4:3/1) drew with GLAMORGAN (8:4/4) at Birmingham. Glamorgan 311–3 closed (100 overs) (R. C. Ontong 135*, A. Jones 92) and 156 (D. J. Brown 7–73). Warwickshire 276–9d (J. Whitehouse 81, A. I. Kallicharran 66) and 4–0.

25, 26, 27 July
DERBYSHIRE (8:4/4) drew with GLOUCESTER-SHIRE (5:3/2) at Derby. Gloucestershire 281 (A. W. Stovold 93, Zaheer Abbas 93) and 233 (M. D. Partridge 70, M. J. Procter 52). Derbyshire 334–6 closed (103 overs) (J. G. Wright 70, G. Miller 69*, A. Hill 68) and 17–0. *Derbyshire's score after 100 overs was 316–6.*

ESSEX (20:4/4) beat HAMPSHIRE (4:0/4) by an innings and 33 runs at Bournemouth. Hampshire 128 (J. K. Lever 7–40) and 219 (C. G. Greenidge 67, D. L. Acfield 5–61). Essex 380 (105.5 overs) (B. R. Hardie 146*, G. A. Gooch 70).

LANCASHIRE (3:2/1) drew with WARWICKSHIRE (8:4/4) at Manchester. Warwickshire 359–4 closed (100 overs) (D. L. Amiss 184, T. A. Lloyd 75). Lancashire 208 (C. H. Lloyd 75, C.

C. Clifford 5–96) and 469–9 (J. Lyon 123, R. M. Ratcliffe 101*, C. H. Lloyd 93).
Lyon and Ratcliffe, who each scored their maiden fist-class hundreds, set a new Lancashire eighth-wicket record with their partnership of 158.

MIDDLESEX (15:0/3) beat LEICESTERSHIRE (7: 3/4) by 2 runs at Leicester. Middlesex 97 and 317 (R. O. Butcher 106, C. T. Radley 81). Leicestershire 303 (107.2 overs) (D. I. Gower 98, J. C. Balderstone 56) and 109.

NORTHAMPTONSHIRE (8:4/4) drew with KENT (5:3/2) at Northampton. Northamptonshire 363–6 closed (100 overs) (W. Larkins 103, R. G. Williams 85, G. Cook 67) and 183 (A. J. Lamb 71, D. L. Underwood 5–55). Kent 285 (G. R. Dilley 81, R. A. Woolmer 71) and 127–5.

NOTTINGHAMSHIRE (20:4/4) beat YORKSHIRE (3:1/2) by 8 wickets at Worksop. Nottinghamshire 371–6d (J. D. Birch 94*, P. A. Todd 73, M. J. Harris 64, H. T. Tunnicliffe 62) and 149–2 (D. W. Randall 53*). Yorkshire 159 and 360 (G. Boycott 175* carried his bat through the innings, D. L. Bairstow 61).

WORCESTERSHIRE (20:4/4) beat SURREY (4:1/3)

by 9 wickets at Guildford. Worcestershire 446-7 closed (100 overs) (G. M. Turner 131, Younis Ahmed 107, D. N. Patel 56, P. A. Neale 55) and 48-1. Surrey 183 (J. Cumbes 5-46) and 309 (G. R. J. Roope 87, G. P. Howarth 58).

28, 30, 31 July
ESSEX (17:1/4) beat GLOUCESTERSHIRE (4:0/4) by 4 wickets at Colchester. Gloucestershire 92 and 205 (A. W. Stovold 52, D. L. Acfield 6-56). Essex 170 (N. Phillip 62, B. M. Brain 5-33) and 129-6.

GLAMORGAN (0) drew with LANCASHIRE (4:4/0) at Swansea. No play possible on third day. Lancashire 304-2d (B. Wood 135*, F. C. Hayes 88). Glamorgan 62-1.

KENT (17:1/4) beat NOTTINGHAMSHIRE (4:0/4) by 125 runs at Folkestone. Kent 161 and 172 (M. K. Bore 8-89). Nottinghamshire 121 (D. L. Underwood 6-36) and 87 (D. L. Underwood 7-35).

LEICESTERSHIRE (5:3/2) drew with WORCESTER-SHIRE (8:4/4) at Leicester. Leicestershire 295 (B. Dudleston 68, B. F. Davison 66) and 131-5. Worcestershire 404 (116.5 overs) (G. M. Turner 120, E. J. O. Hemsley 93). *Worcestershire's score after 100 overs was 364-5.*

NORTHAMPTONSHIRE (20:4/4) beat SUSSEX (3: 0/3) by 1 wicket at Northampton. North-amptonshire 303-8 closed (100 overs) (G. Cook 100, P. Willey 68) and 84-9. Sussex 146 (R. G. Williams 5-57) and 240 (P. W. G. Parker 103, P. Willey 5-67).

SURREY (5:1/4) drew with DERBYSHIRE (8:4/4) at The Oval. Derbyshire 322-9 closed (100 overs) (K. J. Barnett 85, A. J. Borrington 64, D. J. Thomas 6-84) and 174-2d (P. N. Kirsten 103*). Surrey 189 (G. P. Howarth 95) and 132-3 (R. D. V. Knight 72*).

HAMPSHIRE (18:2/4) beat WARWICKSHIRE (4: 0/4) by 290 runs at Nuneaton. Hampshire 200 (C. G. Greenidge 64, T. E. Jesty 52, S. P. Perryman 6-69) and 271-4d (D. J. Rock 104, D. R. Turner 57, C. G. Greenidge 52*). Warwickshire 111 (J. M. Rice 5-17) and 70.

YORKSHIRE (18:2/4) beat MIDDLESEX (8:4/4) by 6 wickets at Scarborough. Middlesex 307-9d (C. T. Radley 51) and 111-6d (P. Carrick 5-32). Yorkshire 202-9d (G. Boycott 76) and 217-4 (R. G. Lumb 91*).

1, 2, 3 August
NORTHAMPTONSHIRE (17:3/2) beat DERBYSHIRE (8:4/4) by 8 wickets at Burton upon Trent. Derbyshire 300-6d (J. G. Wright 131, A. Hill

After a fortnight of net practices with the England Prudential Cup squad, Mike Gatting found runs hard to come by when he returned to the round of Championship matches.

99) and 125. Northamptonshire 292 (A. J. Lamb 140*) and 134–2 (W. Larkins 69*).

MIDDLESEX (19:3/4) beat ESSEX (3:0/3) by 10 wickets at Colchester. Essex 106 (W. W. Daniel 6–38) and 225 (K. R. Pont 59, K. W. R. Fletcher 57). Middlesex 299 (105.3 overs) (C. T. Radley 55, K. W. R. Fletcher 5–41) and 36–0.

GLOUCESTERSHIRE (17:4/1) beat LEICESTER-SHIRE (7:4/3) by 8 wickets at Bristol. Leicestershire 314–4 closed (100 overs) (J. C. Balderstone 95, B. Dudleston 78, N. E. Briers 66*) and 134 (J. C. Balderstone 56, M. J. Procter 7–26 including the hat-trick). Gloucestershire 388–8 closed (100 overs) (Sadiq Mohammad 137, M. J. Procter 122, M. D. Partridge 74*) and 61–2.
M. J. Procter became the first player in the history of first-class cricket to take a hat-trick and score a century in the same match on two occasions.

HAMPSHIRE (4:2/2) drew with SOMERSET (7:4/3) at Southampton. Hampshire 225–7 closed (100 overs) (D. R. Turner 94) and 23–2. Somerset 366–6d (P. M. Roebuck 81, P. A. Slocombe 70, P. W. Denning 56, I. V. A. Richards 51).

SURREY (19:3/4) beat KENT (3:0/3) by 10 wickets at Folkestone. Surrey 259–8 closed (100 overs) (G. P. Howarth 75, G. R. J. Roope 57) and 8–0. Kent 94 (R. D. Jackman 5–21) and 171 (R. D. V. Knight 5–63).

SUSSEX (5:2/3) drew with GLAMORGAN (2:0/2) at Eastbourne. No play possible on first day. Sussex 215–5d (Imran Khan 60) and 140–3d (K. C. Wessels 101). Glamorgan 127–8d (A. E. Cordle 51, Imran Khan 5–59) and 144–6 (A. Jones 54).

WORCESTERSHIRE (7:4/3) drew with NOTTING-HAMSHIRE (4:4/0) at Worcester. Worcestershire 400–2 closed (100 overs) (P. A. Neale 163*, E. J. O. Hemsley 81*, J. A. Ormrod 73, G. M. Turner 56) and 273–1d (G. M. Turner 150*, P. A. Neale 84*). Nottinghamshire 328–7 closed (100 overs) (C. E. B. Rice 91, P. A. Todd 86) and 208–9 (M. J. Harris 53, N. Gifford 5–57).

YORKSHIRE (19:3/4) beat WARWICKSHIRE (4:0/4) by 10 wickets at Sheffield. Yorkshire 259 (P. Carrick 65, S. P. Perryman 5–60) and 32–0. Warwickshire 35 (G. B. Stevenson 6–14) and 255 (D. L. Amiss 58, K. D. Smith 52, P. Carrick 5–80).

4, 6, 7 August
DERBYSHIRE (3:0/3) drew with WARWICKSHIRE (6:2/4) at Chesterfield. Derbyshire 122 (D. J. Brown 5–59) and 233–3 (D. S. Steele 122*, A. Hill 92). Warwickshire 267 (109.2 overs) (A. I. Kallicharran 62, K. D. Smith 61).

D. J. Brown became the sixth bowler to take 1,000 fist-class wickets for Warwickshire.

GLAMORGAN (6:2/4) drew with HAMPSHIRE (6:2/4) at Cardiff. No play possible on third day. Glamorgan 205 (A. L. Jones 54) and 49–2. Hampshire 204 (A. H. Wilkins 5–91).

LANCASHIRE (6:2/4) drew with SOMERSET (8: 4/4) at Manchester. Lancashire 200–9 closed (100 overs) (F. C. Hayes 65) and 90–3. Somerset 388–9 closed (100 overs) (P. W. Denning 106, B. C. Rose 87, V. J. Marks 60).

NORTHAMPTONSHIRE (8:4/4) drew with MIDDLE-SEX (6:4/2) at Northampton. Northamptonshire 311–5 closed (100 overs) (W. Larkins 136, P. Willey 76, A. J. Lamb 65) and 269–7d (P. Willey 113*). Middlesex 314 (M. J. Smith 114, G. D. Barlow 50) and 75–1.

NOTTINGHAMSHIRE (2:1/1) drew with SURREY (8:4/4) at Nottingham. Surrey 321–4 closed (100 overs) (G. S. Clinton 120, A. R. Butcher 103, R. D. V. Knight 60*) and 88–5d. Nottinghamshire 156 (M. J. Harris 67) and 11–1.

SUSSEX (8:4/4) drew with KENT (5:2/3) at Eastbourne. Sussex 374–8d (K. C. Wessels 187, P. W. G. Parker 74, Imran Khan 52) and 109–4 (K. C. Wessels 62). Kent 249.

WORCESTERSHIRE (20:4/4) beat ESSEX (5:1/4) by an innings and 22 runs at Worcester. Worcestershire 353–9 closed (100 overs) (J. A. Ormrod 134). Essex 185 (J. Cumbes 5–31) and 146 (J. D. Inchmore 6–35).

YORKSHIRE (5:2/3) drew with LEICESTERSHIRE (7:4/3) at Bradford. Yorkshire 211–8 closed (100 overs) and 156–5. Leicestershire 317–7 closed (100 overs) (J. F. Steele 77, B. F. Davison 58, B. Dudleston 55).

11, 13, 14 August
GLOUCESTERSHIRE (6:3/3) drew with YORK-SHIRE (7:4/3) at Cheltenham. Gloucestershire 288–5d closed (100 overs) (A. J. Hignell 102, A. W. Stovold 62). Yorkshire 303–8d (P. Carrick 128*, G. Boycott 95, M. J. Procter 6–107 including a hat-trick of lbw's).

SURREY (19:3/4) beat HAMPSHIRE (5:2/3) by 10 wickets at Portsmouth. Hampshire 207 (M. N. S. Taylor 53, P. I. Pocock 8–61) and 157 (P. I. Pocock 5–61). Surrey 303 (105.3 overs) (G. P. Howarth 109*, Intikhab Alam 52) and 62–0.
G. R. J. Roope took his 500th first-class catch in the first innings. Gales on the third day caused the bails to be dispensed with, prevented the scoreboard from functioning and necessitated the wicket-keeper (G. R. Stephenson) taping his cap under his chin like a bonnet.

Shrewdly and surely, Norman Gifford led Worcestershire to second in the table.

KENT (4:1/3) drew with WORCESTERSHIRE (7:3/4) at Canterbury. Kent 160 (G. W. Johnson 71) and 386–5d (A. G. E. Ealham 153, C. J. Tavaré 112). Worcestershire 286 (102.2 overs) (Younis Ahmed 170) and 30–2.
Ealham and Tavaré added 251 for the fourth wicket.

MIDDLESEX (20:4/4) beat GLAMORGAN (5:1/4) by an innings and 34 runs at Lord's. Middlesex 323–9 closed (100 overs) (P. H. Edmonds 141*). Glamorgan 159 (M. W. W. Selvey 5–42) and 130.

NORTHAMPTONSHIRE (7:4/3) drew with LEICESTERSHIRE (4:2/2) at Wellingborough. No play possible on third day. Northamptonshire 300–6 closed (100 overs) (W. Larkins 115, A. J. Lamb 77). Leicestershire 211–7 (B. Dudleston 60).

NOTTINGHAMSHIRE (4:0/4) drew with DERBYSHIRE (6:3/3) at Nottingham. Derbyshire 265 (P. N. Kirsten 75, W. K. Watson 6–51) and 57–3d. Nottinghamshire 138–7d and 158–6.

SOMERSET (17:1/4) beat SUSSEX (5:1/4) by 6 wickets at Weston-super-Mare. Sussex 154 and 64 (J. Garner 5–45). Somerset 150 (I. V. A. Richards 65, Imran Khan 5–52) and 71–4.

WARWICKSHIRE (5:4/1) drew with LANCASHIRE (3:1/2) at Birmingham. No play possible on third day. Warwickshire 370–6 closed (100 overs) (G. W. Humpage 81, A. I. Kallicharran 76, D. L. Amiss 61, C. Maynard 53*). Lancashire 179–3 (B. Wood 96*, F. C. Hayes 51).

15, 16, 17 August
GLOUCESTERSHIRE (8:4/4) drew with WORCESTERSHIRE (3:0/3) at Cheltenham. No play possible on third day. Gloucestershire 308–8 closed (100 overs) (Sadiq Mohammad 102, A. J. Hignell 65*, Zaheer Abbas 61). Worcestershire 142–9 (M. J. Procter 5–53).

HAMPSHIRE (8:4/4) drew with MIDDLESEX (2:0/2) at Portsmouth. Middlesex 140 and 8–2. Hampshire 403 (125.5 overs) (C. G. Greenidge 145, N. E. J. Pocock 143*).

KENT (8:4/4) drew with YORKSHIRE (2:0/2) at Canterbury. Kent 345–2 closed (100 overs) (R. A. Woolmer 169, C. J. Tavaré 86*) and 170–3d (C. J. Tavaré 66*). Yorkshire 224 (J. H. Hampshire 82, D. L. Underwood 6–71) and 14–2.

LEICESTERSHIRE (6:4/2) drew with DERBYSHIRE (5:4/1) at Leicester. No play possible on third day. Leicestershire 454–4d (B. Dudleston 202, J. F. Steele 187). Derbyshire 315–5 closed (100 overs) (P. N. Kirsten 135*, J. G. Wright 105).
Dudleston and Steele scored 390 for the first wicket, beating the Leicestershire record set by

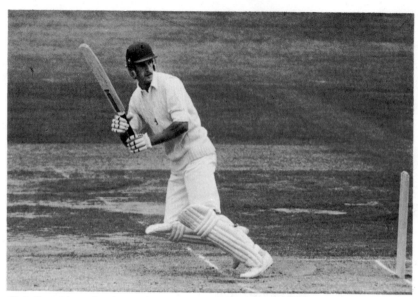

Chris Tavaré kept alive hopes of an England call with 1,239 runs for Kent in the Schweppes Championship, but he failed to shine when put to the test by Bob Willis at the end of the summer.

C. J. B. Wood and H. Whitehead against Worcestershire in 1906.

SOMERSET (2:1/1) drew with NOTTINGHAM-SHIRE (4:0/4) at Weston-super-Mare. No play possible on third day. Somerset 191 (E. E. Hemmings 5–75). Nottinghamshire 37–4.

SURREY (6:2/4) drew with SUSSEX (5:1/4) at The Oval. Surrey 240 (A. R. Butcher 71*, Intikhab Alam 50, Imran Khan 5–31) and 113–3d (G. P. Howarth 68*). Sussex 189 (Imran Khan 60, R. D. Jackman 5–64).

18, 20, 21 August
DERBYSHIRE (5:1/4) drew with WORCESTER-SHIRE (8:4/4) at Derby. Derbyshire 194 (J. D. Inchmore 6–46) and 158 (D. S. Steele 56). Worcestershire 328–9d (P. A. Neale 111, Younis Ahmed 76) and 17–1.

LEICESTERSHIRE (18:2/4) beat GLAMORGAN (3:0/3) by an innings and 60 runs at Cardiff. Glamorgan 59 and 183 (A. L. Jones 79, A. Jones 58, K. Higgs 6–33). Leicestershire 302 (125.3 overs) (J. C. Balderstone 79).

SURREY (15:2/1) beat GLOUCESTERSHIRE (5:3/2) by 1 wicket off last ball. No play possible on first day. Gloucestershire 250–3d (Sadiq Mohammad 126, Zaheer Abbas 64, M. J. Procter 50*) and 216–7d (M. J. Procter 102, Zaheer Abbas 52, R. D. V. Knight 5–44). Surrey 200–5d (G. S. Clinton 82, R. D. V.

Knight 58) and 267–9 (G. R. J. Roope 84).
Procter reached his hundred in 76 minutes off 78 balls, his second fifty taking 17 minutes.

LANCASHIRE (7:3/4) drew with HAMPSHIRE (7:3/4) at Manchester. Hampshire 254 (R. M. Ratcliffe 6–84) and 207 (M. N. S. Taylor 50). Lancashire 287–9d (D. Lloyd 110, B. Wood 61, K. Stevenson 5–106) and 94–2.

MIDDLESEX (6:2/4) drew with SOMERSET (4:4/0) at Lord's. Somerset 315–9d (I. V. A. Richards 156) and 116–6d (P. M. Roebuck 57). Middlesex 218–1d (M. J. Smith 105, M. W. Gatting 93*) and 94–4.
Richards (4 to 104*) scored a hundred before lunch on the second day.*

ESSEX (17:1/4) beat NORTHAMPTONSHIRE (6:2/4) by 7 wickets at Northampton. Northamptonshire 224 (P. Willey 131, S. Turner 5–70) and 203 (A. J. Lamb 66, S. Turner 5–56). Essex 199 (K. S. McEwan 70, K. W. R. Fletcher 52*, Sarfraz Nawaz 6–60) and 229–3 (B. R. Hardie 103*, M. H. Denness 51).
Essex won their first County Championship title at 6.00pm on 21 August with four games still to play.

SUSSEX (19:3/4) beat YORKSHIRE (5:1/4) by 143 runs at Hove. Sussex 267 (G. D. Mendis 84, A. C. S. Pigott 55, G. A. Cope 6–37) and 184–6d (J. R. T. Barclay 55). Yorkshire 198 (R. G. Lumb 61, S. Oldham 50, G. G. Arnold 6–41) and 110 (R. G. L. Cheatle 6–32).

25, 27, 28 August

ESSEX (20:4/4) beat SURREY (7:3/4) by 15 runs at Chelmsford. Essex 300-9 closed (100 overs) (B. R. Hardie 76, N. Phillip 66, M. H. Denness 61) and 101. Surrey 287 (G. P. Howarth 103, G. R. J. Roope 61) and 99.

On 28 August, J. K. Lever became the first bowler to take 100 wickets in first-class matches in the 1979 season.

GLAMORGAN (4:3/1) drew with DERBYSHIRE (1:0/1) at Swansea. No play possible on first day. Glamorgan 250-3d (J. A. Hopkins 94, A. L. Jones 66) and 144 (G. Miller 6-53). Derbyshire 137-3d and 237-8.

KENT (19:3/4) beat HAMPSHIRE (3:0/3) by an innings and 56 runs at Bournemouth. No play possible on first day. Hampshire 144 and 82 (D. L. Underwood 8-28). Kent 282-7d (R. A. Woolmer 105, C. J. Tavaré 101).

LEICESTERSHIRE (8:4/4) drew with NORTHAMP-TONSHIRE (6:4/2) at Leicester. Northampton-shire 366 (A. J. Lamb 178, P. Willey 67) and 250 (P. Willey 69, T. J. Yardley 57, G. Cook 6-72). Leicestershire 357-5 closed (104 overs) (B. Dudleston 93, D. I. Gower 84*) and 87-4.

SOMERSET (4:2/2) drew with GLOUCESTERSHIRE (5:2/3) at Taunton. No play possible on first day. Somerset 200-7d (V. J. Marks 65, B. M. Brain 5-61) and 263-2d (B. C. Rose 133, P. A. Slocombe 103*). Gloucestershire 200-6d (M. J. Procter 93) and 246-8 (Zaheer Abbas 147).

Procter scored 93 in 46 minutes with eight sixes including six off successive balls (two in one over, four in the next) off D. Breakwell.

SUSSEX (4:0/4) drew with MIDDLESEX (2:1/1) at Hove. No play possible on first day. Middlesex 188 (R. G. L. Cheatle 5-52) and 151 (Imran Khan 5-50). Sussex 136-3d (G. D. Mendis 54*, Imran Khan 51*) and 111-6.

WARWICKSHIRE (18:3/3) beat WORCESTERSHIRE (6:4/2) by 4 wickets with 8 balls to spare at Worcester. Worcestershire 300-7d (Younis Ahmed 152*) and 259-2 (G. M. Turner 108, P. A. Neale 101*). Warwickshire 264-5d (A. I. Kallicharran 107*, G. W. Humpage 96) and 298-6 (K. D. Smith 69).

Warwickshire were set to score 296 in a minimum of 219 minutes after Turner and Neale had each scored hundreds before lunch on the third day.

YORKSHIRE (18:2/4) beat LANCASHIRE (3:1/2) by 6 wickets with 3 balls to spare at Leeds. Lancashire 155 and 270 (C. H. Lloyd 103, J. Abrahams 53). Yorkshire 322 (123.4 overs) (G. Boycott 94, J. H. Hampshire 53, A. Sidebottom 51, R. M. Ratcliffe 5-82) and 104-4 (S. N. Hartley 53*).

29, 30, 31 August

ESSEX (19:4/3) beat NORTHAMPTONSHIRE (8:4/4) by 5 wickets at Chelmsford. Northamptonshire 314-7 closed (100 overs) (W. Larkins 91, A. J. Lamb 69) and 137 (R. G. Williams 51, S. Turner 5-39). Essex 303-9d (B. R. Hardie 93, N. Smith 63, B. J. Griffiths 5-76) and 154-5 (K. W. R. Fletcher 50*).

SUSSEX (18:2/4) beat HAMPSHIRE (2:0/2) by 9 wickets at Bournemouth. Hampshire 123 and 179 (C. G. Greenidge 76). Sussex 282 (125.5 overs) (J. R. T. Barclay 73, G. D. Mendis 61) and 24-1.

WORCESTERSHIRE (18:2/4) beat MIDDLESEX (4:0/4) by 165 runs at Lord's. Worcestershire 218 (R. Herkes 6-60) and 234 (G. M. Turner 87, D. J. Humphries 50). Middlesex 145 (N. Gifford 5-12) and 142.

NOTTINGHAMSHIRE (17:4/1) beat WARWICK-SHIRE (7:4/3) by 7 wickets at Birmingham. Warwickshire 327-4 closed (100 overs) (D. L. Amiss 130, T. A. Lloyd 104, A. I. Kallicharran 53*) and 197 (A. I. Kallicharran 60, E. E. Hemmings 5-74). Nottinghamshire 315-8 closed (100 overs) (C. E. B. Rice 85, H. T. Tunnicliffe 68) and 212-3 (M. J. Harris 65*, D. W. Randall 62).

1, 3, 4 September

KENT (19:3/4) beat GLAMORGAN (6:2/4) by an innings and 21 runs in 2 days at Cardiff. Glamorgan 232 (J. A. Hopkins 82, D. L. Underwood 8-88) and 46 (D. L. Underwood 5-14). Kent 299 (Asif Iqbal 152, C. J. Tavaré 50).

GLOUCESTERSHIRE (6:4/2) drew with WARWICK-SHIRE (5:4/1) at Bristol. Gloucestershire 383-3 closed (100 overs) (Zaheer Abbas 151*, C. B. Broad 96, Sadiq Mohammad 66) and 404-4d (Sadiq Mohammad 141, M. J. Procter 92, A. W. Stovold 67). Warwickshire 438-5 closed (100 overs) (D. L. Amiss 232*, A. I. Kallicharran 125) and 105-2 (K. D. Smith 57*).

This match produced 1,330 runs and only 14 wickets. Procter scored 92 off 45 balls in 35 minutes. Amiss and Kallicharran added 262 for the fourth wicket.

LANCASHIRE (5:1/4) drew with NOTTINGHAM-SHIRE (6:2/4) at Blackpool. Nottinghamshire 200 (M. F. Malone 7-88) and 178-9d (D. Lloyd 5-70). Lancashire 155 (D. Lloyd 52, M. K. Bore 5-63) and 126-3 (B. Wood 65*).

LEICESTERSHIRE (20:4/4) beat ESSEX (4:1/3) by 197 runs at Leicester. Leicestershire 310-7 closed (100 overs) (B. Dudleston 62, J. F. Steele 56, J. C. Balderstone 55) and 226-1 (J. F. Steele

107*, J. C. Balderstone 66*). Essex 167 and 172 (B. R. Hardie 59* carried his bat through the innings, N. G. B. Cook 6–57).

SOMERSET (5:1/4) drew with DERBYSHIRE (5:1/4) at Taunton. Somerset 199 (V. J. Marks 52) and 313–7d (B. C. Rose 116, I. V. A. Richards 89). Derbyshire 179 (J. G. Wright 53) and 207–5 (J. G. Wright 142*).

5, 6, 7 September

GLOUCESTERSHIRE (20:4/4) beat NORTHAMPTON-SHIRE (6:3/3) by 135 runs at Bristol. Gloucestershire 395–7d (A. J. Hignell 149*, C. B. Broad 129) and 196–6d (M. J. Procter 105, Sadiq Mohammad 56). Northamptonshire 250 (W. Larkins 59, D. A. Graveney 5–59) and 206 (D. A. Graveney 5–88).
Procter scored 100 in 57 minutes (the fastest of the season) with 2 sixes and 15 fours. His second fifty took 16 minutes.

LANCASHIRE (18:2/4) beat LEICESTERSHIRE (4:0/4) by 10 wickets at Manchester. Leicestershire 148 (M. F. Malone 6–60) and 94 (M. F. Malone 5–32). Lancashire 237 (F. C. Hayes 85*, K. Higgs 6–84) and 7–0.

NOTTINGHAMSHIRE (7:4/3) drew with MIDDLE-SEX (7:4/3) at Nottingham. Nottinghamshire 376–8 closed (100 overs) (D. W. Randall 209, M. W. W. Selvey 5–109) and 279–2d (D. W. Randall 146, M. J. Harris 58*). Middlesex 362–7d (G. D. Barlow 133, W. H. Slack 66, M. W. Gatting 56) and 101–2 (G. D. Barlow 60*).
Randall became the first Nottinghamshire batsman to score 200 and 100 in the same match.

SURREY (20:4/4) beat HAMPSHIRE (3:2/1) by 8 wickets at The Oval. Hampshire 243 (C. G. Greenidge 118, S. T. Clarke 6–90) and 228 (J. M. Rice 61, R. D. Jackman 5–64). Surrey 432 (126.1 overs) (G. P. Howarth 183, D. M. Smith 79, G. S. Clinton 60) and 41–2.

SUSSEX (20:4/4) beat SOMERSET (7:4/3) by 9 wickets at Hove. Somerset 322 (100 overs) (P. M. Roebuck 63) and 232 (P. W. Denning 64, D. J. S. Taylor 50*, Imran Khan 6–53). Sussex 419–8d (K. C. Wessels 146, P. W. G. Parker 90, G. D. Mendis 61) and 139–1 (K. C. Wessels 81*, J. R. T. Barclay 56).

WARWICKSHIRE (18:4/4) beat KENT (2:0/2) by an innings and 174 runs at Birmingham. Kent 143 and 117 (R. G. D. Willis 5–41). Warwickshire 434 (D. L. Amiss 96, C. Maynard 85, P. R. Oliver 79, A. I. Kallicharran 51).

WORCESTERSHIRE (18:4/2) beat GLAMORGAN (6:4/2) by 6 wickets at Worcester. Glamorgan 341–6 closed (100 overs) (A. L. Jones 83, R. C. Ontong 78, J. A. Hopkins 60) and 241 (A. Jones 108, D. N. Patel 5–95). Worcestershire 304–6d (Younis Ahmed 77, P. A. Neale 74, G. M. Turner 70) and 279–4 (G. M. Turner 135, E. J. O. Hemsley 59).

YORKSHIRE (20:4/4) beat ESSEX (6:4/2) by 1 wicket at Scarborough. Essex 339–9d (K. S. McEwan 124, G. A. Gooch 69, K. W. R. Fletcher 50) and 154 (P. Carrick 5–61). Yorkshire 329–6d (R. G. Lumb 110, P. Carrick 59) and 167–9 (S. Turner 5–35).
G. B. Stevenson (23) and G. A. Cope (5* despite a damaged hand) scored 33* for the last wicket to win the match.*

COUNTY CHAMPIONS 1864–1979

1864	Surrey	1896	Yorkshire	1938	Yorkshire
1865	Nottinghamshire	1897	Lancashire	1939	Yorkshire
1866	Middlesex	1898	Yorkshire	1946	Yorkshire
1867	Yorkshire	1899	Surrey	1947	Middlesex
1868	Nottinghamshire	1900	Yorkshire	1948	Glamorgan
1869	{ Nottinghamshire / Yorkshire	1901	Yorkshire	1949	{ Middlesex / Yorkshire
		1902	Yorkshire		
1870	Yorkshire	1903	Middlesex	1950	{ Lancashire / Surrey
1871	Nottinghamshire	1904	Lancashire		
1872	Nottinghamshire	1905	Yorkshire	1951	Warwickshire
1873	{ Gloucestershire / Nottinghamshire	1906	Kent	1952	Surrey
		1907	Nottinghamshire	1953	Surrey
1874	Gloucestershire	1908	Yorkshire	1954	Surrey
1875	Nottinghamshire	1909	Kent	1955	Surrey
1876	Gloucestershire	1910	Kent	1956	Surrey
1877	Gloucestershire	1911	Warwickshire	1957	Surrey
1878	Undecided	1912	Yorkshire	1958	Surrey
1879	{ Nottinghamshire / Lancashire	1913	Kent	1959	Yorkshire
		1914	Surrey	1960	Yorkshire
1880	Nottinghamshire	1919	Yorkshire	1961	Hampshire
1881	Lancashire	1920	Middlesex	1962	Yorkshire
1882	{ Nottinghamshire / Lancashire	1921	Middlesex	1963	Yorkshire
		1922	Yorkshire	1964	Worcestershire
1883	Nottinghamshire	1923	Yorkshire	1965	Worcestershire
1884	Nottinghamshire	1924	Yorkshire	1966	Yorkshire
1885	Nottinghamshire	1925	Yorkshire	1967	Yorkshire
1886	Nottinghamshire	1926	Lancashire	1968	Yorkshire
1887	Surrey	1927	Lancashire	1969	Glamorgan
1888	Surrey	1928	Lancashire	1970	Kent
1889	{ Nottinghamshire / Lancashire / Surrey	1929	Nottinghamshire	1971	Surrey
		1930	Lancashire	1972	Warwickshire
		1931	Yorkshire	1973	Hampshire
1890	Surrey	1932	Yorkshire	1974	Worcestershire
1891	Surrey	1933	Yorkshire	1975	Leicestershire
1892	Surrey	1934	Lancashire	1976	Middlesex
1893	Yorkshire	1935	Yorkshire	1977	{ Middlesex / Kent
1894	Surrey	1936	Derbyshire		
1895	Surrey	1937	Yorkshire	1978	Kent
				1979	Essex

COUNTY CAPS AWARDED 1979

Derbyshire	D. S. Steele
Glamorgan	R. N. S. Hobbs, R. C. Ontong, P. D. Swart
Gloucestershire	J. C. Foat
Hampshire	K. Stevenson
Kent	C. S. Cowdrey, P. R. Downton
Middlesex	R. O. Butcher
Northamptonshire	R. G. Williams
Somerset	J. Garner, V. J. Marks
Sussex	G. G. Arnold, P. W. G. Parker
Worcestershire	D. N. Patel, Younis Ahmed

Essex, Lancashire, Leicestershire, Nottinghamshire, Surrey, Warwickshire and Yorkshire did not award any new caps.

Essex – Schweppes county champions of 1979. Back row (l–r): Mike McEvoy, Alan Lilley, Graham Gooch, Keith Pont, Stephen Malone, Neil Smith, Brian Hardie, Mike Denness. Front row: Ken McEwan, John Lever, Keith Fletcher (captain), Ray East, Stuart Turner, David Acfield. Photo: Press Association.

DERBYSHIRE

President:	The Duke of Devonshire
Chairman:	F. Burton
Secretary:	D. A. Harrison
Captain:	1979 D. S. Steele and G. Miller
	1980 G. Miller
Colours:	Chocolate, amber and pale blue
Headquarters:	

County Cricket Ground,
Nottingham Road, Derby
DE2 6DA.

Honours: County Champions (1) 1936
Gillette Cup Finalists (1) 1969
Benson and Hedges Cup Finalists (1) 1978
1st XI Home Grounds 1980:
Derby; Chesterfield (Queen's Park); Burton upon Trent (Allied Breweries Ground); Ilkeston.

Only a blind man could maintain that all was sweetness and light at Derby during 1979. Quite clearly, the period following the departure of the county's inspirational leader, Eddie Barlow, was taxing for all concerned, and despite reaching the semi-final of the Benson and Hedges Cup, Derbyshire's results painted a forlorn picture. They finished one place off the bottom in both the Schweppes Championship and the John Player League, and were put out by Somerset in their opening Gillette Cup match. A sharper indictment is that they won only one of their 22 three-day matches in the Championship.

The reasons for their poverty are deep and varied. By no means the slightest of these was their regular sacrifice of three players, currently irreplaceable within their squad, to the England team. No other county suffered so severely from Test calls. The captaincy changes, however, were almost equally restricting. Barlow, with his obsessional enthusiasm, demanding dedication and boundless optimism, was an impossibly charismatic man to follow and no-one could envy David Steele, who was recruited from a long career at Northampton and installed in the job. It was an interesting move, contemplated only as an interim measure, but it simply did not work. Steele, for all his adhesive qualities at the crease, is not a natural leader, and after more than one painful episode, he handed over to Geoff Miller on 1 July.

Miller would appear to have the temperament and resource to become an admirable skipper, but his early offerings were naturally tentative. Derbyshire must persevere with him over a long period and then, perhaps, his qualities as a man to mould team spirit will emerge. Having observed him on a number of overseas tours, I do not doubt the ability of this serious and intelligent young man in that respect. Miller's amiable personality also contains a droll side, best shown when he combines with team-mate Mike Hendrick in a hysterical impression of two flat-cap Derbyshire miners chatting over their pints. Miller's frequent departures to the Test squad, however, left his county with a real problem. There was no other obvious leader on the staff, and the job was left between Phil Russell, the 35-year-old coach, and South African Peter Kirsten, a man who always seems to have been around longer than his 24 years insist.

There was, once again, a certain disappointment over Kirsten's batting contribution. He averaged 31, five fewer than in 1978, but everyone, not least the player himself, remains puzzled that a batsman of such natural fluency – rated by many good judges the best of South Africa's rich batting crop – has not scored many more runs in his first two seasons of full-time English cricket. His problem was scoring 30 or 40 with almost ridiculous ease and then presenting an undeserving bowler with an unexpected gift.

Steele and John Wright, the tall, left-handed New Zealand opener, were the most prolific of the county's batsmen. The grey-haired trencher-man

Bob Taylor, like county colleagues Miller and Hendrick, served England well, but Derbyshire were hardly in a position to give so generously to the national side.

produced his 1,190 runs with much of his well-known obduracy but also revealed the occasional refreshing dash of enterprise. Wright confirmed his vast promise and at times looked a player of world class. But probably the most encouraging feature of a bleak summer was the emergence of Kim Barnett as one of the country's most promising batsmen. He made his début in May and by September had scored more than 700 first-class runs – scored them, what is more, with the style of a thoroughbred. Of him, we are all to hear a great deal more.

With Hendrick available, Derbyshire's attack had some of the incision of old. Without him, there was no obvious spearhead: Colin Tunnicliffe's 37 wickets were gained expensively and the other seamers, Bob Wincer and John Walters, would not claim to be more than change bowlers. Miller's off-spin, too, was not consistently productive, and it is something of a commentary that the leading wicket-taker was Steele, previously ranked as little more than an occasional left-arm spin option.

There is to be no easy return to prominence for Derbyshire. But, unlike some of the teams who struggled with them in 1979, they do have a nucleus of genuine talent. Much now depends on Miller's ability to pull the strings.

Schweppes County Championship:	16th	Won 1	Lost 6	Drawn 14	(Abandoned 1)
All First-Class Matches:		Won 1	Lost 6	Drawn 16	(Abandoned 1)
Gillette Cup:	Lost to Somerset in 2nd round				
Benson and Hedges Cup:	Lost to Surrey in semi-final				
John Player League:	16th	Won 4	Lost 9	No result 3	

DERBYSHIRE CHAMPIONSHIP AVERAGES   *Not out

BATTING and FIELDING	M	I	NO	HS	R	Av	100	50	Ct	St
J. G. Wright	17	31	2	142*	1135	39.13	5	4	8	—
D. S. Steele	21	35	7	122*	1025	36.60	1	7	20	—
G. Miller	11	14	4	82	348	34.80	—	2	7	—
F. W. Swarbrook	6	7	2	52	163	32.60	—	1	4	—
P. N. Kirsten	21	35	2	135*	1067	32.33	2	5	20	—
M. Hendrick	9	8	6	29*	63	31.50	—	—	9	—
A. Hill	18	33	2	99	749	24.16	—	4	8	—
A. J. Borrington	18	26	4	64	521	23.68	—	3	8	—
K. J. Barnett	21	33	5	96	661	23.60	—	3	13	—
C. J. Tunnicliffe	19	21	4	57	382	22.47	—	2	8	—
R. W. Taylor	10	10	2	43*	173	21.62	—	—	22	3
I. S. Anderson	4	7	2	38	83	16.60	—	—	1	—
J. Walters	20	25	6	54	264	13.89	—	1	7	—
R. C. Wincer	10	11	4	26	88	12.57	—	—	2	—
A. J. McLellan	11	10	3	41	72	10.28	—	—	23	1
A. J. Mellor	6	6	4	3*	7	3.50	—	—	3	—
P. E. Russell	5	4	0	4	8	2.00	—	—	1	—

Also batted: H. Cartwright (2 matches) 72, 0; J. W. Lister (2 matches) 44, 14, 7, 3.

BOWLING	O	M	R	W	Av	BB	5wI	10wM
Hendrick	286.4	82	588	26	22.61	4-32	—	—
Miller	355	106	851	33	25.78	6-53	2	—
Steele	476.4	127	1393	47	29.63	6-91	2	—
Tunnicliffe	437.5	101	1260	37	34.05	4-35	—	—
Kirsten	263.3	63	736	19	38.73	4-44	—	—
Wincer	215	36	785	20	39.25	4-81	—	—
Walters	343	71	1088	24	45.33	4-100	—	—

Also bowled: Anderson 4-0-13-0; Barnett 87.5-11-333-4; Hill 9-1-46-2; Mellor 90.1-19-276-7; Russell 121-29-335-6; Swarbrook 41-5-161-0.

ESSEX

President: T. N. Pearce
Chairman: A. G. Waterman
Secretary/Manager:
P. J. Edwards
Captain: K. W. R. Fletcher
Colours: Blue, gold and red
Headquarters:
The County Ground, New
Writtle Street, Chelmsford
CM2 0RW.

Honours: County Champions
(1) 1979
Benson and Hedges Cup
Winners (1) 1979
John Player League Runners-
up (3) 1971, 1976, 1977
1st XI Home Grounds 1980:
Chelmsford; Colchester (Castle
Park); Ilford (Valentine's Park);
Southend-on-Sea (Southchurch
Park).

Little of relevance can be added to all the superlatives heaped on Essex for their triumphant 1979. They are talented, enterprising, amusing and vastly popular, and it would come as a surprise if there is a cricket follower in England who begrudges them the first honours of their 103-year history. No-one, surely, would contest captain Keith Fletcher's assertion that this was the best Essex side he has played in – and that over a period of 18 years – nor his prediction that they are capable of remaining at this peak for a further three or four years.

From the time that they burst into an outrageous lead during June, carried chiefly by the spectacular returns of John Lever at a stage when many believed he should have been in England's World Cup side, the Championship virtually descended to an argument over the minor placings. Essex never seemed likely to be caught, and their ultimate advantage of 77 points over runners-up Worcestershire was no fewer than their average lead over the last two months.

One oddity was that, despite the lack of challengers, Essex totalled only eight points more than in 1978, when they were second to Kent. The reason lies with the rain, which damaged the county programme so severely last season and which Essex avoided more than most. That, however, merely made up for their ill-luck in previous years; and by winning six matches more than any other county they stalled claims of an unfair advantage.

The great thing about Essex's success was that it was a genuine team effort. Whereas other counties consistently looked to two or three outstanding individuals, Essex had no dominant stars; only an impressive depth in each department. Naturally, however, there were some telling solo achievements, none more significant than that of Lever, who took more than 100 wickets for the second successive year – something only Derek Underwood, of his contemporaries, equals. The infectiously cheerful 'Jake', never visibly downcast or bitter at his shortage of Test calls, employed his left-arm angle and prodigious swing to enormous benefit. Although not among the country's quickest bowlers, he was often a devastating spearhead.

If Lever didn't get you then, almost inevitably, Phillip or Turner would. 'Nobby' Phillip, the quiet Dominican who served West Indies so well when their Packer players were absent, dabbled with the odd sweet Martini, marvelled in apparent bewilderment at the lunatic humour of most of his

Stuart Turner will have good reason to remember his benefit season: two county titles in addition to gathering more than 500 runs and 50 wickets in the first-class game.

team-mates . . . then went out to bowl with deceptive pace, movement off the seam, and great heart. He took 70 first-class wickets at 21 apiece, while Stuart Turner celebrated his benefit year with 61 first-class victims, *plus* a regular generous share of success in the one-day competitions, wheeling his medium-pace seamers with an intensity that suggested every ball might be his last.

With such a seam attack, there was a stage of the season when the county's spinners were redundant – which at least enabled Ray East to polish up his impressions of a piano player in the outfield. Their time came, of course, and East and the droll David Acfield were responsible for several dramatic wins in the closing weeks.

The Championship was won, not with a fanfare at Chelmsford or Southend, but with something of an anticlimax at Northampton, in front of only a few hundred spectators. It was no damp squib, however, for the stocky Scot, Brian Hardie, whose unbeaten century confirmed the crucial victory. Hardie epitomised the Essex ideal of depth. Coming in at number 5, or sometimes opening, he was rarely spectacular but seldom failed. For the second consecutive year, he averaged 40.

Kenny McEwan, laconic to the point of looking lazy, once again scored the most runs and did it in a manner which mocked the weird fact that his native South Africa still fails to recognise him as a top-class player. When he and Graham Gooch were in form and together – as occurred in the Benson and Hedges Cup final – there was probably no finer sight in 1979 cricket. While McEwan was elegant, wristy and graceful, Gooch punched and savaged the ball with an assurance grown remarkably in the past 18 months.

Then there was 'Gnome', the captain Fletcher. If things were going wrong – and, even for Essex, they did occasionally – more often than not it was Fletcher who steered them out. His Test career may have been cut short by the pacemen of Australia and West Indies, but there are precious few better players on the county circuit.

Haggis, Sammy and Monty – Mike Denness, Neil Smith and Keith Pont – complete the regular side and played their parts; Denness lending his vast experience to the early batting, Smith keeping wicket with agility to belie his bulk and scoring runs at number 9, and Pont, a wit to rival East, admirably filling the all-rounder role yet unable to command a regular place.

Essex did more than merely win matches. They won them in a way which reminded us all that cricket can still be played well *and* enjoyed.

Schweppes County Championship: 1st	Won 13	Lost 4	Drawn 4	(Abandoned 1)
All First-Class Matches:	Won 13	Lost 4	Drawn 6	(Abandoned 1)
Gillette Cup:	Lost to Lancashire in 1st round			
Benson and Hedges Cup:	Winners			
John Player League:	6th	Won 8	Lost 6	No result 2

ESSEX CHAMPIONSHIP AVERAGES   *Not out

BATTING and FIELDING	M	I	NO	HS	R	Av	100	50	Ct	St
B. R. Hardie	21	31	5	146*	1111	42.73	3	4	27	—
K. S. McEwan	21	32	2	208*	1254	41.80	3	5	18	—
G. A. Gooch	10	15	2	109	535	41.15	1	4	14	—
K. W. R. Fletcher	21	31	4	140*	880	32.59	1	6	19	—
M. H. Denness	20	33	2	136	973	31.38	2	3	8	—
S. Turner	21	28	4	102	525	21.87	1	1	14	—
R. E. East	19	25	5	70	390	19.50	—	1	8	—
K. R. Pont	11	17	2	77	292	19.46	—	2	6	—
N. Phillip	21	28	4	66	417	17.37	—	2	6	—
N. Smith	21	26	6	90*	297	14.85	—	2	48	3
A. W. Lilley	3	4	0	35	46	11.50	—	—	1	—
D. L. Acfield	17	15	9	12*	55	9.16	—	—	5	—
M. S. A. McEvoy	7	12	0	28	108	9.00	—	—	11	—
J. K. Lever	17	13	4	14	72	8.00	—	—	3	—

G. E. Sainsbury (1 ct) played in one match but did not bat.

BOWLING	O	M	R	W	Av	BB	5wI	10wM
Lever	575.5	138	1460	99	14.74	8-49	8	2
Turner	537.3	151	1211	57	21.24	5-35	4	1
Phillip	523.1	124	1445	66	21.89	5-23	1	—
Acfield	453.2	131	991	39	25.41	6-56	3	—
East	541.3	162	1253	43	29.13	5-56	1	—

Also bowled: Fletcher 22.3-3-85-8; Gooch 24-4-75-1; Hardie 5-0-39-2; Pont 57-12-154-4; Sainsbury 23-2-79-1.

GLAMORGAN

Patron:	Sir Edward Lewis
President:	Judge Rowe Harding
Chairman:	O. S. Wheatley
Secretary:	P. B. Clift
Captain:	R. N. S. Hobbs
Colours:	Blue and gold
Headquarters:	
6 High Street, Cardiff CF1 1YU.	

Honours: County Champions (2) 1948, 1969
Gillette Cup Finalists (1) 1977
1st XI Home Grounds 1980:
Cardiff (Sophia Gardens);
Ebbw Vale (Welfare Ground);
Swansea (St Helen's).

On the face of it, there is no escaping the facts. Glamorgan endured what was probably the most disastrous season of their 92 years and, for the first time ever, failed to win a single Championship match. It was a traumatic introduction to captaincy for Robin Hobbs, who finished his comeback season dismayed by results and disabled by a mysterious knee injury. Even in the limited-overs competitions, hope was scarce: equal 12th in the John Player League and first-round casualties in the Gillette Cup. Their season was partially redeemed only by reaching the quarter-finals of the Benson and Hedges Cup for the third successive year. They have never gone farther.

Glamorgan's batting remained their most acute problem during 1979. Although Alan Jones inevitably produced his annual 1,000 runs for the 19th successive summer, and Rodney Ontong achieved four figures for the first time, the remainder of the order was erratic, even untrustworthy. Peter Swart, the burly Rhodesian all-rounder, averaged under 30 and, although occasionally batting with pleasing fluency, was too often out early. John Hopkins, a pressing candidate for an England opener's place only two years ago, fell away badly and was subsequently dropped down the order to regain confidence. Mike Llewellyn, the left-hander of awesome shoulder-power who looked to have made such progress in 1978, could not even make the side by the end of the season.

With these senior players struggling, it was small wonder that highly promising youngsters such as Alan Lewis Jones did not make the strides that might have been expected. Jones's average was only around the 20 mark; but when given the responsibility of opening late in the summer, he gave indications of a growing maturity to confirm the ability he has shown for England Young Cricketers. Still more encouraging was the emergence of a Geordie called Geoffrey Holmes, given his chance in the middle order and responding with a maiden century before his 21st birthday. There was much to admire in his batting during the latter weeks of the season, and he could be one of the county's stalwarts through the eighties.

The side's bowling limitations are exposed by the fact that one has to glance 33 places down the national averages to find a Glamorgan name – left-arm seamer Alan Wilkins who, in fact, was thwarted by injury to the extent that he took only 30 wickets. With Malcolm Nash also a victim of fitness worries, and providing only 16 wickets, much of the burden fell on the ever-willing Tony Cordle. Born in 1940, this cheerful Barbadian was in his

Like many in Wales, Alan Lewis Jones will not want 1979 to linger in the memory. Yet the wheel of fortune could so easily turn for Glamorgan in the 1980s.

17th season with Glamorgan. He not only collected 58 wickets but also, in a John Player League match at Portsmouth, the first hat-trick of his career. Hobbs and Barry Lloyd, the spinners, failed to take 50 wickets between them, but the real and urgent deficiency was an incisive spearhead bowler – something the county have not possessed for a number of seasons.

With the powers of Alan Jones and Nash – whose reliability could never be questioned over so many years – now apparently waning, things may be said to look bleak down Cardiff way. Swart, too, has decided to retire from the full-time game and return to the northern leagues, but his place as the imported all-rounder goes to the precocious Pakistani, Javed Miandad. As the odd-man-out in a strange overcrowding of overseas players at Sussex, Miandad has felt rightly aggrieved to be deprived of senior cricket, and his capture represents a major coup and a great source of hope for Glamorgan. Hobbs, despite the sadness of his first summer since unexpectedly returning as the only English leg-spinner in our game – just as he was in his Essex days – has two years of his contract to run. Perhaps if Holmes, Lewis Jones and others continue to develop, the future holds less gloom than of late for him and his committee.

Schweppes County Championship:	17th	Won 0	Lost 10	Drawn 11	(Abandoned 1)
All First-Class Matches:		Won 1	Lost 11	Drawn 12	(Abandoned 1)
Gillette Cup:	Lost to Kent in 1st round				
Benson and Hedges Cup:	Lost to Derbyshire in quarter-final				
John Player League:	12th	Won 6	Lost 10		

GLAMORGAN CHAMPIONSHIP AVERAGES   *Not out

BATTING and FIELDING	M	I	NO	HS	R	Av	100	50	Ct	St
R. C. Ontong	21	37	5	135*	1120	35.00	3	7	8	—
A. Jones	20	36	0	115	1106	30.72	2	7	10	—
P. D. Swart	18	31	4	122	754	27.92	1	2	12	—
J. A. Hopkins	20	36	1	94	945	27.00	—	6	15	—
D. A. Francis	13	23	7	56*	381	23.81	—	1	3	—
G. C. Holmes	8	11	3	100*	190	23.75	1	—	1	—
A. L. Jones	13	23	2	83	461	21.95	—	4	9	—
M. J. Llewellyn	9	14	1	106*	258	19.84	1	1	4	—
B. J. Lloyd	15	23	6	43	266	15.64	—	—	11	—
A. E. Cordle	21	27	6	51	316	15.04	—	1	11	—
E. W. Jones	19	31	6	108	351	14.04	1	—	37	2
G. Richards	9	12	1	34	142	12.90	—	—	3	—
M. A. Nash	9	11	0	41	123	11.18	—	—	5	—
R. N. S. Hobbs	17	19	7	29	101	8.41	—	—	8	—
A. H. Wilkins	8	9	1	17	34	4.25	—	—	1	—
A. J. Mack	7	10	4	5	13	2.16	—	—	1	—
N. J. Perry	4	4	1	1	1	0.33	—	—	—	—

BOWLING	O	M	R	W	Av	BB	5wI	10wM
Wilkins	204.5	45	603	22	27.40	6–79	2	—
Cordle	587.3	124	1572	56	28.07	6–49	1	—
Ontong	255	48	802	28	28.64	5–40	2	—
Swart	192	40	563	17	33.11	4–61	—	—
Mack	160.3	25	513	14	36.64	4–62	—	—
Nash	226.3	66	619	16	38.68	4–50	—	—
Lloyd	372.1	85	1038	26	39.92	4–55	—	—
Hobbs	231.3	62	720	17	42.35	2–8	—	—

Also bowled: Holmes 5.1–1–28–0; Perry 113–19–386–7; Richards 42–9–138–4.

GLOUCESTERSHIRE

Patron:	The Duke of Beaufort
President:	B. O. Allen
Chairman:	J. K. R. Graveney
Secretary/Manager:	A. S. Brown
Captain:	1979 M. J. Procter
Colours:	Blue, gold, brown, sky-blue, green and red
Headquarters:	Phoenix County Ground, Nevil Road, Bristol BS7 9EJ.

Honours: County Champions (3) 1874, 1876, 1877
Joint Champions (1) 1873
Gillette Cup Winners (1) 1973
Benson and Hedges Cup Winners (1) 1977
1st XI Home Grounds 1980: Bristol; Cheltenham (College Ground); Gloucester (Winget Sports Ground); Moreton-in-Marsh.

Any talk of Gloucestershire during 1979 inevitably centred around Mike Procter, whose feats once more raised the tragedy of the politics which have deprived Test cricket of a remarkable individual. Not that Gloucestershire are complaining.

In brief, Procter scored the fastest hundred of the season, took a hat-trick twice in consecutive matches, and picked up almost every Player of the Year award available. Scarcely a match passed without some spectacular contribution from this amiable South African, who now believes that he may play only one more season of county cricket before returning home for good. He has already decided to relinquish the county captaincy, which he held for three years, and hand over to a younger man.

His personal figures for last season were 1,241 runs and 81 wickets, agonisingly close to the 'double', probably his final consuming ambition in English cricket. Fred Titmus was the last to achieve it, back in 1967, but there were times last summer when Procter threatened to do what many insist is now impossible. His hat-tricks against Leicestershire – accompanied by a century – and Yorkshire in early August revived memories of the early 1970s, when his pace rivalled the world's fastest, and his batting, which he has sometimes sacrificed to the need for long spells of bowling, was often destructive genius. Three times he made outrageous attempts on the fastest century, only to fall in the 90s, and it was 6 September and his final innings of the season when Northamptonshire were taken apart for a 57-minute hundred.

Even Procter's manly efforts at a one-man team could not entirely camouflage the deficiencies that still exist, however. Tenth position in the Championship for the second successive year is probably a fair reflection of a team which was short on both depth and consistency. The batting, on paper at least, was plentiful, with the two Pakistanis, Sadiq and Zaheer, to complement Procter's raw aggression with their own brand of delicate elegance. Sadiq averaged 56, Zaheer 46, so the platform was frequently there for those who followed.

Andy Stovold, 26 years old but already in his seventh season, scored more runs than ever before and provided solidity among the strokeplayers. He was

Scores of 86 and 49 on his début against Cambridge helped Chris Broad establish himself in the Gloucestershire first team, and against Northants he scored a maiden century.

also quite naturally a candidate to succeed Procter as captain, as was Alastair Hignell, the England rugby fullback. Hignell missed much of the season on a rugby tour with England but on his return batted with high promise on occasions. In the final match, Northamptonshire were not only destroyed by Procter, but also ground into the September dust by Hignell and a young, Bristolian left-hander named Chris Broad. Together, they put on 228 for the fifth wicket, both men scoring centuries and Broad confirming the promise he had shown since the early-season one-day games.

With all this batting success, one would have thought Gloucestershire deserved a higher rating in the Championship. Sadly, for they are a popular county, they frequently failed to bowl sides out. Despite the perennial threat of Procter, the rest of their seam attack is limited to the efforts of Brian Brain and sundry developing youngsters. Brain has often been vaunted as the most difficult English seamer to play, particularly when the conditions suit him. By his own standards, however, 1979 was not a fruitful year: just 47 wickets, in fact. He will be 40 this season and Gloucestershire may rapidly be faced with replacing their entire new-ball attack.

Neither of the spinners, John Childs and David Graveney, was as productive as before, and perhaps the major addition to the side was Mike Garnham, a 19-year-old wicket-keeper-batsman with a multi-national background. Born in South Africa, he went to school in Melbourne and Perth before completing his education in Devon, for whom he played before going to Gloucestershire. However, the new season will see him at Leicestershire, and Andy Brassington, surely one of the finest young 'keepers in England, should retain his place behind the stumps.

On a sadder note was the departure of Jim Foat, not retained at the end of the season. A brilliant fielder and a batsman who has never fulfilled his undoubted potential, Foat was a memorable character off the field, one of cricket's comedians.

Schweppes County Championship:	10th	Won 5	Lost 4	Drawn 11 (Abandoned 2)
All First-Class Matches:		Won 6	Lost 4	Drawn 13 (Abandoned 2)
Gillette Cup:	Lost to Hampshire in 1st round			
Benson and Hedges Cup:	Failed to qualify for Q-F (4th in Group A)			
John Player League:	8th	Won 7	Lost 7	No result 2

GLOUCESTERSHIRE CHAMPIONSHIP AVERAGES   *Not out

BATTING and FIELDING	M	I	NO	HS	R	Av	100	50	Ct	St
Sadiq Mohammad	15	27	2	171	1504	60.16	8	4	12	—
Zaheer Abbas	16	28	1	151*	1192	44.18	3	6	8	—
M. J. Procter	20	34	3	122	1200	38.70	3	7	11	—
A. J. Hignell	15	25	6	149*	695	36.57	2	3	19	—
A. W. Stovold	20	35	0	156	1220	34.85	1	8	18	—
M. D. Partridge	20	28	9	90	613	32.26	—	5	8	—
C. B. Broad	7	13	1	129	334	27.83	1	1	3	—
J. C. Foat	9	15	2	126	343	26.38	1	1	5	—
M. A. Garnham	3	4	2	18	50	25.00	—	—	2	2
D. R. Shepherd	6	9	1	70	197	24.62	—	1	—	—
D. A. Graveney	19	24	8	56*	283	17.68	—	1	5	—
M. W. Stovold	6	9	1	27	84	10.50	—	—	1	—
J. H. Childs	19	15	9	9	47	7.83	—	—	5	—
B. M. Brain	20	18	0	24	123	6.83	—	—	3	—
A. J. Brassington	17	19	7	17	73	6.08	—	—	14	4
P. Bainbridge	7	13	1	19	68	5.66	—	—	—	—

Also batted: N. H. Finan (1 match) 4*.

BOWLING	O	M	R	W	Av	BB	5wI	10wM
Procter	547.2	128	1491	74	20.14	8–30	6	1
Brain	436.5	109	1191	42	28.35	5–33	2	—
Graveney	389	91	1238	38	32.57	5–59	3	1
Childs	602.3	178	1704	46	37.04	5–118	1	—
Partridge	236.4	41	833	20	41.65	5–29	1	—

Also bowled: Bainbridge 54–15–184–5; Foat 1–0–3–0; Hignell 1–0–4–0; Sadiq 48–7–180–4; A. W. Stovold 6.4–2–22–1; Zaheer 2–0–2–0.

HAMPSHIRE

President: R. Aird	*Honours:* County Champions
Chairman: G. Ford	(2) 1961, 1973
Secretary: A. K. James	John Player League Champions
Captain: 1979 G. R. Stephenson	(2) 1975, 1978
1980 N. E. J. Pocock	*1st XI Home Grounds 1980:*
Colours: Blue, gold and	Southampton; Basingstoke
white	(May's Bounty); Bournemouth
Headquarters:	(Dean Park); Portsmouth
County Ground, Northlands	(United Services Officers'
Road, Southampton SO9 2TY.	Ground).

It is impossible to lose two players of the calibre of Barry Richards and Andy Roberts, plus a respected and talented captain like Richard Gilliat, without suffering for it. The effect is that of a hangover. Unless you have the resilience, or in this case the reserves of talent, to counter the deficiencies, life will become an arduous struggle.

Hampshire managed to avoid disgracing themselves but never hinted at aspiring to their heights of recent years. They finished 12th in the Championship and their problem was that they seldom scored enough runs. One could count on the fingers of one hand – and still have some left – the number of occasions they reached the magical 300 in the first innings, and the result was a meagre total of 39 batting bonus points, fewer than all but two counties. They were regularly beaten by an innings and at one stage lost three matches in succession in this ignominious fashion. The new captain, Bob Stephenson – the amiable man from Derby who makes a winter-living from repairing sports equipment – faced more crises than even his phlegmatic nature would have liked.

All that is on the debit side, but there was not a complete absence of encouragement for the faithful of Southampton, Portsmouth and Bourne-mouth. The arrival of Malcolm Marshall, for instance, effectively ensured that Roberts, whose contributions had deteriorated steadily, was barely missed. Hampshire, not surprisingly, had turned back to the Caribbean for a replacement when Roberts departed. Thanks to a recommendation from Peter Short, former secretary of the West Indies Board, they were able to approach and secure Marshall even before he began his Test career with three matches against India in the winter of 1978–79. He bounced into English cricket with a match-winning spell against Glamorgan in the first week of May, amid flurries of snow which can scarcely have been a familiar sight to him. And despite missing a fortnight to join the West Indies World Cup squad, he took 47 first-class wickets at a very reasonable outlay. At times he was genuinely fast, generating pace and bounce from a physique and run-up rather reminiscent of Michael Holding's.

As a partner, Marshall had that able medium-pacer, Keith Stevenson. It is an odd coincidence, but nothing more, that Hampshire's two namesakes – one spells his name with a 'v', the other 'ph' – were born and bred in Derby. Keith made his début for Derbyshire five years after Bob had left,

Hampshire wasted no time finding a replacement for Andy Roberts, producing in Malcolm Marshall another fast bowler of genuine pace who will trouble most in a drier summer.

then followed him to the south coast for the 1978 season, seeking the regular cricket he had never achieved in the Midlands. He took 56 wickets in his first season, 69 in his second; evidence of another shrewd signing.

These two apart, the county's bowling was somewhat stereotyped; unlimited medium-pace, the off-spin of Nigel Cowley, and the left-arm spin of John Southern, which has not yet developed to expectations. Southern took only 29 wickets, partly because an attack of appendicitis sidelined him for some while.

Hampshire's batting has long relied on its top four. When Richards and Gordon Greenidge were opening, with David Turner and Trevor Jesty to follow, they rarely needed more. But things are different now. Richards has gone, Greenidge played almost the entire season with knee and ankle ailments, Turner endured a nightmare summer, and Jesty, although consistent, never scored above 76. Greenidge, in my view, deserved a benefit on the spot for refusing to rest despite a permanent limp. He batted better on one good leg than most can on two, rode some cynical criticism from opposing captains, and finished the year with an average of 50 and his reputation as one of the most loyal and unselfish overseas players intact.

John Rice was promoted from the lower reaches to open and did enough to suggest the job may be his for some years. Far from spectacular, he nevertheless applied his considerable frame diligently, and began to bat with some fluency in the later weeks of the season. Of the younger players on the staff, Tim Tremlett continued to advance, albeit slowly, and Paul Terry, born in West Germany but educated in the cricket academy of Millfield, displayed the occasional touch of class which augurs well for a more prosperous future for Hampshire.

Schweppes County Championship:	12th	Won 3	Lost 9	Drawn 9	(Abandoned 1)
All First-Class Matches:		Won 3	Lost 9	Drawn 11	(Abandoned 1)
Gillette Cup:	Lost to Middlesex in 2nd round				
Benson and Hedges Cup:	Failed to qualify for Q-F (5th in Group B)				
John Player League:	10th	Won 7	Lost 8	No result 1	

HAMPSHIRE CHAMPIONSHIP AVERAGES

*Not out

BATTING and FIELDING	M	I	NO	HS	R	Av	100	50	Ct	St
C. G. Greenidge	17	30	2	145	1404	50.14	3	8	27	—
T. E. Jesty	18	33	3	76	1025	34.16	—	9	16	—
J. M. Rice	21	38	3	84*	804	22.97	—	3	15	—
D. R. Turner	20	36	1	129	766	21.88	1	3	3	—
N. E. J. Pocock	10	19	2	143*	359	21.11	1	—	8	—
M. N. S. Taylor	20	28	3	75	480	19.20	—	3	9	—
J. W. Southern	14	20	8	61*	228	19.00	—	1	5	—
N. G. Cowley	21	36	6	85	523	17.43	—	2	6	—
D. J. Rock	14	24	1	104	397	17.26	1	—	8	—
M. A. Bailey	4	6	1	24	76	15.20	—	—	1	—
V. P. Terry	5	7	0	21	86	12.28	—	—	4	—
G. R. Stephenson	21	30	2	43	308	11.00	—	—	29	4
M. D. Marshall	17	22	1	38	168	8.00	—	—	10	—
K. Stevenson	21	28	15	24	96	7.38	—	—	5	—
T. M. Tremlett	5	10	1	18	43	4.77	—	—	3	—
M. C. J. Nicholas	3	6	0	10	28	4.66	—	—	1	—

BOWLING	O	M	R	W	Av	BB	5wI	10wM
Marshall	440	142	957	46	20.80	5–56	1	—
Stevenson	509.3	121	1459	61	23.91	5–30	3	—
Taylor	249.5	68	696	27	25.77	5–33	1	—
Rice	257.4	55	707	24	29.45	5–17	1	—
Southern	333.2	114	829	28	29.60	6–81	1	—
Cowley	475.4	144	1184	37	32.00	5–44	1	—

Also bowled: Bailey 50.4–9–151–3; Jesty 31–9–105–1; Nicholas 0.1–0–1–0; Pocock 5–3–12–1; Stephenson 1–1–0–0; Tremlett 76.2–13–236–6; Turner 14.5–5–65–2.

KENT

Patron:	HRH The Duke of Kent
President:	T. A. Pearce
Chairman:	W. C. W. Brice
Secretary:	Gp. Capt. M. D. Fenner
Captain:	A. G. E. Ealham
Colours:	Red and white
Headquarters:	St Lawrence Ground, Old Dover Road, Canterbury CT1 3NZ.

Honours: County Champions (6) 1906, 1909, 1910, 1913, 1970, 1978
Joint Champions (1) 1977
Gillette Cup Winners (2) 1967, 1974
Benson and Hedges Cup Winners (3) 1973, 1976, 1978
John Player League Champions (3) 1972, 1973, 1976
1st XI Home Grounds 1980: Canterbury (St Lawrence Ground); Dartford (Hesketh Park); Folkestone (Cheriton Road); Maidstone (The Mote); Tunbridge Wells (Nevill Ground).

For the first time since 1975, Kent finished a season without a single honour. It was a rank failure by their extraordinary standards, as captain Alan Ealham was quick to point out. Yet it could hardly be called a disaster, even by the fervently committed fans of Canterbury. They lost only three times in the Championship, though dropped from first to fifth place. They were also beaten three times in the John Player League, and the last of those defeats, by Middlesex on 9 September, sent the title to Somerset, leaving them with only runners-up prizemoney as compensation.

So what went wrong? Basically, the same squad that has won 10 major titles during the seventies has not grown too old to challenge, as a glance at their ages confirms. As Ealham agrees, it was simply a case of ailing form. 'We played badly as a team for most of the season. I was surprised we won as many games as we did', he said at the season's death.

Such a generalisation, although accurate in many senses, could not be applied to Derek Underwood, who refuted all claims that his powers were waning. The country's leading wicket-taker during 1978, he this time finished level with Essex's John Lever – 106 apiece. After his sequence of devastating spells towards the end of the season, the selectors could no longer ignore him and he quite rightly became the first English Packer player to be recalled to the Test squad. Underwood is unique and the game may well not see his like again. Those who dismiss him as 'just a wet-wicket bowler' should try facing him themselves; try scoring quickly against him and see what happens. A master of containing tactics, a demon when the wicket favours him, this sensitive 35-year-old with the look of a man from a bygone era has it in him to contort and deceive for at least another five years, in which time heaven knows how many records will have succumbed.

What Kent lacked was support for the maestro, and in truth it came only from the newly discovered talent of Graham Dilley, 6 feet 3 inches of 20-year-old from Dartford. Dilley made a place his own, often displacing the more seasoned Kevin Jarvis, took 49 wickets at 23 apiece, and earned himself

Having to wait until the winter tour for his England recall, 'Deadly' Derek Underwood spent the summer months capturing more than 100 wickets for the second successive season.

an England blooding in Australia. Even his batting was impressive – he averaged 20 – and he showed every sign of becoming a genuine all-rounder. Jarvis and the vastly popular beneficiary John Shepherd both had unhappy terms with the ball, the support bowlers shared precious few wickets, and 'Deadly' Derek was left with all eyes turning on him rather too often for team comfort.

The batting was almost similarly reliant, but this time on two individuals. Bob Woolmer and Chris Tavaré, both pushing without profit for a place in England's thinking, each totalled more than 1,300 runs. Both suffered their lean spells and Tavaré was periodically accused of making his runs without grace. But the figures alone suggest that there are very few more prolific players in the country than these two.

Frankly, the rest were mediocre. Apart from Asif Iqbal, who played only 16 first-class innings, no-one else averaged above 30. Charles Rowe, Chris Cowdrey, Ealham, Shepherd and Graham Johnson failed to provide the mighty strength in depth which has made Kent batting so formidable over recent years. The tail was sometimes alarmingly long.

With three English WSC players on their staff, Kent were quite naturally a vehicle for the cricket politicians. Scarcely a week passed without some media discussion about which, if any, of the rebels should merit England comebacks; and the fact that Underwood was the only one favoured reflects no discredit on the performances of the other two. Woolmer, with his efficient opening and his invaluable seam bowling, particularly in one-day cricket, I have already mentioned, but what of Alan Knott?

Many, with a blinkered cynicism typical of the troubled Packer era, insisted that his extraordinary talents, both as wicket-keeper and batsman, had diminished the moment he signed a WSC contract; some of his displays in Australia added weight to the argument. But in his half-season with Kent in 1979 he proved them all wrong. His 'keeping was at times inspired, never less than exceptional, and his batting, despite the poverty of opportunity at number 8, pulled Kent out of the occasional dilemma. It was unfortunate for Paul Downton to return from university in mid-season, his place guaranteed under a weird arrangement but with every pressure on him to emulate the tutor. How long Knott will go on few could predict, but he certainly gave continuous pleasure to all who saw him in 1979 ... one of the most memorable features of a season that those indomitable early-morning campers who populate the Kent grounds might have forgotten very swiftly over their winter fires.

Schweppes County Championship:	5th	Won 6	Lost 3	Drawn 13	
All First-Class Matches:		Won 6	Lost 3	Drawn 15	
Gillette Cup:	Lost to Somerset in quarter-final				
Benson and Hedges Cup:	Failed to qualify for Q-F (4th in Group D)				
John Player League:	2nd	Won 11	Lost 3	No result 2	

KENT CHAMPIONSHIP AVERAGES *Not out

BATTING and FIELDING	M	I	NO	HS	R	Av	100	50	Ct	St
C. J. Tavaré	22	35	5	150*	1239	41.30	3	6	19	—
R. A. Woolmer	22	36	4	169	1193	37.28	3	4	10	—
Asif Iqbal	10	16	1	152	506	33.73	1	—	3	—
C. J. C. Rowe	21	36	5	147*	932	30.06	3	3	6	—
G. W. Johnson	22	29	7	71	634	28.81	—	4	15	—
A. G. E. Ealham	22	31	3	153	745	26.60	1	3	12	—
C. S. Cowdrey	19	27	4	83	611	26.56	—	4	11	—
A. P. E. Knott	9	10	2	63	200	25.00	—	1	13	1
J. N. Shepherd	15	19	1	86	366	20.33	—	1	8	—
G. R. Dilley	20	22	9	81	248	19.07	—	1	15	—
D. L. Underwood	22	23	5	45	210	11.66	—	—	17	—
R. W. Hills	8	8	2	27	64	10.66	—	—	4	—
P. R. Downton	13	16	1	29	141	9.40	—	—	25	4
K. B. S. Jarvis	17	14	5	8	38	4.22	—	—	3	—

BOWLING	O	M	R	W	Av	BB	5wI	10wM
Underwood	779.2	329	1521	104	14.62	8–28	10	4
Dilley	427.3	108	1096	46	23.82	6–66	1	—
Jarvis	372.2	96	1112	36	30.88	4–42	—	—
Shepherd	395.3	103	1039	33	31.48	4–55	—	—
Johnson	416	126	1034	23	44.95	5–12	1	—

Also bowled: Asif 17–3–71–1; Cowdrey 9.4–1–49–4; Ealham 8.3–2–49–1;
Hills 114–26–341–8; Rowe 47–14–128–6; Tavaré 9.5–2–39–1; Woolmer 94–16–266–2.

LANCASHIRE

Patroness:	Her Majesty The Queen
President:	W. D. Crumblehulme
Chairman:	C. S. Rhoades
Secretary:	C. D. Hassell
Captain:	F. C. Hayes
Colours:	Red, green and blue
Headquarters:	
Old Trafford Cricket Ground, Manchester M16 0PX.	

Honours: County Champions (8) 1881, 1897, 1904, 1926, 1927, 1928, 1930, 1934 Joint Champions (4) 1879, 1882, 1889, 1950 Gillette Cup Winners (4) 1970, 1971, 1972, 1975 John Player League Champions (2) 1969, 1970

1st XI Home Grounds 1980: Manchester (Old Trafford); Blackpool (Stanley Park); Liverpool (Aigburth); Southport.

There are plausible reasons for any side suffering a decline, but for Lancashire, who finished in the low reaches of the Championship for the third consecutive season, continued failure is not easy to explain away. Traditionally among the most powerful of counties, Lancashire have now gone 30 years without winning the title – and that was only a share of the honour with the Surrey team who were about to dominate the fifties. Their large and loyal support has begun to demand rather more than further demonstrations of their penchant for the Gillette Cup.

In 1979, even that was denied them. Finalists six times in the previous nine years, Lancashire were put out in the second round by Kent, having already accounted for champions-elect Essex. They slipped from fifth to equal 10th in the John Player League, failed to progress beyond the group stage of the Benson and Hedges Cup, and dropped one place to 13th in the Championship.

If that seems a startlingly undistinguished campaign for such a club, it must be said that they suffered more from injuries than any other county. At one stage during July, a number of seniors were playing on, while palpably unfit, to avoid a completely embarrassing situation. Perhaps the most damaging injury was to Willie Hogg, the broadly built young quick bowler from Ulverston, who had begun to emerge with such lively promise during the previous season that he gained selection for MCC against the tourists and was a well-backed tip to win rapid England honours. Those, so far, have been denied him by an injury which he aggravated by further bowling. His Championship work was restricted to just 213 overs and 25 wickets, and Lancashire had no-one of comparable pace to replace him.

Not that they could be accused of sitting back in idle resignation. Apart from shuffling their own staff of seamers – Paul Allott, Bob Ratcliffe, Alan Worsick and, when fit, the luckless Peter Lee – they first signed the mountainous South African Paul Robinson and then, more profitably, the Australian swing and seam exponent, Mick Malone.

At 6 feet 9 inches, a height to make even Joel Garner raise his eyebrows, Robinson certainly had the physical credentials to frighten a few.

A member of the 1977 Australians, Mick Malone helped Haslingden in the Lancashire League before joining Lancashire, with stunning success, at the end of last season. This summer his swing bowling could add essential incisiveness to the county's injury-prone attack.

Unfortunately, his performances never quite matched his appearance, and after hovering over New South Wales's Geoff Lawson, Lancashire swooped for Malone with immediate results. He played only a couple of games at the tail-end of the season, yet took a remarkable 19 wickets to finish at the head of the national averages. Malone began with seven for 88 against Nottinghamshire at Blackpool, then produced match figures of 11 for 92 against Leicestershire as the county improved their final placing with a two-day win.

If Malone is to be a fixture, then Lancashire's attack will instantly assume new and more forbidding proportions in the coming season . . . especially if the unfortunate Hogg and Lee, who has now been troubled by unfitness for several seasons, are fully mobile again. Last summer, only the remarkably reliable Jack Simmons, a deserving beneficiary this year, took more than 40 wickets, which explains the low return on bowling bonus points.

The batting failures are not so easily understood. With four Test players in the side, in Barry Wood, Clive and David Lloyd and the captain Frank Hayes, one always expects enterprise and entertainment from Lancashire's batting. This particular quartet rarely disappointed: only David Lloyd averaged less than 40, and his season was far from gloomy. But in batting, as in bowling, the county are short of depth and must hope for the rapid development of Manchester-born opener Geoffrey Trim. Indeed they would welcome a further influx of young blood.

Schweppes County Championship: 13th	Won 4 Lost 4 Drawn 14
All First-Class Matches:	Won 4 Lost 4 Drawn 16
Gillette Cup:	Lost to Kent in 2nd round
Benson and Hedges Cup:	Failed to qualify for Q-F (3rd in Group B)
John Player League:	10th Won 6 Lost 7 No result 3

LANCASHIRE CHAMPIONSHIP AVERAGES   *Not out

BATTING and FIELDING	M	I	NO	HS	R	Av	100	50	Ct	St
C. H. Lloyd	16	22	4	104*	880	48.88	3	3	11	—
F. C. Hayes	17	21	4	88	746	43.88	—	6	8	—
B. Wood	21	33	7	135*	1094	42.07	2	6	11	—
D. Lloyd	21	32	3	135*	1043	35.96	4	4	12	—
R. M. Ratcliffe	15	14	5	101*	232	25.77	1	—	3	—
B. W. Reidy	16	24	5	131*	482	25.36	1	—	4	—
J. Abrahams	13	23	1	79	545	24.77	—	5	11	—
R. Arrowsmith	7	6	3	39	72	24.00	—	—	3	—
J. Simmons	22	25	5	74*	469	23.45	—	1	17	—
J. Lyon	20	22	8	123	313	22.35	1	—	29	2
G. E. Trim	6	11	0	91	228	20.72	—	1	9	—
D. P. Hughes	13	12	3	60*	158	17.55	—	1	14	—
A. Kennedy	9	11	3	21	135	16.87	—	—	—	—
P. G. Lee	15	14	7	19	68	9.71	—	—	—	—
P. J. W. Allott	12	6	2	14	19	4.75	—	—	4	—
W. Hogg	11	8	1	11	33	4.71	—	—	4	—

Also batted: I. Cockbain (1 match) 23; G. Fowler (1 match) 2, 2; M. F. Malone (2 matches) 0, 0; P. A. Robinson (1 match) 15; C. J. Scott (2 matches) 0, 0 (8 ct, 1 st).
H. Pilling played in one match but did not bat.

BOWLING	O	M	R	W	Av	BB	5wI	10wM
Malone	83.3	26	191	18	10.61	7–88	3	1
Lloyd D.	59.3	19	164	11	14.90	6–60	2	—
Simmons	454	112	1231	51	24.13	7–86	1	—
Ratcliffe	413.5	120	1017	38	26.76	6–84	3	1
Hogg	212.4	45	704	25	28.16	4–26	—	—
Reidy	143.4	21	462	16	28.87	5–61	1	—
Wood	137.5	26	455	14	32.50	3–51	—	—
Lee	277.5	58	874	22	39.72	3–50	—	—
Hughes	198.2	49	592	13	45.53	4–77	—	—
Allott	223.2	41	609	13	46.84	5–39	1	—

Also bowled: Arrowsmith 82.1–20–280–9; Robinson 20–4–58–2.

LEICESTERSHIRE

President: W. Bentley
Chairman: C. H. Palmer
Secretary/Manager: F. M.
Turner
Captain: K. Higgs
Colours: Scarlet and dark
green
Headquarters:
County Ground, Grace Road,
Leicester LE2 8AD.

Honours: County Champions
(1) 1975
Benson and Hedges Cup
Winners (2) 1972, 1975
John Player League Champions
(2) 1974, 1977
1st XI Home Ground 1980:
Leicester (Grace Road).

Whether Ken Higgs, aged 42, or Nick Cook, aged 22, was the star of Leicestershire's season is purely a matter for local bickering. The county should simply be happy that their apparently ageless captain is still as mean and effective in his bowling, while old enough to be the father of the new, young protégé. Higgs took 47 wickets, conceded barely more than two runs per over, and still bustled in with that air of purpose and belligerence which once made him such an able new-ball partner to John Snow for England. Always difficult to hurry against, he also moves the ball off the seam as much as anyone in the game, and wears the look of someone who could play until he is 50.

Cook, whose career record before the season comprised two matches and three wickets, forced his way into the side and took 36 wickets with left-arm spin, oblivious to the opposition of three such bowlers already in the team. Born in Leicester, and a second-team player since the age of 18, Cook is just the sort of home-bred product the counties must encourage, and Leicestershire are to be applauded for giving him such exposure.

There was appreciably more to admire in a county which started the season as if destined for a dire struggle without their retired leader, Ray Illingworth, and then rallied to finish respectably in sixth position, just as they had done in 1978. That they were basically strong in most departments is evidenced by their collection of 128 bonus points, more than any other county. Their 60 points for batting was also unsurpassed, garnered by the doggedness of John Steele and Chris Balderstone and the more flamboyant approach of Barry Dudleston, Brian Davison and David Gower.

Dudleston and Steele were responsible for one of the more memorable highspots of Leicestershire's season when they built an opening stand of 390 against Derbyshire in August. It was a record for any Leicestershire wicket, beating a figure set 73 years ago, and brought the likeable Dudleston his first double-century – a suitable recompense after two years of injuries.

Earlier in the season, the county's fifth-wicket record had also fallen as Nigel Briers and Roger Tolchard turned what had been a crisis against Joel Garner into a commendable total against Somerset. The batting, as can be seen, did not end with the top five, and the fact that Tolchard, vice-captain for the first time, was left out of the team in mid-season is further proof that they felt confident of their depth.

Briers faded from a trumpeting start and some premature talk of England potential to an average of just 20, but he surely has the ability to come again. Gower, despite carping criticism that he makes many more runs for country than county, personified class and style when casualness did not get the better of him. Neither Steele nor Balderstone is the type of batsman to drag spectators in off the streets, but each explored the limits of his own potential once more and they came up with some invaluably resilient innings.

Leicestershire supporters may view David Gower with mixed feelings: pride at his England performances and disappointment that his talents are so rarely on show at Grace Road.

Davison, who failed to score a century, and his Rhodesian friend and countryman, Paddy Clift, just occasionally set Grace Road buzzing with the type of thunderous hitting of which both are capable.

If Higgs and Cook were the most striking contributors to the bowling, that should not detract from Les Taylor, the sturdy one-time miner who has answered Leicestershire's need for a penetrating fast bowler. With his strong body action and economical run, Taylor presented himself before the England selectors with a number of impressive displays, and may well have been a winter tourist but for a muscle injury under the ribs which robbed him of the season's final three weeks.

Clift was the only bowler to reach 50 wickets, but the county always seemed to have such a wide-ranging attack that it scarcely mattered. Ken Shuttleworth, relishing a regular place to stage a rally late in his career, and Peter Booth made a total of five seamers; Steele, Balderstone, Jack Birkenshaw and even Dudleston provided spin. It remained a well-balanced side, despite the inescapable fact that several seniors are past their best. With youngsters like Cook and Briers, not to mention Gower, they should not struggle.

Schweppes County Championship: 6th	Won 4	Lost 5	Drawn 12	(Abandoned 1)	
All First-Class Matches:	Won 5	Lost 5	Drawn 14	(Abandoned 1)	
Gillette Cup:	Lost to Northamptonshire in quarter-final				
Benson and Hedges Cup:	Failed to qualify for Q-F (4th in Group B)				
John Player League:	6th	Won 7	Lost 5	No result 4	

LEICESTERSHIRE CHAMPIONSHIP AVERAGES   *Not out

BATTING and FIELDING	M	I	NO	HS	R	Av	100	50	Ct	St
J. C. Balderstone	21	36	5	95	1221	39.38	—	11	14	—
J. F. Steele	20	34	3	187	1196	38.58	3	6	18	—
B. Dudleston	18	31	0	202	1111	35.83	2	6	14	1
D. I. Gower	10	18	3	98	515	34.33	—	5	4	—
B. F. Davison	21	35	0	84	1149	32.82	—	8	11	—
R. W. Tolchard	18	27	6	109	643	30.61	1	2	40	3
P. B. Clift	21	30	8	64	600	27.27	—	2	7	—
K. Shuttleworth	16	19	9	44	265	26.50	—	—	16	—
J. Birkenshaw	9	10	5	33*	119	23.80	—	—	7	—
M. Schepens	4	6	2	57	91	22.75	—	1	5	—
N. E. Briers	17	28	1	119	574	21.25	2	1	9	—
P. Booth	8	7	3	20	63	15.75	—	—	2	—
N. G. B. Cook	13	11	4	18*	66	9.42	—	—	3	—
K. Higgs	18	13	6	9	42	6.00	—	—	18	—
L. B. Taylor	13	8	4	9*	14	3.50	—	—	1	—

Also batted: J. P. Agnew (2 matches) 9; G. J. Parsons (2 matches) 17, 0.

BOWLING	O	M	R	W	Av	BB	5wI	10wM
Higgs	399.5	131	865	46	18.80	6-33	4	—
Taylor	316.3	68	861	39	22.07	6-61	2	—
Cook	336.5	113	806	32	25.18	6-57	2	—
Clift	502.1	138	1264	45	28.08	5-17	1	—
Steele	237.4	75	596	20	29.80	3-20	—	—
Shuttleworth	382	78	1142	38	30.05	4-60	—	—
Balderstone	246.5	73	645	21	30.71	3-38	—	—
Birkenshaw	151.3	40	381	12	31.75	3-20	—	—

Also bowled: Agnew 46–14–124–4; Booth 82–19–307–7; Briers 3–2–1–0; Davison 0.5–0–7–0; Dudleston 55–25–104–6; Parsons 32–10–125–4.

MIDDLESEX

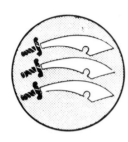

Patron:	HRH The Prince Philip, Duke of Edinburgh	*Honours:* County Champions (6) 1866, 1903, 1920, 1921, 1947, 1976
President:	G. O. B. Allen	Joint Champions (2) 1949, 1977
Chairman:	F. G. Mann	Gillette Cup Winners (1) 1977
Secretary:	A. J. Burridge	Benson and Hedges Cup
Captain:	J. M. Brearley	Finalists (1) 1975
Colours:	Blue	*1st XI Home Ground 1980:*

Headquarters:
Lord's Cricket Ground,
St John's Wood Road,
London NW8 8QN.

1st XI Home Ground 1980:
Lord's.

The dramatic demise of Middlesex, potentially the most formidable team in England, remains the greatest mystery of the 1979 county season. After three seasons in the leading three, they spent much of last summer languishing in some embarrassment at the foot of the table before scrambling up to joint 13th. In the other competitions, they were more of a force – fourth in the John Player League, semi-finalists in the Gillette and in the last eight of the Benson and Hedges. But for a squad containing eight Test players and the inspirational qualities of Mike Brearley, the season was still bewilderingly barren.

The absence of Brearley for lengthy and frequent periods was no doubt contributory. Ideally, a team needs continuation in its leadership and Brearley, at the peak of his England successes, was not able to give it. One of the county's most pressing tasks is to decide on a suitable successor for the time, probably not too distant, when Brearley turns his attentions outside cricket.

There were times last summer when Middlesex's cricket appeared short of the urgency and purpose that marked their triumphs of recent seasons. The batting lacked solidity and the bowling did not have the bite of old. But, just like Kent, Middlesex have too much ability to linger long among the also-rans.

It was pleasing to see Graham Barlow back in the mood which gained him three England caps. This adventurous left-hander had been disappointing for two years but, as is his character, he bounced back to average 41. Barlow is a fluent and attractive player when in form and could conceivably force himself back into Test contention. Clive Radley, whose brief Test opportunity came so late in his career, was as reliably resilient, in his own scuttling, unorthodox fashion, as ever. Mike Smith, the tall and angular opener with the exaggerated shuffle across his crease, scored more than 1,100 runs with a sprinkling of centuries in a season he almost denied himself. Smith had considered retiring at the end of 1978 to run a hotel, but has delayed his departure for at least another year and will be playing again this summer.

Without in any way slighting this trio, it is probably true to say that Middlesex would have preferred the bulk of their runs to have come from the

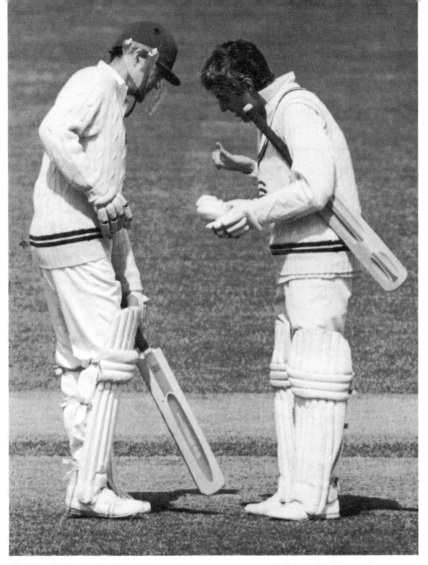

Smith and Brearley in mid-wicket conference over a sore point for the Middlesex skipper.

younger brigade in whom they are trusting their future. Instead, Mike Gatting took a step backwards, Roland Butcher flattered only to deceive, and Ian Gould scored only half as many runs as in 1978. A sorry commentary, perhaps, on the county's youngsters, yet all three played the occasional innings to prove their talent is intact, only waiting to re-emerge.

The most startling innings of their season came from Phil Edmonds, who arrived in a Saturday morning crisis against Glamorgan and smote a career-best 141 not out in remarkably quick time. Edmonds is a cricketer of flourishing ability who has not yet fulfilled his potential either as batsman or spin bowler. His omission from England's tour squad in controversial circumstances prompted interest in his services from at least five other counties during the close-season.

While on spin, it must be said that John Emburey – to many good judges, the best off-break bowler in England – fell short of expectations. His 59 wickets were collected at 27 apiece and, on occasions, his accuracy failed him. A back injury deterred him further in a season he will not remember fondly.

The pace bowling was once again in the capable hands of West Indian Wayne Daniel and that most typical of English seamers, Mike Selvey. Neither could be said to have failed – they took 108 wickets between them – but by comparison with past campaigns, Daniel was not so consistently sharp and Selvey, bravely battling on against a foot injury, rather less penetrating. The third seamer's job passed rapidly between the experienced Allan Jones and two newcomers – Robin Herkes, who took six wickets on his bowling début in the Championship, and Bill Merry, who bowls with full length and deceptive whip.

In 1980 the club will have a change of secretary – Alan Burridge succeeds Arthur Flower. Perhaps the new season will also bring a change of fortunes from those which produced the past year's baffling results.

Schweppes County Championship:	13th	Won 3	Lost 3	Drawn 14	(Abandoned 2)
All First-Class Matches:		Won 3	Lost 3	Drawn 14	(Abandoned 2)
Gillette Cup:	Lost to Somerset in semi-final				
Benson and Hedges Cup:	Lost to Yorkshire in quarter-final				
John Player League:	4th	Won 9	Lost 5	No result 2	

MIDDLESEX CHAMPIONSHIP AVERAGES   *Not out

BATTING and FIELDING	M	I	NO	HS	R	Av	100	50	Ct	St
P. H. Edmonds	10	12	5	141*	398	56.85	1	1	9	—
G. D. Barlow	20	33	9	133	1000	41.66	1	5	9	—
C. T. Radley	20	35	6	118*	1128	38.89	2	8	23	—
J. M. Brearley	8	13	2	148*	415	37.72	1	1	10	—
M. J. Smith	19	34	4	137	1109	36.96	5	1	2	—
M. W. Gatting	14	21	4	93*	557	32.76	—	2	11	—
J. E. Emburey	18	20	5	91*	437	29.13	—	1	20	—
N. G. Featherstone	10	14	3	59*	260	23.63	—	1	10	—
R. O. Butcher	14	22	0	106	513	23.31	1	2	13	—
W. N. Slack	6	12	0	66	236	19.66	—	1	2	—
I. J. Gould	18	21	1	89	347	17.35	—	2	24	2
M. W. W. Selvey	20	18	1	45	237	13.94	—	—	7	—
W. W. Daniel	17	13	6	18	72	10.28	—	—	5	—
A. A. Jones	11	8	3	12	29	5.80	—	—	3	—
W. G. Merry	8	6	4	4*	7	3.50	—	—	1	—

Also batted: P. B. Fisher (2 matches) 6, 0 (5 ct); R. Herkes (2 matches) 0, 0*, 0*, 0; F. J. Titmus (2 matches) 25, 5 (1 ct); K. P. Tomlins (1 match) 4 (1 ct).

BOWLING	O	M	R	W	Av	BB	5wI	10wM
Daniel	429.2	100	1170	52	22.50	6–38	2	—
Featherstone	191.1	40	568	23	24.69	4–28	—	—
Emburey	681.2	206	1457	57	25.56	4–31	—	—
Selvey	578.3	177	1443	56	25.76	5–42	3	—
Edmonds	387.4	122	878	32	27.43	4–30	—	—
Jones	221.2	49	646	17	38.00	3–39	—	—
Merry	150	36	431	10	43.10	3–46	—	—

Also bowled: Barlow 2–1–1–0; Butcher 1–0–4–0; Gatting 34.4–7–106–1; Herkes 25.4–2–84–6; Radley 2–0–9–1; Slack 6–3–3–0; Smith 5–0–22–0; Titmus 76–16–177–3; Tomlins 2–0–13–0.

NORTHAMPTONSHIRE

President: R. R. Garratt
Chairman: H. W. Wright
Secretary: K. C. Turner
Captain: P. J. Watts
Colours: Maroon
Headquarters:
County Ground,
Wantage Road,
Northampton NN1 4TJ.

Honours: County Championship Runners-up (4) 1912, 1957, 1965, 1976
Gillette Cup Winners (1) 1976
1st XI Home Grounds 1980:
Northampton; Luton, Bedfordshire; Milton Keynes, Buckinghamshire; Tring, Hertfordshire; Wellingborough (School Ground).

By scoring 78 in the Gillette Cup final, before a Lord's full house and millions of television viewers, Allan Lamb moved out of parochial fame in Northampton and established himself as a real star. This short man, with the trendily long hair, Mexican moustache and the odd-sounding birthplace of Langebaanweg in Cape Province, made the sort of batting impact in 1979 that only the indomitable Geoff Boycott and the spectacular Younis Ahmed could match. He totalled 1,747 runs in first-class innings alone, fashioned in a style pleasing to the eye and the scorebook. He is a little craftsman, with the ability to improvise and the temperament to ride storms. He was the undoubted triumph of Northamptonshire's season.

Lamb came to Northampton in 1978 when Derbyshire, from three available South Africans, chose Peter Kirsten. They might, temporarily anyway, be rueing that decision. For it was largely on the back of Lamb's superb batting, and the consistent support from Wayne Larkins, Geoff Cook and Peter Willey, that Northamptonshire were able to negotiate the season with far more comfort and respect than many had predicted.

If Lamb was the front man, none must forget the catalyst role played by captain Jim Watts, who is approaching his 40th birthday with the satisfaction of a job capably done. When he returned, for the third time, to lead the county in 1978, the team was in disarray and in dispute. They were both unhappy and unsuccessful, and Watts reasoned that by curing the first ill, the second should cure itself. His theory has been proved; Northamptonshire now have one of the happiest dressing-rooms in the country, and the results are improving appreciably.

Their strength, without question, was their batting. Apart from those already mentioned, the season was notable for the sudden maturing of Richard Williams. From a middle-order man with his place insecure and his runs inconsistent, Williams became a media target almost overnight as he followed his maiden century with three more in rapid succession and was promptly capped. Watts had given him the number 3 place for the season, and he did not waste the chance.

Larkins survived some untimely injuries to average more than 40 and earn his first England tour, while Cook, who must be unfortunate to remain unrecognised at international level, was a model opening partner, stable and assured. Willey, back at his punishing best after an uncertain start to the

Badly timed injuries robbed Wayne Larkins of the opportunity to translate county form into Test match runs, but compensation came with selection to tour Australia.

season, joined Larkins en route for Australia. Runs even came from down the order, where Jim Yardley added useful scores to some splendid slip catching.

It was a lack of bowling class which prevented Northamptonshire from capitalising on these strengths to become a power. Only Sarfraz, the moody but often devastating Pakistani, gave bite to an attack which often allowed promising positions to slip away. Sarfraz can be almost unplayable when the ball is new and the day damp and cloudy, but there was little to support him. Jim Griffiths, a locally born seamer who began his first-class career late and has reached 30 with few noticing it, took 49 wickets reasonably cheaply, but injuries continued to dog the ginger-haired Geordie, Alan Hodgson, and an experiment with Les McFarlane, the coloured demon bowler of the town league, was no great success.

Willey and Williams, as a spin combination, have neither the resource nor the experience to bowl sides out regularly when conditions favour them. However, both improved enough to suggest that their time may be near.

One thing is certain. With Lamb only 25, Larkins 26 and Williams a precocious 22, the county's batting looks assured for years to come. Their need is for a strike bowler, and with that they could easily become a force during the eighties.

Schweppes County Championship: 11th	Won 3	Lost 6	Drawn 12	(Abandoned 1)
All First-Class Matches:	Won 3	Lost 6	Drawn 13	(Abandoned 1)
Gillette Cup:	Lost to Somerset in final			
Benson and Hedges Cup:	Failed to qualify for Q-F (4th in Group C)			
John Player League:	12th Won 5 Lost 9 No result 2			

NORTHAMPTONSHIRE CHAMPIONSHIP AVERAGES   *Not out

BATTING and FIELDING	M	I	NO	HS	R	Av	100	50	Ct	St
A. J. Lamb	20	32	6	178	1614	62.07	3	11	19	—
W. Larkins	13	22	1	136	965	45.95	3	6	10	—
P. Willey	19	30	6	131	957	39.87	2	5	9	—
G. Cook	21	36	2	130	1132	33.29	2	4	18	—
R. G. Williams	21	34	3	151*	937	30.22	3	3	6	—
T. J. Yardley	19	29	6	66*	623	27.08	—	4	17	—
I. M. Richards	10	15	1	47	312	22.28	—	—	2	—
P. J. Watts	18	24	7	42*	323	19.00	—	—	11	—
Sarfraz Nawaz	13	15	2	46	220	16.92	—	—	7	—
G. Sharp	21	26	2	51	386	16.08	—	1	31	5
R. M. Carter	9	10	3	26*	94	13.42	—	—	4	—
T. M. Lamb	16	17	7	14	72	7.20	—	—	2	—
A. Hodgson	10	11	3	10	39	4.87	—	—	4	—
B. J. Griffiths	13	14	6	10*	36	4.50	—	—	2	—
L. McFarlane	8	2	0	0	0	0.00	—	—	3	—

BOWLING	O	M	R	W	Av	BB	5wI	10wM
Sarfraz	407.5	130	913	45	20.28	6–60	2	—
Griffiths	385	79	1112	43	25.86	5–76	1	—
Williams	415	115	1142	36	31.72	5–57	1	—
Willey	624.2	166	1464	46	31.82	5–46	3	—
Lamb T. M.	296.5	85	872	22	39.63	4–58	—	—
McFarlane	181	34	569	13	43.76	3–83	—	—
Hodgson	205	36	706	15	47.06	3–41	—	—

Also bowled: Carter 80–23–219–7; Cook 11.3–4–31–0; Lamb A. J. 6–1–15–1; Larkins 25–8–76–1; Richards 2–2–0–0; Watts 107–24–304–7; Yardley 0.3–0–3–0.

NOTTINGHAMSHIRE

President: H. T. Milnes
Chairman: J. R. Heatley
Chief Executive: P. G. Carling
Captain: 1979 M. J. Smedley
         and C. E. B. Rice
         1980 C. E. B. Rice
Colours: Green and gold
Headquarters:
Trent Bridge Cricket Ground,
Nottingham NG2 6AG.

Honours: County Champions
(12) 1865, 1868, 1871, 1872,
1875, 1880, 1883, 1884, 1885,
1886, 1907, 1929
Joint Champions (5) 1869,
1873, 1879, 1882, 1889
1st XI Home Grounds 1980:
Nottingham (Trent Bridge);
Worksop (Town Ground);
Cleethorpes, Lincolnshire.

With an attack led menacingly by Clive Rice and Richard Hadlee, plus some high-grade batting of both the forcing and defensive forms, Nottinghamshire had been widely tipped for a breakthrough as the team of 1979. That they failed was possibly due as much to tension off the field as deficiencies on it.

When Mike Smedley was relieved of the captaincy in July, and Rice inserted in his place, it was the upshot of months of split feelings among players and committee. Finally, it was fairly unanimously agreed that the ambitions of the county were not nearing fruition under the gentle, unassuming leadership of the 37-year-old Yorkshireman. The fire in the belly of the South African all-rounder was needed. The heavy irony of the situation was that Rice had been previously appointed to the job for the 1978 season, Smedley voluntarily stepping down. But the position was returned to its previous owner when Rice made it known that he had signed for World Series Cricket. Now, with peace apparently reached by the cricket politicians, no barriers prevented the change.

No-one could have expected Rice to provide an overnight transition, and of course, he did not. Nottinghamshire finished ninth in the Championship, a disappointing drop of two places, rose to eighth in the John Player League, and picked up the small consolation of defeating the Indian tourists in the Holt-sponsored three-day match. But the 30-year-old from Johannesburg freely confesses that he was feeling the symptoms that finished Barry Richards as a county player – no lure of Test selection, the same challenges repeated, and now, even WSC disbanded. Appointment to the captaincy injected him with new incentives just in time to halt disillusionment.

Rice's all-round efforts during 1979 could not be faulted: he finished well up both batting and bowling averages, scoring 1,297 runs and taking 58 wickets. Hadlee was up there, too, in the bowling section, and Nottinghamshire were left to ponder just how different their position might have been had the New Zealand seamer managed to stay fully fit. As it was, a hamstring injury sustained in July cut deeply into his effectiveness and forced Nottinghamshire to turn back to their third overseas player, South African pace bowler Kenny Watson.

The imports allowed little opportunity for locally born seamer Kevin Cooper, whose output dropped from 53 wickets in 1978 to 15. But the two

Highlights of Derek Randall's county season were 100 before lunch against Leicestershire and a unique double-hundred and hundred against Middlesex in the final game of the Championship.

acquisitions from less distance, Mike Bore and Eddie Hemmings, both settled in admirably. Together these two spin bowlers, neither of whom had been held in high regard by their previous employers, donated 113 wickets to the Championship cause. Bore, the slow left-armer kept out of the Yorkshire side by Phil Carrick, accounted for 56 while Hemmings, no mean all-rounder but eventually discarded by Warwickshire, went one better. In addition he also played some invaluable innings, equalling his previous career best with 85 not out against Hampshire.

If Rice, with his erect, watchful stance and quite destructive driving, was a mainstay of the batting, then even he was upstaged by the Retford imp, Derek Randall. Despite an unprofitable season with England, Randall averaged over 50 for the county and wagged his finger at the selectors who had rested him for the final Test by amassing 209 and 146 in the county's closing Championship match, against Middlesex. As is his wont, he was irritatingly inconsistent; one day uncontrollably brilliant, the next a shuffling disaster.

It was as well, with two such belligerent players to follow, that Nottinghamshire had one of the most stable opening pairs in England in Mike Harris and Paul Todd. Both passed 1,000 runs quite comfortably, and while Todd's style won him an increasing number of supporters for an England place, the vigilant Harris just went on accumulating.

Trevor Tunnicliffe and John Birch both made good progress in the middle order and are the age to develop further. Indeed, given a fair share of fortune and fitness, Nottinghamshire may well give a better return to their backers in 1980.

Schweppes County Championship:	9th	Won 6	Lost 4	Drawn 9	(Abandoned 3)
All First-Class Matches:		Won 8	Lost 4	Drawn 10	(Abandoned 3)
Gillette Cup:	Lost to Sussex in quarter-final				
Benson and Hedges Cup:	Failed to qualify for Q-F (3rd in Group D)				
John Player League:	8th	Won 6	Lost 6	No result 4	

NOTTINGHAMSHIRE CHAMPIONSHIP AVERAGES   *Not out

BATTING and FIELDING	M	I	NO	HS	R	Av	100	50	Ct	St
D. W. Randall	10	20	1	209	980	51.57	3	3	7	—
M. J. Harris	19	35	4	133*	1273	41.06	2	9	8	—
C. E. B. Rice	18	30	2	129	1095	39.10	1	8	20	—
C. C. Curzon	3	4	3	18*	36	36.00	—	—	3	1
P. A. Todd	16	29	1	174	922	32.92	1	4	13	—
H. T. Tunnicliffe	19	35	10	97	793	31.72	—	5	12	—
J. D. Birch	11	18	4	94*	397	28.35	—	2	9	—
K. E. Cooper	9	6	3	18*	67	22.33	—	—	3	—
M. J. Smedley	10	14	1	47*	260	20.00	—	—	11	—
B. Hassan	8	12	0	49	235	19.58	—	—	5	—
R. J. Hadlee	10	14	4	41	193	19.30	—	—	4	—
B. N. French	16	17	5	41	210	17.50	—	—	31	3
W. K. Watson	9	9	5	22*	64	16.00	—	—	4	—
E. E. Hemmings	19	29	6	85*	350	15.21	—	1	9	—
M. K. Bore	19	14	7	13*	37	5.28	—	—	5	—
P. J. Hacker	10	11	3	9	40	5.00	—	—	2	—

Also batted: R. E. Dexter (1 match) 1; K. S. Mackintosh (1 match) 8, 8 (2 ct); R. T. Robinson (1 match) 28, 40.

BOWLING	O	M	R	W	Av	BB	5wI	10wM
Hadlee	265.1	86	625	37	16.89	7–23	2	—
Rice	385	112	984	45	21.86	6–49	2	—
Watson	188.5	60	508	19	26.73	6–51	1	—
Hemmings	692	204	1682	57	29.50	5–74	2	—
Bore	669.4	199	1758	56	31.39	8–89	3	—
Cooper	123.5	33	358	11	32.54	4–42	—	—
Hacker	177	42	639	15	42.60	4–46	—	—

Also bowled: Birch 24–5–76–1; Harris 10–2–31–0; Mackintosh 10–3–23–0; Tunnicliffe 143.2–41–445–8.

SOMERSET

President: C. R. M. Atkinson
Chairman: R. C. Kerslake
Secretary: D. G. Seward
Captain: B. C. Rose
Colours: Black, white and
           maroon
Headquarters:
County Cricket Ground,
St James's Street,
Taunton TA1 1JT.

Honours: Third in County
Championship (4) 1892, 1958,
1963, 1966
Gillette Cup Winners (1) 1979
John Player League Champions
(1) 1979
1st XI Home Grounds 1980:
Taunton; Bath (Recreation
Ground); Weston-s-Mare
(Clarence Park).

By an uncanny coincidence, Somerset won the first two trophies of their history on the final weekend of the season, having failed in an identical situation 12 months earlier. Nobody was surprised that this highly talented team finally rewarded their loud and long-suffering band of supporters. It had seemed a probability from the season's outset that at least one honour would come their way, and their qualities are fashioned ideally for the one-day game.

Although it would be wrong to level Somerset as exclusively a limited-overs team, their final position of eighth in the Schweppes Championship was certainly unexpectedly modest. For much of the season they were to the fore among the pack of counties forlornly chasing Essex. But with their momentous climax beckoning inevitably, with its obvious pressures, they fell away to the extent that only 22 points were gleaned from the last five matches.

Their forbidding power was based on the extraordinary Joel Garner, freakishly built and awesomely adept at utilising his physical gifts to their limit. No other bowler on the English circuit is able to extract such startling bounce from only fractionally short of a length, and it is commonly agreed that Garner is not only a great destroyer but also a remarkably difficult bowler to score runs against. He took 55 wickets at only 13 runs apiece and conceded an average of fewer than two runs per over. In one-day cricket, he was, if anything, even more effective. Batsmen, forced to attempt attacking shots, were hustled out by his deceptive pace. His Gillette Cup figures were astonishing: five for 11 in the quarter-final against Kent, four for 24 against Middlesex in the semi-final, and then six for 29 in the final victory over Northamptonshire. Fifteen wickets for just 64 runs in the last three rounds!

Big Bird, as Garner is commonly known, was the bowling hammer. Viv Richards, his fellow West Indian star, was the equivalent in batting terms. Although by his standards a first-class average of 40 was disappointing, Richards was frequently devastating in one-day matches, never more so than in his century which virtually won the Gillette Cup final.

It was refreshing, however, to see three English batsmen standing out for Somerset. Peter 'Dasher' Denning, 30 and with a decade of service to the county, had his most consistent and prolific season, while captain Brian

Rose – nicknamed Harry because of his admiration for gardener Harry Wheatcroft – topped 1,300 runs and enlivened speculation that he could be the next man to lead England. Heading both these openers in the national averages, though, was Peter Roebuck, the bespectacled, studious-looking middle-order man. One of five Somerset players to have come through Millfield School, Roebuck, who was born in Oxford but went to Cambridge University, turned 24 this year and is probably ready for his chance at Test level. He bats in a determined fashion somewhat reminiscent of Boycott and is just one of many splendid fielders in this side.

With Joel Garner away for much of the summer with the West Indians, Somerset will be looking to Hallam Moseley to produce 'substitute' performances similar to last year's.

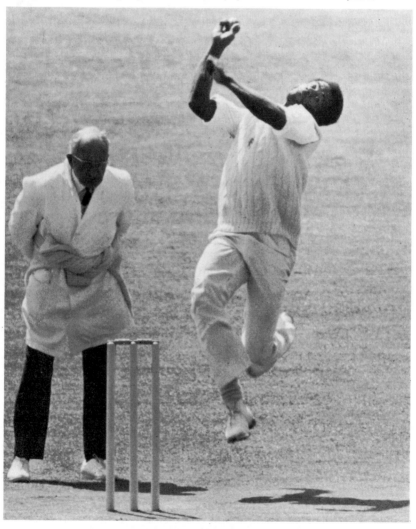

With the bulk of runs coming from Rose, Denning, Richards and Roebuck, it hardly mattered that Ian Botham was so often absent on national business. Botham's contributions to the season, in fact, were not of the sensational sort we normally associate him with. In Championship games for the county, he scored fewer than 500 runs and took only 26 wickets; but he was, naturally, invaluable in the limited-overs triumphs.

When Botham was playing for England, Colin Dredge and Keith Jennings performed admirably in the seam-bowling department. Barbadian Hallam Moseley, whose chances were severely restricted by the overseas players rule, took his limited chances so well that he led the national bowling averages for some weeks.

Vic Marks, developing so fast as off-spinner, batsman and a generally intelligent cricketer that he must be a real rival to Miller and Willey in the England squad, shared the slow bowling with Dennis Breakwell. Both took their share of wickets. And always, of course, there were that genial, burly pair of Graham Burgess and Derek Taylor rejoicing in winning something at last, and Phil Slocombe, willing to fill any place in the batting order. Now that Somerset have broken their duck, there is the feeling – depressing for all opposition – that they will not stop at one good year.

Schweppes County Championship: 8th	Won 5	Lost 1	Drawn 15	(Abandoned 1)
All First-Class Matches:	Won 6	Lost 1	Drawn 17	(Abandoned 1)
Gillette Cup:	**Winners**			
Benson and Hedges Cup:	Expelled from competition (Winners Group A)			
John Player League:	**1st**	Won 12	Lost 3	No result 1

SOMERSET CHAMPIONSHIP AVERAGES   *Not out

BATTING and FIELDING	M	I	NO	HS	R	Av	100	50	Ct	St
P. M. Roebuck	20	32	7	89	1125	45.00	—	10	19	—
P. W. Denning	20	31	5	106	1114	42.84	2	6	16	—
B. C. Rose	20	31	1	133	1270	42.33	2	8	11	—
I. V. A. Richards	15	24	0	156	996	41.50	3	4	12	—
C. H. Dredge	9	10	5	55	196	39.20	—	1	4	—
V. J. Marks	21	27	7	93	762	38.10	—	7	7	—
I. T. Botham	11	15	1	120	487	34.78	1	1	11	—
D. J. S. Taylor	20	20	10	50*	318	31.80	—	1	30	10
P. A. Slocombe	20	32	3	103*	804	27.72	1	6	6	—
D. Breakwell	21	26	8	54*	441	24.50	—	2	8	—
J. W. Lloyds	3	5	0	43	92	18.40	—	—	1	—
J. Garner	14	10	4	53	106	17.66	—	1	3	—
M. J. Kitchen	5	6	0	34	87	14.50	—	—	7	—
H. R. Moseley	6	4	1	15	25	8.33	—	—	1	—
N. F. M. Popplewell	6	8	1	13	50	7.14	—	—	1	—
K. F. Jennings	16	9	5	11*	16	4.00	—	—	6	—

Also batted: T. Gard (1 match) 7* (3 ct); D. R. Gurr (3 matches) 11*.

BOWLING	O	M	R	W	Av	BB	5wI	10wM
Garner	393.1	137	761	55	13.83	6–80	4	—
Moseley	144.1	35	385	17	22.64	5–18	1	—
Marks	498.2	138	1377	50	27.54	6–33	4	—
Breakwell	508.3	168	1200	40	30.00	6–41	1	—
Dredge	204	43	659	21	31.38	4–40	—	—
Botham	257.4	62	846	26	32.53	6–81	1	—
Jennings	204	63	537	16	33.56	4–25	—	—

Also bowled: Gurr 69.3–17–185–2; Lloyds 4–1–14–0; Popplewell 84–28–215–5; Richards 57–4–208–3; Roebuck 6–0–22–1.

SURREY

Patroness: Her Majesty The Queen
President: W. E. E. Gerrish
Chairman: R. Subba Row
Secretary: I. F. B. Scott-Browne
Captain: R. D. V. Knight
Colours: Chocolate
Headquarters: Kennington Oval, London SE11 5SS.

Honours: County Champions (18) 1864, 1887, 1888, 1890, 1891, 1892, 1894, 1895, 1899, 1914, 1952, 1953, 1954, 1955, 1956, 1957, 1958, 1971
Joint Champions (2) 1889, 1950
Benson and Hedges Cup Winners (1) 1974
1st XI Home Grounds 1980: The Oval; Guildford (Woodbridge Road).

Mickey Stewart, Surrey's captain for a number of years, returned to The Oval in 1979 as the county attempted to revive its spirit and results. Nothing tangible was won, but Stewart, in his first year as team manager, achieved a minor miracle. A team that, for several years, had meandered along to mediocrity and scantily concealed its troubles off the field, began playing with purpose and clearly enjoying it. They rose from dismal 16th in 1979 to finish third in the Championship, taking their share of the Schweppes prizemoney, and reached the final of the Benson and Hedges Cup, in which they gave Essex a memorable match.

Stewart adopted his new duties as those of a football manager. He became a quick-change artist, appearing in tracksuit for training sessions with the players, and then in a smartly-cut suit. He wanted no clashes of personality and ensured there were none; he made players with skulking, untapped talent suddenly believe in themselves again.

Credit for the transformation must also go to Roger Knight, who survived a torrid first season as captain and doubtless enjoyed his second much more. A very different man from Stewart, Knight nevertheless worked in effective partnership and one had only to be near the dressing-room at The Oval to know that harmony had returned.

The greatest single difference to the team itself was the arrival of Sylvester Theophilus Clarke. Exotically named, this muscular Barbadian did the job that West Indians are almost born to do – he bowled fast, even off a short run. In doing so, he lightened the load on the willing Robin Jackman who, suitably inspired by his new partner, bowled with great skill and enthusiasm to take 93 wickets and prompt the thought once more that he would surely have been recognised at Test level but for having to bowl on the soul-destroying slow pitches of The Oval. He seams the ball as violently as anyone in England and has been injured so seldom that it is difficult to recall him missing a match. Clarke, however, was troubled by injury.

When Jackman and Clarke left an innings, it was frequently destroyed by Pat Pocock, who took 70 wickets and reinforced the impression that, at 34, he is still maturing as an off-spinner. 'Percy' will often point out that both Fred Titmus and Ray Illingworth enjoyed their best seasons when older than him, and he retains the ambition of reclaiming his England place.

Three men who played an important part in the Surrey revival of 1979: (above) captain Roger Knight with team manager Mickey Stewart; (below) Geoff Howarth.

Last season finally saw the best of Geoff Howarth, the Kiwi who has for so long been a disappointment at county level. His 1,238 runs were made at an average of 47 and on many occasions he looked a truly world-class batsman, all effortless grace and timing. Alan Butcher, who had appeared to slip back after being prematurely tipped as a Test batsman before he was even capped by Surrey, was another who progressed dramatically under the new hierarchy. His runs came at such a flood early in the season that he looked destined for 2,000 runs, and although he fell away slightly, he still won his first England cap on his home ground.

Knight himself and the chirpy Graham Roope were both reliable producers in the middle order, where David Smith – sacked and reinstated a year earlier – fulfilled his early promise. A South London boy, Smith was only 17 when he made his début. Now, at 24, he is maturing into an attractive left-hander and can finally hold down a regular place.

There were those around who smiled smugly when Younis Ahmed began his astonishing runmaking exploits for Worcestershire and pointed out that Surrey were foolish to let him go. There will be few assenters at The Oval, though. Success so nearly came their way this past year, and with young talent like Smith and the bouncy wicket-keeper Jack Richards still maturing, the years ahead look prosperous . . . particularly if Mr Stewart stays to continue his work.

Schweppes County Championship: 3rd	Won 6	Lost 3	Drawn 12 (Abandoned 1)
All First-Class Matches:	Won 7	Lost 3	Drawn 13 (Abandoned 1)
Gillette Cup:	Lost to Northamptonshire in 2nd round		
Benson and Hedges Cup:	Lost to Essex in final		
John Player League:	12th	Won 5	Lost 9 No result 2

SURREY CHAMPIONSHIP AVERAGES   *Not out

BATTING and FIELDING	M	I	NO	HS	R	Av	100	50	Ct	St
G. P. Howarth	18	30	4	183	1238	47.61	4	7	12	—
A. R. Butcher	21	38	4	169	1231	36.20	3	6	12	—
G. R. J. Roope	21	34	7	114	920	34.07	1	5	40	—
G. S. Clinton	21	37	4	134	1075	32.57	2	6	13	—
D. M. Smith	17	22	6	79	497	31.06	—	3	6	—
R. D. V. Knight	20	32	4	100*	829	29.60	1	4	13	—
Intikhab Alam	14	21	4	52	345	20.29	—	2	8	—
R. D. Jackman	19	25	8	82	287	16.88	—	1	11	—
P. H. L. Wilson	16	11	7	15	48	12.00	—	—	3	—
M. A. Lynch	6	11	2	22	108	12.00	—	—	3	—
S. T. Clarke	9	11	3	25	90	11.25	—	—	5	—
P. I. Pocock	20	19	7	20	131	10.91	—	—	5	—
C. J. Richards	21	20	1	29	183	9.63	—	—	48	7
D. J. Thomas	7	8	2	15*	48	8.00	—	—	2	—

Also batted: A. Needham (1 match) 2 (2 ct).

BOWLING	O	M	R	W	Av	BB	5wI	10wM
Jackman	603.1	169	1515	87	17.41	8–64	7	—
Clarke	287.1	95	684	38	18.00	6–61	3	—
Pocock	573.3	176	1406	63	22.31	9–57	3	1
Knight	260	66	728	29	25.10	5–44	2	—
Wilson	284.5	63	861	30	28.70	4–39	—	—
Thomas	169	32	556	13	42.76	6–84	1	—
Intikhab	318.1	91	886	16	55.37	3–44	—	—

Also bowled: Butcher 27–8–114–1; Howarth 20–6–46–1; Roope 40.4–6–167–5; Smith 12–1–55–0.

SUSSEX

President:	H. T. Bartlett
Chairman:	A. Crole-Rees
Captain:	A. Long
Colours:	Dark blue, light blue and gold

Headquarters:
County Ground, Eaton Road, Hove BN3 3AN.

Honours: County Championship Runners-up (6) 1902, 1903, 1932, 1933, 1934, 1953
Gillette Cup Winners (3) 1963, 1964, 1978
John Player League Runners-up (1) 1976
1st XI Home Grounds 1980:
Hove; Eastbourne (The Saffrons); Hastings (Central Ground); Horsham.

Controversy having followed them about over the past few years, it was pleasant to see Sussex developing well during 1979 in peace and tranquility. Well, almost . . . The one ripple on the surface concerned the South African giant, Garth le Roux, who had played for the county once the previous year – many believe, purely as a qualifying measure for World Series Cricket – but had then looked certain to sign for Worcestershire. Negotiations had been continuing for some time, Worcester having paid le Roux's fare to England and provided him with a car, when the burly fast bowler suddenly announced he had decided to play for Sussex.

Bitterness was added to the conflict by the memory of Imran Khan's acrimonious defection from Worcestershire to Sussex in 1977. Worcestershire's objections, however, were overruled by a TCCB tribunal, who ruled that Sussex had acted quite fairly, but that le Roux would not be free to play for them until 1980.

As the county already had three world-class overseas players on their staff, there was a fair amount of head-scratching and speculation over who would be the one – or two – to go. Eventually, although Imran had hinted that he might not return for another season, it was Javed Miandad. The young Pakistani, whose talents had been wasted owing to the presence of the superb South African lefthander, Kepler Wessels, joined Glamorgan and Sussex are back to three imports. However, they can still use only two in any one match. Their plan, at this distance, is apparently to share the strike-bowler load between Imran and le Roux, which means that opponents will largely be spared the awesome ordeal of facing them in partnership.

Imran, whose threat is accentuated by bowling from a wide angle and slanting the ball into the batsman from short of a length, took 73 wickets at minimal cost last year, and also averaged 35 with the bat. His most spectacular effort was an unbeaten 154 against luckless Hampshire. His bowling and the batting of Wessels were the biggest single factors in the county's jump to fourth place in the Championship. They won three of their last four matches, completing a gratifying run-in with victory over Somerset by nine wickets, Wessels scoring 146 and 81 not out.

Wessels married an Australian girl during the summer – he is taking out Australian citizenship in an attempt to play Test cricket – and there were

Imran Khan – all-rounder of action-packed performances to delight the seasiders.

fears that he might not return to Hove next season. That would be a minor disaster after his total of 1,800 runs, more than anyone in the country, during 1979.

More relevant from England's viewpoint were the strides taken by Paul Parker in his first full season of county cricket. He averaged 44 and batted well enough to command support for a place on the England tour. His time will surely come. John Barclay, liable to be the county captain at some time in the future, batted in his characteristically dogged fashion and put together his regular 1,000 runs. He also took 52 wickets with off-spin he visibly enjoys and which is just as clearly improving. The Ceylonese batsman, Gehan

Mendis, was consistent again, but remained uncapped and also ran into disciplinary trouble which led to his omission from one match.

Seam bowling, traditionally the strength of Sussex cricket, was naturally spearheaded by Imran, but there were times when Geoff Arnold – 'Horse' to all in the game – bowled with the control and movement of his Test days. John Spencer, no longer certain of a regular place, took 33 wickets but might soon turn his attentions to his teaching career, especially with the emergence at Hove of two splendid seam-bowling prospects in Tony Pigott and Colin Wells. Old Harrovian Pigott takes a long, sprinted run and bowls genuinely fast, though as yet in short spells. At 21, he is a precious commodity in England, and covetous glances have been thrown his way by other counties. Wells, making his début at the age of 19, is medium pace, but he took 10 wickets so cheaply in his late-season blooding that he finished second in the national averages.

Arnold Long, who succeeded the controversial Tony Greig as captain, may well stand down after the coming year and, at 40 years old, concentrate on his business interests. By then, he should know he is leaving behind a thriving concern.

Schweppes County Championship: 4th	Won 6	Lost 4	Drawn 10	(Abandoned 2)
All First-Class Matches:	Won 7	Lost 4	Drawn 12	(Abandoned 2)
Gillette Cup:	Lost to Northamptonshire in semi-final			
Benson and Hedges Cup:	Failed to qualify for Q-F (3rd in Group C)			
John Player League:	12th	Won 6	Lost 10	

SUSSEX CHAMPIONSHIP AVERAGES   *Not out

BATTING and FIELDING	M	I	NO	HS	R	Av	100	50	Ct	St
K. C. Wessels	18	31	2	187	1619	55.82	6	9	15	—
P. W. G. Parker	18	29	5	103	1003	41.79	2	5	11	—
Imran Khan	16	25	5	154*	700	35.00	1	6	6	—
T. J. Head	4	2	1	22	33	33.00	—	—	15	—
J. R. T. Barclay	20	35	4	104*	893	28.80	1	6	16	—
A. Long	16	17	10	35*	200	28.57	—	—	36	5
G. D. Mendis	19	32	3	118	762	26.27	1	5	20	—
P. J. Graves	16	22	2	59	437	21.85	—	1	5	—
A. C. S. Pigott	12	17	2	55	289	19.26	—	1	6	—
C. P. Phillipson	20	27	5	47	383	17.40	—	—	16	—
J. Spencer	15	15	4	35	145	13.18	—	—	2	—
S. P. Hoadley	4	6	0	23	77	12.83	—	—	1	—
C. E. Waller	14	12	7	18*	64	12.80	—	—	12	—
C. M. Wells	4	5	1	29	42	10.50	—	—	1	—
G. G. Arnold	17	17	0	51	151	8.88	—	1	5	—
R. G. L. Cheatle	6	4	1	15	25	8.33	—	—	8	—

Also batted: Javed Miandad (1 match) 0, 30* (2 ct).

BOWLING	O	M	R	W	Av	BB	5wI	10wM
Imran	415.4	106	1091	73	14.94	6–37	7	—
Arnold	422.5	144	900	50	18.00	6–41	2	—
Cheatle	159.3	40	405	20	20.25	6–32	2	—
Barclay	336	63	1054	44	23.95	6–101	1	—
Phillipson	152.2	37	358	12	29.83	2–2	—	—
Waller	441.1	114	1147	37	31.00	4–18	—	—
Spencer	305	74	783	22	35.59	6–42	1	—
Pigott	240	42	828	23	36.00	4–65	—	—

Also bowled: Wells 41.1–16–87–6; Wessels 1–0–4–0.

WARWICKSHIRE

President:	Brig. Sir R. A. G. Calthorpe
Chairman:	C. C. Goodway
Secretary:	A. C. Smith
Captain:	1979 J. Whitehouse
	1980 R. G. D. Willis
Colours:	Blue, gold and silver
Headquarters:	
County Ground, Edgbaston, Birmingham B5 7QU.	

Honours: County Champions (3) 1911, 1951, 1972
Gillette Cup Winners (2) 1966, 1968
1st XI Home Grounds 1980: Birmingham (Edgbaston); Nuneaton (Griff & Coton).

A county captain's job is not always a glamorous one. For John Whitehouse, leading Warwickshire through one of the worst seasons in their history, it was distinctly unenviable. There must have been times when the quiet, fresh-faced Whitehouse, his options tied by a remarkable sequence of injuries and a playing staff without depth of strength, longed for the accountant's office where he spends his winters. It was that bad a year.

Yet it began well enough with a string of victories in the Benson and Hedges Cup group games. That little dream ended with defeat by Essex in the quarter-final, and from that moment on the season assumed a bleak note. They failed to survive a match in the Gillette Cup, slumped to 15th place in the Championship, and were convincingly bottom of the John Player League, in which their quite extraordinary ineptitude prompted an unfeeling band of Edgbaston followers – I hesitate to call them supporters – to adopt and adapt the chorus: 'We've got the worst team in the land.' Warwickshire won only two matches on Sundays – ironically, two in succession – and such an appalling record in a competition which can sometimes assume the proportions of a lottery is quite bewildering.

The reasons for their Championship demise demanded rather more sympathy. All three strike bowlers on the staff, Bob Willis, David Brown and Steve Rouse, spent more of the season out of the side than in it, and there were occasions when Whitehouse's bowling resources were pitifully thin. Rouse, suffering from a severe knee injury, did not play at all until the closing weeks of the season, while Brown, despite periodically returning to the side and picking up wickets, could never fully shake off problems with his ankle joints, which are clearly threatening to end his distinguished playing career.

Willis, of course, was often absent on England business. But he, too, endured fitness problems – once with a rib muscle and then with a knee – and before shattering Kent with five for 41 to give Warwickshire an unexpected innings victory in their final Championship game, he had taken only six wickets for Warwickshire all season.

A heavy burden, then, was passed on to Steve Perryman, the slightly built swing bowler, and Anton Ferreira, the county's new acquisition from South Africa. Perryman, who can be a most difficult proposition when conditions are right for him, produced the occasional destructive spell but finished with 51 wickets at 32 apiece; 'Yogi' Ferreira, who does not bowl as fast as his huge

Bob Willis, taking over a side in need of all his enthusiasm and energy, will be hoping Warwickshire's times are a-changin' in 1980.

frame would suggest, took only 31 at a cost of almost 40 runs each.

There was no improvement when Whitehouse turned to spin. The county having allowed Eddie Hemmings to depart for Nottinghamshire, the slow bowlers were Chris Clifford, a 37-year-old former Yorkshire off-break bowler, and Phil Oliver who, at 23, is still only learning the art. Although Clifford totalled 49 wickets, both spinners were generally expensive, and Warwickshire had such difficulty dismissing opposition that they finished with appreciably fewer bowling points than any other county.

Batting was not such a problem. Dennis Amiss, having initially been dismissed for allegiance to WSC, followed his 2,000 runs in 1978 with a slightly more modest total, but his 1,672 at an average of all but 50 must have brought relief to those who agreed to his reinstatement to the county. With Alvin Kallicharran, once he was released from the World Cup, recovering his most attractive form, Warwickshire had the basis for some formidable scores. Unfortunately, with the younger players still developing, there were many times when the innings fell into rapid decline.

Andy Lloyd, the red-headed chatterbox from Shropshire, finally found himself a niche at number 3 and celebrated with his maiden century against Nottinghamshire in late August. Oliver, too, played with crisp assurance at times, but there were disappointing setbacks for the highly promising opener, David Smith. Geoff Humpage sacrificed his wicket-keeping job to devote himself to batting, giving Chris Maynard an opportunity which he accepted with several smart shows, in addition to some useful innings. He may well be a name for the future.

And Whitehouse himself? Well, he averaged only 20 with the bat, a sharp decline for one hovering over the England side not many months ago. But then, with all the endless problems at Edgbaston last year, perhaps it was no surprise.

Schweppes County Championship:	15th	Won 3	Lost 7	Drawn 11 (Abandoned 1)
All First-Class Matches:		Won 4	Lost 7	Drawn 11 (Abandoned 1)
Gillette Cup:	Lost to Nottinghamshire in 2nd round			
Benson and Hedges Cup:	Lost to Essex in quarter-final			
John Player League:	17th	Won 2	Lost 13	No result 1

WARWICKSHIRE CHAMPIONSHIP AVERAGES   *Not out

BATTING and FIELDING	M	I	NO	HS	R	Av	100	50	Ct	St
A. I. Kallicharran	16	25	5	170*	1080	54.00	4	6	14	—
D. L. Amiss	21	35	3	232*	1613	50.40	6	6	13	—
C. Maynard	12	12	3	85	310	34.44	—	2	27	1
G. W. Humpage	16	23	2	96	716	34.09	—	2	21	2
T. A. Lloyd	15	26	5	104	613	29.19	1	1	16	—
R. G. D. Willis	8	5	2	42*	83	27.66	—	—	1	—
P. R. Oliver	15	17	3	83	355	25.35	—	2	7	—
K. D. Smith	19	32	2	71	664	22.13	—	6	9	—
A. M. Ferreira	15	15	5	57	219	21.90	—	1	7	—
J. Whitehouse	20	32	4	98	554	19.78	—	3	10	—
D. J. Brown	9	7	1	33	103	17.16	—	—	2	—
R. LeQ. Savage	6	8	5	15*	39	13.00	—	—	3	—
R. N. Abberley	5	8	2	22*	63	10.50	—	—	3	—
D. C. Hopkins	12	14	2	34*	103	8.58	—	—	3	—
S. P. Perryman	18	13	4	12	68	7.55	—	—	4	—
C. C. Clifford	20	17	5	26	88	7.33	—	—	4	—

Also batted: J. A. Claughton (2 matches) 0, 12 (1 ct); S. J. Rouse (1 match) 21 (1 ct); G. P. Thomas (1 match) 9.

BOWLING	O	M	R	W	Av	BB	5wI	10wM
Brown	243.4	60	653	21	31.09	7–73	2	—
Hopkins	275	59	886	27	32.81	6–67	1	—
Perryman	653	214	1635	48	34.06	6–69	4	1
Ferreira	412	93	1198	30	39.93	5–66	1	—
Clifford	682.4	154	2166	49	44.20	5–37	3	—
Savage	155.4	29	525	10	52.50	4–83	—	—

Also bowled: Humpage 16–1–96–0; Kallicharran 114.1–19–384–4; Lloyd 10–2–57–1; Oliver 121–21–425–5; Rouse 20.3–3–80–6; Whitehouse 9–2–21–1; Willis 134–39–378–9.

WORCESTERSHIRE

President: Rev. Prebendary
W. R. Chignell
Chairman: J. G. E. Lampard
Secretary: M. D. Vockins
Captain: N. Gifford
Colours: Dark green and
black
Headquarters:
County Ground, New Road,
Worcester WR2 4QQ.

Honours: County Champions
(3) 1964, 1965, 1974
John Player League Champions
(1) 1971
Gillette Cup Finalists (2) 1963,
1966
Benson and Hedges Cup
Finalists (2) 1973, 1976
1st XI Home Grounds 1980:
Worcester; Stourport-on-
Severn (Chain Wire).

Disregarding Essex and Somerset, the undoubted teams of the year, it could be argued that the biggest, and most surprising, success story of 1979 was that of Worcestershire. There seemed no reason to suggest that the club which had laboured to 13th and 15th places in the past two seasons should be a major threat in any of the competitions. Yet they finished runners-up to Essex in the Championship and took third place in the John Player League.

There was no dark secret to their success. Quite simply, they batted as well, if not better, than any other side, making so many runs that their deficiencies in the bowling department were camouflaged. Younis Ahmed, whose registration was something of a gamble after his comparatively poor return in his last few years at Surrey, amassed an astonishing 1,539 runs, averaged almost 70, and played as if he could not stop making big scores. His transformation was one of the most remarkable features of the season and emphasised what a talented player he has always been. Glenn Turner's equally productive batting was less of a surprise. He finished fourth in the national averages – Younis was second – and completed 1,000 runs for the county for the 12th time in a career of superb service.

The runs did not begin and end with these two, either. Opener Alan Ormrod totalled more than 1,100, Phil Neale had the best of his five seasons at Worcester and scored 1,305, and depth was provided by Ted Hemsley and Dipak Patel – the Kenyan whose all-round progress earned him one of the four Whitbread scholarships in Australia.

Cynics will scoff that any batsman would like to carry the Worcester wicket around with him, and certainly it is a delight of consistent pace and bounce. But that should not detract from the purposeful manner in which Worcestershire exploited the conditions. They amassed some mighty scores, and made them with enterprise.

Although John Inchmore returned after lengthy injury problems to collect 62 wickets in lively style, the attack was short of penetration. Van Holder, in his 12th and benefit season, had lost much of his bite, and Jim Cumbes, for all his honest endeavours, knows too well he will not often bowl teams out himself. Garth le Roux would have been the man to complete the team, so Worcestershire's chagrin is forgivable over the episode which saw the South African pace bowler join Sussex.

Norman Gifford, however, showed no signs of exhausted powers. At the age of 39, and in his 22nd year on the county staff, this Lancastrian left-arm spinner picked up 78 wickets with that mix of skill and cunning that has been snaring opponents for so long. He also captained the side with considerable enthusiasm and enterprise, although there were a few incidents he will not wish to recall. Somerset's outrageous declaration after one over of their Benson and Hedges tie is one; his own declaration against Northampton-shire, when he confused the rules and was asked to follow on, another. Finally, as they pursued the victory over Derbyshire that would have kept Essex waiting to crack their champagne, there was more controversy. The umpires gave Gifford the impression that Worcestershire had four overs in which to score 25 to win. In fact, they were allowed only 10 minutes – time for two overs – and the game was drawn, leaving Essex celebrating down the motorway at Northampton while an enraged Gifford protested to everyone in earshot.

If the 1979 season had one overriding sadness for Worcestershire supporters, it was that Basil D'Oliveira, ambassador and cricket artist with the county for 15 years, seems finally to have decided he has had enough. By the evidence of his birth certificate, he was 48 in October . . . but he is in truth an ageless character whose presence on the circuit will be missed.

Schweppes County Championship: 2nd	Won 7	Lost 4	Drawn 10	(Abandoned 1)
All First-Class Matches:	Won 7	Lost 4	Drawn 12	(Abandoned 1)
Gillette Cup:	Lost to Leicestershire in 2nd round			
Benson and Hedges Cup:	Lost to Surrey in quarter-final			
John Player League:	3rd	Won 9	Lost 4	No result 3

WORCESTERSHIRE CHAMPIONSHIP AVERAGES   *Not out

BATTING and FIELDING	M	I	NO	HS	R	Av	100	50	Ct	St
Younis Ahmed	20	29	7	221*	1508	68.54	4	7	4	—
G. M. Turner	18	31	2	150*	1669	57.55	8	5	10	—
P. A. Neale	21	35	5	163*	1214	40.46	4	4	9	—
J. A. Ormrod	21	36	4	134	1037	32.40	2	6	14	—
E. J. O. Hemsley	21	33	5	93	830	29.64	—	5	20	7
J. D. Inchmore	20	22	9	37*	283	21.76	—	—	8	—
D. J. Humphries	21	28	4	50	496	20.66	—	1	48	8
V. A. Holder	13	12	6	24*	119	19.83	—	—	5	—
D. N. Patel	19	25	2	68	453	19.69	—	2	19	—
B. L. D'Oliveira	5	6	1	51*	58	11.60	—	1	—	—
B. J. R. Jones	4	8	0	19	89	11.12	—	—	—	—
J. Cumbes	18	15	9	13*	59	9.83	—	—	3	—
N. Gifford	17	16	5	35	102	9.27	—	—	12	—
G. G. Watson	8	11	1	18*	75	7.50	—	—	—	—
A. P. Pridgeon	5	1	1	0*	0	—	—	—	—	—

BOWLING	O	M	R	W	Av	BB	5wI	10wM
Gifford	798.3	237	1848	78	23.69	5–12	2	—
Inchmore	500.4	91	1547	59	26.22	6–35	3	—
Cumbes	552.2	100	1550	47	32.97	6–103	3	—
Holder	375	71	962	28	34.35	4–76	—	—
Patel	374.3	91	1224	34	36.00	5–95	1	—
Watson	231.5	43	711	17	41.82	4–29	—	—

Also bowled: D'Oliveira 78–24–175–6; Hemsley 8–3–22–1; Neale 1–0–5–0; Ormrod 1–0–14–0; Pridgeon 97–15–324–5; Younis 59.5–12–151–3.

Now that Basil D'Oliveira has retired, the all-rounder's rôle at Worcestershire is in the hands of the 21-year-old Nairobi-born Dipak Patel. After four years in the side he needs to translate promise into consistent performances.

YORKSHIRE

Patroness: HRH The Duchess of Kent
President: Sir Kenneth Parkinson
Chairman: A. H. Connell
Secretary: J. Lister
Captain: J. H. Hampshire
Colours: Oxford blue, Cambridge blue and gold
Headquarters: Headingley Cricket Ground, Leeds LS6 3BU.
Honours: County Champions (31) 1867, 1870, 1893, 1896, 1898, 1900, 1901, 1902, 1905, 1908, 1912, 1919, 1922, 1923, 1924, 1925, 1931, 1932, 1933, 1935, 1937, 1938, 1939, 1946, 1959, 1960, 1962, 1963, 1966, 1967, 1968
Joint Champions (2) 1869, 1949
Gillette Cup Winners (2) 1965, 1969
Benson and Hedges Cup Finalists (1) 1972
John Player League Runners-up (1) 1973
1st XI Home Grounds 1980: Leeds (Headingley); Bradford (Park Avenue); Harrogate (St George's Road); Huddersfield (Fartown); Hull (The Circle, Anlaby Road); Middlesbrough (Acklam Park); Scarborough; Sheffield (Abbeydale Park).

The immediate problem confronting Ray Illingworth as he began his first season as manager of his native Yorkshire was a delicate one: his two senior players were not talking to each other. Since the now notorious go-slow in mid-1978, by which John Hampshire chose to protest against the tactics of his then captain, Geoffrey Boycott, the rift between these two stubborn, strong-minded individuals had grown wider, unhealed by several meetings in Australia. For Boycott, the situation had been made almost intolerable by the fact that he had been stripped of the captaincy in favour of Hampshire. Illingworth, then, had a touchy issue on his hands.

It says much for the influence of this shrewd man of powerful will that Boycott and Hampshire publicly settled their differences. Although one is left to wonder on whether their relationship resumed actual chumminess, the county were at least able to get on with the cricket relatively unhampered by personal side-issues.

Illingworth had never pretended that he could wave a magic wand and make Yorkshire great again, which is just as well. They slid from fourth to seventh in the Championship, and despite varying degrees of progress in each of the limited-overs competitions, a semi-final in the Benson and Hedges Cup was the most they had to show.

It was certainly not the fault of Boycott. Test calls, and a nagging back injury, ruled that he played only 15 first-class innings for Yorkshire, but in those he scored 1,160 runs at an awesome average of 116. Even after adding his England record, his season's average was in three figures, and had he taken one more wicket – he picked up nine in first-class matches – he could have topped the national bowling averages as well. The revival of Boycott's singular bowling style was one of the features of the season. He was used chiefly in one-day games, both by county and country, and, with cap immovable from his head, he visibly enjoyed every delivery. Moreover, he produced some remarkably useful spells.

With the hopes of Yorkshire weighing heavily on him, John Hampshire found the actuality of captaincy as demanding as his predecessor had, and his 1978 form proved elusive.

Yorkshire's seam attack was, as ever, well served, but it suffered from the continuing fitness problems of Chris Old, seldom totally free from strains and restricted to a haul of 42 wickets. Graham Stevenson reached 50, and the rest of the spoils were shared between Arnie Sidebottom, Steve Oldham, Howard Cooper and Alan Ramage.

The county's leading wicket-taker was Phil Carrick, who responded to the new leadership by producing his best season yet at the age of 27. He bowled almost 700 overs of left-arm spin to capture 55 wickets, and proved his claim to all-round rating by averaging 33 with the bat and improving his career-best score with an unbeaten 128.

But if Carrick's season was a contented one, the same could not be said for Geoff Cope. The likeable but long-suffering off-spinner, twice banned from bowling because of a suspect action, had worked tirelessly with his mentor, Johnny Wardle, and the MCC coach and ex-Yorkshire spinner, Don Wilson. Finally given what he assumed to be his last chance, he came back into the side in mid-season but finished with only 13 wickets, almost half of them from one heady spell of six for 37 against Sussex. His new action, at least, remained apparently unquestioned, and one hopes that he enjoys a suitably successful benefit this year.

Much of Yorkshire's batting was surprisingly barren during 1979. There were two major exceptions – Boycott and Richard Lumb, 30 this year but reviving talk of England selection with consistent good form which amassed 1,465 runs, his best since 1975.

Perhaps everyone expected too great an impact to be made by the two highly rated youngsters, Bill Athey and Kevin Sharp, for they were both acutely disappointing. Athey, who appears to be slipping backwards, followed a 1979 average of 25 with one of 21, while Sharp seemed to lose confidence and was ultimately left out of the side with an average of 25. At 22 and 21 respectively, there is ample time for both to come good, and they will probably benefit from less premature talk of England.

While David Bairstow, boisterous and bouncy, earned his first England cap as wicket-keeper-batsman after a season notable for some quite stunning catches standing back, John Hampshire slipped to a batting average of just 30 – a sharp decline from his 53 of the previous summer. Perhaps the problems of captaincy weighed heavily . . . but Yorkshire will not mind if he, and their respected manager, can now achieve the results their talent should merit.

Schweppes County Championship: 7th	Won 5	Lost 3	Drawn 13	(Abandoned 1)
All First-Class Matches:	Won 6	Lost 3	Drawn 13	(Abandoned 1)
Gillette Cup:	Lost to Middlesex in quarter-final			
Benson and Hedges Cup:	Lost to Essex in semi-final			
John Player League: 4th	Won 8	Lost 4	No result 4	

YORKSHIRE CHAMPIONSHIP AVERAGES

*Not out

BATTING and FIELDING	M	I	NO	HS	R	Av	100	50	Ct	St
G. Boycott	11	15	5	175*	1160	116.00	4	7	3	—
R. G. Lumb	21	33	2	159	1400	45.16	5	4	11	—
P. Carrick	21	26	8	128*	621	34.50	1	3	11	—
S. N. Hartley	3	5	1	53*	126	31.50	—	1	1	—
G. A. Cope	9	9	6	39*	92	30.66	—	—	3	—
J. H. Hampshire	20	30	2	96	847	30.25	—	6	20	—
J. D. Love	11	19	3	170*	417	26.06	1	—	6	—
K. Sharp	14	21	2	80	483	25.42	—	2	2	—
H. P. Cooper	6	3	0	40	69	23.00	—	—	1	—
C. W. J. Athey	20	32	3	79*	642	22.13	—	2	14	1
D. L. Bairstow	21	32	8	61	527	21.95	—	2	40	9
A. Sidebottom	13	14	5	51	184	20.44	—	1	2	—
G. B. Stevenson	16	19	4	42	244	16.26	—	—	8	—
A. Ramage	4	3	3	8*	14	—	—	—	—	—
S. Oldham	12	5	1	50	52	13.00	—	1	4	—
C. M. Old	13	15	5	23	110	11.00	—	—	8	—
J. P. Whiteley	11	6	2	20	43	10.75	—	—	3	—

Also batted: P. G. Ingham (2 matches) 17, 4, 11; C. Johnson (1 match) 1, 13; B. Leadbeater (2 matches) 15, 1*, 1, 49.

BOWLING	O	M	R	W	Av	BB	5wI	10wM
Old	360.5	96	904	36	25.11	5–72	1	—
Sidebottom	294	72	826	31	26.64	4–59	—	—
Stevenson	468.2	115	1364	46	29.65	6–14	1	—
Ramage	112	34	305	10	30.50	3–63	—	—
Carrick	646.2	210	1678	51	32.90	5–32	3	—
Cooper	142	36	387	11	35.18	2–16	—	—
Cope	191.3	58	490	13	37.69	6–37	1	—
Oldham	247.2	52	720	18	40.00	4–76	—	—
Whiteley	203.2	66	529	10	52.90	3–85	—	—

Also bowled: Athey 96.3–21–311–1; Bairstow 5–1–16–1; Boycott 45.2–20–84–9; Love 10–1–35–0.

OTHER FIRST-CLASS MATCHES 1979

MCC

KENT at Lord's, 21, 22, 23 April. Match drawn. Kent 195 (G. W. Johnson 82, C. M. Old 6–34). MCC 278–9 (D. I. Gower 66).

INDIANS at Lord's, 30 June, 2, 3 July. Match drawn. *(See Indian Tour section for scores.)*

Ireland v Scotland

Played at Rathmines, Dublin, 28, 29, 30 July. Ireland won by 7 wickets. Scotland 191 (F. Robertson 51) and 142 (T. M. Black 57, M. Halliday 5–39). Ireland 195 (G. F. Goddard 7–56) and 142–3 (J. F. Short 80*).

Cambridge University
Played 10   Won 1   Drawn 7   Lost 2

ESSEX at Cambridge, 21, 23, 24 April. Match drawn. Cambridge U. 197 and 90–4. Essex 308–8d (B. R. Hardie 59, K. W. R. Fletcher 56).

LEICESTERSHIRE at Cambridge, 25, 26, 27 April. Match drawn. Leicestershire 88–1d (B. Dudleston 52) and 135–3 (D. I. Gower 72). Cambridge U. 137 (A. R. Dewes 64, J. F. Steele 6–36).

SURREY at Cambridge, 2, 3 *(no play)*, 4 *(no play)* May. Match drawn. Surrey 41–0.

NOTTINGHAMSHIRE at Cambridge, 9, 10, 11 *(no play)* May. Match drawn. Nottinghamshire 342 (M. J. Smedley 91, C. E. B. Rice 76, E. E. Hemmings 73, M. J. Harris 53, N. C. Crawford 6–80). Cambridge U. 111–5.

GLOUCESTERSHIRE at Cambridge, 16, 17, 18 May. Match drawn. Gloucestershire 360–5d (J. C. Foat 117, C. B. Broad 86, A. W. Stovold 54, S. J. Windaybank 53) and 201–4d (A. W. Stovold 69*). Cambridge U. 303–6d (A. R. Dewes 84, D. R. Pringle 58, N. H. C. Cooper 54) and 104–0 (A. M. Mubarak 58*). *Broad and Windaybank were making their first appearance in first-class cricket and shared an opening partnership of 126 in the first innings.*

YORKSHIRE at Cambridge, 9, 11, 12 June. Yorkshire won by 151 runs. Yorkshire 283 (G. B. Stevenson 73*) and 170–5d (J. D. Love 79). Cambridge U. 156 and 146.

SUSSEX at Cambridge, 13, 14, 15 June. Match drawn. Cambridge U. 222–8d (D. C. Holliday 55*, I. A. Greig 53) and 115–6. Sussex 183–7d.

LANCASHIRE at Cambridge, 20, 21, 22 June. Match drawn. Lancashire 236 (B. W. Reidy 65) and 205–8d (J. Abrahams 69). Cambridge U. 252 (N. F. M. Popplewell 92, D. R. Pringle 53) and 80–2.

SOMERSET at Bath, 23, 24, 25 June. Somerset won by 6 wickets. Cambridge U. 195 (I. A. Greig 58, H. R. Moseley 6–52) and 98. Somerset 168 and 128–4.

OXFORD UNIVERSITY at Lord's, 4, 5, 6 July. Cambridge U. won by an innings and 52 runs. (See p. 144 for full scorecard.)

Oxford University
Played 11   Won 0   Drawn 4   Lost 7

GLAMORGAN at Oxford, 25, 26, 27 April. Glamorgan won by 8 wickets. Oxford U. 77 (A. H. Wilkins 5–25) and 101. Glamorgan 143 (G. V. Marie 5–46) and 39–2.

HAMPSHIRE at Oxford, 9, 10, 11 *(no play)* May. Match drawn. Hampshire 251–7d (M. C. J. Nicholas 105*). Oxford U. 59 (K. Stevenson 7–22, N. E. J. Pocock held five catches).

GLOUCESTERSHIRE at Oxford, 23, 24 *(no play)*, 25 May. Match drawn. Gloucestershire 121–3 (Sadiq Mohammad 56).

WARWICKSHIRE at Oxford, 2 *(no play)*, 4, 5 June. Warwickshire won by 69 runs. Warwickshire 187–7d and 140–3d (K. D. Smith 64*). Oxford U. 121–2d and 137.

SOMERSET at Oxford, 9 *(no play)*, 11, 12 June. Match drawn. Somerset 205–5d (P. W. Denning 91) and 163–4d. Oxford U. 149–5d (R. P. Moulding 56*) and 78–6 (S. M. Clements 57*).

LEICESTERSHIRE at Oxford, 13, 14, 15 June. Leicestershire won by 8 wickets. Oxford U. 146 and 180 (Aamer Hameed 52). Leicestershire 307–6d (P. B. Clift 88*) and 20–2.

Two bowlers who opened for MCC in 1979 and were both handicapped by injuries as the season progressed.
Left: Lancashire's Willie Hogg, who was being viewed as an England prospect in the match against the Indian tourists.
Below: Chris Old, of Yorkshire, who found conditions much to his liking in the opening match of the season and took 6–34 against county champions Kent.

WORCESTERSHIRE at Oxford, 16, 18, 19 June. Match drawn. Worcestershire 311–5d (P. A. Neale 65, D. N. Patel 64, B. L. D'Oliveira 51) and 147–2d (J. A. Ormrod 56). Oxford U. 179 and 259–8 (J. A. Claughton 82, S. M. Clements 56).

SURREY at Oxford, 20, 21, 22 June. Surrey won by an innings and 73 runs. Surrey 351–3d (R. D. V. Knight 117*, A. R. Butcher 102, D. M. Smith 58*). Oxford U. 121 (P. I. Pocock 5–17) and 157 (R. D. Jackman 5–56).

SRI LANKANS at Guildford, 24, 25 June. Sri Lanka won by an innings and 86 runs in 2 days.

Oxford U. 63 (G. R. A. De Silva 6–30) and 146 (D. S. De Silva 8–46). Sri Lanka 295–8d (R. L. Dias 84*, B. Warnapura 73, A. P. B. Tennekoon 63).

SUSSEX at Pagham, 27, 28, 29 June. Sussex won by 115 runs. Sussex 357–4d (P. W. G. Parker 101, G. D. Mendis 95, K. C. Wessels 55, J. R. T. Barclay 54) and 165–6d. Oxford U. 217 (J. O. D. Orders 70, J. Spencer 6–40) and 190 (M. G. L'Estrange 63).

CAMBRIDGE UNIVERSITY at Lord's, 4, 5, 6 July. Cambridge U. won by an innings and 52 runs. (See p. 144 for full scorecard.)

THE UNIVERSITY MATCH 1979

Played at Lord's, London, 4, 5, 6 July *captain
Toss: Oxford   Result: Cambridge U. won by an innings and 52 runs   †wicket-keeper

OXFORD UNIVERSITY

J. A. Claughton	lbw b Surridge	7	c Mills b Greig	6
J. J. Rogers	b Surridge	22	c Cottrell b Greig	4
S. M. Clements*	c Cottrell b Greig	1	c Greig b Pringle	30
R. P. Moulding	b Greig	0	c Greig b Surridge	1
J. O. D. Orders	c Cottrell b Greig	1	b Popplewell	15
M. G. L'Estrange†	c Holliday b Surridge	24	c Cottrell b Popplewell	18
N. D. Morrill	c Cooper b Pringle	14	c and b Surridge	20
Aamer Hameed	c Greig b Pringle	11	c and b Surridge	34
C. J. Ross	not out	3	not out	9
J. M. Knight	c Holliday b Surridge	1	b Pringle	9
J. P. Pearce	b Pringle	0	b Surridge	0
Extras	(lb 9, w 2, nb 2)	13	(b 3, lb 4)	7
TOTAL		**97**		**153**

CAMBRIDGE UNIVERSITY

N. H. C. Cooper	c Orders b Ross	54
A. M. Mubarak	b Ross	25
J. P. C. Mills	b Knight	6
B. Bennett	lbw b Knight	0
N. F. M. Popplewell	lbw b Aamer	40
D. R. Pringle	not out	103
I. A. Greig*	b Ross	10
D. C. Holliday	b Knight	16
N. C. Crawford	c Claughton b Aamer	13
P. R. Cottrell†	b Knight	7
D. Surridge	not out	1
Extras	(b 4, lb 9, w 7, nb 7)	27
TOTAL	(9 wickets declared)	**302**

CAMBRIDGE UNIVERSITY

	O	M	R	W	O	M	R	W
Surridge	14	4	22	4	23.4	8	56	4
Greig	9	1	33	3	6	1	19	2
Crawford	7	2	19	0				
Pringle	11	4	10	3	22	12	27	2
Cooper					3	0	9	0
Popplewell					11	2	35	2

OXFORD UNIVERSITY

	O	M	R	W
Knight	30	4	69	4
Aamer	28	3	85	2
Ross	26.3	4	78	3
Pearce	11	2	43	0
Orders	1	1	0	0

FALL OF WICKETS

Wkt	O	C	O
1st	19	41	10
2nd	20	74	17
3rd	20	74	20
4th	28	130	51
5th	38	148	71
6th	71	166	82
7th	85	203	126
8th	91	251	137
9th	92	270	152
10th	97		153

CAMBRIDGE UNIVERSITY

BATTING AND FIELDING

*Not out   †Blue 1979

	M	I	NO	R	HS	Av	100	50	Ct	St
†D. R. Pringle	10	13	3	404	103*	40.40	1	2	7	—
†N. H. C. Cooper	7	8	1	264	54	37.71	—	2	3	—
†N. F. M. Popplewell	9	10	1	281	92	31.22	—	1	3	—
†I. A. Greig	8	11	1	249	58	24.90	—	2	7	—
A. R. Dewes	9	13	1	269	84	22.41	—	2	2	—
†D. Surridge	9	8	6	40	14*	20.00	—	—	3	—
†A. M. Mubarak	9	13	2	201	58*	18.27	—	1	6	—
†J. P. C. Mills	10	13	0	198	46	15.23	—	—	4	—
†P. R. Cottrell	10	9	1	119	34	14.87	—	—	17	4
†N. C. Crawford	9	9	1	107	46	13.37	—	—	2	—
†D. C. Holliday	10	14	3	145	55*	13.18	—	1	6	—

Played in three matches: N. Russom 12, 12, 8*. *Played in two matches:* †B. Bennett 4, 0; T. D. W. Edwards 18, 7*, 2 (1 ct); M. G. Howat, did not bat. *Played in one match:* I. G. Peck 4, 0.

BOWLING

	O	M	R	W	Av	BB	5wI	10wM
D. Surridge	208.2	44	583	27	21.59	4–22	—	—
N. C. Crawford	131.2	31	429	18	23.83	6–80	1	—
D. R. Pringle	247.3	74	559	22	25.40	4–43	—	—
N. F. M. Popplewell	149	33	476	16	29.75	3–18	—	—
N. H. C. Cooper	72	15	216	6	36.00	2–11	—	—
I. A. Greig	90	18	277	6	46.16	3–33	—	—

Also bowled: D. C. Holliday 53–12–181–4; M. G. Howat 30–3–116–1; J. P. C. Mills 1–0–5–0; A. M. Mubarak 1–0–6–0; N. Russom 27–5–88–2.

OXFORD UNIVERSITY

BATTING AND FIELDING

*Not out   †Blue 1979

	M	I	NO	R	HS	Av	100	50	Ct	St
†S. M. Clements	11	19	3	420	57*	26.25	—	1	2	—
†J. O. D. Orders	5	10	0	201	70	20.10	—	2	1	—
†J. A. Claughton	7	14	0	277	82	19.78	—	1	1	—
†Aamer Hameed	9	13	0	217	52	16.69	—	1	2	—
†M. G. L'Estrange	11	19	1	278	63	15.44	—	1	12	—
N. J. C. Gandon	8	13	1	170	38	14.16	—	—	6	—
†J. J. Rogers	11	19	2	237	33*	13.94	—	—	3	—
†N. D. Morrill	9	14	2	158	45	13.16	—	—	2	—
S. R. Northcote-Green	6	10	2	100	38*	12.50	—	—	1	—
†R. P. Moulding	8	13	1	146	57*	12.16	—	1	4	—
†J. M. Knight	11	16	0	117	20	7.31	—	—	2	—
J. L. Rawlinson	4	6	2	27	13*	6.50	—	—	2	—
†C. J. Ross	10	14	7	40	16*	5.71	—	—	3	—
†J. P. Pearce	5	8	2	16	8*	2.66	—	—	2	—

Played in two matches: S. M. Skala 2, 5, 11 (6 ct, 1 st). *Played in one match:* T. E. O. Bury did not bat; G. V. Marie 6*, 11*; R. Marsden 3 (2 ct); J. F. W. Sanderson 2 (1 ct).

BOWLING

	O	M	R	W	Av	BB	5wI	10wM
G. V. Marie	21	4	46	5	9.20	5–46	1	—
C. J. Ross	263.5	60	691	26	26.57	4–66	—	—
J. M. Knight	259.1	46	795	21	37.85	4–69	—	—
J. P. Pearce	97.2	17	344	7	49.14	4–94	—	—
N. D. Morrill	145.4	29	490	8	61.25	3–53	—	—
Aamer Hameed	150	25	521	7	74.57	2–85	—	—

Also bowled: S. M. Clements 38–9–160–3; J. O. D. Orders 34–5–104–1; J. J. Rogers 8–1–39–1; J. F. W. Sanderson 23–8–66–2.

FIRST-CLASS AVERAGES 1979

BATTING (Qualification: 8 innings, average 10.00)   *Not out

	M	I	NO	HS	Runs	Av	100	50
G. Boycott	15	20	5	175*	1538	102.53	6	7
Younis Ahmed	22	30	8	221*	1539	69.95	4	7
A. J. Lamb	21	34	8	178	1747	67.19	4	11
G. M. Turner	18	31	2	150*	1669	57.55	8	5
Sadiq Mohammad	17	30	2	171	1595	56.96	8	5
K. C. Wessels	21	36	2	187	1800	52.94	6	11
A. I. Kallicharran	17	26	5	170*	1098	52.28	4	6
C. G. Greenidge	17	30	2	145	1404	50.14	3	8
D. L. Amiss	22	37	3	232*	1672	49.17	6	6
C. H. Lloyd	17	22	4	104*	880	48.88	3	3
G. P. Howarth	19	30	4	183	1238	47.61	4	7
D. W. Randall	14	25	1	209	1138	47.41	3	5
P. M. Roebuck	23	37	10	89	1273	47.14	—	11
Zaheer Abbas	17	30	2	151*	1304	46.57	3	8
P. H. Edmonds	15	17	6	141*	490	44.54	1	1
R. G. Lumb	22	35	2	159	1465	44.39	5	4
P. W. G. Parker	23	37	7	103	1330	44.33	4	5
F. C. Hayes	18	22	5	88	747	43.94	—	6
P. W. Denning	22	35	6	106	1222	42.13	2	7
P. A. Neale	22	37	6	163*	1305	42.09	4	5
K. S. McEwan	23	35	2	208*	1387	42.03	3	6
C. E. B. Rice	21	34	3	129	1297	41.83	1	10
G. D. Barlow	20	33	9	133	1000	41.66	1	5
D. I. Gower	17	27	4	200*	957	41.60	1	8
C. J. Tavaré	24	38	6	150*	1328	41.50	3	7
W. Larkins	16	27	1	136	1079	41.50	3	7
B. C. Rose	21	33	1	133	1317	41.15	2	8
P. Willey	22	34	7	131	1109	41.07	2	6
J. C. Balderstone	24	41	7	122*	1393	40.97	1	11
B. Wood	22	35	7	135*	1144	40.85	2	6
R. A. Woolmer	24	39	5	169	1382	40.64	4	5
D. R. Pringle	10	13	3	103*	404	40.40	1	2
B. R. Hardie	23	34	5	146*	1170	40.34	3	5
M. J. Harris	21	38	4	133*	1368	40.23	2	10
I. V. A. Richards	16	26	0	156	1043	40.11	3	4
D. S. Steele	23	38	8	127*	1190	39.66	2	7
J. F. Steele	23	38	5	187	1301	39.42	3	6
J. G. Wright	19	35	3	142*	1249	39.03	5	5
C. T. Radley	20	35	6	118*	1128	38.89	2	8
M. J. Procter	21	36	4	122	1241	38.78	3	7
I. T. Botham	15	20	1	137	731	38.47	2	1
A. R. Butcher	24	42	5	169	1398	37.78	4	6
N. H. C. Cooper	7	8	1	54	264	37.71	—	2
V. J. Marks	24	33	9	93	894	37.25	—	7
M. J. Smith	19	34	4	137	1109	36.96	5	1
G. Miller	16	19	5	82	512	36.57	—	4
C. B. Broad	9	16	2	129	512	36.57	1	2
A. W. Stovold	22	39	1	156	1388	36.52	1	10
G. A. Gooch	17	25	2	109	838	36.43	1	6

	M	I	NO	HS	Runs	Av	100	50
P. A. Todd	19	34	2	176	1164	36.37	2	4
B. Dudleston	21	35	0	202	1258	35.94	2	8
C. H. Dredge	11	11	5	55	215	35.83	—	1
G. Cook	22	37	2	130	1241	35.45	3	4
A. J. Hignell	16	27	6	149*	736	35.04	2	3
Imran Khan	16	25	5	154*	700	35.00	1	6
D. Lloyd	22	34	3	135*	1078	34.77	4	4
D. M. Smith	19	23	7	79	555	34.68	—	4
C. Maynard	12	12	3	85	310	34.44	—	2
T. E. Jesty	19	35	3	76	1100	34.37	—	10
G. W. Humpage	17	24	2	96	755	34.31	—	2
M. D. Partridge	23	31	10	90	717	34.14	—	6
R. C. Ontong	23	41	7	135*	1157	34.02	3	7
R. D. V. Knight	22	33	5	117*	946	33.78	2	4
Asif Iqbal	10	16	1	152	506	33.73	1	—
P. Carrick	22	27	8	128*	639	33.63	1	3
G. R. J. Roope	23	35	7	114	939	33.53	1	5
K. W. R. Fletcher	23	34	4	140*	1006	33.53	1	8
J. M. Brearley	14	20	3	148*	564	33.17	1	1
J. A. Ormrod	22	38	4	134	1126	33.11	2	7
R. G. Williams	22	35	3	151*	1057	33.03	4	3
G. S. Clinton	22	38	5	134	1082	32.78	2	6
H. T. Tunnicliffe	22	39	12	97	883	32.70	—	6
R. G. D. Willis	12	8	5	42*	98	32.66	—	—
J. R. T. Barclay	23	39	5	104*	1093	32.14	2	7
B. L. D'Oliveira	7	9	1	112	257	32.12	1	2
B. F. Davison	24	39	0	84	1245	31.92	—	8
P. N. Kirsten	23	38	2	135*	1148	31.88	2	5
D. J. S. Taylor	20	20	10	50*	318	31.80	—	1
M. H. Denness	21	35	2	136	1032	31.27	2	4
P. B. Clift	24	34	10	88*	741	30.87	—	3
J. C. Foat	10	17	2	126	463	30.86	2	1
G. A. Cope	9	9	6	39*	92	30.66	—	—
M. W. Gatting	16	24	5	93*	580	30.52	—	2
J. H. Hampshire	21	31	2	96	880	30.34	—	6
G. W. Johnson	24	31	7	82	726	30.25	—	5
E. J. O. Hemsley	23	34	6	93	842	30.07	—	5
A. Jones	22	40	0	115	1198	29.95	2	8
R. W. Tolchard	20	30	7	109	688	29.91	1	2
J. E. Emburey	20	22	6	91*	477	29.81	—	1
P. D. Swart	21	36	5	122	918	29.61	1	4
T. A. Lloyd	15	26	5	104	613	29.19	1	1
J. A. Hopkins	23	42	1	94	1174	28.63	—	8
A. Long	16	17	10	35*	200	28.57	—	—
G. D. Mendis	22	37	4	118	929	28.15	1	6
D. N. Patel	21	29	4	118*	698	27.92	1	3
D. R. Shepherd	8	10	2	70	223	27.87	—	1
C. J. C. Rowe	23	39	5	147*	945	27.79	3	3
A. Hill	19	35	3	99	887	27.71	—	6
J. D. Love	12	21	3	170*	496	27.55	1	1
J. D. Birch	13	21	5	94*	440	27.50	—	2
B. W. Reidy	18	26	6	131*	547	27.35	1	1
P. A. Slocombe	23	38	3	103*	956	27.31	1	6
T. J. Yardley	19	29	6	66*	623	27.08	—	4
A. P. E. Knott	10	11	2	63	243	27.00	—	1
C. S. Cowdrey	21	30	4	83	692	26.61	—	4
J. Abrahams	15	25	1	79	633	26.37	—	6
P. R. Oliver	16	18	3	83	394	26.26	—	2
S. M. Clements	11	19	3	57*	420	26.25	—	1
A. G. E. Ealham	24	33	4	153	760	26.20	1	3
R. W. Taylor	14	14	3	64	286	26.00	—	1
R. M. Ratcliffe	17	16	5	101*	285	25.90	1	—
K. Sharp	16	24	2	80	566	25.72	—	2
K. Shuttleworth	19	20	9	44	279	25.36	—	—

Geoffrey Boycott returned from an unhappy winter in Australia to re-affirm his status as the leading English batsman, averaging more than 100 for the second time in his career.

	M	I	NO	HS	Runs	Av	100	50
K. J. Barnett	23	36	6	96	752	25.06	—	4
I. A. Greig	8	11	1	58	249	24.90	—	2
J. M. Rice	23	41	3	84*	927	24.39	—	4
D. L. Bairstow	24	37	9	61	680	24.28	—	3
K. D. Smith	20	34	3	71	739	23.83	—	7
J. Birkenshaw	9	10	5	33*	119	23.80	—	—
N. G. Featherstone	10	14	3	59*	260	23.63	—	1
D. A. Francis	15	26	7	56*	446	23.47	—	1
A. J. Borrington	19	28	4	64	563	23.45	—	3
J. Simmons	23	25	5	74*	469	23.45	—	1
M. J. Smedley	12	16	1	91	351	23.40	—	1
R. O. Butcher	14	22	0	106	513	23.31	1	2
D. Breakwell	24	31	9	54*	510	23.18	—	2
P. J. Graves	17	24	2	59	501	22.77	—	1
A. R. Dewes	9	13	1	84	269	22.41	—	2
C. J. Tunnicliffe	20	22	4	57	403	22.38		
G. C-. Holmes	10	14	3	100*	246	22.36	1	—
J. Lyon	21	22	8	123	313	22.35	1	—
I. M. Richards	11	15	1	47	312	22.28	—	—
N. F. M. Popplewell	16	20	2	92	400	22.22	—	1
D. J. Humphries	22	30	4	68	575	22.11	—	2
C. W. J. Athey	21	34	3	79*	679	21.90	—	2
J. D. Inchmore	21	22	9	37*	283	21.76	—	—
S. Turner	23	30	4	102	561	21.57	1	1
D. R. Turner	22	39	1	129	815	21.44	1	3
G. B. Stevenson	17	20	5	73*	317	21.13	—	1
J. Whitehouse	21	34	4	98	624	20.80	—	3
A. L. Jones	15	27	3	83	498	20.75	—	4
N. E. Briers	19	32	2	119	620	20.66	2	1
J. W. Southern	16	21	9	61*	247	20.58	—	1
A. Sidebottom	13	14	5	51	184	20.44	—	1
K. R. Pont	13	20	3	77	346	20.35	—	2
M. J. Llewellyn	10	15	1	106*	285	20.35	1	1
Intikhab Alam	15	21	4	52	345	20.29	—	2
G. R. Dilley	21	23	10	81	262	20.15	—	1
J. O. D. Orders	5	10	0	70	201	20.10	—	2
M. Hendrick	15	12	7	36	100	20.00	—	—
D. Surridge	9	8	6	14*	40	20.00	—	—
A. M. Ferreira	16	17	6	57	219	19.90	—	1
G. E. Trim	8	13	0	91	258	19.84	—	1
V. A. Holder	14	12	6	24*	119	19.83	—	—
W. N. Slack	6	12	0	66	236	19.66	—	1
N. E. J. Pocock	12	22	2	143*	393	19.65	1	—
J. N. Shepherd	16	20	1	86	370	19.47	—	1
A. C. S. Pigott	14	20	3	55	328	19.29	—	1
R. E. East	20	26	5	70	401	19.09	—	1
P. J. Watts	18	24	7	42*	323	19.00	—	—
N. Smith	23	29	7	90*	417	18.95	—	3
N. G. Cowley	23	39	6	85	611	18.51	—	2
C. P. Phillipson	23	31	6	47	460	18.40	—	—
M. N. S. Taylor	21	30	3	75	495	18.33	—	3
A. M. Mubarak	9	13	2	58*	201	18.27	—	1
D. J. Rock	16	27	1	104	473	18.19	1	1
E. E. Hemmings	21	31	6	85*	453	18.12	—	2
J. A. Claughton	9	16	0	82	289	18.06	—	1
W. K. Watson	10	10	5	25	89	17.80	—	—
D. A. Graveney	22	27	10	56*	301	17.70	—	1
J. Garner	14	10	4	53	106	17.66	—	1
I. J. Gould	19	22	1	89	370	17.61	—	2
B. Hassan	11	16	1	49	257	17.13	—	—
D. P. Hughes	15	14	3	60*	188	17.09	—	1
N. Phillip	22	30	5	66	425	17.00	—	2
Sarfraz Nawaz	13	15	2	46	220	16.92	—	—
R. D. Jackman	21	25	8	82	287	16.88	—	1

	M	I	NO	HS	Runs	Av	100	50
A. Kennedy	9	11	3	21	135	16.87	—	—
Aamer Hameed	9	13	0	52	217	16.69	—	1
I. S. Anderson	5	9	3	38	98	16.33	—	—
G. Sharp	22	26	2	51	386	16.08	—	1
R. J. Hadlee	12	16	4	41	193	16.08	—	—
K. E. Cooper	12	9	4	18*	79	15.80	—	—
M. G. L'Estrange	11	19	1	63	278	15.44	—	1
B. J. Lloyd	16	25	6	43	293	15.42	—	—
M. A. Lynch	7	12	2	45	153	15.30	—	—
J. P. C. Mills	10	13	0	46	198	15.23	—	—
P. R. Cottrell	10	9	1	34	119	14.87	—	—
B. N. French	19	20	5	41	223	14.86	—	—
M. J. Kitchen	7	10	0	36	146	14.60	—	—
B. J. R. Jones	6	12	0	39	174	14.50	—	—
A. E. Cordle	22	28	6	51	316	14.36	—	1
N. J. C. Gandon	8	13	1	38	170	14.16	—	—
J. J. Rogers	11	19	2	33*	237	13.94	—	—
M. W. W. Selvey	20	18	1	45	237	13.94	—	—
J. Walters	22	28	7	54	291	13.85	—	1
R. M. Carter	10	10	3	26*	94	13.42	—	—
N. C. Crawford	9	9	1	46	107	13.37	—	—
D. C. Holliday	10	14	3	55*	145	13.18	—	1
N. D. Morrill	9	14	2	45	158	13.16	—	—
E. W. Jones	21	34	6	108	368	13.14	1	—
R. LeQ. Savage	7	8	5	15*	39	13.00	—	—
G. Richards	10	13	1	34	155	12.91	—	—
P. Booth	10	8	3	20	64	12.80	—	—
R. C. Wincer	11	11	4	26	88	12.57	—	—
S. R. Northcote-Green	6	10	2	38*	100	12.50	—	—
P. Bainbridge	8	14	2	81*	149	12.41	—	1
R. P. Moulding	8	13	1	57*	146	12.16	—	1
P. H. L. Wilson	17	11	7	15	48	12.00	—	—
C. E. Waller	16	13	7	18*	69	11.50	—	—
R. N. Abberley	6	9	2	22*	79	11.28	—	—
S. T. Clarke	11	11	3	25	90	11.25	—	—
M. A. Nash	9	11	0	41	123	11.18	—	—
J. Spencer	17	16	3	35	145	11.15	—	—
G. R. Stephenson	23	33	3	43	333	11.10	—	—
D. L. Underwood	23	24	5	45	210	11.05	—	—
P. I. Pocock	22	19	7	20	131	10.91	—	—
N. G. B. Cook	14	12	5	18*	74	10.57	—	—
R. W. Hills	10	11	4	27	73	10.42	—	—
W. W. Daniel	17	13	6	18	72	10.28	—	—
A. J. McLellan	12	10	3	41	72	10.28	—	—
C. M. Old	14	16	5	23	112	10.18	—	—

BOWLING (Qualification: 10 wickets)

	O	M	R	W	Av	BB	5wI	10wM
J. Garner	393.1	127	761	55	13.83	6–80	4	—
D. L. Underwood	799.2	335	1575	106	14.85	8–28	10	4
Imran Khan	415.4	106	1091	73	14.94	6–37	7	—
H. R. Moseley	196.4	50	495	31	15.96	6–52	2	1
R. J. Hadlee	317	103	753	47	16.02	7–23	2	—
R. D. Jackman	628.1	173	1595	93	17.15	8–64	8	—
J. K. Lever	700	166	1834	106	17.30	8–49	8	2
S. T. Clarke	320.1	106	757	43	17.60	6–61	3	—
G. G. Arnold	435.5	147	950	52	18.26	6–41	2	—
K. Higgs	404.5	133	872	47	18.55	6–33	4	—
M. J. Procter	574.5	140	1532	81	18.91	8–30	7	1
C. E. B. Rice	448	134	1139	58	19.63	6–49	3	—
Sarfraz Nawaz	408.5	130	913	45	20.28	6–60	2	—

Joel Garner, devastating for Somerset in the Gillette Cup, was also a force to be reckoned with in the first-class game and headed the national bowling averages.

	O	M	R	W	Av	BB	5wI	10wM
P. I. Pocock	595.5	189	1435	70	20.50	9–57	4	1
N. Phillip	548.1	128	1506	70	21.51	5–23	1	—
S. Turner	576.3	164	1285	61	21.06	5–35	4	1
M. Hendrick	456	150	885	42	21.07	4–32	—	—
D. Surridge	208.2	44	583	27	21.59	4–22	—	—
L. B. Taylor	352.3	77	958	44	21.77	6–61	2	—
R. G. L. Cheatle	185.1	49	467	21	22.23	6–32	2	—
C. M. Old	381.1	103	938	42	22.33	6–34	2	—
M. D. Marshall	467	146	1051	47	22.36	5–56	1	—
W. W. Daniel	429.2	100	1170	52	22.50	6–38	2	—
K. Stevenson	548.3	133	1567	69	22.71	7–22	4	—
A. Ramage	129	38	348	15	23.20	3–24	—	—
G. R. Dilley	446.4	110	1151	49	23.48	6–66	1	—
N. Gifford	798.3	237	1848	78	23.69	5–12	2	—
N. C. Crawford	131.2	31	429	18	23.83	6–80	1	—
C. P. Phillipson	203.5	53	477	20	23.85	4–24	—	—
A. H. Wilkins	248.5	56	717	30	23.90	6–79	3	—
J. R. T. Barclay	412.4	85	1250	52	24.03	6–61	2	—
J. Simmons	454	112	1231	51	24.13	7–86	1	—
N. G. B. Cook	359.5	119	870	36	24.16	6–57	2	—
J. F. Steele	273.2	91	654	27	24.22	6–36	1	—
B. J. Griffiths	422.5	89	1222	50	24.44	5–76	1	—
N. G. Featherstone	191.1	40	568	23	24.69	4–28	—	—
R. D. V. Knight	260	66	728	29	25.10	5–44	2	—
J. D. Inchmore	521.4	102	1572	62	25.35	6–35	3	—
D. R. Pringle	247.3	74	559	22	25.40	4–43	—	—
D. L. Acfield	489.2	143	1048	41	25.56	6–56	3	—
M. W. W. Selvey	578.3	177	1443	56	25.76	5–42	3	—
C. J. Ross	263.5	60	691	26	26.57	4–66	—	—
A. Sidebottom	294	72	826	31	26.64	4–59	—	—
J. Spencer	365.1	107	888	33	26.90	6–40	2	—
J. E. Emburey	746.2	225	1619	59	27.44	4–31	—	—
B. L. D'Oliveira	122	37	275	10	17.50	2–15	—	—
M. N. S. Taylor	265.5	70	746	27	27.62	5–33	1	—
A. E. Cordle	609.3	133	1604	58	27.65	6–49	1	—
B. M. Brain	495.5	125	1355	49	27.65	5–33	2	—
V. J. Marks	568.4	153	1581	57	27.73	6–33	4	—
D. Breakwell	567.3	193	1311	47	27.89	6–41	1	—
W. K. Watson	213.5	69	560	20	28.00	6–51	1	—
P. B. Clift	560.1	151	1412	50	28.24	5–57	1	—
K. Shuttleworth	444	101	1273	45	28.28	4–59	—	—
G. Miller	452.1	138	1047	37	28.29	6–53	2	—
B. Wood	161.2	30	513	18	28.50	4–58	—	—
E. E. Hemmings	738	226	1770	62	28.54	5–74	2	—
I. T. Botham	436.4	111	1318	46	28.65	6–81	3	—
P. H. L. Wilson	284.5	63	861	30	28.79	4–39	—	—
G. B. Stevenson	498.3	124	1440	50	28.80	6–14	1	—
R. C. Ontong	302	62	927	32	28.96	5–40	2	—
R. M. Ratcliffe	450.5	131	1103	38	29.02	6–84	3	1
B. W. Reidy	148.4	22	468	16	29.25	5–61	1	—
W. Hogg	240.4	48	791	27	29.29	4–26	—	—
J. C. Balderstone	265.5	80	681	23	29.60	3–38	—	—
R. E. East	561.3	168	1290	43	30.00	5–56	1	—
C. H. Dredge	251	60	759	25	30.36	4–40	—	—
D. S. Steele	503.4	135	1459	48	30.39	6–91	2	—
M. K. Bore	731	226	1885	61	30.90	8–89	3	—
K. F. Jennings	245.3	78	620	20	31.00	4–25	—	—
D. J. Brown	243.4	60	653	21	31.09	7–73	2	—
P. Carrick	668.2	218	1717	55	31.21	5–32	3	—
R. W. Hills	151	34	437	14	31.21	4–58	—	—
P. H. Edmonds	564.4	181	1230	39	31.53	4–30	—	—
R. Arrowsmith	96.1	22	316	10	31.60	2–22	—	—
J. N. Shepherd	418.3	114	1075	34	31.61	4–55	—	—
J. M. Rice	270.4	58	760	24	31.66	5–17	1	—

	O	M	R	W	Av	BB	5wI	10wM
J. Birkenshaw	151.3	40	381	12	31.75	3–20	—	—
P. D. Swart	234.3	48	673	21	32.04	4–61	—	—
C. E. Waller	487.1	126	1262	39	32.35	4–18	—	—
V. A. Holder	405	75	1041	32	32.53	4–76	—	—
S. P. Perryman	671	224	1662	51	32.58	6–69	4	1
P. Willey	716.1	190	1697	52	32.63	5–46	3	—
A. C. S. Pigott	269	48	917	28	32.75	4–40	—	—
J. W. Southern	370.2	120	951	29	32.79	6–81	1	—
D. C. Hopkins	275	59	886	27	32.81	6–67	1	—
R. G. Williams	430	119	1184	36	32.88	5–57	1	—
J. Cumbes	577.3	108	1591	48	33.14	6–103	3	—
R. G. D. Willis	261	68	699	21	33.28	5–41	1	—
K. B. S. Jarvis	414.2	104	1275	38	33.55	4–42	—	—
D. A. Graveney	417	98	1311	39	33.61	5–59	3	1
N. F. M. Popplewell	251	66	747	22	33.95	3–18	—	—
H. P. Cooper	142	36	387	11	35.18	2–16	—	—
N. G. Cowley	507.4	146	1306	37	35.29	5–44	1	—
C. J. Sunnicliffe	454.5	107	1307	37	35.32	4–35	—	—
K. E. Cooper	177.4	45	536	15	35.73	4–42	—	—
R. C. Wincer	235.5	40	864	24	36.00	4–79	—	—
S. Oldham	279.2	64	803	22	36.50	4–76	—	—
R. N. S. Hobbs	269.3	77	805	22	36.59	3–21	—	—
G. G. Watson	272.5	49	825	22	37.50	4–29	—	—
G. A. Cope	191.3	58	490	13	37.69	6–37	1	—
J. M. Knight	259.1	46	795	21	37.85	4–69	—	—
P. Booth	111	28	379	10	37.90	3–46	—	—
A. A. Jones	221.2	49	646	17	38.00	3–39	—	—
M. A. Nash	226.3	66	619	16	38.68	4–50	—	—
J. H. Childs	658.3	195	1861	48	38.77	5–118	1	—

One of 21 catches taken by Mike Brearley in 1979: a low left-handed effort to dismiss Gavaskar at Lord's and give Ian Botham his 100th Test wicket.

	O	M	R	W	Av	BB	5wI	10wM
A. M. Ferreira	426	102	1210	31	39.03	5–66	1	—
P. G. Lee	288.5	61	901	23	39.17	3–50	—	—
H. T. Tunnicliffe	166.2	50	511	13	39.30	4–30	—	—
D. N. Patel	452.3	109	1461	37	39.48	5–95	1	—
P. N. Kirsten	269.3	65	752	19	39.57	4–44	—	—
A. J. Mack	176.3	27	572	14	40.85	4–62	—	—
T. M. Lamb	329.5	94	997	24	41.54	4–58	—	—
J. Walters	380	80	1209	29	41.68	4–100	—	—
B. J. Lloyd	396.1	89	1102	26	42.38	4–55	—	—
P. J. Hacker	177	42	639	15	42.60	4–46	—	—
D. J. Thomas	169	32	556	13	42.76	6–84	1	—
D. P. Hughes	226.2	56	646	15	43.06	4–77	—	—
W. G. Merry	150	36	431	10	43.10	3–46	—	—
N. J. Perry	174.4	39	563	13	43.30	3–51	—	—
L. McFarlane	181	35	569	13	43.76	3–83	—	—
C. C. Clifford	682.4	154	2166	49	44.20	5–37	3	—
G. W. Johnson	448	143	1087	24	45.29	5–12	1	—
A. Hodgson	234	39	819	18	45.50	3–41	—	—
P. J. W. Allott	223.2	41	609	13	46.84	5–39	1	—
M. D. Partridge	296.4	51	1072	21	51.04	5–29	1	—
R. LeQ. Savage	177.4	39	566	11	51.45	4–83	—	—
Intikhab Alam	345.1	100	959	18	53.27	3–44	—	—
J. P. Whiteley	209.2	67	546	10	54.60	3–85	—	—

The following bowlers took 10 wickets but bowled in fewer than 10 innings:

M. F. Malone	102.3	32	230	19	12.10	7–88	3	1
C. M. Wells	73.1	30	137	10	13.70	4–23	—	—
D. Lloyd	59.3	19	164	11	14.90	6–60	2	—

FIELDING STATISTICS

Wicket-keepers

59	D. L. Bairstow (50 ct, 9 st)
58	C. J. Richards (50 ct, 8 st)
57	D. J. Humphries (49 ct, 8 st)
54	N. Smith (51 ct, 3 st)
46	R. W. Tolchard (43 ct, 3 st)
42	B. N. French (38 ct, 4 st)
42	E. W. Jones (39 ct, 3 st)
41	A. Long (36 ct, 5 st)
40	G. Sharp (34 ct, 6 st)
39	D. J. S. Taylor (29 ct, 10 st)
35	G. R. Stephenson (31 ct, 4 st)
34	R. W. Taylor (31 ct, 3 st)
32	J. Lyon (30 ct, 2 st)
30	P. R. Downton (26 ct, 4 st)
28	C. Maynard (27 ct, 1 st)
27	I. M. Gould (24 ct, 3 st)
26	A. J. McLellan (24 ct, 2 st)
23	G. W. Humpage (21 ct, 2 st)
22	T. J. Head (21 ct, 1 st)
21	A. J. Brassington (17 ct, 3 st)

Fieldsmen

41	G. R. J. Roope
30	B. R. Hardie
29	E. J. O. Hemsley
28	G. A. Gooch
27	C. G. Greenidge
24	G. D. Mendis
23	C. T. Radley
22	C. E. B. Rice
22	P. M. Roebuck
22	D. S. Steele
21	I. T. Botham
21	J. M. Brearley
21	J. E. Emburey
21	J. H. Hampshire
21	P. N. Kirsten
21	J. F. Steele
21	C. J. Tavaré
21	K. C. Wessels
20	D. N. Patel

One that got away . . . much to the frustration of Ian Botham. A true competitor, he gives 100 per cent whether batting or bowling and has the confidence to expect success.

IAN BOTHAM – AN APPRECIATION

Trevor Bailey

One of the greatest joys of having been fortunate enough to have played a game at the highest level is that it enables one to appreciate the outstanding performer in any sport immediately, almost instinctively. Ken Rosewall's backhand, Liam Brady's talking left leg, the long approach shot by Jack Nicklaus, and the style and perfect timing of Pekka Vasala on the track have all given me enormous pleasure. But inevitably the exploits of cricketers have a special appeal.

I admire Geoff Boycott's defensive technique and abnormal appetite for runs, the dexterity of Bob Taylor behind the stumps, Greg Chappell's on-driving, the teasing flight of Bishan Bedi, the sheer virtuosity of Vivian Richards, and the pace and grace of Michael Holding. However, I have a special regard for the genuine all-rounder, which is why I have been so delighted by the exploits of Ian Botham. During last summer Ian completed his Test match 'double' in a shorter time than anybody else – a magnificent performance – but it should not be forgotten that he did play a high number of Tests in a very short period against opposition, much of which was not up to the standard normally associated with international cricket.

There never has, and never will be, any shortage of all-rounders in school and club cricket. I was once, in fact, asked to captain an England Schools XI containing 10, which did pose certain problems as to the batting order and employing all the bowlers. The large number of players who are able to combine run-making and wicket-taking at these two levels is hardly surprising. There is no great strain physically in scoring 75 runs and capturing five wickets once, or twice, a week. The majority of first-class cricketers would certainly be capable of doing well with bat and ball in club cricket.

The number of all-rounders starts to decline when they realise that, in competition with the top-class specialist, they have to produce the figures in both departments; day after day, month after month, year after year. It is at this stage that so many decide to specialise and concentrate on either their batting or their bowling. This is why England, more than other countries, produces many batsmen who can turn their arm over, and bowlers who can score runs when they are really needed, as distinct from genuine all-rounders.

The all-rounder provides cricket with the balance that is so essential to all sports. Five bowlers are generally regarded as the ideal number for a Test match, and are essential in limited-overs cricket. But if none of them can bat, the team, even with a wicket-keeper-batsman, will have a long tail. There is a need for one, or ideally two all-rounders to increase the run potential without reducing the penetration of the attack.

The perfect all-rounder should be sufficiently proficient in both departments to justify selection in either. The higher the standard, the rarer dual excellence of this nature becomes, which is why England's selectors have so often had problems and why they are so delighted with the arrival of Ian Botham. The competent 'bits and pieces' cricketer, so useful to a county XI, is usually not quite good enough with either bat or ball for international cricket. Consequently, the selectors are forced to settle for a specialist in one department who is no more than competent in the other. An example of such a compromise was Ted Dexter, who was a brilliant batsman, but as a bowler came closer to a fourth, rather than a third, seamer at Test level.

There are, and always have been, very few English all-rounders who are good enough to command a regular place in a strong county team purely as a batsman, if unable to bowl, or simply as a bowler. Even taking all the cricketing countries into account, the number who have justified selection in either rôle at international level can be counted on the fingers of two hands. They include Sir Gary Sobers, Mike Procter, Wilfred Rhodes, Vinoo Mankad and Keith Miller. To this illustrious band can now be added the name of Ian Botham, and he has not even reached his prime.

Although many might query the assessment that Ian is the best seam bowler in England at the present moment, and some would pick the estimable Mike Hendrick, the fact remains that Ian has a far more impressive record in Test cricket. He is forever picking up five or more wickets in an innings, a feat which always eludes Mike, while in the all-important comparison of wickets taken per overs bowled, he is way ahead. The prime task of any bowler in Test, as distinct from limited-overs, cricket is to take as many wickets as possible as quickly as possible, which is exactly what Ian has done.

Why has Botham been so successful as a fast-medium bowler in Test and first-class cricket but, comparatively speaking, less effective in the one-day game? I believe the main reasons to be six-fold.

First, he is essentially an attacking bowler, prepared to concede runs in his pursuit of wickets. He likes to experiment. Secondly, he is able to swing the ball in the air, later and rather more than most of his type. To his natural outswinger, he has added a big inswinger which is not simply pushed into the batsman, but does swerve. In addition he is able to seam the ball. But what has really made his swing and seam bowling so deadly is that he keeps the ball up to the bat, thus encouraging batsmen to play him off the front foot. By avoiding the common complaint of bowling too short, he *gives the ball sufficient time to swing.*

Thirdly, he has a strong, high action and a physique which enables him to keep bowling for long spells without tiring. Fourthly, he has a useful lively bouncer, though at present he is inclined to telegraph it, and is close to acquiring a really good slower ball. Fifthly, he loves bowling and detests batsmen. He appreciates that most fast bowlers like giving bouncers, but rather resent being on the receiving end. Ian delights in rousing their resentment.

Finally, I think it would be true to say he is a lucky bowler. And it would be equally true to say that he makes his own luck.

Any bowler must have fancied his chances against Mike Brearley's somewhat anaemic batting line-up of 1978–79. Therefore it was easier for Ian to justify his place purely as a batsman in that particular England team than it might have been in another era. Nevertheless, he is an exciting, match-winning strokemaker, whom I do not think has reached his peak. At the moment he looks safer, and is more impressive, against speed than spin. His tendency to hit slow bowlers firm-footed has caused problems, but on the other hand he gives the ball such a thump that he has the considerable advantage of being able to mishit a six. When he middles the ball, it is liable to disappear out of the ground. His ability to reach the boundary off front or back foot with straight-bat strokes on either side of the wicket means that he is hard to contain, and runs quickly accrue when he is at the crease.

Brian Close, no mean judge, believes Ian has the ability to develop into a great batsman, but he needs to tighten up his defence off his back foot and curb some of his natural impulsiveness, *without cutting out his aggressive strokes*. He can hardly ask for a better model than Vivian Richards, who combines handsome shots with big innings.

Nobody can claim to be a true all-rounder unless he is an expert in that third, vital department, the field. Ian Botham is not only a fieldsman of the very highest class, with a superb pair of hands, but he is the dream of every captain – an all-round fieldsman. It does not matter much where you place Ian. In the slips, the covers, the deep, at silly mid-off, or standing suicidally close in a bat-pad position, he is just as good; and frequently he is better than the expert specialist.

As an attacking bowler, exciting strokemaker, and brilliant all-purpose fieldsman with the build and stamina of a mobile heavyweight, Ian must automatically be of great value to England and Somerset: indeed, to any side. But in addition he has two very vital assets. He is a true competitor, who hates losing, and a real team-man who is able to pull out that little extra in a crisis. The odds are that in any tense finish – the final Test against India last year or that breathtaking Gillette Cup semi-final with Essex in 1978 – Ian will be making a catch, hitting a six, capturing a wicket, or running somebody out. He is that type of player. He reminds me so much of Keith Miller in his prime, but is more personally involved and ruthless; a truly dynamic cricketer.

Left: Phil Edmonds takes aggressive measures to bolster the Middlesex innings during the Gillette Cup semi-final against Somerset. But his fine, unbeaten 63 was not enough to halt the confident West Countrymen.
Below: The capacity crowd at Lord's for the Gillette Cup final enjoys a perfect late-summer day.

GILLETTE CUP 1979

SOMERSET

1ST ROUND 27 June	2ND ROUND 18, 19 July	QUARTER-FINALS 8, 9 August	SEMI-FINALS 22 August	FINAL 8 September
SOMERSET (Bye)	SOMERSET†			
DERBYSHIRE (Bye)	Derbyshire	SOMERSET†		
Glamorgan†	KENT†		SOMERSET	
KENT	Lancashire	Kent		
Essex				SOMERSET
LANCASHIRE†				
Gloucestershire†	Hampshire			
HAMPSHIRE	MIDDLESEX†	MIDDLESEX†		
MIDDLESEX (Bye)			Middlesex†	
Berkshire	Durham†	Yorkshire		
DURHAM†	YORKSHIRE			
YORKSHIRE (Bye)				
NOTTINGHAMSHIRE (Bye)	NOTTINGHAMSHIRE			
WARWICKSHIRE (Bye)	Warwickshire†	Nottinghamshire		
SUSSEX (Bye)	SUSSEX†		Sussex†	
Buckinghamshire†	Suffolk	SUSSEX†		
SUFFOLK				Northamptonshire
Devon				
LEICESTERSHIRE†	LEICESTERSHIRE†	Leicestershire		
WORCESTERSHIRE (Bye)	Worcestershire		NORTHAMPTONSHIRE	
NORTHAMPTONSHIRE (Bye)	NORTHAMPTONSHIRE†	NORTHAMPTONSHIRE†		
SURREY (Bye)	Surrey			

†Home team.   Winning team in small capitals.

SEMI-FINAL

Middlesex v Somerset
The myth that a limited-overs game is invariably entertaining and exciting
was again exploded in the Gillette Cup semi-final between Somerset and
Middlesex at Lord's. On this occasion the villain of the piece was the pitch,
which assisted the bowlers in the early stages and then eased out into a good
one. A really bad wicket would have been preferable, as that at least would
have been the same for both sides.

Immediately Rose won the toss and inserted Middlesex there was never
much serious doubt about the outcome. Indeed, if Botham had enjoyed any
luck in his opening spell, when he regularly beat the bat at least twice an over,
Somerset's victory would have been even more complete. As it was,
Middlesex at lunch were 87 for five, with 37 overs expended and Smith, 42
not out, still somewhat puzzled how he had survived the initial onslaught.
Rather surprisingly, the main destroyer was the medium-paced Burgess, who
was able to wobble the ball about enough to worry, contain, and secure
wickets.

After the interval, on a noticeably easier pitch, Edmonds and Gould enjoyed a sprightly stand of fifty and the former went on to complete an undefeated half-century before running out of partners. Despite this spirited rearguard, the eventual total of 185 did not represent a sufficiently testing objective for a side with Somerset's batting power. Rose and Denning experienced some early problems, especially outside the off stump, against the excessive pace of Daniel, but they provided the sound foundation required. To make Somerset's task even easier, Daniel pulled a muscle and had to leave the field. Subsequently Rose's team cruised comfortably home, with Denning, a hustling left-hander, accumulating an unbeaten 90 with ever-increasing freedom and confidence. Botham finished off the game in the grand manner with a six.

The behaviour of some of the Somerset supporters, who appeared to outnumber, and certainly to out-shout, those of the home side, was over-boisterous, and much of their chanting was almost as mindless as that of the average football crowd.

MIDDLESEX v SOMERSET
Played at Lord's, London, 22 August
Toss: Somerset   Result: **Somerset** won by 7 wickets   *captain*
Man of the Match: P. W. Denning   †*wicket-keeper*

MIDDLESEX				SOMERSET	O	M	R	W
M. J. Smith	c Taylor b Jennings	45		Botham	11	3	28	0
J. M. Brearley*	c Taylor b Garner	2		Garner	10.5	3	24	4
M. W. Gatting	b Jennings	11		Burgess	12	3	25	3
C. T. Radley	c and b Burgess	3		Jennings	12	0	38	2
G. D. Barlow	st Taylor b Burgess	11		Breakwell	7	2	22	0
N. G. Featherstone	lbw b Burgess	0		Richards	5	0	27	0
P. H. Edmonds	not out	63						
I. J. Gould†	run out (Botham/Richards)	22		MIDDLESEX				
M. W. W. Selvey	c Taylor b Garner	7		Selvey	11.2	5	31	1
W. W. Daniel	b Garner	0		Daniel	8	0	16	0
A. A. Jones	b Garner	0		Jones	9	1	44	1
Extras	(b 5, lb 6, w 2, nb 8)	21		Featherstone	8	1	31	1
TOTAL	(57.5 overs)	**185**		Edmonds	12	2	39	0
				Gatting	2	0	12	0

SOMERSET			FALL OF WICKETS		
B. C. Rose*	b Jones	19	Wkt	M	Sm
P. W. Denning	not out	90	1st	11	49
I. V. A. Richards	c Edmonds b Featherstone	32	2nd	33	99
P. M. Roebuck	b Selvey	26	3rd	46	183
I. T. Botham	not out	6	4th	74	—
V. J. Marks			5th	74	—
G. I. Burgess	⎫		6th	103	—
D. Breakwell	⎪ did not bat		7th	160	—
D. J. S. Taylor	⎬		8th	179	—
J. Garner	⎪		9th	185	—
K. F. Jennings	⎭		10th	185	—
Extras	(b 5, lb 6, nb 6)	17	Umpires: D. J. Halfyard		
TOTAL	(3 wickets – 50.2 overs)	**190**	R. Julian		

Left: Peter Denning, Man of the Match at Lord's, confidently struck 90 not out to ensure that Somerset would revisit Lord's in September for the second successive year.

SEMI-FINAL

Sussex v Northamptonshire

Northamptonshire beat Sussex by 37 runs in a stirring match that illustrated the best features of the one-day game: fine batting, tight bowling, including some spin, and brilliant fielding. It must be mentioned, too, that the entertaining spectacle owed much to the essential requirement – a good, true pitch which positively encouraged the playing of strokes. The game revolved around an outstanding fourth-wicket partnership of 157 between Allan Lamb and Peter Willey, which not only rescued Northamptonshire when they appeared to be heading for defeat but took them to a commanding position from which they were never dislodged. In addition to his splendidly judged innings, Willey also sent down 12 very tidy overs of off-spin.

The Midlanders started badly, having two of their quintet of consistent run-getters back in the pavilion for 16. However, Lamb, after some anxious moments, gradually settled and produced strokes of real authority. Willey began quietly, and sensibly, against tight bowling, with the result that runs came at no more than a trickle, but he cut loose after lunch. One memorable

over from Imran Khan, who went for 55 runs in his allotted 12 overs, saw Willey improve his score by 13. He outscored Lamb in this period of positive aggression and both departed in the same over with 234 on the board. In the last four overs a further 21 were scrambled to produce a total of 255, which looked, and proved, too many for Sussex.

If the Seasiders were to win, at least two of their major batsmen needed to play major innings. Against the Midlanders' attack, missing their one class bowler, Sarfraz, this was highly possible on this lovely Hove pitch. But only Mendis came off. Barclay, Parker and Imran Khan all failed, while the most dangerous threat of all, Wessels, was dismissed by Tim Lamb when he was batting with a fluency that looked especially ominous.

Mendis and Graves led a brave recovery without ever quite establishing the necessary tempo. When both departed Sussex were still 109 behind with only three wickets and 16 overs remaining. The tail responded admirably to this severe challenge. Long, Pigott, Spencer and Arnold all swung sufficiently well to keep alive the hopes of their supporters, yet they never quite suggested bringing off the nearly impossible.

SUSSEX v NORTHAMPTONSHIRE
Played at Hove, 22 August
Toss: Northamptonshire   Result: **Northamptonshire** won by 37 runs   *captain
Man of the Match: P. Willey   †wicket-keeper

NORTHAMPTONSHIRE			SUSSEX	O	M	R	W
G. Cook	c Long b Arnold	5	Imran	12	1	55	0
W. Larkins	run out (Parker)	11	Arnold	12	2	45	3
R. G. Williams	b Spencer	16	Pigott	6	0	39	0
A. J. Lamb	c Pigott b Arnold	101	Spencer	12	2	34	1
P. Willey	b Arnold	89	Phillipson	6	1	27	1
T. J. Yardley	c Spencer b Phillipson	7	Barclay	12	0	41	0
G. Sharp†	run out	4					
P. J. Watts*	not out	8	NORTHAMPTONSHIRE				
A. Hodgson			Griffiths	10	0	48	1
T. M. Lamb	} did not bat		Hodgson	9.2	0	37	2
B. J. Griffiths			T. M. Lamb	12	2	52	4
Extras	(b 9, nb 5)	14	Watts	12	1	33	1
TOTAL	(7 wickets – 60 overs)	255	Willey	12	2	32	1

SUSSEX			FALL OF WICKETS		
J. R. T. Barclay	c Sharp b Griffiths	2	*Wkt*	*Nh*	*Sx*
K. C. Wessels	c Sharp b T. M. Lamb	28	1st	13	11
G. D. Mendis	lbw b Hodgson	69	2nd	16	45
P. W. G. Parker	lbw b T. M. Lamb	2	3rd	77	56
Imran Khan	c Sharp b Watts	11	4th	234	85
P. J. Graves	c and b Willey	21	5th	234	138
C. P. Phillipson	run out	0	6th	241	139
A. C. S. Pigott	lbw b T. M. Lamb	30	7th	255	146
A. Long*†	b T. M. Lamb	15	8th	—	185	
G. G. Arnold	not out	18	9th	—	201
J. Spencer	lbw b Hodgson	6	10th	—	218
Extras	(lb 11, w 2, nb 3)	16	Umpires: W. E. Alley		
TOTAL	(55.2 overs)	218		D. G. L. Evans	

Left: South African Allan Lamb's century at Hove, full of authority and true class, provided the basis for the winning Northamptonshire total.

Joel Garner's six wickets, for a mere 29 runs, made certain that Somerset would not be disappointed a second year at Lord's and, with his not out 24, made him a contender for the Man of the Match award.

GILLETTE CUP FINAL 1979

Twelve months after those two disastrous days of 1978, when Somerset saw their dreams of the 'double' within their grasp disappear, they achieved the honour they had been seeking for more than one hundred years. At Lord's, on a perfect September day, they beat Northamptonshire without undue difficulty in a good Gillette Cup final, even if the result from lunchtime onwards was rarely seriously in doubt.

In the false hope that there would be moisture and life in the Lord's pitch at 10.30 a.m. – as indeed there had been in the semi-final – and possibly influenced by the fact that this match had been won by the side batting second for the past five years, Jim Watts inserted the opposition. It turned out to be a fatal mistake. Somerset, assisted by some wayward bowling, began at a fierce gallop, providing the ideal platform for Vivian Richards to score a masterful century, in which he showed exceptional judgement and control. He did not lift a ball off the ground until after lunch and remained in charge until the final over. Somerset's match-winning total of 269 owed nearly everything to the virtuosity of this great player. When a batsman of Vivian's calibre produces a major innings in a limited-overs contest, a win, all things being equal and provided the bowlers perform adequately, is almost assured. So it was proved. Apart from the bright start, sensible support from Rose, a few mighty blows from Botham and a flourish from Garner, Somerset relied on the genius of their West Indian import. The rest of their batting, against an insipid attack, was undistinguished.

Apart from Sarfraz, who came in for some rough treatment in the closing stages, the Midlanders' bowling was well below that expected from a county eleven. This point was illustrated by their captain, Watts. In his prime no more than a county third or fourth seamer, he was easily the most successful and inexpensive member of the attack, simply by obeying the fundamental precept of maintaining a line and length.

How did Northamptonshire reach the final with quite such an anaemic bowling line-up? The answer is that, in limited-overs cricket, the key to success is usually runs scored in quantity and at speed. The main function of the attack is the denial of runs rather than the taking of wickets. The first five of the Northamptonshire batting line-up all scored well and heavily during the season. On this occasion it needed at least three of their talented quintet to produce a major innings. The massive Joel Garner saw that this did not occur by shooting out Larkins and Williams in his first spell, coming back to remove Willey, and finishing with six wickets for 29 runs in 10.3 overs. This on a pitch on which the Northants' bowlers had difficulty in restricting batsmen to four per over and Tim Lamb went for 70 in his 12 overs.

The abrupt dismissal of Larkins and Williams meant that everything depended on the talented Allan Lamb, who is international class. The South African played a great innings which, considering the near-hopeless position and the superior bowling, was in many respects an even better knock than that of Richards. As long as he was at the crease, the more optimistic of Northamptonshire supporters felt Allan could conjure up a miracle to give them victory. He did play uncommonly well, but in the end Somerset simply had to prevail. Just as they had batted to greater effect, so their bowling was superior, and they were better in the field, with Richards, Botham and Roebuck especially outstanding.

NORTHAMPTON v SOMERSET
Played at Lord's, London, 8 September
Toss: Northamptonshire   Result: **Somerset** won by 45 runs
Man of the Match: I. V. A. Richards   *Captain   †Wicket-keeper

SOMERSET		Runs	Mins	Balls	6s	4s
B. C. Rose*	*b* Watts	41	91	83	—	5
P. W. Denning	*c* Sharp *b* Sarfraz	19	27	21	—	3
I. V. A. Richards	*b* Griffiths	117	189	136	—	11
P. M. Roebuck	*b* Willey	14	39	52	—	1
I. T. Botham	*b* T. M. Lamb	27	21	17	—	5
V. J. Marks	*b* Griffiths	9	17	17	—	1
G. I. Burgess	*c* Sharp *b* Watts	1	2	4	—	—
D. Breakwell	*b* T. M. Lamb	5	5	9	—	1
J. Garner	*not out*	24	34	26	—	2
D. J. S. Taylor†	*not out*	1	1	1	—	—
K. F. Jennings	*did not bat*					
Extras	(*b* 5, *lb* 3, *nb* 3)	11				
TOTAL	(8 wickets – 60 overs)	**269**				

NORTHAMPTONSHIRE		Runs	Mins	Balls	6s	4s
G. Cook	*run out (Roebuck/Jennings)*	44	122	97	—	5
W. Larkins	*lbw b* Garner	0	3	5	—	—
R. G. Williams	*hit wkt b* Garner	8	9	8	—	2
A. J. Lamb	*st* Taylor *b* Richards	78	145	127	—	9
P. Willey	*c* Taylor *b* Garner	5	12	15	—	—
T. J. Yardley	*c* Richards *b* Burgess	20	37	34	—	2
G. Sharp†	*b* Garner	22	33	30	—	—
Sarfraz Nawaz	*not out*	16	31	21	—	1
T. M. Lamb	*b* Garner	4	7	8	—	—
B. J. Griffiths	*b* Garner	0	1	2	—	—
P. J. Watts*	*absent hurt*					
Extras	(*b* 6, *lb* 9, *w* 5, *nb* 7)	27				
TOTAL	(56.3 overs)	**224**				

NORTHAMPTONSHIRE

	O	M	R	W
Sarfraz	12	3	51	1
Griffiths	12	1	58	2
Watts	12	2	34	2
T. M. Lamb	12	0	70	2
Willey	12	2	45	1

SOMERSET	O	M	R	W
Garner	10.3	3	29	6
Botham	10	3	27	0
Jennings	12	1	29	0
Burgess	9	1	37	1
Marks	4	0	22	0
Richards	9	0	44	1
Breakwell	2	0	9	0

FALL OF WICKETS

Wkt	Sm	Nh
1st	34	3
2nd	95	13
3rd	145	126
4th	186	138
5th	213	170
6th	214	186
7th	219	218
8th	268	224
9th	—	224
10th	—	—

Umpires: D. J. Constant
          J. G. Langridge

GILLETTE CUP RECORDS

Highest Total	371–4	Hampshire v Glamorgan at Southampton	1975
Highest Total Batting Second	297–4	Somerset v Warwickshire at Taunton	1978
Lowest Total	41	Cambridgeshire v Buckinghamshire at Cambridge	1972
	41	Middlesex v Essex at Westcliff-on-Sea	1972
	41	Shropshire v Essex at Wellington	1974
Biggest Victories	10 wkts	Northamptonshire beat Leicestershire at Leicester	1964
	10 wkts	Warwickshire beat Cambridgeshire at Birmingham	1965
	10 wkts	Sussex beat Derbyshire at Hove	1968
	10 wkts	Hampshire beat Nottinghamshire at Southampton	1977
	214 runs	Leicestershire beat Staffordshire at Stoke	1975
Highest Individual Score	177	C. G. Greenidge: Hampshire v Glamorgan at Southampton	1975

(86 hundreds have been scored in these matches)

Fastest Hundred	77 minutes	R. E. Marshall (140): Hampshire v Bedfordshire at Goldington	1968

Highest Partnerships for Each Wicket *Unbroken*

1st	227	R. E. Marshall and B. L. Reed: Hampshire v Bedfordshire, Goldington	1968
2nd	223	M. J. Smith and C. T. Radley: Middlesex v Hampshire, Lord's	1977
3rd	160	B. Wood and F. C. Hayes: Lancashire v Warwickshire, Birmingham	1976
4th	234*	D. Lloyd and C. H. Lloyd: Lancashire v Gloucestershire, Manchester	1978
5th	135	J. F. Harvey and I. R. Buxton: Derbyshire v Worcestershire, Derby	1972
6th	105	G. St A. Sobers and R. A. White: Nottinghamshire v Worcestershire, Worcester	1974
7th	107	D. R. Shepherd and D. A. Graveney: Gloucestershire v Surrey, Bristol	1973
8th	69	S. J. Rouse and D. J. Brown: Warwickshire v Middlesex, Lord's	1977
9th	87	M. A. Nash and A. E. Cordle: Glamorgan v Lincolnshire, Swansea	1974
10th	45	A. T. Castell and D. W. White: Hampshire v Lancashire, Manchester	1970
Best Bowling		7–15 A. L. Dixon: Kent v Surrey at The Oval	1967

Hat-tricks

J. D. F. Larter	Northamptonshire v Sussex at Northampton	1963
D. A. D. Sydenham	Surrey v Cheshire at Hoylake	1964

(Sydenham took four wickets in five balls)

R. N. S. Hobbs	Essex v Middlesex at Lord's	1968
N. M. McVicker	Warwickshire v Lincolnshire at Birmingham	1971

Wicket-keeping – Most Dismissals

5	Seven instances: R. Booth (Worcestershire); F. E. Collyer (Hertfordshire); A. P. E. Knott (Kent); D. L. Murray, twice (Nottinghamshire); J. T. Murray (Middlesex); S. C. Owen (Staffordshire)

Fielding – Most Catches

4	A. S. Brown: Gloucestershire v Middlesex at Bristol	1963
4	G. Cook: Northamptonshire v Glamorgan at Northampton	1972

GILLETTE CUP FINALISTS

1963 SUSSEX beat Worcestershire by 14 runs
1964 SUSSEX beat Warwickshire by 8 wickets
1965 YORKSHIRE beat Surrey by 175 runs
1966 WARWICKSHIRE beat Worcestershire by 5 wickets
1967 KENT beat Somerset by 32 runs
1968 WARWICKSHIRE beat Sussex by 4 wickets
1969 YORKSHIRE beat Derbyshire by 69 runs
1970 LANCASHIRE beat Sussex by 6 wickets
1971 LANCASHIRE beat Kent by 24 runs
1972 LANCASHIRE beat Warwickshire by 4 wickets

1973 GLOUCESTERSHIRE beat Sussex by 40 runs
1974 KENT beat Lancashire by 4 wickets
1975 LANCASHIRE beat Middlesex by 7 wickets
1976 NORTHAMPTONSHIRE beat Lancashire by 4 wickets
1977 MIDDLESEX beat Glamorgan by 5 wickets
1978 SUSSEX beat Somerset by 5 wickets
1979 SOMERSET beat Northamptonshire by 45 runs

Graham Gooch's relentless attack on a weakened Surrey attack in the Benson and Hedges Cup final, put Essex within striking distance of their first-ever major trophy.

BENSON AND HEDGES CUP 1979

Zonal Results

GROUP A	P	W	L	NR	Pts
SOMERSET	4	3	1	0	9*
WORCESTERSHIRE	4	3	1	0	9
Glamorgan	4	2	1	1	7
Gloucestershire	4	1	3	0	3
Minor Counties (South)	4	0	3	1	1

GROUP B					
WARWICKSHIRE	4	4	0	0	12
DERBYSHIRE	4	2	1	1	7†
Lancashire	4	2	1	1	7
Leicestershire	4	1	3	0	3
Hampshire	4	0	4	0	0

GROUP C					
ESSEX	4	3	1	0	9
SURREY	4	3	1	0	9
Sussex	4	2	2	0	6
Northamptonshire	4	2	2	0	6
Combined Universities	4	0	4	0	0

GROUP D					
MIDDLESEX	4	3	0	1	10
YORKSHIRE	4	2	0	2	8
Nottinghamshire	4	2	1	1	7
Kent	4	1	3	0	3
Minor Counties (North)	4	0	4	0	0

*In Group A, Somerset were disqualified and their place in the quarter-finals taken by Glamorgan.
†Qualified for the quarter-finals on higher wicket-taking rate.

Final Rounds

QUARTER-FINALS 6 June	SEMI-FINALS 4 July	FINAL 21 July	†Home team Winning team in small capitals

ESSEX†

Warwickshire
} ESSEX†

Middlesex†

YORKSHIRE
} Yorkshire

} ESSEX

Glamorgan†

DERBYSHIRE
} Derbyshire†

Worcestershire†

SURREY
} SURREY

} Surrey

} ESSEX

SEMI-FINALS

There were a remarkable number of similarities about the two Benson and Hedges Cup semi-finals. Both were tight, comparatively low-scoring matches, Essex beating Yorkshire by three wickets in the 54th over, and Derbyshire failing by only seven runs in the 54th over to make the 167 required. Both losing teams played themselves into winning positions on more than one occasion and then, through their own deficiencies rather than the skill of the opposition, allowed their opponents to escape and go on to win.

Essex v Yorkshire

Although Boycott had declared himself unfit, Yorkshire could hardly have had a better start at Chelmsford. Lumb and Hampshire put on 107 for the first wicket at a sprightly speed and without taking undue chances. At this stage everything suggested a massive total and victory, for counties do not

Kevin Sharp falls lbw to Norbert Phillip for 0 as Essex strike back after a commanding start to the Yorkshire innings at Chelmsford.

often make large scores against Yorkshire's tight attack. However, when Hampshire departed – rather needlessly – the Northerners' batting disintegrated. The middle order of Sharp, Athey and Love disappeared quickly for single figures, and even though Lumb went to 75, and Bairstow and Stevenson struck the odd blow, the Essex bowlers were able to take control and restrict Yorkshire to 173. One could not help wondering why no use was made of Old, who is such a dangerous striker. How some of the great Yorkshire players of the past would have viewed such a classic illustration of batting panic was not to be contemplated!

The Yorkshire bowlers, who should have been bowling with a total in excess of 200 behind them, performed very well and were splendidly supported in the field. They made the initial break with the new ball, but found Gooch in dominating form. Though they bowled and fielded their way back into the game, worrying Essex supporters, they encountered further purposeful opposition from Pont and Hardie, and this eventually proved too much. Yorkshire were left musing that, if only their batsmen had picked up those extra 20 or 30 runs that were there for the taking, they would have been on their way to Lord's instead of an understandably jubilant Essex.

ESSEX v YORKSHIRE
Played at Chelmsford, 4 July
Toss: Essex   Result: **Essex** won by 3 wickets   *captain*
Gold Award: K. R. Pont   †*wicket-keeper*

YORKSHIRE			ESSEX	O	M	R	W
R. G. Lumb	*b* Phillip	75	Lever	11	2	31	2
J. H. Hampshire*	*c* Turner *b* East	53	Phillip	11	2	28	2
K. Sharp	*lbw b* Phillip	0	Turner	11	2	31	1
C. W. J. Athey	*b* East	1	Pont	11	0	45	1
J. D. Love	*c* McEwan *b* Pont	2	East	11	1	25	2
D. L. Bairstow†	*run out (Pont)*	10					
A. Sidebottom	*c* Fletcher *b* Turner	0	YORKSHIRE				
P. Carrick	*b* Lever	1	Old	11	2	19	0
G. B. Stevenson	*b* Lever	13	Stevenson	11	4	43	2
C. M. Old	*not out*	1	Sidebottom	11	1	35	3
H. P. Cooper	*not out*	4	Cooper	10	1	29	1
Extras	(*lb* 7, *nb* 6)	13	Carrick	11	0	32	1
TOTAL	(9 wickets – 55 overs)	**173**					

ESSEX			FALL OF WICKETS		
G. A. Gooch	*c* Bairstow *b* Sidebottom	49	*Wkt*	*Y*	*E*
A. W. Lilley	*c* Bairstow *b* Stevenson	0	1st	107	2
K. S. McEwan	*c* Bairstow *b* Sidebottom	18	2nd	109	42
K. W. R. Fletcher*	*c* Sidebottom *b* Stevenson	7	3rd	114	68
B. R. Hardie	*c* Bairstow *b* Sidebottom	24	4th	123	99
K. R. Pont	*c* Love *b* Cooper	36	5th	146	112
N. Phillip	*c* Sidebottom *b* Carrick	9	6th	152	139
S. Turner	*not out*	11	7th	153	169
N. Smith†	*not out*	4	8th	159	—
R. E. East	} *did not bat*		9th	168	—
J. K. Lever			10th	—	—
Extras	(*b* 4, *lb* 3, *w* 3, *nb* 6)	16	Umpires: D. Oslear		
TOTAL	(7 wickets – 54 overs)	**174**	A. G. T. Whitehead		

Derbyshire v Surrey

Surrey began well in their semi-final against Derbyshire at Derby with Butcher and Lynch putting on 52 for the first wicket. But their formidable middle order of Howarth, Knight and Roope failed to function. Once Lynch departed for 49, they owed everything to Smith and, rather surprisingly, wicket-keeper Richards who guided them – not all that convincingly – to a total of 166. If this was certainly not grand, it proved sufficient.

In Clarke, Surrey's above-average county attack had a distinctly menacing bowler, and the Derbyshire batting last summer tended to be short of runs and class. None the less, 167 in 55 overs was definitely on, provided two accredited batsmen could each play a reasonable innings and the other nine could scramble 60 or 70 between them. Unfortunately, only Kirsten obliged and his fine 70 was almost, but not quite, enough to take them into the final. To make it even more frustrating, Wright, Hill and Steele all stayed long enough at the crease to settle, but were still unable to establish themselves. So near, but yet so far: it just needed a 20 or 30 from one of that experienced trio and the next stop would have been Lord's for the second year running.

DERBYSHIRE v SURREY
Played at Derby, 4 July
Toss: Surrey   Result: **Surrey** won by 6 runs
Gold Award: P. N. Kirsten

*captain
†wicket-keeper

SURREY

A. R. Butcher	c Taylor b Hendrick	19
M. A. Lynch	c Taylor b Walters	49
G. P. Howarth	c Steele b Hendrick	2
R. D. V. Knight*	c Hendrick b Miller	6
G. R. J. Roope	c Tunnicliffe b Miller	9
D. M. Smith	c Kirsten b Walters	34
R. D. Jackman	run out (Kirsten/Miller)	1
S. T. Clarke	lbw b Miller	1
C. J. Richards†	not out	25
P. I. Pocock	not out	5
P. H. L. Wilson	did not bat	
Extras	(lb 7, w 4, nb 4)	15
TOTAL	(8 wickets – 55 overs)	**166**

DERBYSHIRE

A. Hill	b Wilson	9
J. G. Wright	c Richards b Wilson	10
P. N. Kirsten	c Richards b Jackman	70
D. S. Steele	b Wilson	14
A. J. Borrington	lbw b Jackman	1
G. Miller*	lbw b Clarke	5
K. J. Barnett	b Clarke	14
J. Walters	c Richards b Clarke	2
R. W. Taylor†	not out	8
C. J. Tunnicliffe	b Roope	7
M. Hendrick	b Knight	3
Extras	(b 6, lb 6, w 4, nb 1)	17
TOTAL	(53.2 overs)	**160**

DERBYSHIRE

	O	M	R	W
Hendrick	11	2	38	2
Tunnicliffe	11	1	41	0
Walters	11	2	28	2
Steele	11	5	21	0
Miller	11	2	23	3

SURREY

	O	M	R	W
Clarke	11	5	31	3
Jackman	11	2	31	2
Wilson	11	0	33	3
Knight	7.2	2	23	1
Pocock	11	4	22	0
Roope	2	1	3	1

FALL OF WICKETS

Wkt	Sy	D
1st	52	19
2nd	54	38
3rd	68	114
4th	88	116
5th	98	116
6th	101	123
7th	108	138
8th	158	141
9th	—	157
10th	—	160

Umpires: R. Julian
            P. B. Wight

Right: Roger Knight, in his second season as Surrey's captain, saw early signs of the long-awaited revival at The Oval. A close Benson and Hedges semi-final win over Derbyshire was followed several weeks later by a spirited attempt to match the formidable Essex total in the final. Knight himself scored 52 as Surrey went down fighting.

BENSON AND HEDGES CUP FINAL

Essex, after more than 100 years, won their first major honour by defeating Surrey at Lord's in the best Benson and Hedges Cup final since the competition's inception. The manner in which this breakthrough was achieved suggested that this could well prove to be the first of several triumphs in the next few seasons.

Having won the toss, Roger Knight decided to insert the opposition on a plumb, flat pitch and Graham Gooch and company proceeded to capitalise fully on their good fortune, storming their way to a massive 290 for six against a depleted attack. With Clarke unable to play, and Jackman clearly not fully fit, some of the Surrey bowling wilted under a non-stop assault that began in the first over. Pocock, usually so dependable, strayed off line, and the tidiest spell came from Intikhab. Wilson, who captured four of the wickets, looked an excellent prospect, especially if he can reduce a run-up which would necessitate him running through the sightscreen on some of the smaller grounds. Knight illustrated the virtues of line and length.

Gooch and Denness, who considering the occasion and his current form was correctly preferred to the talented Lilley, opened the innings with a flurry of handsome strokes and impressive boundaries. They gave Essex the right, bright start required for a match-winning total. The departure of the former Kent and England captain was followed by a peaceful period as McEwan, after two extravagant waves outside the off stump without making contact, played himself in. It proved to be the calm before the storm. The South African, in the course of a brilliant partnership of 124, overtook and passed Gooch, who was also batting quite beautifully. McEwan was eventually caught behind off Wilson, but there was no reduction in the impetus. Fletcher, the Essex captain, played spectacular strokes from the moment he arrived at the crease, and his 34 was a gem of improvisation. All the while, at the other end, Gooch was striding purposefully and powerfully towards a chanceless century.

Majestic would be an appropriate adjective with which to describe Graham's knock of 120. It began with a square cover-drive in the opening over and contained numerous spectacular strokes, such as the lofted on-drive for six off Knight, just when he was threatening to arrest the tempo, and a heave against a reasonable ball from Wilson which finished up on top of the stand. Pont added several impressive blows in the closing overs, leaving Essex well content with their final score. It was easily the highest in a Benson and Hedges Cup final and other records were shattered along the run-strewn way, among them the highest individual innings.

South African Ken McEwan took advantage of a Lord's final to impress his glorious stroke-play on a large audience, hitting 72 in an entertaining, match-winning partnership with Gooch.

Nobody could have fancied their chances of scoring 291 in 55 overs against the Essex bowling and fielding. Yet Surrey did extremely well to reach 255 before they were all out in the 52nd over. Perhaps the sheer improbability – near impossibility – of their task was one of the reasons they scored quite so many runs. Because they had to be taken, they took chances they would not have done had their target been, say, 230 to 240.

As a result there were moments during the splendid stand between Knight and Howarth, and later between Howarth and Smith and Smith and Roope, when there appeared to be a chance of achieving the impossible. Logic eventually prevailed, however, as Surrey forfeited wickets in their efforts to maintain the tempo. It is one thing to score àt over five runs per over – or seven – for a limited period, but it is an altogether different story when the rate has to be maintained for a total of nearly 300. Fortune may favour the brave, but not indefinitely. The Surrey batsmen eventually ran out of luck and runs, though not before Messrs Knight, Howarth, Smith and Roope had delighted the crowd, given hope to their supporters, and seriously worried the Essex team and their followers.

It was a match to remember and to treasure. The high-quality batting of both sides, the fielding, and lastly, but by no means least, the impeccably sporting way it was played ensured it would be so.

ESSEX v SURREY
Played at Lord's, London, 21 July
Toss: Surrey   Result: **Essex** won by 35 runs
Man of the Match: G. A. Gooch

*captain
†wicket-keeper

ESSEX		Runs	Mins	Balls	6s	4s
M. H. Denness	c Smith b Wilson	24	43	36	—	4
G. A. Gooch	b Wilson	120	203	141	3	11
K. S. McEwan	c Richards b Wilson	72	96	99	—	10
K. W. R. Fletcher*	b Knight	34	37	30	—	3
B. R. Hardie	c Intikhab b Wilson	4	14	6	—	—
K. R. Pont	not out	19	19	13	—	3
N. Phillip	c Howarth b Jackman	2	5	6	—	—
S. Turner	not out	1	5	2	—	—
N. Smith†	} did not bat					
R. E. East						
J. K. Lever						
Extras	(b 3, lb 8, nb 3)	14				
TOTAL	(6 wickets – 55 overs)	290				

SURREY		Runs	Mins	Balls	6s	4s
A. R. Butcher	c Smith b Lever	13	20	22	—	2
M. A. Lynch	c McEwan b East	17	53	32	—	2
G. P. Howarth	c Fletcher b Pont	74	131	99	—	6
R. D. V. Knight*	c Smith b Pont	52	66	64	—	8
D. M. Smith	b Phillip	24	45	34	—	2
G. R. J. Roope	not out	39	64	32	1	2
Intikhab Alam	c Pont b Phillip	1	9	5	—	—
R. D. Jackman	b East	1	3	5	—	—
C. J. Richards†	b Turner	1	5	5	—	—
P. I. Pocock	b Phillip	7	21	17	—	1
P. H. L. Wilson	b Lever	0	3	1	—	—
Extras	(b 4, lb 16, w 1, nb 5)	26				
TOTAL	(51.4 overs)	255				

SURREY	O	M	R	W
Jackman	11	0	69	1
Wilson	11	1	56	4
Knight	11	1	40	1
Intikhab	11	0	38	0
Pocock	11	0	73	0
ESSEX				
Lever	9.4	2	33	2
Phillip	10	2	42	3
East	11	1	40	2
Turner	11	1	47	1
Pont	10	0	67	2

FALL OF WICKETS

Wkt	E	Sy
1st	48	21
2nd	172	45
3rd	239	136
4th	261	187
5th	273	205
6th	276	219
7th	—	220
8th	—	226
9th	—	250
10th	—	255

Umpires: H. D. Bird and B. J. Meyer

BENSON AND HEDGES CUP RECORDS

Highest Total	350–3	Essex v Combined Universities at Chelmsford	1979
Highest Total Batting Second	282	Gloucestershire v Hampshire at Bristol	1974
Lowest Total	61	Sussex v Middlesex at Hove	1978
Highest Match Aggregate	593	Hampshire (311–4) v Gloucestershire (282) at Bristol	1974
Lowest Match Aggregate *(55-overs match)*	123	Sussex (61) v Middlesex (62–2) at Hove	1978
Biggest Victories	10 wkts	Eight instances (one each by Essex, Kent, Leicestershire, Northamptonshire, Somerset, Warwickshire, Worcestershire and Yorkshire).	
	214 runs	Essex beat Combined Universities at Chelmsford	1979
Highest Individual Score	173*	C. G. Greenidge: Hampshire v Minor Counties (S) at Amersham	1973

62 hundreds have been scored in these matches.

Fastest Hundred	62 minutes	M. A. Nash (103*): Glamorgan v Hampshire, Swansea	1976

Highest Partnerships for Each Wicket   *Unbroken*

1st	223	G. A. Gooch and A. W. Lilley: Essex v Combined Universities, Chelmsford	1979
2nd	285*	C. G. Greenidge and D. R. Turner: Hampshire v Minor Counties (S), Amersham	1973
3rd	227	{ M. E. J. C. Norman and B. F. Davison: Leicestershire v Warwickshire, Coventry	1972
		D. Lloyd and F. C. Hayes: Lancashire v Minor Counties (N), Manchester	1973
4th	165*	Mushtaq Mohammad and W. Larkins: Northants v Essex, Chelmsford	1977
5th	134	M. Maslin and D. N. F. Slade: Minor Counties (E) v Notts, Nottingham	1976
6th	114	Majid Khan and G. P. Ellis, Glamorgan v Gloucestershire, Bristol	1975
7th	102	E. W. Jones and M. A. Nash, Glamorgan v Hampshire, Swansea	1976
8th	109	R. E. East and N. Smith: Essex v Northamptonshire, Chelmsford	1977
9th	81	J. N. Shepherd and D. L. Underwood: Kent v Middlesex, Lord's	1975
10th	61	J. M. Rice and A. M. E. Roberts: Hampshire v Gloucestershire, Bristol	1975
Best Bowling	7–12	W. W. Daniel: Middlesex v Minor Counties (E), Ipswich	1978
Most Economical Bowling	11–9–3–1	C. M. Old, Yorkshire v Middlesex, Lord's	1979
Most Expensive Bowling	11–0–80–0	J. Smith: Minor Counties (S) v Hampshire, Amersham	1973
Hat-tricks		G. D. McKenzie: Leicestershire v Worcestershire, Worcester	1972
		K. Higgs: Leicestershire v Surrey, Lord's	1974
		A. A. Jones: Middlesex v Essex, Lord's	1977
		M. J. Procter: Gloucestershire v Hampshire, Southampton	1977

Fifty Runs and Five Wickets in a Match

M. J. Procter	154*	5–26	Gloucestershire v Somerset, Taunton	1972
B. E. A. Edmeades	50	5–22	Essex v Leicestershire, Ilford	1973
Imran Khan	65*	5–8	Sussex v Northamptonshire, Northampton	1978

Wicket-keeping – Most Dismissals

5 (all ct)	G. Sharp: Northamptonshire v Middlesex, Lord's	1974
5 (all ct)	D. L. Bairstow: Yorkshire v Derbyshire, Bradford	1975

Fielding – Most Catches

5	V. J. Marks: Combined Universities v Kent, Oxford	1976

PREVIOUS WINNERS   1972 Leicestershire   1973 Kent   1974 Surrey   1975 Leicestershire
1976 Kent   1977 Gloucestershire   1978 Kent

Captain victorious. After a controversial start to their season, Brian Rose and Somerset emerged triumphant, clinching the John Player League title the day after winning the Gillette Cup.

JOHN PLAYER LEAGUE 1979

FINAL TABLE		*P*	*W*	*L*	*NR*	*Pts*	*6s*	*4w*	*Prize-money*
1	SOMERSET (2)	16	12	3	1	50	21	1	£5,500
2	Kent (10)	16	11	3	2	48	16	4	£2,750
3	Worcestershire (4)	16	9	4	3	42	22	2	£1,500
4	Middlesex (15)	16	9	5	2	40	27	2	
	Yorkshire (7)	16	8	4	4	40	29	0	
6	Essex (6)	16	8	6	2	36	18	5	
	Leicestershire (3)	16	7	5	4	36	21	3	
8	Gloucestershire (17)	16	7	7	2	32	12	2	
	Nottinghamshire (13)	16	6	6	4	32	21	2	
10	Hampshire (1)	16	7	8	1	30	34	2	
	Lancashire (5)	16	6	7	3	30	21	2	
	Glamorgan (10)	16	6	10	0	24	21	4	
11	Northamptonshire (13)	16	5	9	2	24	20	3	
	Surrey (10)	16	5	9	2	24	35	3	
	Sussex (8)	16	6	10	0	24	13	3	
16	Derbyshire (8)	16	4	9	3	22	13	3	
17	Warwickshire (16)	16	2	13	1	10	34	3	

Figures in brackets show the 1978 positions.

PREVIOUS CHAMPIONS

1969 Lancashire	1973 Kent	1977 Leicestershire
1970 Lancashire	1974 Leicestershire	1978 Hampshire
1971 Worcestershire	1975 Hampshire	
1972 Kent	1976 Kent	

Once again the John Player League produced a close, exciting race for the title. The issue was not decided until the final Sunday of the season when Somerset beat Nottinghamshire at Trent Bridge to finish first, and Kent, by losing at home to Middlesex, had to be content with second place.

Nobody can deny that Brian Rose's team deserved to carry off the title, for they were indisputably the best limited-overs side in the country. The doubly sweet taste of success was also a compensation for the disappointments of 1978, when they were beaten at the post on successive days. Somerset possessed powerful, fast-scoring batting, a tidy and varied attack, and above-average ability in the field. Most important of all, they had, in Richards, Garner and Botham three outstanding match-winners.

In addition to carrying off the Sunday League, Somerset could rejoice at the great support they received in the competition. This is reflected in the £36,000 taken in gate receipts, while their club membership rose from 5,200 to 6,700. As a result their gates had to be closed on several occasions. Such figures are good not only for Somerset but also for cricket. But though they can show a great increase in interest and enthusiasm throughout the county, unfortunately the club do also appear to have acquired a large and noisy moronic element. These undesirable fugitives from the football world will not only upset the true Somerset supporters with their behaviour and loud, mindless chanting; they could well drive them away.

The Kent attack, which was superbly backed up in the field, did enough to win the John Player League, but their batting was not sufficiently consistent. Batting was certainly not the weakness of Worcestershire, where runs flowed like drink at a publican's wedding. With so many of their batsmen in outstanding form, it was inevitable that they would do well in this competition, in which the acquiring of quick runs is the chief essential. They finished third, one place higher than in 1978, and should again be up with the leaders this summer.

For Warwickshire the John Player League represented sheer disaster. Although their teams, over the years, have never really come to terms with the particular demands of this form of truncated cricket, their performances in 1979 were ridiculous. Even if short of talent, they were not completely

By hitting 163 not out in the John Player League against Warwickshire, Gordon Greenidge became the batsman with the highest score in all three major limited-overs competitions.

Younis Ahmed found the move west to Worcestershire a fruitful one. In addition to his Championship form he was also among the runs in the John Player League.

devoid of it. Not only did they end up with the 'wooden spoon', but they finished with the lowest number of points ever (10), recorded the fewest victories (2), and suffered the highest number of defeats (13).

After Somerset, Kent and Worcestershire, the most impressive of the other counties was Middlesex, who made a big advance up the table to finish fourth equal with Yorkshire. For a time the Tykes looked like serious contenders for the title, but their young batsmen failed to live up to expectations. If they strike form this summer they could make an even more serious challenge. Their bowling and fielding, when it comes to the denial of runs, are well above average.

Essex, with other honours within their grasp, lost some of their usual urgency on Sundays, as typified in losing at home to struggling Glamorgan. Although Leicestershire are efficient and experienced, they did not always score fast enough, while the 1978 champions Hampshire perhaps inevitably fell away. They are at present over-dependent on the genius of Greenidge, who even on one leg managed to conjure up some marvellous match-winning innings.

1979 AWARDS AND DISTRIBUTION OF PRIZE-MONEY

The total prize-money was £29,170.
£5,500 and Trophy to League Champions: **SOMERSET**.
£2,750 to runners-up: Kent.
£1,500 to third placing: Worcestershire.
£120 each match to winners (shared in event of a 'no result').

£1,200 batsmen's pool. One share for every six hit. 378 sixes were hit by 120 players – each six being worth £3.17.
Six-hitters:
- 15 – C. G. Greenidge (**£225** award for most sixes).
- 11 – P. R. Oliver.
- 10 – J. D. Love, G. R. J. Roope, P. D. Swart.
- 9 – K. R. Pont.
- 8 – G. D. Barlow, J. D. Birch, I. T. Botham, R. O. Butcher, E. J. O. Hemsley, T. E. Jesty, W. Larkins, Younis Ahmed.
- 7 – B. F. Davison, J. N. Shepherd, J. Whitehouse.
- 6 – Imran Khan, P. N. Kirsten, I. V. A. Richards.
- 5 – N. E. Briers, J. H. Hampshire, Javed Miandad, G. W. Johnson, R. D. V. Knight, C. H. Lloyd, R. C. Ontong, G. R. Stephenson.
- 4 – D. L. Amiss, D. L. Bairstow, S. T. Clarke, B. Dudleston, N. G. Featherstone, B. Hassan, G. W. Humpage, Intikhab Alam, A. J. Lamb, D. Lloyd, B. W. Reidy, J. Simmons, D. M. Smith.
- 3 – C. W. J. Athey, A. R. Butcher, A. M. Ferreira, G. A. Gooch, D. P. Hughes, Sadiq Mohammad, J. G. Wright, Zaheer Abbas.
- 2 – Asif Iqbal, M. K. Bore, J. E. Emburey, D. A. Francis, J. Garner, M. W. Gatting, D. I. Gower, S. N. Hartley, E. E. Hemmings, D. J. Humphries, A. L. Jones, K. S. McEwan, C. W. Maynard, C. M. Old, M. D. Partridge, M. J. Procter, C. E. B. Rice, B. C. Rose, Sarfraz Nawaz, C. J. Tunnicliffe, D. R. Turner, P. Willey, P. H. L. Wilson.
- 1 – J. M. Brearley, P. Carrick, R. M. Carter, P. B. Clift, K. E. Cooper, C. S. Cowdrey, N. G. Cowley, P. W. Denning, G. R. Dilley, P. H. Edmonds, K. W. R. Fletcher, P. J. Graves, F. C. Hayes, A. J. Hignell, A. Hill, G. P. Howarth, A. I. Kallicharran, A. W. Lilley, M. J. Llewellyn, R. G. Lumb, M. A. Lynch, L. McFarlane, P. A. Neale, J. A. Ormrod, P. W. G. Parker, D. N. Patel, N. Phillip, P. I. Pocock, C. T. Radley, D. W. Randall, J. M. Rice, G. Richards, M. J. M. Roebuck, S. J. Rouse, K. Sharp, P. A. Slocombe, M. J. Smedley, K. D. Smith, D. S. Steele, J. F. Steele, A. W. Stovold, M. N. S. Taylor, V. P. Terry, R. W. Tolchard, G. M. Turner, S. Turner, R. G. Williams, T. J. Yardley.

£1,200 bowlers' pool. One share for taking four or more wickets in a match. 44 instances (fewer than in any other season of the competition) by 37 bowlers – each share being worth £27.27.
Shareholders:
- 2 – B. M. Brain, R. W. Hills, Imran Khan, T. M. Lamb, M. D. Marshall, N. Phillip, L. B. Taylor (share **£225** award for most instances).
- 1 – I. T. Botham, D. J. Brown, A. E. Cordle, W. W. Daniel, R. E. East, N. Gifford, R. J. Hadlee, W. Hogg, V. A. Holder, G. P. Howarth, G. W. Humpage, P. N. Kirsten, P. G. Lee, K. S. Mackintosh, R. C. Ontong, P. I. Pocock, K. R. Pont, J. Spencer, M. W. W. Selvey, D. S. Steele, J. F. Steele, P. D. Swart, S. Turner, D. L. Underwood, J. Walters, R. G. Williams, A. H. Wilkins, R. G. D. Willis, P. H. L. Wilson, R. A. Woolmer.

£250 for the fastest fifty in a match televised on BBC2:
B. F. Davison (Leicestershire) who scored 50 off 34 balls against Glamorgan at Leicester on 17 June.

JOHN PLAYER LEAGUE RECORDS

Highest Total	307–4	Worcestershire v Derbyshire at Worcester	1975
Highest Total Batting Second	261–8	Warwickshire v Nottinghamshire at Birmingham	1976
Lowest Total	23	Middlesex v Yorkshire at Leeds	1974
Highest Match Aggregate	525	Somerset (270–4) v Glos. (255) at Bristol (Imperial)	1975
Lowest Match Aggregate	117	Middlesex (76) v Northamptonshire (41) at	
(40 overs matches)		Northampton	1972

Biggest Victories

10 wkts — Sixteen instances by Derbyshire, Essex, Glamorgan, Hampshire, Leicestershire (2), Middlesex, Somerset, Surrey (3), Warwickshire (2), Worcestershire and Yorkshire (2).

190 runs		Kent beat Northamptonshire at Brackley	1973
Highest Individual Score	163*	C. G. Greenidge: Hampshire v Warwickshire at Birmingham	1979

134 hundreds have been scored in the League, including nine by B. A. Richards and six by J. H. Hampshire.

Fastest Hundred	50 minutes	C. H. Lloyd (100*) Lancashire v Nottinghamshire at Nottingham	1974

Highest Partnership for Each Wicket *Unbroken

1st	218	A. R. Butcher and G. P. Howarth: Surrey v Gloucestershire, The Oval	1976
2nd	179	B. W. Luckhurst and M. H. Denness: Kent v Somerset, Canterbury	1973
3rd	182	H. Pilling and C. H. Lloyd: Lancashire v Somerset, Manchester	1970
4th	175*	M. J. K. Smith and D. L. Amiss: Warwickshire v Yorkshire, Birmingham	1970
5th	163	A. G. E. Ealham and B. D. Julien: Kent v Leicestershire, Leicester	1977
6th	121	C. P. Wilkins and A. J. Borrington: Derbyshire v Warwickshire, Chesterfield	1972
7th	96*	R. Illingworth and J. Birkenshaw: Leicestershire v Somerset, Leicester	1971
8th	95*	D. Breakwell and K. F. Jennings: Somerset v Nottinghamshire, Nottingham	1976
9th	86	D. P. Hughes and P. Lever: Lancashire v Essex, Leyton	1973
10th	57	D. A. Graveney and J. B. Mortimore: Gloucestershire v Lancashire, Tewkesbury	1973
Best Bowling	8–26	K. D. Boyce: Essex v Lancashire at Manchester	1971
Most Economical Bowling	8–8–0–0	B. A. Langford: Somerset v Essex at Yeovil	1969
Most Expensive Bowling	8–0–79–1	R. E. East: Essex v Glamorgan at Swansea	1969

Hat-tricks (12)

A. Ward	Derbyshire v Sussex at Derby (*Ward took four wickets with successive balls*)	1970
R. Palmer	Somerset v Gloucestershire at Bristol	1970
K. D. Boyce	Essex v Somerset at Westcliff-on-Sea	1971
G. D. McKenzie	Leicestershire v Essex at Leicester	1972
R. G. D. Willis	Warwickshire v Yorkshire at Birmingham	1973
W. Blenkiron	Warwickshire v Derbyshire at Buxton	1974
A. Buss	Sussex v Worcestershire at Hastings	1974
J. M. Rice	Hampshire v Northamptonshire at Southampton	1975
M. A. Nash	Glamorgan v Worcestershire at Worcester	1975
A. Hodgson	Northamptonshire v Somerset at Northampton	1976
A. E. Cordle	Glamorgan v Hampshire at Portsmouth	1979
C. J. Tunnicliffe	Derbyshire v Worcestershire at Derby	1979

Fifty Runs and Five Wickets in a Match

C. J. R. Black	72*	6–25	Middlesex v Surrey at The Oval	1971
M. A. Buss	69	5–36	Sussex v Derbyshire at Eastbourne	1973
R. D. V. Knight	75	5–42	Sussex v Nottinghamshire at Nottingham	1977
G. W. Johnson	50	5–26	Kent v Surrey at The Oval	1974

Wicket-keeping — Most Dismissals

7 (6ct, 1st)	R. W. Taylor: Derbyshire v Lancashire at Manchester	1975

Fielding – Most Catches

5	J. M. Rice: Hampshire v Warwickshire at Southampton	1978

MISCELLANY

Minor Counties and Other Cricket 1979

Minor Counties Championship 1979

			P	W	L	D	NR	Pts	Av
1	SUFFOLK (3)	G	10	5	2†	3	—	65	6.50
2	Durham (2)	G	12	6	—	5	1	71	5.91
3	Oxfordshire (19)	G	10	5	2§	3	—	59	5.90
4	Devon (1)	G	10	5	2	2	1	54	5.40
5	Cornwall (20)	G	10	4	2	4	—	50	5.00
6	Hertfordshire (13)		10	3	2*	5	—	46	4.60
6	Shropshire (9)		10	3	2	4	1	44	4.40
8	Norfolk (12)		10	3	—	7	—	43	4.30
9	Wiltshire (11)		10	2	6‡	1	1	37	3.70
10	Lincolnshire (14)		10	2	2†	5	1	33	3.30
11	Lancashire II (7)		8	1	1*	6	—	23	2.87
12	Buckinghamshire (4)		12	2	4*	6	—	33	2.75
13	Northumberland (18)		12	—	—	9	3	31	2.58
14	Dorset (6)		10	—	2†	7	1	25	2.50
14	Staffordshire (14)		10	1	2*	4	3	25	2.50
16	Berkshire (5)		10	1	2*	7	—	24	2.40
17	Bedfordshire (8)		10	1	3*	6	—	23	2.30
17	Cambridgeshire (17)		10	1	2	7	—	23	2.30
17	Somerset II (14)		10	1	3*	4	2	23	2.30
20	Cheshire (10)		10	—	5†	4	1	22	2.20
21	Cumberland (21)		8	—	2*	5	1	14	1.75

Figures in brackets show the 1978 positions.
*Signifies 1st innings lead – one match lost.   †Signifies 1st innings lead – two matches lost.
‡Signifies 1st innings lead – four matches lost.   §Signifies tie on 1st innings – one match lost.
A Challenge Match between Suffolk and Durham was played at Ipswich on 10, 11, 12 September. This resulted in a draw, so that Suffolk became Minor County champions under Rule 16 of the competition.

Tilcon Trophy

Played at Harrogate on 4, 5, 6 July

SUSSEX beat NOTTINGHAMSHIRE by 4 wickets.
Nottinghamshire 201 in 53.4 overs (D. W. Randall 103). Sussex 203–6 in 48.1 overs (P. W. G. Parker 67).
Man of the Match: D. W. Randall.

GLOUCESTERSHIRE beat WARWICKSHIRE by 5 wickets.
Warwickshire 265–6 in 55 overs (D. L. Amiss 74, A. I. Kallicharran 54). Gloucestershire 269–5 in 53 overs (Zaheer Abbas 134*, Sadiq Mohammad 57).
Man of the Match: Zaheer Abbas.

FINAL

SUSSEX beat GLOUCESTERSHIRE by 109 runs.
Sussex 225 in 54.2 overs (A. Long 60*). Gloucestershire 116.
Men of the Match: A. Long and C. P. Phillipson (47 and 3–25).

PREVIOUS WINNERS	1976 Hampshire	1977 Nottinghamshire	1978 Yorkshire

RECORDS

Highest Total	269–5	Gloucestershire v Warwickshire	1979
Lowest Total	58	Nottinghamshire v Surrey	1978
Highest Individual Score	134*	Zaheer Abbas: Gloucestershire v Warwickshire	1979
(Three hundreds have been scored in these matches)			
Best Bowling Analysis	5–22	R. D. Jackman: Surrey v Nottinghamshire	1978

Fenner Trophy

Played at Scarborough on 29, 30, 31 August

YORKSHIRE beat GLOUCESTERSHIRE by 33 runs.
Yorkshire 253–5 in 50 overs (R. G. Lumb 115, J. D. Love 86). Gloucestershire 220 in 47.2 overs (A. J. Hignell 58, Sadiq Mohammad 51).

LEICESTERSHIRE beat GLAMORGAN by 60 runs.
Leicestershire 196–8 in 50 overs. Glamorgan 136 in 40.3 overs (K. Shuttleworth 4–29).

FINAL
LEICESTERSHIRE beat YORKSHIRE by 9 runs.
Leicestershire 225–6 in 50 overs. Yorkshire 216 in 49.2 overs (J. D. Love 65).

PREVIOUS WINNERS	1971 Kent	1974 Yorkshire	1977 Hampshire
	1972 Yorkshire	1975 Hampshire	1978 Northamptonshire
	1973 Kent	1976 Hampshire	

RECORDS

Highest Total	290–8	Hampshire v Gloucestershire	1975
Lowest Total	59	Warwickshire v Yorkshire	1974
Highest Individual Score	141*	B. W. Luckhurst: Kent v Lancashire	1973
(Seven hundreds have been scored in these matches – B. W. Luckhurst is alone in scoring two)			
Best Bowling Analysis	5–23	A. G. Nicholson: Yorkshire v Warwickshire	1974

Second Eleven Championship 1979

		P	W	L	D	Bonus Points Bt	Bonus Points Bw	Pts	Av
1	WARWICKSHIRE (4)	21	9	3	9	54	57	216	10.28
2	Middlesex (14)	15	5	5	5	37	50	147	9.80
3	Yorkshire (5)	16	5	—	11	48	46	150	9.37
4	Sussex (1)	12	3	2	7	32	40	112	9.33
5	Kent (13)	11	4	—	7	19	35	102	9.13
6	Lancashire (3)	14	4	2	8	35	40	123	8.78
7	Nottinghamshire (8)	18	4	—	14	46	55	149	8.27
8	Glamorgan (12)	16	4	3	9	35	38	119	7.43
9	Essex (2)	13	2	5	6	42	33	95	7.30
10	Gloucestershire (17)	10	2	2	6	22	24	70	7.00
11	Hampshire (6)	18	3	5	10	36	51	123	6.83
12	Worcestershire (9)	18	3	8	7	36	50	116	6.48
13	Surrey (11)	13	1	3	9	26	37	73	5.61
14	Leicestershire (7)	16	1	4	11	28	47	87	5.43
15	Derbyshire (16)	10	1	3	6	9	9	19	4.00
16	Somerset (10)	7	—	1	6	15	12	27	3.85
17	Northamptonshire (15)	20	—	5	15	35	37	72	3.60

Figures in brackets show the 1978 positions.

LIMITED-OVERS AVERAGES 1979

These combined one-day cricket averages include performances in the Prudential Cup, Gillette Cup, Benson and Hedges Cup and John Player League matches.

BATTING (Qualification: 10 innings, average 23.00)   *Not out

	M	I	NO	HS	Runs	Av	100s	50s
G. M. Turner	23	23	5	83*	978	54.33	—	9
G. A. Gooch	24	24	3	138	1,137	54.14	3	6
Younis Ahmed	20	19	1	113	848	47.11	3	4
I. V. A. Richards	23	22	3	138*	878	46.21	2	4
C. G. Greenidge	24	24	3	163*	944	44.95	2	6
A. J. Lamb	23	22	4	101	801	44.50	1	7
Zaheer Abbas	20	20	2	93*	790	43.88	—	8
B. Wood	19	17	4	116	554	42.61	1	5
G. R. J. Roope	23	23	8	75*	623	41.53	—	2
B. C. Rose	23	23	6	88*	701	41.23	—	5
A. Jones	18	18	1	89	672	39.52	—	5
C. H. Lloyd	23	19	6	164	511	39.30	—	2
J. H. Hampshire	18	16	2	75*	550	39.28	—	6
Javed Miandad	16	15	2	98*	491	37.76	—	4
W. Larkins	21	21	2	111	717	37.73	1	5
P. N. Kirsten	20	19	3	102	595	37.18	1	4
K. W. R. Fletcher	23	21	5	72	593	37.06	—	3
P. D. Swart	20	20	4	75*	587	36.68	—	5
D. Lloyd	21	19	1	74	653	36.27	—	5
M. J. Procter	18	18	3	86*	534	35.60	—	4
B. Dudleston	16	16	2	125	495	35.35	1	4
Sadiq Mohammad	18	18	2	80*	556	34.75	—	5
G. Boycott	20	19	4	92	507	33.80	—	3
G. Cook	23	21	2	114*	626	32.94	1	2
K. D. Smith	14	14	1	68	427	32.84	—	4
E. J. O. Hemsley	19	18	3	75*	491	32.73	—	4
G. P. Howarth	22	21	1	91	650	32.50	—	6
P. Willey	23	23	4	101*	616	32.42	1	4
B. F. Davison	20	18	3	78	480	32.00	—	4
J. G. Wright	23	22	0	101	679	30.86	1	3
P. A. Todd	13	12	1	61	334	30.36	—	2
N. E. Briers	17	17	3	76*	416	29.71	—	3
A. I. Kallicharran	21	20	0	101	593	29.65	1	3
J. F. Steele	20	16	8	76*	235	29.37	—	2
P. W. Denning	23	22	3	90*	558	29.36	—	2
P. B. Clift	20	14	4	49*	293	29.30	—	—
D. R. Turner	21	21	0	80	610	29.04	—	4
M. J. Harris	16	14	3	64	318	28.90	—	1
K. C. Wessels	11	11	0	104	318	28.90	1	1
K. R. Pont	23	18	4	52	404	28.85	—	1
D. W. Randall	18	16	3	103*	371	28.53	1	2
D. M. Smith	20	18	2	61	452	28.25	—	1
J. N. Shepherd	19	17	4	63	362	27.84	—	2
G. D. Mendis	22	21	0	69	584	27.80	—	2
C. W. J. Athey	21	18	3	85	417	27.80	—	2
G. W. Humpage	20	20	4	58	444	27.75	—	3
Imran Khan	25	23	5	65*	498	27.66	—	1

	M	I	NO	HS	Runs	Av	100s	50s
B. Hassan	12	10	1	108	247	27.44	1	2
C. E. B. Rice	17	15	3	72*	324	27.00	—	2
A. J. Hignell	12	11	2	41	243	27.00	—	—
G. Richards	14	10	4	38	162	27.00	—	—
C. J. Tavaré	21	21	2	89	489	25.73	—	3
G. W. Johnson	21	21	1	73	512	25.60	—	3
B. W. Reidy	21	15	5	65*	254	25.40	—	2
A. Hill	13	12	0	56	302	25.16	—	2
J. M. Rice	21	21	1	91	502	25.10	—	3
I. T. Botham	22	16	4	55	301	25.08	—	1
D. L. Amiss	21	21	0	78	521	24.80	—	3
J. D. Birch	18	16	2	85	346	24.71	—	2
A. J. Borrington	17	16	1	63	365	24.33	—	2
J. M. Brearley	22	21	0	76	508	24.19	—	3
P. M. Roebuck	19	17	4	50	309	23.76	—	1
K. J. Barnett	20	18	4	43*	331	23.64	—	—
J. Simmons	22	14	4	54*	235	23.50	—	2
J. D. Love	15	13	2	90	258	23.45	—	1
A. W. Lilley	21	21	9	119	468	23.40	1	1
J. Whitehouse	21	21	1	51	467	23.35	—	2
K. S. McEwan	23	23	2	72	486	23.14	—	2

BOWLING (Qualification: 20 wickets)

	O	M	R	W	Av	5w	BB
J. Garner	214.2	40	575	47	12.23	3	6–29
W. W. Daniel	138.1	24	365	29	12.58	—	4–13
D. L. Underwood	179.3	49	458	35	13.08	—	4–12
J. K. Lever	194.3	34	617	43	14.34	—	4–18
R. J. Hadlee	150	28	423	29	14.58	1	5–21
C. M. Old	217	55	537	36	14.91	—	4–8
R. E. East	107	16	361	24	15.04	1	5–20
P. H. L. Wilson	142.5	12	535	34	15.73	1	5–21
R. G. D. Willis	163	24	585	37	15.81	—	4–11
R. W. Hills	137	15	479	30	15.96	—	4–14
J. N. Shepherd	143.1	24	436	27	16.14	—	4–32
K. Higgs	148	30	426	25	17.04	—	3–16
M. Hendrick	155.3	39	399	23	17.34	—	4–15
S. Oldham	147.2	25	480	27	17.77	—	4–26
L. B. Taylor	140.1	23	502	28	17.92	—	4–27
G. Miller	124.4	18	401	22	18.22	—	3–23
R. A. Woolmer	157	25	481	26	18.50	1	6–9
W. Hogg	122	17	445	24	18.54	—	4–23
H. P. Cooper	173.1	23	596	32	18.62	—	4–28
M. W. W. Selvey	168.2	34	433	22	19.68	—	4–28
J. F. Steele	154.3	23	537	27	19.88	1	5–22
J. R. T. Barclay	144.2	11	558	28	19.92	1	5–43
P. H. Edmonds	177	28	499	25	19.96	—	3–20
I. T. Botham	189.4	37	610	30	20.33	—	4–10
B. M. Brain	137.5	22	553	27	20.48	—	4–28
K. F. Jennings	148.1	21	493	24	20.54	—	4–11
J. D. Inchmore	132.5	14	459	22	20.86	—	3–24
M. D. Marshall	162.2	24	491	23	21.34	1	5–13
J. E. Emburey	162	19	538	25	21.52	—	3–42
M. J. Procter	139.1	28	432	20	21.60	—	3–6
A. E. Cordle	166.4	30	524	24	21.83	1	5–24
A. H. Wilkins	108.5	16	438	20	21.90	—	4–31
K. Stevenson	148.2	17	580	26	22.30	—	3–23
Imran Khan	211.5	39	649	29	22.37	—	4–20
T. M. Lamb	175.5	20	701	31	22.61	1	5–13
P. B. Clift	151.4	16	515	22	23.40	—	3–25
P. D. Swart	144.2	16	560	23	24.34	—	4–35

	O	M	R	W	Av	5w	BB
S. P. Perryman	158.4	19	635	26	24.42	—	4–30
S. Turner	202	27	687	28	24.53	—	4–18
N. Phillip	179.3	16	675	27	25.00	—	4–23
J. Spencer	151.4	22	609	24	25.37	—	4–44
K. R. Pont	183.3	21	745	29	25.68	—	4–24
Sarfraz Nawaz	175.4	37	580	22	26.36	—	3–26
P. Willey	195	25	615	23	26.73	—	3–23
B. J. Griffiths	146.3	14	646	22	29.36	1	5–43
R. D. Jackman	162.3	16	706	22	32.06	—	3–26
P. I. Pocock	188	27	730	21	34.76	—	4–32

MOST ECONOMICAL BOWLING (Qualification: 100 overs, 3.30 runs/over)

	O	M	R	W	Runs/over
C. M. Old	217	55	537	36	2.47
D. L. Underwood	179.3	49	458	35	2.55
M. Hendrick	155.3	39	399	23	2.56
M. W. W. Selvey	168.2	34	433	22	2.57
W. W. Daniel	138.1	24	365	29	2.64
J. Garner	214.2	40	575	47	2.68
S. T. Clarke	117.5	28	331	19	2.80
P. H. Edmonds	177	28	499	25	2.81
R. J. Hadlee	150	28	423	29	2.82
K. Higgs	148	30	426	25	2.87
M. D. Marshall	162.2	24	491	23	3.02
J. N. Shepherd	143.1	24	436	27	3.04
Imran Khan	211.5	39	649	29	3.06
R. A. Woolmer	157	25	481	26	3.06
G. G. Arnold	169.3	26	525	17	3.09
M. J. Procter	139.1	28	432	20	3.10
A. E. Cordle	166.4	30	524	24	3.14
P. Willey	195	25	615	23	3.15
J. K. Lever	194.3	34	617	43	3.17
I. T. Botham	189.4	37	610	30	3.21
G. Miller	124.4	18	401	22	3.21
S. Oldham	147.2	25	480	27	3.25
B. Wood	115.3	13	379	19	3.28
Sarfraz Nawaz	175.4	37	580	22	3.30

WICKET-KEEPING (Most dismissals)

Dismissals		Ct	St
30	I. J. Gould	23	7
28	D. J. S. Taylor	20	8
26	D. L. Bairstow	24	2
25	P. R. Downton	23	2
24	A. Long	21	3
24	G. Sharp	19	5
22	C. J. Richards	18	4
21	J. Lyon	18	3
19	D. J. Humphries	16	3
19	E. W. Jones	14	5
18	N. Smith	15	3
17	G. R. Stephenson	12	5
17	R. W. Taylor	13	4
16	A. J. Brassington	15	1
15	G. W. Humpage	15	0
15	A. P. E. Knott	12	3

FIELDING (Most catches)

Ct	
17	G. M. Turner
13	I. T. Botham
12	P. Willey
11	C. J. Tavaré
11	R. G. Williams
11	B. Wood
11	T. J. Yardley
10	D. L. Amiss
10	J. M. Brearley
10	A. G. E. Ealham
10	J. E. Emburey
10	K. S. McEwan

Right: Derek Randall was a certain selection for Australia after innings of the highest calibre on two previous visits.

AUSTRALIA 1979–80

Selection of the Kent fast bowler Graham Dilley for Australia was a sensible, calculated gamble which was justified by his successful Test début in Perth.

A NEW STYLE OF TOUR

There have always been problems choosing a side to tour Australia. The selectors not only have to pick a party with ability, balance and harmony, but need to take into account the different conditions. A high-scoring county batsmen has often failed out there, through either a lack of pedigree or a faulty technique, while the typical English seamer usually makes little impression.

In choosing the team for the tour of Australia this past winter, the selectors' task was different and more difficult. The visit was unlike anything that had taken place previously. First, the trip was hastily and, in some respects, badly conceived. England, after all, had completed a full Australian tour only the previous winter (1978-79), while in 1977 they had followed up their Indian campaign with the Centenary Test in Melbourne.

Last winter's programme was devised by the Australian Board of Control, in conjunction with World Series Cricket, to save them from virtual bankruptcy following their war with the Packer circus. Their compromise – capitulation might be a more accurate description – left them no alternative but to find a solution which, it is hoped, would save them. As a result the format is unique, consisting of a double tour by England and the West Indies. But, and it is a considerable but, such a tour lacked balance. It necessitated too much travelling and, from the point of view of the tourists, there were too many gaps between matches.

Secondly, England agreed to a trip which included three, instead of the usual six, Tests; a reduced number of matches against Australian sides; and a limited-overs competion involving themselves, Australia and West Indies. This culminated in a three-game Grand Final, under floodlights, between the two most successful sides with lucrative prizemoney at stake.

Such a set of circumstances meant that the England selectors had to find a team which was not only able to win a three-match Test series, but would also give a good account of itself in the limited-overs cricket, which for the first time in Australia was to play a really significant part in the visit.

Although it is sometimes said that an international cricketer should be equally efficient at all forms of the game, this does not always apply. For example, Bishan Bedi, who has been one of the great Test match spinners, did not command a regular place in the Northamptonshire eleven for Sunday matches; and John Hampshire is more likely to win a high-scoring limited-overs game than Geoff Boycott, who is a much more accomplished batsman. At times, of course – say, every decade or so – Boycott is liable to produce a remarkable, uninhibited innings, as in the 1965 Gillette Cup Final and at Sydney last December.

Thirdly, the controlling bodies for cricket in the three countries concerned are only slowly realising how much their power has diminished; and conversely, how much that of international players and sponsors has increased. This has been an outcome of the Packer Revolution, which showed that it was possible to stage top-class cricket with the best players in the world without the approval of the ICC.

Predictably, the first reaction of the players was to ask for more money for this special tour, even though their rewards about quadrupled to prevent them defecting to WSC. They were aware what the Packer cricketers had earned during the previous two winters in Australia and they wanted comparable rewards for what was likely to prove a hard trip. The result was the rather ridiculous situation of the TCCB and the West Indies Board of Control haggling over their respective guarantees from the Australian Board of Control in October; long after their teams, due to arrive in Australia in November, had been chosen.

The TCCB knew that if they gave Mike Brearley and Company what they felt, or imagined, they were worth, there would be little to share out among the seventeen counties, who not only employ the tourists but rely heavily on international cricket to exist. Eventually a compromise was reached so that each county club would finish up with a share of about £2,000 from the trip. Though welcome, this is considerably less than in the past, without taking inflation into consideration!

The West Indies Board of Control was in an especially weak position. Cricket out there has always been short of funds. The receipts and the crowds for Tests are comparatively small and expenses high, while the inter-island first-class cricket has to be subsidised. The majority of their players, already under contract to WSC and county clubs, were virtually independent mercenaries, which placed the West Indies Board in a poor bargaining position. To make matters worse, there must be some uneasiness about future tours to the Caribbean, past tours having too often been disfigured by riots in recent years. These happenings have been especially sad, for the West Indians play cricket so well and enjoy it so much.

Next winter, England are due in the West Indies, and the Board know they will have to find enough money to satisfy the demands of their own players, most of whom are based elsewhere. They will have to be flown home and provided with accommodation throughout the campaign. In addition, increased demands from the visitors are inevitable. It will not be easy for them to find the cash because, unlike in Australia and England, there is also a shortage of sponsors with the kind of resources needed.

One obvious effect of the newly acquired affluence of the best players is that they can afford to be more fussy, and are likely to avoid the problem tour, unless the rewards are very attractive. It is also interesting to note that one does not hear anything these days about staleness and having to play too much cricket. 'Have bat, will travel, anywhere anytime' is the new motto provided the money is right.

Having relied almost entirely on those who defended the Ashes for the summer's somewhat meaningless series against India, it was only natural that the selectors, under chairman Alec Bedser (also manager for the

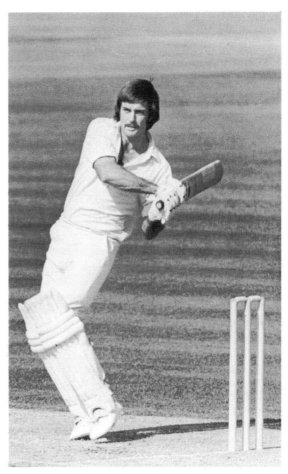

A successful allround season for Northamptonshire saw Peter Willey return to the England side at The Oval, where a convincing display won him a trip to Australia.

Australian trip), would follow the same policy for the winter. They chose to ignore that the success had been gained against an insipid and Packerless Australia and that England had never faced top-class opposition since Mike Brearley took over. Nevertheless, it should be pointed out in their defence that, in general, the most promising of the young batsmen and bowlers failed to translate their potential into runs and wickets on a scale that demanded instant international recognition.

For England to beat an Australian team reinforced by Packer players – even though some of these have an inflated view of their own ability, and others are no more than good, honest State cricketers – was likely to prove a tough but by no means impossible project. Although England would probably need to play above their ability to be successful, there were several factors in their favour. They possessed a thoroughly professional attack made even more formidable by the brilliance in the field. They had, as a result of their international record, built up a belief in themselves, a very strong team spirit and, last but by no means least, a certain arrogance that would ensure a fight to the bitter end. Nothing, however, could really camouflage the frailty of their batting line-up, and one was left to wonder how much could depend on the five newcomers to the party.

Wayne Larkins, an exciting strokemaker of considerable ability, had still to prove himself at the highest level. He was undoubtedly fortunate to have batted so often last summer at Northamptonshire, where the pitches were plumb and the runs plentiful. This advantage could also be said to apply to Peter Willey, who has an impressive record against pace and hits the ball uncommonly hard. But there was still a question mark against his ability to cope with the lifter outside the off stump, and his much-improved off-break bowling had yet to be proved at international level.

The choice of Graham Dilley represented a sensible, calculated gamble. It is not unreminiscent of the time Brian Statham was flown out as replacement on the evidence of half a dozen county games and the fact that he had impressed Sir Len Hutton in a Roses match. If Dilley turns into half as good a bowler, his selection will go down as positively inspired. Tall and strongly built, he could become genuinely quick, as distinct from sharp.

The recall of Derek Underwood, after two years in the international wilderness as a result of his WSC contract, was an entirely logical step. It may have been hard on Phil Edmonds, and a case might have been made for taking two contrasting left-armers rather than two off-spinners, although it should be remembered that Miller and Emburey, also a shade unfortunate, were far more effective than Edmonds in Australia the previous winter. For the second successive summer Underwood captured over 100 wickets for Kent. He is the best spinner in the country, possibly the world, and in an entirely different class from Edmonds. Deadly on a helpful pitch, he can be used as a stock bowler on an easy wicket in a test and is the ideal brake bowler for limited-overs cricket. Furthermore, he knew Australian conditions well.

In drawing up their programme, the Australian authorities banked on several natural winners. In the West Indians, they had currently the best, most attractive team in the world. And by inviting England for a second successive summer, they were giving their strengthened team – and their supporters – a welcome opportunity to exact revenge for the humiliating defeat inflicted on them a year earlier by their oldest adversary.

The TCCB refused to put up the Ashes for a three-match series with many unusual features on the grounds that it would cheapen them. Their decision, if somewhat predictable, was not well received by the Australians; not the least because the Ashes are a highly marketable asset. It produced typically Australian accusations that the English were 'chicken', and in some ways increased the pressure on the England players.

In the circumstances, it would probably have been wiser to have said the three Tests were for the Ashes, or alternatively to have cried off the tour. There is certainly no set pattern in the number of games needed to qualify for an Ashes series, and in the past there have been as few as two Tests in a tour. It would have been the same for both sides, except that the Australians, with three Tests against West Indies – for the Sir Frank Worrell Trophy, incidentally – had a much more demanding schedule.

AUSTRALIA v ENGLAND 1979–80 – 1st Test

Played at Perth, Australia, 14, 15, 16, 18, 19 December
Toss: England   Result: **Australia** won by 138 runs
Man of the Match: I. T. Botham

AUSTRALIA

Batsman	1st innings		2nd innings	
J. M. Weiner	run out	11	c Randall b Underwood	58
B. M. Laird	lbw b Botham	0	c Taylor b Underwood	33
A. R. Border	lbw b Botham	4	c Taylor b Willis	115
G. S. Chappell*	c Boycott b Botham	19	st Taylor b Underwood	43
K. J. Hughes	c Brearley b Underwood	99	c Miller b Botham	4
P. M. Toohey	c Underwood b Dilley	19	c Taylor b Botham	3
R. W. Marsh†	c Taylor b Dilley	42	c Gower b Botham	4
R. J. Bright	c Taylor b Botham	17	lbw b Botham	12
D. K. Lillee	c Taylor b Botham	18	c Willey b Dilley	19
G. Dymock	b Botham	5	not out	20
J. R. Thomson	not out	1	b Botham	8
Extras	(b 4, lb 3, nb 2)	9	(b 4, lb 5, w 2, nb 7)	18
TOTAL		**244**		**337**

ENGLAND

Batsman	1st innings		2nd innings	
D. W. Randall	c Hughes b Lillee	0	lbw b Dymock	1
G. Boycott	lbw b Lillee	0	not out	99
P. Willey	c Chappell b Dymcock	9	lbw b Dymock	12
D. I. Gower	c Marsh b Lillee	17	c Thomson b Dymock	23
G. Miller	c Hughes b Thomson	25	c Chappell b Thomson	8
J. M. Brearley*	c Marsh b Lillee	64	(7) c Marsh b Bright	11
I. T. Botham	c Toohey b Thomson	15	(6) c Marsh b Lillee	18
R. W. Taylor†	b Chappell	14	b Lillee	15
G. R. Dilley	not out	38	c Marsh b Dymock	16
D. L. Underwood	lbw b Dymock	13	c Weiner b Dymock	0
R. G. D. Willis	b Dymock	11	c Chappell b Dymock	0
Extras	(lb 7, nb 15)	22	(lb 3, w 1, nb 8)	12
TOTAL		**228**		**215**

ENGLAND	O	M	R	W	O	M	R	W
Dilley	18	1	47	2	18	3	50	1
Botham	35	9	78	6	45.5	14	98	5
Willis	23	7	47	0	26	7	52	1
Underwood	13	4	33	1	41	14	82	3
Miller	11	2	30	0	10	0	36	0
Willey					1	0	1	0

AUSTRALIA	O	M	R	W	O	M	R	W
Lillee	28	11	73	4	23	5	74	2
Dymock	29.1	14	52	3	17.2	4	34	6
Chappell	11	6	5	1	6	4	6	0
Thomson	21	3	70	2	11	3	30	1
Bright	1	0	6	0	23	11	30	1
Weiner					8	3	22	0
Border					2	0	7	0

FALL OF WICKETS

Wkt	A 1st	E 1st	A 2nd	E 2nd
1st	2	0	91	8
2nd	17	12	100	26
3rd	20	14	168	64
4th	88	41	183	75
5th	127	74	191	115
6th	186	90	204	141
7th	219	123	225	182
8th	219	185	303	211
9th	243	203	323	211
10th	244	228	337	215

Umpires: M. G. O'Connell and D. Weser
*Captain   †Wicket-keeper

High points: The bowling of Botham in both Australian innings, often into the strong Perth wind . . . Dilley's encouraging Test début . . . Hughes' spirited 50 out of 70 in 95 minutes . . . Lillee's sustained fast-medium and Dymock's swing bowling which revealed the flaws in England's batting . . . Border's century, his third of a year in which he scored more runs than any previous Australian in his first year of Test cricket . . . the supreme technique of Boycott, who carried his bat through England's second innings – the first Englishman to do so since Hutton at Adelaide in 1951.

Low point: Lillee's (mis)use of his much-publicised aluminium bat and the subsequent nine and a half minutes' undignified dispute involving both captains and the umpires.

AUSTRALIA v ENGLAND 1979–80 – 2nd Test
Played at Sydney, Australia, 4, 5, 7, 8 January
Toss: Australia   Result: **Australia** won by 6 wickets
Man of the Match: G. S. Chappell

ENGLAND

G. A. Gooch	*b* Lillee	18		*c* G. Chappell *b* Dymock	4
G. Boycott	*b* Dymock	8		*c* McCosker *b* Pascoe	18
D. W. Randall	*c* G. Chappell *b* Lillee	0	(6)	*c* Marsh *b* G. Chappell	25
P. Willey	*c* Wiener *b* Dymock	8	(3)	*b* Pascoe	3
J. M. Brearley*	*c* Pascoe *b* Dymock	7	(4)	*c* Marsh *b* Pascoe	19
D. I. Gower	*b* G. Chappell	3	(7)	*not out*	98
I. T. Botham	*c* G. Chappell *b* Pascoe	27	(8)	*c* Wiener *b* G. Chappell	0
R. W. Taylor†	*c* Marsh *b* Lillee	10	(9)	*b* Lillee	8
G. R. Dilley	*not out*	22	(10)	*b* Dymock	4
R. G. D. Willis	*c* Wiener *b* Dymock	3	(11)	*c* G. Chappell *b* Lillee	1
D. L. Underwood	*c* Border *b* Lillee	12	(5)	*c* Border *b* Dymock	43
Extras	(*nb* 5)	5		(*b* 1, *lb* 10, *w* 1, *nb* 2)	14
TOTAL		**123**			**237**

AUSTRALIA

R. B. McCosker	*c* Gower *b* Willis	1	(2)	*c* Taylor *b* Underwood	41
J. M. Wiener	*run out*	22	(1)	*b* Underwood	13
I. M. Chappell	*c* Brearley *b* Gooch	42		*c* Botham *b* Underwood	9
G. S. Chappell*	*c* Taylor *b* Underwood	3		*not out*	98
K. J. Hughes	*c* Taylor *b* Botham	18		*c* Dilley *b* Willis	47
A. R. Border	*c* Gooch *b* Botham	15		*not out*	2
R. W. Marsh†	*c* Underwood *b* Gooch	7			
D. K. Lillee	*c* Brearley *b* Botham	5			
G. Dymock	*c* Taylor *b* Botham	4			
L. S. Pascoe	*not out*	10			
J. D. Higgs	*b* Underwood	2			
Extras	(*b* 2, *lb* 12, *w* 2)	16		(*lb* 8, *w* 1)	9
TOTAL		**145**		(4 wickets)	**219**

AUSTRALIA	O	M	R	W	O	M	R	W
Lillee	13.3	4	40	4	24.3	3	63	2
Dymock	17	6	42	4	28	8	48	3
Pascoe	9	4	14	1	23	3	76	3
G. Chappell	4	1	19	1	21	10	36	2
Higgs	1	0	3	0				

ENGLAND	O	M	R	W	O	M	R	W
Botham	17	7	29	4	23.3	12	43	0
Willis	11	3	30	1	12	2	26	1
Underwood	13.2	3	39	2	26	6	71	3
Dilley	5	1	13	0	12	0	33	0
Willey	1	0	2	0	4	0	17	0
Gooch	11	4	16	2	8	2	20	0

FALL OF WICKETS

Wkt	E 1st	A 1st	E 2nd	A 2nd
1st	10	18	6	31
2nd	13	52	21	51
3rd	31	71	29	98
4th	38	92	77	203
5th	41	100	105	—
6th	74	114	156	—
7th	75	121	174	—
8th	90	129	211	—
9th	98	132	218	—
10th	123	145	237	—

Umpires: R. C. Bailhaiche and W. J. Copeland
*Captain   †Wicket-keeper

High points: The determination of Gooch (batting 90 minutes) and Brearley (70 minutes) and the lively assault by the tail in England's first innings . . . Ian Chappell's fighting 42 to nullify the threat of Underwood on a wet wicket . . . Underwood's second innings, having gone in as nightwatchman . . . Randall's and Gower's sparkling return to form to give England hope (as at Perth, Willis was out with his partner approaching 100) . . . Underwood's bowling on the fourth morning . . . the stylish innings under pressure of Greg Chappell, though England were sure he was caught behind off Dilley when on 32.

Low points: The decision to commence play on the first day in conditions totally unsuitable for the commencement of a five-day Test. Play began at 3.30 pm and at stumps England, put in, were 90–7.

AUSTRALIA v ENGLAND 1979–80 – 3rd Test
Played at Melbourne, Australia, 1, 2, 3, 5, 6 February
Toss: England   Result: **Australia** won by 8 wickets
Man of the Match: D. K. Lillee

ENGLAND

G. A. Gooch	*run out* (Pascoe/Hughes)	99		*b* Mallett	51
G. Boycott	*c* Mallett *b* Dymock	44		*b* Lillee	7
W. Larkins	*c* G. Chappell *b* Pascoe	25		*lbw b* Pascoe	3
D. I. Gower	*lbw b* Lillee	0		*b* Lillee	11
P. Willey	*lbw b* Pascoe	1		*c* Marsh *b* Lillee	2
I. T. Botham	*c* Marsh *b* Lillee	8	(7)	*not out*	119
J. M. Brearley*	*not out*	60	(6)	*c* Border *b* Pascoe	10
R. W. Taylor†	*b* Lillee	23		*c* Border *b* Lillee	32
D. L. Underwood	*c* I. Chappell *b* Lillee	3		*b* Pascoe	0
J. K. Lever	*b* Lillee	22		*c* Marsh *b* Lillee	12
R. G. D. Willis	*c* G. Chappell *b* Lillee	4		*c* G. Chappell *b* Pascoe	2
Extras	(*b* 1, *lb* 2, *nb* 14)	17		(*b* 2, *lb* 12, *nb* 10)	24
TOTAL		**306**			**273**

AUSTRALIA

R. B. McCosker	*c* Botham *b* Underwood	33		*lbw b* Botham	2
B. M. Laird	*c* Gower *b* Underwood	74		*c* Boycott *b* Underwood	25
I. M. Chappell	*c and b* Underwood	75		*not out*	26
K. J. Hughes	*c* Underwood *b* Botham	15			
A. R. Border	*c and b* Lever	63			
G. S. Chappell*	*c* Larkins *b* Lever	114	(4)	*not out*	40
R. W. Marsh†	*c* Botham *b* Lever	17			
D. K. Lillee	*c* Willey *b* Lever	8			
G. Dymock	*b* Botham	19			
A. A. Mallett	*lbw b* Botham	25			
L. S. Pascoe	*not out*	1			
Extras	(*b* 13, *lb* 12, *w* 1, *nb* 7)	33		(*lb* 8, *nb* 2)	10
TOTAL		**477**			**103**

AUSTRALIA	O	M	R	W	O	M	R	W
Lillee	33.1	9	60	6	33	6	78	5
Dymock	28	6	54	1	11	2	30	0
Mallett	35	9	104	0	14	1	45	1
Pascoe	32	7	71	2	29.5	3	80	4
Border					4	0	16	0

ENGLAND	O	M	R	W	O	M	R	W
Lever	53	15	111	4	7.4	1	18	0
Botham	39.5	15	105	3	12	5	18	1
Willis	21	4	61	0	5	3	8	0
Underwood	53	19	131	3	14	2	49	1
Willey	13	2	36	0				

FALL OF WICKETS

Wkt	E 1st	A 1st	E 2nd	A 2nd
1st	116	52	25	20
2nd	170	179	46	42
3rd	175	196	64	—
4th	177	219	67	—
5th	177	345	88	—
6th	192	411	92	—
7th	238	421	178	—
8th	242	432	179	—
9th	296	465	268	—
10th	306	477	273	—

Umpires: R. C. Bailhache and P. M. Cronin
*Captain   †Wicket-keeper

Australia's victory in the third Test gave them a clean sweep of the series and put into perspective England's results over the past two years. The main difference between the teams lay in the performances of Greg Chappell and Dennis Lillee. Lillee, at 30, cut his pace to a brisk fast-medium, moved the ball disconcertingly in the air and off the wicket, bowled with much thought, and took 23 wickets at a cost of 16 apiece. He was named Man of the Series. Chappell, in his six innings, aggregated 317 runs (average 79.25) whereas no other player on either side scored more than 200 runs.

An ugly side of the series was the boorish behaviour of certain sections in the crowd, who booed the English players throughout and treated Brearley with a hostile incivility that would have shamed the patrons of Newgate.

AUSTRALIA v WEST INDIES 1979–80 – 1st Test
Played at Brisbane, Australia, 1, 2, 3, 4, 5 December
Toss: Australia   Result: Match drawn
Man of the Match: G. S. Chappell

AUSTRALIA

B. M. Laird	*c* Murray *b* Garner	92	(2)	*c* sub (Marshall) *b* Garner	75
R. B. McCosker	*c* Kallicharran *b* Croft	14	(1)	*b* Holding	33
A. R. Border	*c* Murray *b* Garner	1		*c* Richards *b* Garner	7
G. S. Chappell*	*c* King *b* Roberts	74		*b* Croft	124
K. J. Hughes	*b* Croft	3		*not out*	130
D. W. Hookes	*c* Holding *b* Croft	43		*b* Roberts	37
R. W. Marsh†	*c* Murray *b* Garner	3		*c* Kallicharran *b* King	19
R. J. Bright	*b* Holding	13		*not out*	2
D. K. Lillee	*lbw b* Garner	0			
R. M. Hogg	*b* Roberts	8			
J. R. Thomson	*not out*	0			
Extras	(*b* 1, *lb* 4, *nb* 12)	17		(*b* 2, *lb* 11, *w* 2, *nb* 6)	21
TOTAL		**268**		(6 wickets declared)	**448**

WEST INDIES

D. L. Haynes	*c* Marsh *b* Thomson	42	(2)	*lbw b* Hogg	4
C. G. Greenidge	*c* Marsh *b* Lillee	34	(1)	*c* McCosker *b* Thomson	0
I. V. A. Richards	*c* Marsh *b* Lillee	140			
A. I. Kallicharran	*c* Marsh *b* Thomson	38		*not out*	10
L. G. Rowe	*b* Chappell	50	(3)	*b* Hogg	3
C. L. King	*c* Marsh *b* Lillee	0	(5)	*not out*	8
D. L. Murray*†	*c* McCosker *b* Thomson	21			
A. M. E. Roberts	*run out*	7			
J. Garner	*lbw b* Lillee	60			
M. A. Holding	*b* Bright	11			
C. E. H. Croft	*not out*	2			
Extras	(*b* 5, *lb* 3, *nb* 28)	36		(*b* 5, *w* 1, *nb* 9)	15
TOTAL		**441**		(3 wickets)	**40**

WEST INDIES	O	M	R	W	O	M	R	W
Roberts	18.1	5	50	2	27	5	70	1
Holding	16	3	53	1	30	4	94	1
Croft	25	6	80	3	28	3	106	1
Garner	22	5	55	4	41	13	75	2
King	5	1	13	0	22	6	50	1
Kallicharran					18	2	32	0

AUSTRALIA	O	M	R	W	O	M	R	W
Lillee	29.1	8	104	4	2	0	3	0
Hogg	25	6	55	0	5	2	11	2
Thomson	24	4	90	3	3	2	3	1
Bright	32	9	97	1	4	3	8	0
Chappell	12	2	25	1				
Border	5	1	19	0				
Hookes	5	2	15	0				

FALL OF WICKETS

Wkt	A 1st	WI 1st	A 2nd	WI 2nd
1st	19	68	40	2
2nd	26	93	55	15
3rd	156	198	179	16
4th	174	317	297	—
5th	228	317	371	—
6th	242	341	442	—
7th	246	365	—	—
8th	252	366	—	—
9th	268	385	—	—
10th	268	441	—	—

Umpires: A. R. Crafter and R. C. Bailhaiche
*Captain   †Wicket-keeper

High points: The stand of 130 between Chappell and the gritty Laird, who batted on after having a blood blister lanced . . . 72 runs coming off Lillee's first 66 balls . . . Richards' 140 despite a painful hip injury . . . 5 successive boundaries, flashing along the ground, by Rowe (2 off Bright) and Richards (3 off Hogg) . . . 4 enormous sixes by Garner . . . Richards' breathtaking left-handed catch at third slip to dismiss Border . . . Chappell's match-saving 124, his fifteenth Test century.

Low points: West Indies over-rate of fewer than 14 per hour . . . Holding bowling off a short run in the second over of the match . . . Lillee's histrionics in West Indies' second innings . . . the number of no balls (55).

AUSTRALIA v WEST INDIES 1979–80 – 2nd Test
Played at Melbourne, Australia, 29, 30, 31 December, 1 January
Toss: Australia   Result: **West Indies** won by 10 wickets
Man of the Match: I. V. A. Richards

AUSTRALIA

Batsman	Dismissal 1	Score	Dismissal 2	Score
J. M. Weiner	*lbw b* Garner	40	*c* Murray *b* Croft	24
B. M. Laird	*c* Lloyd *b* Holding	16	*c* Garner *b* Holding	69
A. R. Border	*c* Richards *b* Garner	17	*lbw b* Holding	15
G. S. Chappell*	*c* Murray *b* Garner	19	*c* Murray *b* Roberts	22
K. J. Hughes	*c* Rowe *b* Holding	4	*lbw b* Roberts	70
P. M. Toohey	*c* Roberts *b* Holding	10	*c* Murray *b* Croft	7
R. W. Marsh†	*c* Kallicharran *b* Holding	0	*b* Croft	7
D. K. Lillee	*c* Lloyd *b* Croft	12		
			c and *b* Roberts	0
G. Dymock	*c* Kallicharran *b* Croft	7	*c* Lloyd *b* Garner	17
R. M. Hogg	*c* Greenidge *b* Croft	14	*c* Holding *b* Garner	11
J. D. Higgs	*not out*	0	*not out*	0
Extras	(*b* 9, *lb* 4, *w* 2, *nb* 2)	17	(*b* 2, *lb* 10, *nb* 5)	17
TOTAL		**156**		**259**

WEST INDIES

Batsman	Dismissal 1	Score	Dismissal 2	Score
C. G. Greenidge	*c* Higgs *b* Dymock	48	*not out*	9
D. L. Haynes	*c* Hughes *b* Lillee	29	*not out*	9
I. V. A. Richards	*c* Toohey *b* Dymock	96		
A. I. Kallicharran	*c* Laird *b* Higgs	39		
L. G. Rowe	*b* Lillee	26		
C. H. Lloyd*	*c* Marsh *b* Dymock	40		
D. L. Murray†	*b* Dymock	24		
A. M. E. Roberts	*lbw b* Lillee	54		
J. Garner	*c* Dymock *b* Higgs	29		
M. A. Holding	*not out*	1		
C. E. H. Croft	*lbw b* Higgs	0		
Extras	(*lb* 4, *nb* 7)	11	(*lb* 4)	4
TOTAL		**397**	(no wicket)	**22**

WEST INDIES	O	M	R	W	O	M	R	W
Roberts	14	1	39	0	21	1	64	3
Holding	14	3	40	4	23	7	61	2
Croft	13.3	4	27	3	22	2	61	3
Garner	15	7	33	3	20.4	2	56	2

AUSTRALIA	O	M	R	W	O	M	R	W
Lillee	36	7	96	3	3	0	9	0
Hogg	6	0	59	0				
Dymock	31	2	106	4	3	0	5	0
Higgs	34.4	4	122	3				
Chappell	5	2	3	0				
Hughes					1	1	0	0
Toohey					0.2	0	4	0

*Captain   †Wicket-keeper

FALL OF WICKETS

Wkt	A 1st	WI 1st	A 2nd	WI 2nd
1st	38	46	43	—
2nd	69	156	88	—
3rd	97	215	121	—
4th	108	226	187	—
5th	112	250	205	—
6th	118	305	228	—
7th	123	320	228	—
8th	133	390	233	—
9th	143	396	258	—
10th	156	397	259	—

West Indies' victory, with a day and a half to spare, was their first-ever on the Melbourne Cricket Ground.

High points: The fast bowling of Holding, Croft and Garner on a day when temperatures topped 100°F and humidity was high . . . 4 fours by Haynes off Hogg's second over . . . Chappell's insisting that a catch (Greenidge would have been given out) did not carry . . . Richards' courage: hit in the mouth hooking at Hogg, he hooked the next delivery for six and in 42 minutes hit 45 sweetly obtained runs . . . the swing bowling of Dymock, who frustrated even the great Richards into error . . . another superb bowling performance by the West Indian pace quartet on a wicket described as a fast bowlers' graveyard.

AUSTRALIA v WEST INDIES 1979–80 – 3rd Test
Played at Adelaide, Australia, 26, 27, 28, 29, 30 January
Toss: Australia   Result: **West Indies** won by 408 runs
Man ot the Match: C. H. Lloyd

WEST INDIES

C. G. Greenidge	*lbw b* Lillee	6		*st* Marsh *b* Mallett	76
D. L. Haynes	*c* Lillee *b* Mallett	28		*c* Marsh *b* Pascoe	27
I. V. A. Richards	*c* Marsh *b* Lillee	76		*b* Border	74
A. I. Kallicharran	*c* I. Chappell *b* Mallett	9		*b* Mallett	106
L. G. Rowe	*c* Lillee *b* Dymock	40		*c* Marsh *b* Dymock	43
C. H. Lloyd*	*lbw b* Lillee	121	(7)	*c* Marsh *b* Dymock	40
D. L. Murray†	*c* Marsh *b* Dymock	4	(8)	*c* G. Chappell *b* Dymock	28
A. M. E. Roberts	*b* Lillee	9	(9)	*c* Laird *b* Dymock	8
J. Garner	*c* Hughes *b* Lillee	16	(10)	*not out*	1
M. A. Holding	*b* Pascoe	9	(11)	*lbw b* Dymock	1
C. E. H. Croft	*not out*	1	(6)	*c* Border *b* Pascoe	12
Extras	(*b* 2, *nb* 7)	9		(*b* 1, *lb* 10, *nb* 21)	32
TOTAL		**328**			**448**

AUSTRALIA

J. M. Wiener	*c* Haynes *b* Holding	3	*c* Murray *b* Roberts	8
B. M. Laird	*c* Garner *b* Croft	52	*lbw b* Garner	36
I. M. Chappell	*c* Greenidge *b* Roberts	2	*c* Murray *b* Holding	4
G. S. Chappell*	*c* Garner *b* Roberts	0	*lbw b* Croft	31
K. J. Hughes	*c* Lloyd *b* Croft	34	*lbw b* Garner	11
A. R. Border	*b* Roberts	54	*c* Greenidge *b* Roberts	24
R. W. Marsh†	*c* Murray *b* Croft	5	*not out*	23
D. K. Lillee	*c* Haynes *b* Holding	16	*c* Kallicharran *b* Croft	0
G. Dymock	*c* Rowe *b* Croft	10	*c* Richards *b* Holding	2
A. A. Mallett	*c* Rowe *b* Garner	0	*b* Holding	12
L. S. Pascoe	*not out*	5	*b* Holding	5
Extras	(*b* 1, *lb* 14, *nb* 7)	22	(*lb* 2, *w* 2, *nb* 5)	9
TOTAL		**203**		**165**

AUSTRALIA	O	M	R	W	O	M	R	W
Lillee	24	3	78	5	26	6	75	0
Dymock	25	7	74	2	33.5	7	104	5
Pascoe	15.3	1	90	1	25	3	93	2
Mallett	27	5	77	2	38	7	134	2
Border					4	2	10	1

WEST INDIES	O	M	R	W	O	M	R	W
Roberts	16.5	3	43	3	15	5	30	2
Holding	15	5	31	2	13	2	40	4
Garner	18	4	43	1	11	3	39	2
Richards	2	0	7	0				
Croft	22	4	57	4	11	1	47	2

FALL OF WICKETS

	WI	*A*	*WI*	*A*
Wkt	*1st*	*1st*	*2nd*	*2nd*
1st	11	23	48	12
2nd	115	26	184	21
3rd	115	26	213	71
4th	126	83	299	83
5th	239	110	331	98
6th	252	127	398	130
7th	300	165	417	131
8th	303	188	443	135
9th	326	189	446	159
10th	328	203	448	165

Umpires: M. G. O'Connell and M. W. Johnson
*Captain   †Wicket-keeper

West Indies victory in the series by two Tests to none gave them their first series win in Australia. Vivian Richards was named Man of the Series.

High points: Once more the sheer brilliance of Richards' batting. His first innings 50 came off 50 deliveries; his second off 55 . . . the economy of Rowe's artistry . . . Lloyd's century, his 12th in Test cricket, resplendent with all his former majesty and especially memorable for four fours in one over from Pascoe . . . the power of Greenidge as his confidence grew and Kallicharran's sparkling footwork and sure timing . . . again, the control and relentless authority of the West Indian fast bowlers . . . Lloyd's quiet assimilation of a team brimming with massive individual talents and tinder-like emotions.

Low point: The number of no balls bowled by the Australians, especially by Pascoe.

BENSON AND HEDGES WORLD SERIES CUP

Mr Kerry Packer, having loudly propounded his expertise on promoting cricket, discovered the truth in that old cliché: cricket is an unpredictable game. With his eye on advertising revenue, Packer was obviously counting on the final of the Benson and Hedges World Series Cup being fought out by Australia, replete with their WSC players, and West Indies. Instead, Mike Brearley's 'poms' put their professionalism to the fore and proudly topped the table after their eight qualifying matches. Australia, essential ingredients for a crowd-attracting final series – especially in Sydney – were relegated to also-rans as their visitors went home with the prize-money: £16,000 to the winners of the final, £8,000 to the losers, and £1,500 to the winners of the qualifying matches. Australian cricket, unhappily, was in little better sorts than it was before the rift was healed.

England began their task of qualifying by beating West Indies on scoring-rate, the West Indians' target of 212 (50 overs) being cut to 199 (47 overs) when play paused for a shower – and was further delayed while the playing regulations were sorted out! They needed three off the last ball, with which Botham bowled Croft. England's innings was built around openers Brearley and Randall (49), Gower and Willey (58 not out). In the field, they were well served by their modern virtues of astute captaincy, accurate, frugal bowling, and superb fielding. Randall, at short mid-wicket, took a magnificent catch running backwards.

In their final match of the qualifying series, Botham took an equally memorable caught and bowled, knocking Kallicharran's drive in the air, twisting and turning to his left, and holding the ball in his left hand. England lost that match convincingly but were through to the finals by then, having beaten Australia in all four matches. These four victories owed much to Yorkshiremen. Boycott, originally not considered part of the one-day-and-night thinking, dominated the first three with innings of 68 (England won by three wickets), 105 (by 72 runs), and 86 not out (by four wickets). Willey's 37, 64, and 51 in these matches justified his selection for the tour. In the fourth match, which England won by two wickets with seven balls to spare, Stevenson (4–33 in Australia's innings) and Bairstow hammered England from apparent defeat to an unexpected two points after all but Gooch (69) and Emburey had failed to reach double figures.

Qualifying table

	P	W	L	NR	Pts
England	8	5	2	1	11
West Indies	8	3	4	1	7
Australia	8	3	5	0	6

FINAL: FIRST MATCH

So, so close. England required four off the last ball of the match, but with everyone save Murray on the boundary it was never on. So West Indies won by two runs and took a significant 1–0 lead in the best-of-three finals.

But for dropped catches the game could have been England's. Boycott, at deep square leg, missed Kallicharran when he was 25; Gower put down King before his onslaught took West Indies past 200. King was again fortunate when given not out though beaten by Gooch's direct throw at the stumps. Greenidge, surviving a hard-driven caught and bowled to Botham at six, held the West Indians together until Botham, with three wickets in six balls, put England back in the game.

West Indies, in contrast, held their catches magnificently, King and Lloyd both making brilliant diving efforts. The England run-outs, however, were entirely of their own making . . . and, with Willey and Larkins batting confidently, were disastrous. Botham and Brearley took England closer and closer, and with three overs remaining they needed 25. When Holding began the 50th over, it was down to 15. Amid mounting excitement, 10 came off the first four balls; the fifth brought a single. Lloyd pushed his fielders back, and Brearley's hit found one of them. For England, it was a case of 'if only . . .'.

ENGLAND v WEST INDIES at Melbourne on 20 January 1980
West Indies won by 2 runs   *captain*
Toss: England   †*wicket-keeper*

WEST INDIES				ENGLAND	O	M	R	W
C. G. Greenidge	c Larkins b Botham	80		Willis	10	1	51	1
D. L. Haynes	c Bairstow b Willis	9		Botham	10	2	33	3
I. V. A. Richards	c Bairstow b Dilley	23		Emburey	10	0	31	0
A. I. Kallicharran	b Botham	42		Dilley	10	0	39	2
C. H. Lloyd*	b Botham	4		Willey	10	0	48	0
C. L. King	not out	31						
D. L. Murray†	c Bairstow b Dilley	4		WEST INDIES				
A. M. E. Roberts	run out	1		Roberts	10	1	30	3
J. Garner	run out	3		Holding	10	1	43	1
M. A. Holding	not out	5		Garner	10	1	27	0
C. E. H. Croft	did not bat			Croft	10	1	23	0
Extras	(lb 11, nb 1, w 1)	13		King	4	0	30	0
TOTAL	(8 wickets – 50 overs)	**215**		Richards	6	1	34	0

ENGLAND			FALL OF WICKETS		
G. A. Gooch	c King b Holding	9	*Wkt*	*WI*	*E*
G. Boycott	c Greenidge b Roberts	35	1st	17	13
P. Willey	run out	51	2nd	66	74
D. I. Gower	c Holding b Roberts	10	3rd	161	96
W. Larkins	run out	34	4th	168	152
I. T. Botham	c Lloyd b Roberts	19	5th	168	164
J. M. Brearley*	not out	25	6th	181	190
D. L. Bairstow†	run out	4	7th	183	213
J. E. Emburey			8th	197	
G. R. Dilley	did not bat				
R. G. D. Willis					
Extras	(b 12, lb 12, nb 1, w 1)	26			
TOTAL	(7 wickets – 50 overs)	**213**			

FINAL: SECOND MATCH

West Indies confirmed their standing as world champions of the one-day game by beating England convincingly in the day-and-night match at Sydney and so winning the Benson and Hedges World Series Cup. Their victory also meant that the third match of the finals would not be played.

Brearley chose to bat in the daylight, and Gooch and Boycott gave England a sound start, Boycott, at his best, playing the fast bowlers with confidence and using his feet well to drive Richards. A straight-driven four off Croft and a square drive off Garner were vintage strokes. Gower effected some sparkling drives and pulls and Botham gave the total respectability with his belligerent hitting, including a six off Roberts over mid-wicket.

Greenidge and Haynes began West Indies' reply as if intent to be away by lighting-up time, and England's jubilation at Haynes' dismissal was quelled as Richards warmed to his evening's work. Greenidge, with savagery and sweetly timed drives, hammered his 50 off 85 balls (Boycott's took 79) while Richards, dropped by Willis at long-on at 34, purred to his 50 in 66 deliveries. Derek Underwood and John Lever, watching from the pavilion, must have wondered why they were there.

ENGLAND v WEST INDIES at Sydney on 22 January 1980
West Indies won by 8 wickets
Toss: England   *captain*
Man of the Finals: C. G. Greenidge   †*wicket-keeper*

ENGLAND			WEST INDIES	O	M	R	W
G. A. Gooch	*lbw b* Garner	23	Roberts	10	3	31	2
G. Boycott	*c* Greenidge *b* Roberts	63	Holding	10	1	34	1
P. Willey	*b* Garner	3	Croft	10	3	29	1
D. I. Gower	*c* Murray *b* Holding	27	Garner	10	0	44	2
W. Larkins	*b* Croft	14	Richards	3	0	19	0
I. T. Botham	*c* King *b* Roberts	37	King	7	1	38	0
D. L. Bairstow†	*not out*	18					
J. M. Brearley*	*run out*	4	ENGLAND				
J. E. Emburey	*run out*	6	Willis	10	0	35	0
G. R. Dilley	} *did not bat*		Dilley	7	0	37	0
R. G. D. Willis			Botham	10	1	28	1
Extras	(*b* 1, *lb* 11, *nb* 1)	13	Emburey	9.3	0	48	0
TOTAL	(8 wickets – 50 overs)	**208**	Willey	10	2	35	1
			Gooch	1	0	5	0

WEST INDIES			FALL OF WICKETS		
C. G. Greenidge	*not out*	98	*Wkt*	*E*	*WI*
D. L. Haynes	*lbw b* Botham	17	1st	40	61
I. V. A. Richards	*c* Botham *b* Willey	65	2nd	54	180
A. I. Kallicharran	*not out*	8	3rd	118	
C. H. Lloyd*			4th	126	
D. L. Murray†			5th	155	
C. L. King			6th	188	
A. M. E. Roberts	} *did not bat*		7th	194	
M. A. Holding			8th	208	
C. E. H. Croft					
J. Garner					
Extras	(*b* 5, *lb* 10, *nb* 1, *w* 5)	21			
TOTAL	(2 wickets – 47.3 overs)	**209**			

BENSON AND HEDGES WORLD SERIES CUP 1979–80
Qualifying Rounds

27 November at Sydney: AUSTRALIA beat WEST INDIES by 5 wickets. West Indies 193 (49.3 overs) (A. I. Kallicharran 49, L. S. Pascoe 4–29, A. R. Border 3–36). Australia 196–5 (47.1 overs) (G. S. Chappell 74*, K. J. Hughes 52).

28 November at Sydney: ENGLAND beat WEST INDIES by 2 runs (on faster scoring-rate). England 211–8 (50 overs) (P. Willey 58*, D. W. Randall 49, J. Garner 3–31). West Indies 196 (47 overs) (L. G. Rowe 60, A. I. Kallicharran 44, C. G. Greenidge 42, D. L. Underwood 4–44).

8 December at Melbourne: ENGLAND beat AUSTRALIA by 3 wickets. Australia 207–9 (50 overs) (G. S. Chappell 92, P. Willey 3–33). England 209–7 (49 overs) (G. Boycott 68, P. Willey 37, R. M. Hogg 3–26).

9 December at Melbourne: WEST INDIES beat AUSTRALIA by 80 runs. West Indies 271–2 (48 overs) (I. V. A. Richards 153*, D. L. Haynes 80). Australia 191–8 (48 overs) (A. R. Border 44, G. S. Chappell 31).

11 December at Sydney: ENGLAND beat AUSTRALIA by 72 runs. England 264–7 (49 overs) (G. Boycott 105, P. Willey 64, D. W. Randall 42, D. K. Lillee 4–56). Australia 192 (T. J. Laughlin 74, K. D. Walters 34).

21 December at Sydney: AUSTRALIA beat WEST INDIES by 7 runs. Australia 176–6 (50 overs) (I. M. Chappell 63*, R. W. Marsh 33). West Indies 169 (42.5 overs) (I. V. A. Richards 62, C. G. Greenidge 33, D. K. Lillee 4–28).

23 December at Brisbane: WEST INDIES beat ENGLAND by 9 wickets. England 217–8 (50 overs) (G. Boycott 68, D. I. Gower 59, P. Willey 34, A. M. E. Roberts 3–26). West Indies 218–1 (46.5 overs) (C. G. Greenidge 85*, I. V. A. Richards 85*, D. L. Haynes 41).

26 December at Sydney: ENGLAND beat AUSTRALIA by 4 wickets. Australia 194–6 (47 overs) (I. M. Chappell 60*, G. S. Chappell 52). England 195–6 (45.1 overs) (G. Boycott 86*, P. Willey 51, R. M. Hogg 4–46).

12 January at Melbourne: ENGLAND V WEST INDIES abandoned. No play.

14 January at Sydney: ENGLAND beat AUSTRALIA by 2 wickets. Australia 163 (48.4 overs) (R. B. McCosker 41, G. S. Chappell 34, K. J. Hughes 34, J. M. Wiener 33, G. R. Stevenson 4–33). England 164–8 (48.5 overs) (G. A. Gooch 69, D. K. Lillee 4–12).

16 January at Adelaide: WEST INDIES beat ENGLAND by 107 runs. West Indies 246–5 (50 overs) (I. V. A. Richards 88, A. I. Kallicharran 57, C. G. Greenidge 50). England 139 (42.5 overs) (A. M. E. Roberts 5–22, C. L. King 4–23).

18 January at Sydney: AUSTRALIA beat WEST INDIES by 9 runs. Australia 190 (48.3 overs) (R. B. McCosker 95, J. M. Wiener 50, M. A. Holding 4–17). West Indies 181 (49.1 overs) (A. I. Kallicharran 66, D. A. Murray 35, C. H. Lloyd 34, D. K. Lillee 3–17, L.S. Pascoe 3–34).

Man of the Series: I. V. A. Richards (West Indies).

Right: Peter Willey can look back over 1979 with a sense of achievement: his England place regained and Northamptonshire in the Gillette Cup final. Will 1980 bring further honours for the County Durham-born all-rounder?

LOOKING AHEAD TO 1980

Captain of West Indies since 1974 – apart from his self-imposed exile in Packerland – Clive Lloyd commands a batting line-up and fast bowling battery that almost defies defeat.

THE WONDERFUL WEST INDIANS

Currently world champions of limited-overs cricket, West Indies are arguably the best and certainly the most exciting Test team in the world. Although both Australia and England did their best to change this assessment during last winter's Packer-packaged cricket panorama, Clive Lloyd's team are bound to provide formidable opposition in England this summer. They will also be the strongest touring party to visit this country since the WSC revolution.

Having won on their last two visits, the West Indians must remain firm favourites to make it three in a row. Apart from the quality of their players, they are at their most effective under English conditions, because this is where the majority of them play most of their cricket. As their last manager, Clyde Walcott, said, 'The time is fast approaching when the West Indian manager will meet his side for the first time after he has stepped off the plane at Heathrow'.

The fact that most of the tourists are, or have been, county cricketers is an advantage from the playing angle, but it inevitably detracts from their overall appeal. Their stars lack the mystique and drawing power that Bradman, Lindwall, Worrell, Hall or Miller had in the past. Vivian Richards can be seen any summer, playing for Somerset, either live or on the television.

Despite this disadvantage the West Indians are bound to draw large crowds. The big West Indian immigrant population will once again turn out to support their fellow countrymen, not entirely for the cricket, but also for ethnic reasons. It is to be hoped that in this series their natural exuberance is better controlled than on the last tour. There are those, and one suspects they are in the majority, who would prefer to watch the game without a drum ceaselessly beating in their ear.

The strength of West Indian cricket today stems from their collection of brilliant, world-class strokemakers – including Vivian Richards, Gordon Greenidge and Alvin Kallicharran – their battery of international pace bowlers, and their natural, uninhibited approach to the game. These three ingredients help to explain their effectiveness in both limited-overs and Test cricket. Provided at least one of their front-line batsmen produces a major innings in a one-day game, they are virtually assured of victory, for it is highly improbable that the opposing batsmen will be able to score as fast against the West Indian pace attack.

High calibre strokemakers are also a big asset in Test matches. As well as attracting the paying customers, they are able to dominate an international attack, while the speed at which they acquire runs automatically gives their bowlers more time to dismiss the other side, increasing their chances of victory – or defeat. The danger of defeat, however, is largely offset by the increased importance of pace bowling in recent international series.

The arrival of several top-quality batsmen and fast bowlers during the past few years has been responsible for the successes enjoyed by West Indies, especially against England. But their real and lasting power is derived from their seemingly inexhaustible supply of young players fighting to reach the top; in the West Indies the game is popular, the weather suitable, the competition fierce – and success provides a practical escape route to a higher standard of living. In Barbados today there must be at least three fast bowlers who could walk into a county eleven, while it would be impossible to estimate the number of batsmen with more basic potential than the average young cricketer taken on a county staff.

One important reason why a little island like Barbados has produced so many outstanding cricketers, and supplied 40 per cent of the players for WSC and the official West Indian eleven in 1978–79, is soft-ball cricket. This is not only a good and exciting game on its own, but it provides the best possible introduction to cricket for a child. It teaches him to move into line without the fear of being hit, to strike the ball on the rise, to catch, to bowl and play straight, and to attack a delivery which lifts steeply. Soft-ball cricket can be played on almost any surface and the costs of staging an eleven-a-side match are far less than for, say, soccer!

The increasing number of the West Indian 'have bat, will travel' brigade has provided their administrators with financial, playing and administrative problems. Their star players are demanding an ever-larger slice of the cake, which means there is less left to share out among the islands, who have always lacked adequate finance. The cost of bringing their mercenaries back to the Caribbean, keeping them throughout the tour, and paying them the type of salaries they received from Kerry Packer is crippling the West Indies Board of Control. Apart from at Trinidad, Test gates are small; few can afford the type of admission charges needed to produce high wages for players, and there are few big sponsors.

One of the great advantages enjoyed by cricketers in the Caribbean used to be that their Test stars would automatically take part in local club cricket. This naturally raised the overall standard, increasing the competition and the interest. Because so many of them are virtually resident abroad, their finest players no longer need domestic club cricket to provide them with the necessary practice.

The defection of most of the West Indian side to WSC weakened the power of what had always been an uneasy and divided Board of Control – representatives of a group of islands who are inclined to be jealous of each other and are in no sense a nation. The outcome is that their WSC contingent, with Clive Lloyd as prime minister and Deryck Murray as trade union leader and chancellor, has become far more important than the WIBC. This was illustrated when all the Packer players immediately went on strike after the selectors decided to drop Murray against the Australians in 1978. It is very significant that a number of West Indian administrators

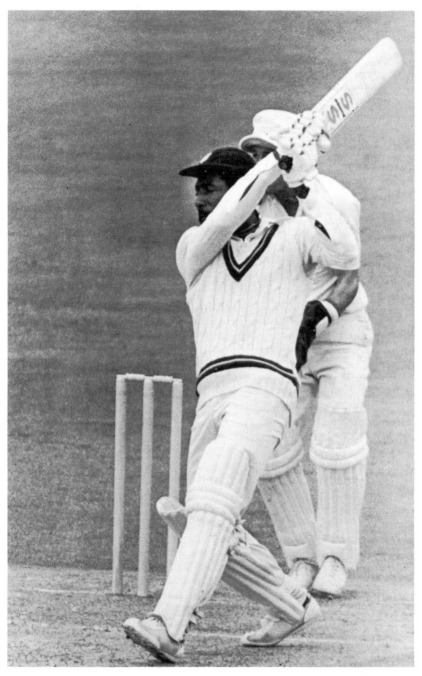

In the 1976 series against England Viv Richards scored 232, 63, 4, 135, 66, 38, and 291 – 829 runs. Since then he has grown in stature!

refused to consider going to Australia as manager, because they knew there would be disciplinary problems.

The increase in the power of a small clique of cricketers, who have considerable financial reasons for continuing to play, will tend to restrict the youngsters because the 'old order' will inevitably settle for an established colleague, rather than gamble on a comparative unknown. A team of experienced players is always more likely to succeed in England, where knowledge of conditions is so vital.

Although the 'glorious uncertainties of cricket' has become a classical cliché, it fortunately still applies. It would therefore be unwise to write off England's chances in the 1980 series, despite the visitors being individually more talented and exciting. Even if Clive Lloyd is fit to lead them, West Indies will lack England's spirit, which can enable them to perform above themselves. Although Lloyd has the confidence of, and is admired by, his players, he can hardly be classified as a tactical genius. It will be remembered how, in Australia in 1975–76, what should have been a great side simply disintegrated under his command.

England would walk the series if the groundsmen could prepare exactly the same pitches as the Australians encountered in 1956, when the England spinners captured over 60 wickets. Not only do West Indies lack high-class slow bowlers but, if their batsmen have a weakness, it must be against spin. The absence of a quality spinner, since the retirement of Lance Gibbs, puts a question mark against them. They are too dependent on their battery of pace and are therefore vulnerable in certain conditions. It also lessens their spectator appeal; unless wickets are falling at regular intervals, the sight of four or five bowlers, with long run-ups and the 'keeper standing back, is one of the game's more monotonous sights. The over-rate is inevitably slow and the range of strokes restricted.

Although the West Indian batting line-up contains batsmen with the virtuosity which enables them to transform the whole course of a match by the quality of their performance, they also have a distinctly suspect tail. Unreliable would probably be the best description, for their hard-hitting fast bowlers can, and do, score runs; but nobody is surprised when they fail, especially when the pressure is on. This weakness means that a fine spell with the new ball, a couple of blinding catches, or a bad call could see them collapse and in deep trouble. The West Indian temperament is essentially effervescent, and if things go wrong, they often fail to play to their true potential.

One final factor working against the West Indians is the way they seem to suffer rather more through injury than other touring sides. Although in some cases this is simply the outcome of too much cricket, there is also a suspicion that they have their fair share of hypochondriacs. Certainly their massage table is permanently occupied, and at times one wonders whether they should also be accompanied by a couple of psychoanalysts as well as an overworked masseur.

REGISTER OF COUNTY PLAYERS

All first-class and Test match career statistics are complete to the end of the 1979 season.

The forename by which a player is known is shown in bold type.

The county in which a player is born is given only when this differs from the one he now represents. For registration purposes a cricketer's 'county of birth' is determined in accordance with boundaries existing at the time of his birth and the County of London is divided between Essex, Kent, Middlesex, and Surrey. Similarly, for overseas players, names of countries given are those in being at the time of their birth.

Abbreviations			
*	Not out	LHB	Bats left-handed
av	Average	LM	Bowls left-arm medium
b	Born	OB	Bowls off-breaks
BB	Best innings bowling analysis	occ	Occasional
cap	Awarded county 1st XI cap	RF	Bowls right-arm fast
ct	Catches	RFM	Bowls right-arm fast-medium
F-c	First-class	RHB	Bats right-handed
HS	Highest score	RM	Bowls right-arm medium
LB	Bowls leg-breaks	SLA	Bowls orthodox slow-left-arm
LF	Bowls left-arm fast	SLC	Bowls slow left-arm 'chinamen'
LFM	Bowls left-arm fast-medium	st	Stumpings
		WK	Wicket-keeper

ABBERLEY, Robert **Neal,** b Birmingham 22 Apr 44, RHB, occ RM. WARWICKSHIRE cap 1966. F-c career: 261 matches; 10,082 runs (av 24.47); 3 hundreds; 5 wkts (av 58.80); 171 ct. HS 117* v Essex (Birmingham) 1966. BB 2–19 v Oxford U. (Oxford) 1972.

Experienced, neat, rather on-side conscious batsman.

ABRAHAMS, John, b Cape Town, South Africa 21 Jul 52. LHB, occ OB. LANCASHIRE – uncapped. F-c career: 98 matches; 3,174 runs (av 24.41): 2 hundreds; 62 ct. HS 126 v Cambridge U. (Cambridge) 1978.

Attractive left-hand batsman, but never scored as heavily as hoped; brilliant fielder.

ACFIELD, David Laurence, b Chelmsford 24 Jul 47, RHB, OB. ESSEX cap 1970. F-c career: 267 matches; 1,284 runs (av 9.04); 619 wkts (av 28.05); 92ct. HS 42 Cambridge U. v Leicester (Leicester) 1967. BB 7–36 v Sussex (Ilford) 1973.

Extremely accurate off-break bowler who is also effective in limited-overs cricket. He is not a big finger-spinner, but is capable of winning a match on a pitch giving assistance.

AGNEW, Jonathan Philip, b Macclesfield, Cheshire 4 Apr 60. RHB, RF. LEICESTERSHIRE – uncapped. F-c career: 7 matches; 11 runs (av 3.66); 13 wkts (av 31.84); 0 ct. HS 9. BB 3–51 v Northants (Leicester) 1978.

A young fast bowler who went from public school cricket into the Leicestershire side. In the next few years could prove to be an international pace bowler, but will have to fill out.

ALLBROOK, Mark Edward, b Frimley, Surrey 15 Nov 54. RHB, OB. NOTTINGHAMSHIRE – uncapped. F-c career: 44 matches; 320 runs (av 8.64); 75 wkts (av 44.97); 14 ct. HS 39 Cambridge U. v Yorks (Cambridge) 1976. BB 7–79 Cambridge U. v Notts (Cambridge) 1978.

Accurate off-break bowler who, at present, does not spin the ball sufficiently.

ALLOTT, Paul John Walter, b Altrincham, Cheshire 14 Sep 56. RHB, RFM. LANCASHIRE

– uncapped. F-c career: 16 matches; 20 runs (av 4.00); 27 wkts (av 39.44); 5 ct. HS 14 v Warwicks (Manchester) 1979. BB 5–39 v Worcs (Southport) 1979.

Right-arm fast-medium bowler.

AMISS, Dennis Leslie, b Birmingham 7 Apr 43. RHB, occ SLA/LM. WARWICKSHIRE cap 1965. 50 England caps 1966–77, scoring 3,612 runs (av 46.30) with 11 hundreds, HS 262*. F-c career: 459 matches; 30,038 runs (av 43.53), 74 hundreds; 18 wkts (av 38.88); 299 ct. HS 262* England v West Indies (Kingston) 1973–74. BB 3–21 v Middlesex (Lord's) 1970.

Took longer than most to establish himself as an England regular. Originally chosen as a middle-order batsman, but following a rewarding spell with Warwickshire as an opener, he took over this role with enormous success at international level. Has become one of the really great accumulators of runs, with a wide range of strokes, a fine defence, and endless patience. There is now an air of inevitability about his batting, so that, once he has settled in, a century seems probable. It is also noticeable how his concentration never wavers; like all outstanding players, can accelerate when needs dictate. Celebrated his recall to Test cricket after a lean spell against Australian pace with hundreds against both West Indies and India, but lost his place in 1977.

ANDERSON, Iain Stuart, b Derby 24 Apr 60. RHB, occ OB. DERBYSHIRE – uncapped. F-c career: 11 matches; 238 runs (av 15.86); 2 wkts (av 81.50); 4 ct. HS 75 v Worcs (Worcester) 1978. BB 1–24 v Northants (Derby) 1978 – on début.

Locally born opening bat and slow left-arm bowler who flights the ball.

ARNOLD, Geoffrey Graham, b Earlsfield 3 Sep 44. RHB, RFM. SUSSEX cap 1979. Played for Surrey 1963–77 (cap 1967). 34 England caps 1967–75, scoring 421 runs (av 12.02), HS 59, and taking 115 wkts (av 28.29), BB 6–45. F-c career: 323 matches; 3,606 runs (av 13.71); 1,037 wkts (av 21.53), 1 hat-trick; 109 ct. HS 73 MCC under-25 v Central Zone (Sahiwal) 1966–67. BB 8–41 Surrey v Glos (Oval) 1967.

Still one of the best new ball bowlers in England. Has excellent control, a late away swing, and a vicious 'nip-backer'. Although not truly fast, he has the ability to produce a respectable bouncer. Can be used as either a shock or stock bowler. A competent bat in the later order, especially when he remembers to play and hit straight.

ASIF IQBAL RAZVI, b Hyderabad, India 6 Jun 43. RHB, RM. KENT cap 1968. Captain 1977. 52 Pakistan caps 1964–79, scoring 3,308 runs (av 39.85) with 11 hundreds, HS 175, and taking 51 wkts (av 28.03), BB 5–48. F-c career: 391 matches; 20,745 runs (av 37.37), 40

hundreds; 288 wkts (av 29.82); 287 ct. HS 196 National Bank v PIA (Lahore) 1976–77. BB 6–45 Pakistan Eaglets v Cambridge U. (Cambridge) 1963.

An exciting strokemaker, capable of changing the course of any game by the virtuosity of his batting. A graceful and exciting batsman with a two-eyed stance, very quick on his feet, he is at his most effective when attacking. A useful second-line seamer and brilliant all-purpose fieldsman. Current captain of Pakistan.

ATHEY, Charles William Jeffrey, b Middlesbrough 27 Sep 57. RHB, occ OB. YORKSHIRE – uncapped. F-c career: 70 matches; 2,337 runs (av 22.91), 3 hundreds; 14 wkts (av 43.00); 65 ct, 2 st. HS 131* v Sussex (Leeds) 1976. BB 3–38 v Surrey (Oval) 1978.

A young batsman in the true Yorkshire tradition, with a sound technique and plenty of strokes.

BAILEY, Michael John, b Cheltenham, Glos 1 Aug 54. LHB, OB. HAMPSHIRE – uncapped. F-c career: 4 matches; 76 runs (av 15.20); 3 wkts (av 50.33); 1 ct. HS 24 and BB 2–65 v Surrey (Portsmouth) 1979.

Left-arm spinner who showed a marked improvement with his new county but had the misfortune to break his thumb when striving to establish himself in the first team.

BAINBRIDGE, Philip, b Stoke-on-Trent, Staffs 16 Apr 58. RHB, RM. GLOUCESTERSHIRE – uncapped. F-c career: 19 matches; 593 runs (av 22.80); 7 wkts (av 42.71); 8 ct. HS 81* v Indians (Bristol) 1979. BB 2–30 v Somerset (Taunton) 1979.

Promising young all-rounder who failed to live up to his performances at the end of 1978.

BAIRSTOW, David Leslie, b Bradford 1 Sep 51. RHB, WK. YORKSHIRE cap 1973. 1 England cap 1979, scoring 68 runs (av 34.00), HS 59, and making 3 dismissals. F-c career: 237 matches; 5,987 runs (av 20.93), 2 hundreds; 5 wkts (av 33.40); 528 ct, 85 st. HS 106 v Glam (Middlesbrough) 1976 and 106 Griqualand West v Natal B (Pietermaritzburg) 1976–77. BB 3–82 Griqualand West v Transvaal B (Johannesburg) 1976–77.

A very good county wicket-keeper with a somewhat unusual hand placement before the ball is bowled. As he showed in the Test match against India, he has a long way to go before he reaches true international class. A useful aggressive batsman, particularly handy when runs are wanted quickly.

BALDERSTONE, John Christopher, b Huddersfield, Yorks 16 Nov 40. RHB, SLA. LEICESTERSHIRE cap 1973. Played for Yorks 1961–69. 2 England caps 1976, scoring 39 runs (av 9.75), HS 35, and taking 1 wkt (av 80.00).

F-c career: 233 matches; 10,193 runs (av 32.25), 14 hundreds; 268 wkts (av 24.94), 1 hat-trick; 116 ct. HS 178* v Notts (Nottingham) 1977. BB 6–25 v Hants (Southampton) 1978.

A sound, consistent county batsman and also a useful, extremely slow left-arm spinner.

BARCLAY, John Robert Troutbeck, b Bonn, West Germany 22 Jan 54. RHB, OB. SUSSEX cap 1976. F-c career: 142 matches, 5,462 runs (av 24.06), 5 hundreds; 162 wkts (av 29.45); 103 ct. HS 112 v Warwicks (Hove) 1977. BB 6–61 v Sri Lankans (Horsham) 1979.

Watchful opening bat with plenty of determination and concentration. Useful off-spinner in all types of cricket, he is not afraid to give the ball some air.

BARLOW, Graham Derek, b Folkestone, Kent 26 Mar 50. LHB, occ RM. MIDDLESEX cap 1976. 3 England caps 1976–77, scoring 17 runs (av 4.25), HS 7*. F-c career: 131 matches; 5,888 runs (av 32.71), 8 hundreds; 1 wkt (av 14.00); 71 ct. HS 160* v Derbys (Lord's) 1976. BB 1–6.

Exciting left-hand strokemaker. Effective and entertaining, he hits the ball hard and is a superb fieldsman in the covers or in the deep.

BARNETT, Kim John, b Stoke-on-Trent, Staffs 17 Jul 60. RHB, LB. DERBYSHIRE – uncapped. F-c career: 23 matches; 752 runs (av 25.06); 4 wkts (av 96.75); 13 ct. HS 96 v Lancs

(Chesterfield) 1979. BB 1–14 v Hants (Basingstoke) 1979.

Promising hard-hitting middle-order batsman and leg-break bowler who toured Australia with Young England.

BIRCH, John Dennis, b Nottingham 18 Jun 55. RHB, RM. NOTTINGHAMSHIRE – uncapped. F-c career: 62 matches; 1,465 runs (av 18.78); 36 wkts (av 49.77); 40 ct. HS 94* v Yorks (Worksop) 1979. BB 6–64 v Hants (Bournemouth) 1975.

All-rounder whose middle-order batting made good progress and he came close to scoring a maiden century. Useful fielder.

BIRKENSHAW, Jack, b Rothwell, Yorks 13 Nov 40. LHB, OB. LEICESTERSHIRE cap 1965. Played for Yorks 1958–60. 5 England caps 1973–74, scoring 148 runs (av 21.14), HS 64 – on début, and taking 13 wkts (av 36.07), BB 5–57. F-c career: 466 matches; 12,203 runs (av 23.55), 4 hundreds; 1,050 wkts (av 26.91), 2 hat-tricks; 300 ct. HS 131 v Surrey (Guildford) 1969. BB 8–94 v Somerset (Taunton) 1972.

A fine all-rounder who is inclined to be underrated and is unlucky not to have had more opportunities for England. Spins his off-breaks considerably and has a deceptive, dipping flight. Relatively more dangerous on a dry, than a wet, turner. Steady, stubborn batsman, always difficult to remove and a

David Bairstow – pugnacious wicket-keeper-batsman ideal for the modern game.

Ian Botham at Lord's. The Indian batsman is Gavaskar, Botham's 100th Test wicket.

good fighter; especially sound against spin bowling.

BOOTH, Peter, b Shipley, Yorks 2 Nov 52. RHB, RFM. LEICESTERSHIRE cap 1976. F-c career: 79 matches; 576 runs (av 11.75); 143 wkts (av 28.02); 25 ct. HS 58* v Lancs (Leicester) 1976. BB 6–93 v Glam (Swansea) 1978.

Lively seamer with a good high action, but short of real pace.

BORE, Michael Kenneth, b Hull 2 June 47. RHB, LM/SLA. NOTTINGHAMSHIRE – uncapped. Played for Yorkshire 1969–78. F-c career: 96 matches; 526 runs (av 7.96); 223 wkts (av 30.27); 32 ct. HS 37* Yorks v Notts (Bradford) 1973. BB 8–89 v Kent (Folkestone) 1979.

Originally a left-arm seamer, he was converted successfully into a fairly flat off-spinner. Had a remarkably good season for his new county, for whom he acquired over 50 wickets.

BORRINGTON, Anthony John, b Derby 8 Dec 48. RHB, occ LB. DERBYSHIRE cap 1977. F-c career: 116 matches; 4,137 runs (av 24.33), 3 hundreds; 57 ct. HS 137 v Yorks (Sheffield) 1978.

Rather limited, but dependable, batsman and fine field.

BOTHAM, Ian Terrence, b Heswall, Cheshire 24 Nov 55. RHB, RM. SOMERSET cap 1976. 21 England caps 1977–79, scoring 1,035 runs (av 38.33) with 4 hundreds, HS 137, and taking 107 wkts (av 19.60), BB 8–34. F-c career: 127 matches; 4,812 runs (av 27.81), 8 hundreds; 471 wkts (av 22.93), 1 hat-trick; 117 ct. HS 167* v Notts (Nottingham) 1976. BB 8–34 England v Pakistan (Lord's) 1978.

Has developed into a world-class all-rounder and an outstanding entertainer. A fine attacking bowler, he can swing the ball either way and keeps a full length, but also possesses a useful bouncer. A hard-hitting batsman with all the shots; especially impressive against pace. A natural competitor and an outstanding fielder, he should be a key member of the England XI for the next decade. His powerful physique enables him to bowl for long spells and play large innings.

BOYCOTT, Geoffrey, b Fitzwilliam 21 Oct 40. RHB, occ RM. YORKSHIRE cap 1963. Captain 1971–78. 84 England caps 1964–79, 4 as captain, scoring 6,316 runs (av 49.34), with 18 hundreds, HS 246*, and taking 7 wkts (av 52.00), BB 3–47. F-c career: 449 matches; 35,761 runs (av 56.94), 115 hundreds; 32 wkts (av 34.81); 181 ct. Only English batsman to average 100 in a home season: 100.12 in 1971, and 102.53 in 1979. HS 261* MCC v WIBC President's XI (Bridgetown) 1973–74. BB 4–14 v Lancs (Leeds) 1979.

A great opening bat with a magnificent technique. Is especially adept at hitting boundaries through the covers off the back foot and is the best acquirer of runs in the country. He made a dramatic and effective return to international cricket in 1977 against the Australians after his self-imposed exile and has retained his place ever since. Sacked as captain of Yorkshire after eight years without the county attaining an honour. Came back from a disastrous tour in Australia to a magnificent summer when he also became known as an occasional purveyor of medium-pace inswing.

BRAIN, Brian Maurice, b Worcester 13 Sep 40. RHB, RFM. GLOUCESTERSHIRE cap 1977. Played for Worcestershire 1966–75 (cap 1966). F-c career: 228 matches; 1,460 runs (av 8.20); 751 wkts (av 23.93); 44 ct. HS 57 v Essex (Cheltenham) 1976. BB 8–55 Worcs v Essex (Worcester) 1975.

This tall, fast-medium bowler has, like good wine, improved with the years. Has always been capable of producing a very good delivery, but used to send down too many loose ones.

BRASSINGTON, Andrew James, b Bagnall, Staffs 9 Aug 54. RHB, WK. GLOUCESTERSHIRE cap 1978. F-c career: 75 matches; 592 runs (av 8.70); 123 ct, 23 st. HS 28 v Glam (Cardiff) 1975.

Considered by many to be the best young 'keeper in the country, but it is a pity he is not more proficient with the bat.

BREAKWELL, Dennis, b Brierley Hill, Staffs 2 Jul 48. LHB, SLA. SOMERSET cap 1976. Played for Northants 1969–72. F-c career: 205

Mike Brearley, captain of Middlesex.

matches; 4,160 runs (av 19.08), 1 hundred; 381 wkts (av 29.54); 77 ct. HS 100* v New Zealanders (Taunton) 1978. BB 8–39 Northants v Kent (Dover) 1970.

Steady left-arm bowler, but not a match-winner. Useful batsman and fine field.

BREARLEY, John Michael, b Harrow 28 Apr 42, RHB, occ WK. MIDDLESEX cap 1964. Captain since 1971. 31 England caps 1976–79, 23 as captain, scoring 1,125 runs (av 22.95), HS 91. F-c career: 383 matches; 20,878 runs (av 36.75), 31 hundreds; 362 ct. 12 st. HS 312* MCC under-25 v N. Zone (Peshawar) 1966–67. BB 1–21.

Has proved himself to be an accomplished opening bat at county level with much determination, but rather limited shots. Uses plenty of right hand, and has an ugly stance with backlift already raised high. His batting in Tests has been largely unproductive. A fine slip fielder. As a quiet, unspectacular leader with considerable charm and good tactical knowledge, he has a fine record as England captain, though the quality of much of the opposition has been sub-standard. Has the confidence of his players and also possesses high business acumen.

BRIERS, Nigel Edwin, b Leicester 15 Jan 55. RHB. LEICESTERSHIRE – uncapped. F-c career: 51 matches; 1,874 runs (av 23.72), 4 hundreds; 1 wkt (av 41.00); 19 ct. HS 119 v Warwicks (Birmingham) 1979. BB 1–22.

Exceptionally promising young batsman with a relaxed, easy style. He played some attractive innings for Leicestershire but failed to make as many runs as had been expected.

BROAD, Christopher **Brian,** b Bristol 29 Sep 57. LHB, RM. GLOUCESTERSHIRE – uncapped. F-c career: 9 matches; 512 runs (av 36.57), 1 hundred; 3 ct. HS 129 v Northants (Bristol) 1979.

Tall, left-handed opening batsman of considerable potential and a more than useful slip fieldsman.

BROWN, David John, b Walsall, Staffs 30 Jan 42. RHB, RFM. WARWICKSHIRE cap 1964. Captain 1975–77. 26 England caps 1965–69, scoring 342 runs (av 11.79), HS 44* and taking 79 wkts (av 28.31), BB 5–42. F-c career: 387 matches; 4,103 runs (av 12.24); 1,161 wkts (av 24.76); 156 ct. HS 79 v Derbys (Birmingham) 1972. BB 8–60 v Middx (Lord's) 1975.

His height and action enable him to extract bounce and he has refused to be dismayed by the setbacks he has experienced through injury. Stubborn tailender who plays straight.

BULPITT, Neville John, b Coventry 15 Apr 57. RHB, RMF. WARWICKSHIRE – uncapped. Played in 3 JPL matches 1979 but has yet to make his first-class début.

Useful all-rounder: medium-pace inswing bowler, middle-order batsman, and fine field.

BUTCHER, Alan Raymond, b Croydon 7 Jan 54, LHB, LM. SURREY cap 1975. 1 England cap 1979, scoring 34 runs (av 17.00). F-c career: 131 matches; 5,237 runs (av 27.27), 8 hundreds; 78 wkts (av 38.15). HS 188 v Sussex (Hove) 1978. BB 6-48 v Hants (Guildford) 1972.

Talented left-handed opener who has taken over Edrich's rôle in the Surrey team. The runs he scored, and the positive way they were obtained, brought about his selection for the final Test v India, when he unfortunately 'froze'. Clearly an accomplished county batsman, but whether he possesses the class to go higher will be seen in the next few summers. An occasional left-arm seamer or spinner.

BUTCHER, Ian Paul, b Farnborough, Kent 1 Jul 62. Younger brother of A. R. Butcher (Surrey and England). RHB. LEICESTERSHIRE – uncapped. Played in 2 JPL matches 1979 but has yet to make his first-class début.

Originally signed as a wicket-keeper-batsman, but his future will probably be as a batsman with a wide range of shots.

BUTCHER, Roland Orlando, b East Point, St Philip, Barbados 14 Oct 53. RHB, occ RM. MIDDLESEX cap 1979. F-c career: 55 matches; 2,212 runs (av 25.13), 2 hundreds; 59 ct. HS 142 v Glos (Bristol) 1978.

Competent and attractive young batsman who hit a good hundred but failed to take advantage, in terms of runs, of his opportunities. Remains a strong prospect, and is an outstanding fielder.

CARRICK, Phillip ('Fergus'), b Armley 16 July 52. RHB, SLA. YORKSHIRE cap 1976. F-c career: 147 matches; 3,178 runs (av 21.76), 2 hundreds; 410 wkts (av 26.97); 81 ct. HS 128* v Glos (Cheltenham) 1979. BB 8-33 v Cambridge U. (Cambridge) 1973.

Orthodox, dependable slow left-arm spinner who has developed into a fine all-rounder. Does not yet win enough matches with the ball for a true Yorkshire left-arm slow bowler. Showed a pleasing approach to run-scoring when promoted up the order towards the end of the season.

CARTER, Robert Michael, b King's Lynn, Norfolk, 25 May 60. RHB, RM. NORTHAMPTONSHIRE – uncapped. F-c career: 12 matches; 102 runs (av 14.57); 8 wkts (av 44.87); 4 ct. HS 26* v Glos (Northampton) 1979. BB 2-12 v Warwicks (Birmingham) 1979.

Typical 'bits and pieces' cricketer who did well as an all-rounder with Young England in Australia. Professional footballer with Norwich City.

CARTWRIGHT, Harold, b Halfway 12 May 51. RHB. DERBYSHIRE cap 1978. F-c career: 82 matches; 2,384 runs (av 21.28), 1 hundred; 31 ct. HS 141* v Warwicks (Chesterfield) 1977.

Hard-hitting batsman and excellent fieldsman in the covers.

CHEATLE, Robert Giles Lenthall, b Paddington, Middx 31 Jul 53. LHB, SLA. SUSSEX – uncapped. F-c career: 40 matches; 276 runs (av 12.54); 77 wkts (av 31.28); 43 ct. HS 49 v Kent (Tunbridge Wells) 1978. BB 6-32 v Yorks (Hove) 1979.

Slow left-arm bowler. An accurate, but not a big spinner, he was given very few opportunities.

CHILDS, John Henry, b Plymouth, Devon 15 Aug 51. LHB, SLA. GLOUCESTERSHIRE cap 1977. F-c career: 80 matches; 145 runs (av 5.57); 202 wkts (av 31.13); 30 ct. HS 12 v Derbys (Ilkeston) 1977. BB 8-34 v Hants (Basingstoke) 1978.

Orthodox left-arm spinner with a nice flight; spins the ball sufficiently. Length and line were not sufficiently stable last summer, so that his wickets tended to be rather too expensive.

CLARKE, Sylvester Theophilus, b Christchurch, Barbados 11 Dec 54. RHB, RFM. SURREY – uncapped. 6 West Indies caps 1977-79, scoring 50 runs (av 8.33), HS 15, and taking 27 wkts (av 31.55), BB 5-126. F-c career: 31 matches; 256 runs (av 9.84); 121 wkts (av 22.32); 16 ct. HS 25 v Hants (Oval) 1979. BB 6-39 Barbados v Trinidad (Bridgetown) 1977-78.

Yet another West Indian fast bowler with real pace. He impressed everyone during his first season with Surrey and would have been an even greater force had he not missed part of the summer through injury.

CLAUGHTON, John Alan, b Leeds, Yorks 17 Sep 56. RHB, SLA. WARWICKSHIRE – uncapped. 39 matches; 1,377 runs (av 20.86), 2 hundreds; 16 ct. HS 130 Oxford U. v Sussex (Oxford) 1978.

Oxford Blue with a first-class honours degree. A sound opening batsman who has made steady progress over the past three seasons, he was prevented from establishing himself in the county XI at the end of last season by a cartilage operation in August.

CLIFFORD, Christopher Craven, b Hovingham, Yorks 5 Jul 42. RHB, OB. WARWICKSHIRE – uncapped. Played 11 matches for Yorkshire 1972. F-c career: 42 matches; 203 runs (av 7.51); 113 wkts (av 35.85); 16 ct. HS 26 v Surrey (Oval) 1979. BB 6-89 v Somerset (Weston-s-Mare) 1978.

An experienced off-break bowler from the Yorkshire Leagues. Bowled more overs and took more wickets than anybody in the Warwickshire side but, as with the remainder of his colleagues, the cost was far too high.

CLIFT, Patrick Bernard (**'Paddy'**), b Salisbury, Rhodesia 14 Jul 53. RHB, RM. LEICESTERSHIRE cap 1976. F-c career: 145 matches; 3,639 runs (av 22.88); 395 wkts (av 24.77), 1 hattrick; 72 ct. HS 88* v Oxford U. (Oxford) 1979. BB 8–17 v MCC (Lord's) 1976.

Good new ball bowler who moves the ball late, especially in to the batsman. A dangerous striker in the lower middle-order.

CLINTON, Grahame Selvey, b Sidcup 5 May 53. LHB, occ RM. SURREY – uncapped. Played for Kent 1974–78. F-c career: 54 matches; 2,224 runs (av 27.80), 2 hundreds; 23 ct. HS 134 v Kent (Oval) 1979. BB 2–8 Kent v Pakistanis (Canterbury) 1978.

A left-handed batsman with an application not unreminiscent of the former Kent opening batsman, Brian Luckhurst. He is increasing his repertoire of strokes and is not worried by fast bowling. His move to Surrey proved most productive.

COCKBAIN, Ian, b Bootle 19 Apr 58. RHB, SLA. LANCASHIRE – uncapped. F-c. career: 1 match; 23 runs (av 23.00); 0 ct. HS 23 v Leics (Manchester) 1979.

An aggressive number 4 or 5 batsman.

COOK, Geoffrey, b Middlesbrough, Yorks 9 Oct 51. RHB. NORTHAMPTONSHIRE cap 1975. F-c career: 196 matches; 8,956 runs (av 28.25), 10 hundreds; 206 ct. HS 155 v Derbys (Northampton) 1978.

Sound batsman with an excellent technique. Again very consistent and has developed into a really fine player; possible opener for England.

COOK, Nicholas Grant Billson, b Leicester 17 Jun 56. RHB, SLA. LEICESTERSHIRE – uncapped. F-c career: 16 matches; 107 runs (av 13.37); 39 wkts (av 24.43); 4 ct. HS 31 v Northants (Leicester) 1978. BB 6–57 v Essex (Leicester) 1979.

A promising slow left-arm bowler who forced his way into the 1st XI despite the presence of two competent left-arm spinners who also bat, which was no mean feat.

COOPER, Howard Pennett, b Bradford 17 Apr 49, LHB, RM. YORKSHIRE – uncapped. F-c career: 94 matches; 1,134 runs (av 14.53); 222 wkts (av 27.46); 58 ct. HS 56 v Notts (Worksop) 1976. BB 8–62 v Glam (Cardiff) 1975.

An accurate seam bowler who gives little away and also has the happy knack of making runs when needed.

COOPER, Kevin Edward, b Hucknall 27 Dec 57. LHB, RM. NOTTINGHAMSHIRE – uncapped. F-c career: 56 matches; 270 runs (av 7.10); 121 wkts (av 29.27); 19 ct. HS 19 v Cambridge U. (Cambridge) 1978. BB 6–32 v Derbys (Derby) 1978.

A lively seam bowler; unable to command a regular place in a county side possessing an international-class opening attack in the South African Rice and New Zealander Hadlee.

COPE, Geoffrey Alan, b Leeds 23 Feb 47. RHB, OB. YORKSHIRE cap 1970. 3 England caps 1977–78, scoring 40 runs (av 13.33), HS 22, and taking 8 wkts (av 34.62), BB 3–102. F-c career: 225 matches; 2,298 runs (av 14.01); 644 wkts (av 23.89), 1 hat-trick; 68 ct. HS 78 v Essex (Middlesbrough) 1977. BB 8–73 v Glos (Bristol) 1975.

Twice in his career he has been stopped from bowling because of a suspect arm action and has twice fought his way back into the Yorkshire team, which shows considerable courage and dedication. Obviously, having to re-adjust on two occasions has affected his performance.

CORDLE, Anthony Elton, b St Michael, Barbados 21 Sep 40. RHB, RFM. GLAMORGAN cap 1967. F-c career: 307 matches; 5,222 runs (av 14.75); 693 wkts (av 27.28); 139 ct. HS 81 v Cambridge U. (Swansea) 1972. BB 9–49 v Leics (Colwyn Bay) 1969.

Fast-medium seamer who is prepared to bowl all day. Uninhibited striker in the late middle-order.

COWDREY, Christopher Stuart, b Farnborough 20 Oct 1957. RHB. KENT cap 1979. F-c career: 54 matches; 1,408 runs (av 25.60), 1 hundred; 6 wkts (av 30.50); 31 ct. HS 101* v Glam (Swansea) 1977. BB 3–40 v Warwicks (Birmingham) 1979.

Young batsman with considerable potential. At present producing useful small scores in limited-overs cricket but not playing major innings in first-class cricket. Magnificent field; useful seamer.

COWLEY, Nigel Geoffrey, b Shaftesbury, Dorset 1 Mar 53. RHB, OB. HAMPSHIRE cap 1978. F-c career: 90 matches; 2,573 runs (av 21.62), 1 hundred; 139 wkts (av 35.68); 40 ct. HS 109* v Somerset (Taunton) 1977. BB 5–44 v Derbys (Basingstoke) 1979.

Off-spinner and useful middle-order batsman. Another 'bits and pieces' cricketer with a bright future.

CUMBES, James, b East Didsbury, Lancs 4 May 44. RHB, RFM. WORCESTERSHIRE cap 1978. Played for Lancs 1963–67 and 1971, and for Surrey 1968–69. F-c career: 129 matches; 361 runs (av 6.94); 315 wkts (av 28.72), 1 hat-trick; 28 ct. HS 25* Surrey v West Indians (Oval) 1969. BB 6–24 v Yorks (Worcester) 1977.

Tall, athletic soccer goalkeeper who bowls at lively fast-medium and can extract bounce from the deadest pitches. Enthusiastic outfielder.

CURTIS, Timothy Stephen, b Chislehurst, Kent 15 Jan 60. RHB, LB. WORCESTERSHIRE – uncapped. F-c career: 1 match; 42 runs (av 21.00); 1 ct. HS 27 v Sri Lankans (Worcester) 1979.

Sound, confident young batsman who scored heavily in schools cricket and is full of promise. Also an occasional leg-spinner.

CURZON, Christopher Colin, b Nottingham 22 Dec 58. RHB, WK. NOTTINGHAMSHIRE – uncapped. F-c career: 7 matches; 62 runs (av 12.40); 5 ct, 2 st. HS 26 v Glos (Cheltenham) 1978.

Reserve wicket-keeper at Trent Bridge. Made a marked advance in his difficult trade.

DANIEL, Wayne Wendell, b St Philip, Barbados 16 Jan 56. RHB, RF. MIDDLESEX cap 1977. 5 West Indies caps 1976, scoring 29 runs (av 9.66), HS 11, and taking 15 wkts (av 25.40), BB 4–53. F-c career: 84 matches: 414 runs (av 9.85); 277 wkts (av 18.72) 18ct. HS 30* v Notts (Lord's) 1978. BB 6–21 West Indians v Yorks (Sheffield) 1976.

Extremely fast, hostile bowler who is quick enough to beat good batsmen by pace alone. Built on the lines of Charlie Griffith, he has power and enormous potential. His control has improved with Middlesex and he is one of the most feared bowlers in the world, though he failed to make the West Indies side in Australia.

DAVIES, Terry, b St Albans, Herts 25 Oct 60. RHB, WK. GLAMORGAN – uncapped. F-c career: 1 match; did not bat.

Extremely promising wicket-keeper currently on MCC staff.

DAVISON, Brian Fettes, b Bulawayo, Rhodesia 21 Dec 46. RHB, RM. LEICESTERSHIRE cap 1971. F-c career: 303 matches; 17,304 runs (av 38.03), 30 hundreds; 81 wkts (av 31.27); 230 ct. HS 189 v Australians (Leicester) 1975. BB 5–52 Rhodesia v Griqualand West (Bulawayo) 1967–68.

Especially aggressive match-winning batsman who hits the ball uncommonly hard. Superbly athletic fieldsman who regularly stops the unstoppable and catches the uncatchable. A dynamic cricketer in every sense.

DENNESS, Michael Henry, b Bellshill, Lanarks 1 Dec 40. RHB. ESSEX cap 1977. Played for Kent 1962–76 (cap 1964, captain 1972–76). 28 England caps 1969–75 (19 as captain), scoring 1,667 runs (av 39.69), with 4 hundreds, HS 188. F-c career: 483 matches; 25,081 runs (av 33.57), 33 hundreds; 2 wkts (av 31.00); 404 ct. HS 195 v Leics (Leicester) 1977. BB 1–7.

Elegant strokemaker with a lovely stance; handsome driver off the front foot. A most attractive player to watch, especially good against spin. A fine fielder who gave Kent great service over the years and has proved a valuable acquisition for Essex, both in terms of playing ability and experience.

DENNING, Peter William, b Chewton Mendip 16 Dec 49. LHB. SOMERSET cap 1973. F-c career: 182 matches; 7,823 runs (av 27.74), 6 hundreds; 1 wkt (av 70.00); 89 ct. HS 122 v Glos (Taunton) 1977. BB 1–4.

Aggressive young lefthander with a sparkling drive; especially good off his front foot and ideally suited to the needs of limited-overs cricket.

DEXTER, ROY Evatt, b Nottingham 13 Apr 55. RHB. NOTTINGHAMSHIRE – uncapped. F-c career: 9 matches; 172 runs (av 14.33); 3 ct. HS 48 v Derbys (Ilkeston) 1977.

Failed to make expected progress in 1979.

DILLEY, Graham Roy, b Dartford 18 May 59. LHB, RFM. KENT – uncapped. F-c career: 26 matches; 304 runs (av 17.88); 57 wkts (av 24.05); 19 ct. HS 81 v Northants (Northampton) 1979. BB 6–66 v Middx (Lord's) 1979.

Outstanding first full season in which his fast bowling proved so effective that he was chosen to tour Australia. Also a promising left-hand batsman and could well develop into an all-rounder. Well built with a high, if slightly open action, he obviously has an outstanding future.

DOWNTON, Paul Rupert, b Farnborough 4 Apr 57. RHB, WK. KENT cap 1979. F-c career: 52 matches; 405 runs (av 10.65); 114 ct, 12 st. HS 31* v Surrey (Maidstone) 1977 – on début.

Took over behind the stumps when Alan Knott joined WSC. Shared the position with Knott last season and naturally suffered by comparison, especially with the bat.

DREDGE, Colin Herbert, b Frome 4 Aug 54. LHB, RM. SOMERSET cap 1978. F-c career: 58 matches; 758 runs (av 16.12); 127 wkts (av 32.09); 24 ct. HS 56* v Yorks (Harrogate) 1977. BB 5–53 v Kent (Taunton) 1978.

Tall seam bowler whose somewhat slingy action enables him to generate rather more pace and lift than batsmen expect.

DUDLESTON, Barry, b Bebington, Cheshire 16 July 45. RHB, SLA, occ WK. LEICESTERSHIRE cap 1969. F-c career: 276 matches; 13,920 runs (av 32.90), 31 hundreds; 35 wkts (av 28.42); 223 ct, 7 st. HS 202 v Derbys (Leicester) 1979. BB 4–6 v Surrey (Leicester) 1972.

Correct, unspectacular batsman with an admirable technique. Remained uninjured and came back to his best form to finish third in the county averages.

EALHAM, Alan George Ernest, b Ashford 30 Aug 44. RHB, occ OB. KENT cap 1970. Captain since 1978. F-c career: 281 matches; 10,007 runs (av 27.41) 6 hundreds; 3 wkts (av 49.00); 168 ct. HS 153 v Worcs (Canterbury) 1979. BB 1–1.

Pressed into service as captain of Kent, this whole-hearted cricketer has done a splendid job. An outstanding fieldsman with the happy knack of taking a vital catch or making a brilliant run-out when most required; a naturally aggressive batsman, especially useful in one-day cricket.

EAST, Raymond Eric, b Manningtree 20 June 47. RHB, SLA. ESSEX cap 1967. F-c career: 323 matches; 5,643 runs (av 17.85), 1 hundred; 823 wkts (av 25.07), 1 hat-trick; 204 ct. HS 113 v Hants (Chelmsford) 1976. BB 8–30 v Notts (Ilford) 1977.

Spins the ball as much, if not more, than any other left-armer in the country. He has good control while his height makes him an extremely nasty proposition on a helpful pitch. At times he suggests he has the basic ability to develop into a genuine all-rounder and is capable of producing an off-drive of classical proportions. A splendid fieldsman, who seldom drops a catch, and a natural, often very funny, comedian.

EDMONDS, Phillippe Henri, b Lusaka, Northern Rhodesia 8 Mar 51. RHB, SLA. MIDDLESEX cap 1974. 18 England caps 1975–79, scoring 277 runs (av 17.31), HS 50, and taking 49 wkts (av 25.53), BB 7–66. F-c career: 203 matches; 4,654 runs (av 19.88), 2 hundreds; 661 wkts (av 24.91); 214 ct. HS 141* v Glam (Lord's) 1979. BB 8–132 v Glos (Lord's) 1977.

Splendid left-arm spinner with a classical action and all the ingredients needed to become an outstanding slow bowler. He retained his place in the national XI throughout the summer but was not chosen for the Australian tour because of Underwood's return. His batting improved considerably and he topped the Middlesex averages. He is clearly one of the best all-rounders in the country; also a superlative fielder.

EMBUREY, John Ernest, b Peckham, Surrey 20 Aug 52. RHB, OB. MIDDLESEX cap 1977. 5 England caps 1978–79, scoring 69 runs (av 9.85), HS 42, and taking 18 wkts (av 19.22), BB 4–46. F-c career: 91 matches: 1,323 runs (av 17.40); 291 wkts (av 23.12); 96 ct. HS 91* v Surrey (Oval) 1979. BB 7–36 v Cambridge U. (Cambridge) 1977.

A fine off-break bowler with a high action. Has the ability to float the ball away from a righthander, sufficient turn, and a teasing flight. Considered by many to be the best off-spinner in the country, and his batting with Middlesex suggested he is moving into the all-rounder category.

FERREIRA, Anthonie Michael (**Anton** or '**Yogi**'), b Pretoria, South Africa 13 Apr 55. RHB, RM. WARWICKSHIRE – uncapped. F-c career: 34 matches; 1,016 runs (av 29.88); 100 wkts (av 28.00); 22 ct. HS 84 Northern Transvaal v Griqualand West (Pretoria) 1978–79. BB 8–38 Northern Transvaal v Transvaal B (Pretoria) 1977–78.

South African who originally came to England with a multi-racial group of cricketers sponsored by Barclays. An accomplished allrounder, he disappointed in his first season with Warwickshire, scoring too few runs and not taking enough wickets. Given a season's experience of English conditions, he should do much better in 1980.

FISHER, Paul Bernard, b Edmonton 19 Dec 54. RHB, WK. MIDDLESEX – uncapped. F-c career: 43 matches; 540 runs (av 8.85); 65 ct, 9 st. HS 42 Oxford U. v Warwicks (Oxford) 1975. Played in one JPL match 1978.

Reserve 'keeper, formerly in the Oxford University XI.

FLETCHER, Christopher David Bryan, b Harrogate, Yorks 10 Dec 57. LHB, RFM. SUSSEX – uncapped. F-c career: 1 match; did not bat; 1 wkt (av 51.00); 0 ct. BB 1–35 v Oxford U. (Pagham) 1979.

Winner of the Sussex fast bowling competition, in which he displayed considerable pace. His advance in 1979 was held up by injury.

FLETCHER, Keith William Robert, b Worcester, Worcs 20 May 44. RHB, occ LB. ESSEX cap 1963. Captain since 1974. 52 England caps 1968–77, scoring 2,975 runs (av 40.20) with 7 hundreds, HS 216, and taking 1 wkt (av 173.00), BB 1–48. F-c career: 522 matches; 28,521 runs (av 38.38), 48 hundreds; 41 wkts (av 40.09); 487 ct. HS 228* v Sussex (Hastings) 1968. BB 5–41 v Middx (Colchester) 1979.

A highly talented player who is equally adept off front and back foot. Has an unusually large repertoire of attacking strokes, but also possesses a sound technique and patience. For a player who is capable of looking so good, he can, when out of touch, appear ordinary. A good, all-purpose fieldsman and an occasional purveyor of rather untrustworthy leg-breaks. Captained Essex quietly and very efficiently to their most successful season ever. Rated by some as the most astute skipper on the county circuit.

FOWLER, Graeme, b Accrington 20 Apr 57. RHB. LANCASHIRE – uncapped. F-c career: 2 matches; 24 runs (av 6.00); 0 ct. HS 20 v Cambridge U. (Cambridge) 1979.

Good young batsman who needs to establish himself in the county XI if he is going to fulfil the early promise demonstrated in 2nd XI cricket.

FRANCIS, David Arthur, b Clydach 29 Nov 53. RHB, occ OB. GLAMORGAN – uncapped. F-c career: 82 matches; 2,589 runs (av 21.57), 1 hundred; 41 ct. HS 110 v Warwicks (Nuneaton) 1977.

He has a pleasing style and hits the ball exceptionally hard. Like many of his colleagues, he found runs hard to come by last season.

FRENCH, Bruce Nicholas, b Warsop 13 Aug 59. RHB, WK. NOTTINGHAMSHIRE – uncapped. F-c career: 62 matches; 677 runs (av 13.54); 103 ct, 16 st. HS 66 v Cambridge U. (Cambridge) 1978.

This diminutive wicket-keeper has become a vital part of the county team and has proved himself to be a very able practitioner of his chosen profession. Young enough to challenge for higher honours.

Gard, Trevor, b West Lambrook 2 Jun 57. RHB, WK. SOMERSET – uncapped. F-c career: 9 matches; 83 runs (av 20.75); 13 ct, 4 st. HS 51* v Indians (Taunton) 1979.

2nd XI wicket-keeper.

GARNER, Joel, b Barbados 16 Dec 52. 6ft 8in (tallest current first-class cricketer). RHB, RFM. SOMERSET cap 1979. 7 West Indies caps 1977–78, scoring 97 runs (av 24.25) and taking 38 wkts (av 23.23), BB 4–48. F-c career: 40 matches; 522 runs (av 18.64); 185 wkts (av 18.30); 23 ct. HS 53 v Yorks (Harrogate) 1979. BB 8–31 v Glam (Cardiff) 1977.

Exceptionally tall, rather awkward-looking West Indian fast bowler who can extract surprising lift from even the most docile of pitches. As a result he is one of the most difficult bowlers to face in the country. His bowling played a major part in the success of Somerset and he was selected to tour Australia with the West Indies. A useful, hard-hitting, uninhibited batsman in the lower order.

GARNHAM, Michael Anthony, b Johannesburg, South Africa 20 Aug 60. RHB, WK. LEICESTERSHIRE – uncapped. Played 3 matches for Gloucestershire 1979. F-c career: 3 matches; 50 runs (av 25.00); 2 ct, 2 st. HS 21 Glos v Northants (Bristol) 1979. Young Wicket-Keeper of the Year 1979.

A most promising young wicket-keeper who could not claim a regular place in the first team because of Brassington. When Brassington was injured he proved himself to be a very adequate deputy. Showed by his initiative in going to Australia, originally without a sponsor, that he is determined to succeed. A name to watch. Should do very well with his new county, Leicestershire.

GATTING, Michael William, b Kingsbury 6 Jun 57. RHB, occ RM. MIDDLESEX cap 1977. 2 England caps 1978, scoring 11 runs (av 3.66),

HS 6. F-c career: 93 matches; 3,555 runs (av 29.62), 2 hundreds; 56 wkts (av 25.69); 80 ct. HS 128 v Derby (Lord's) 1978. BB 5–59 v Leics (Lord's) 1978.

Exciting young batsman with plenty of strokes and a pleasing technique but suffered a bad patch last summer. Also a useful third or fourth seamer and brilliant field.

GIFFORD, Norman, b Ulverston, Lancs 30 Mar 40. LHB, SLA. WORCESTERSHIRE cap 1961. Captain since 1971. 15 England caps 1964–73, scoring 179 runs (av 16.27), HS 25*, and taking 33 wkts (av 31.09), BB 5–55. F-c career: 510 matches; 5,511 runs (av 13.15); 1,565 wkts (av 21.68), 1 hat-trick; 255 ct. HS 89 v Oxford U. (Oxford) 1963. BB 8–28 v Yorks (Sheffield) 1968.

Fine left-arm spinner who is a natural match-winner in the right circumstances. He tends to bowl from wide of the stumps and has a rather flat trajectory, with the result that he is not easy to hit. He never gives anything away and spins the ball rather more than most. A determined tailender, he has often held up the opposition with his essentially practical approach. A shrewd, thoughtful captain.

GOOCH, Graham Alan, b Leytonstone 23 Jul 53. RHB, RM. ESSEX cap 1975. 17 England caps 1975–79, scoring 754 runs (av 30.16), HS 91*, and taking 1 wkt (av 93.00), BB 1–16. F-c career: 135 matches; 6,518 runs (av 32.42), 9 hundreds; 30 wkts (av 43.86); 113 ct. HS 136 v Worcs (Westcliff-on-Sea) 1976. BB 5–40 v West Indians (Chelmsford) 1976.

Powerfully-built batsman, particularly strong off his back foot. Found opening the innings much to his taste with Essex but normally goes in at three or four for England. Has plenty of time to make his shots but sometimes has problems against pace because of a tendency to play slightly across the line. At present an outstanding county cricketer who seems destined to become a true international-class batsman. Bowls medium-pace away-swingers and is an excellent imitator of the actions of many bowlers. Fine catcher close to the wicket; safe in the outfield with a powerful throw.

GOULD, Ian James, b Slough, Bucks 19 Aug 57. LHB, WK. MIDDLESEX cap 1977. F-c career: 74 matches; 1,653 runs (av 19.22), 1 hundred; 130 ct, 20 st. HS 128 v Worcs (Worcester) 1978.

A useful wicket-keeper-batsman, he failed to make the expected improvement in either department but could well come good in 1980.

GOWER, David Ivon, b Tunbridge Wells, Kent 1 Apr 57. LHB, occ OB. LEICESTERSHIRE cap 1977. 16 England caps 1978–79, scoring 1,147 runs (av 52.13), with 3 hundreds, HS 200*. F-c career: 87 matches; 3,887 runs (av 32.66), 6 hundreds; 3 wkts (av 20.33); 35 ct. HS

200* England v India (Birmingham) 1979. BB
3–47 v Essex (Leicester) 1977.

The most exciting English-born batsman to
appear in international cricket for more than a
decade. A graceful lefthander, he strokes the
ball elegantly with the full flow of the bat.
Plays straight and possesses an excellent
temperament, but it is to be hoped that he
ignores those who will advise him to cut out
'this and that' shot because of the element of
risk. Better that he remembers the glittering list
of West Indian batsmen who have gone on
playing their attacking strokes, an approach
which not only produces enjoyment but also a
vast number of runs. Fine cover who moves
fast without appearing to do so.

GRAVENEY, David Anthony, b Bristol 2 Jan
53. Son of J. K. R. Graveney, former Glos
captain. RHB, SLA. GLOUCESTERSHIRE cap
1976. F-c career: 153 matches; 2,801 runs (av
16.97); 356 wkts (av 29.34); 69 ct. HS 92 v
Warwicks (Birmingham) 1978. BB 8–85 v
Notts (Cheltenham) 1974.

Tall, orthodox left-arm slow bowler. His
batting fell away a little, raising doubts
whether he qualifies as an all-rounder.

GRAVES, Peter John, b Hove 19 May 46.
LHB, occ SLA. SUSSEX cap 1969. F-c career:
288 matches; 11,870 runs (av 26.73), 14
hundreds; 15 wkts (av 53.13); 222 ct. HS 145* v
Glos (Gloucester) 1974. BB 3–69 Orange Free
State v Australians (Bloemfontein) 1969–70.

A naturally aggressive lefthander who has
always been good against pace. Has never
scored quite as many runs as expected.

GREENIDGE, Cuthbert Gordon, b St Peter,
Barbados 1 May 51. RHB, occ RM. HAMPSHIRE
cap 1972. 19 West Indies caps 1974–78 scoring
1,641 runs (av 48.26) with 5 hundreds, HS 134.
F-c career: 235 matches; 16,594 runs (av
43.10), 38 hundreds; 16 wkts (av 26.93); 254 ct.
HS 273* D. H. Robins' XI v Pakistanis
(Eastbourne) 1974. BB 5–49 v Surrey (Southampton) 1971. Holds record for highest
individual score in limited-overs matches (177
in Gillette Cup 1975) and the record scores in
all three one-day county competitions.

A world-class opening batsman who plays
the ball very late. His defensive technique is
good and among a wide range of spectacular
strokes his cutting is perhaps the most exciting.
He is a true match-winner, capable of taking
any attack apart. Gathers his runs at a great
pace and with much charm.

GRIFFITHS, Brian James, b Wellingborough
13 Jun 49. RHB, RM. NORTHAMPTONSHIRE cap
1978. F-c career: 50 matches; 76 runs (av 3.30);
131 wkts (av 29.24); 11 ct. HS 11 v Middx
(Lord's) 1978. BB 5–66 v Surrey (Northampton) 1978. Holds world record for most (10)
scoreless innings in succession in f-c matches.

Has proved himself to be a better bowler
than one might expect from seeing him for the
first time. Had another fine season for
Northants, although missing several matches
through injury.

Graham Gooch in punishing mood at Lord's.

GURR, David Roberts, b Whitchurch, Bucks 27 Mar 56. RHB, RFM. SOMERSET – uncapped. F-c career: 41 matches; 410 runs (av 16.40); 110 wkts (av 27.99); 9 ct. HS 46* Oxford U. v Cambridge U. (Lord's) 1977. BB 6–82 Oxford U. v Warwicks (Birmingham) 1976.

Young fast bowler with a high, rather open action. He looked so promising when he was at Oxford but appears to have lost confidence.

HACKER, Peter John, b Nottingham 16 Jul 52. RHB, LM. NOTTINGHAMSHIRE – uncapped. F-c career: 37 matches; 323 runs (av 10.76); 51 wkts (av 47.86); 8 ct. HS 35 v Kent (Canterbury) 1977. BB 4–46 v Glos (Nottingham) 1979.

Left-arm seam bowler who needs more control. At the moment he is proving rather expensive.

HADLEE, Richard John, b Christchurch, New Zealand, 3 Jul 51. Fourth (youngest) son of former New Zealand captain, W. A. Hadlee, and brother of D. R. and B. G. LHB, RFM. NOTTINGHAMSHIRE cap 1978. 26 New Zealand caps 1973–79, scoring 844 runs (av 20.09), HS 87, and taking 107 wkts (av 30.14), BB 7–23. F-c career: 106 matches; 2,562 runs (av 21.52), 1 hundred; 420 wkts (av 22.24), 1 hat-trick; 44 ct. HS 101* v Derbys (Nottingham) 1978. BB 7–23 New Zealand v India (Wellington) 1975–76, and 7–23 v Sussex (Nottingham) 1979.

World-class fast bowler with fine action, pace, and stamina. Tends to make the ball leave the righthander and brings the odd one back off the seam. Won a number of matches for Notts and would have decided more but for injuries. A hard-hitting left-hand bat, distinctly suspect against fast bowling.

HAMPSHIRE, John Harry, b Thurnscoe 10 Feb 41. Brother of A. W. Hampshire. RHB, occ LB. YORKSHIRE cap 1963. Captain since 1979. 8 England caps 1969–75, scoring 403 runs (av 26.86), with 1 hundred – 107 on début. F-c career: 478 matches; 22,742 runs (av 33.54), 34 hundreds; 29 wkts (av 54.65); 376 ct. HS 183* v Sussex (Hove) 1971. BB 7–52 v Glam (Cardiff) 1963.

One of the best batsmen in county cricket, effective and attractive, and one feels he should have become a regular Test player. Might have been a useful leg-spinner. Has a deep knowledge of the game and could lead Yorkshire to an honour in 1980.

HARDIE, Brian Ross, b Stenhousemuir, Stirlingshire 14 Jan 50. RHB. ESSEX cap 1974. Played for Scotland 1970–72. F-c career: 138 matches; 6,605 runs (av 32.53), 9 hundreds; 2 wkts (av 30.00); 131 ct. HS 162 v Warwicks (Birmingham) 1975. BB 2–39 v Glam (Ilford) 1979.

After several seasons as a determined 'sticker' with a limited range of strokes and a rather ugly style, he blossomed forth into a positive and successful batsman. He scored over 1,000 runs for Essex and had the happy knack of coming off when others failed. Surprised everybody, probably even himself, by heading the Essex averages.

HARRIS, Michael John, b St Just-in-Roseland, Cornwall 25 May 44, RHB, LB. NOTTINGHAMSHIRE cap 1967). F-c career: 322 matches; 18,630 runs (av 37.40), 41 hundreds; 79 wkts (av 42.83); 268 ct. 14 st. HS 201* v Glam (Nottingham) 1973. BB 4–16 v Warwicks (Nottingham) 1969.

Solidly built batsman, with a good technique, who can drive off both the front and the back foot. He can keep wicket tidily.

HARTLEY, Stuart Neil, b Shipley 18 Mar 56. RHB, RFM. YORKSHIRE – uncapped. F-c career: 4 matches; 157 runs (av 26.16); 1 ct. HS 53* v Lancs (Leeds) 1979.

Sound young Yorkshire batsman who played a brilliant innings to win last year's Roses match at Headingley. Despite limited opportunities this young Yorkshire League cricketer could well play a major part in a Yorkshire renaissance in 1980. A possible Yorkshire captain of the future.

HASSAN, Basharat (*not 'S.B.'*), b Nairobi, Kenya 24 Mar 44. RHB, occ WK. NOTTINGHAMSHIRE cap 1970. F-c career: 243 matches; 10,565 runs (av 28.86), 13 hundreds; 6 wkts (av 67.83); 212 ct, 1 st. HS 182* v Glos (Nottingham) 1977. BB 3–33 v Lancs (Manchester) 1976.

Must have the ugliest stance in first-class cricket, but he is an unconventional, cross-bat-minded striker capable of changing the whole course of a match with his far-from-textbook methods. A tremendous enthusiast. Useful stop-gap wicket-keeper and fine field.

HAYES, Frank Charles, b Preston 6 Dec 46. RHB. LANCASHIRE cap 1972. Captain since 1978. 9 England caps 1973–76, scoring 244 runs (av 15.25) with 1 hundred (106* on début). F-c career: 212 matches; 10,313 runs (av 36.57), 18 hundreds; 152 ct. HS 187 v Indians (Manchester) 1974.

A player of polish and charm. Will score plenty of runs for Lancashire, but in international cricket he fell into that category of 'almost but not quite there'. The hook has caused his downfall rather too often, and he tends to be a poor starter, which stems from over-nervousness before going to bat. Like so many Lancashire skippers he has so far failed to get the best out of what should be a formidable team.

HEAD, Timothy John, b Hammersmith, Middx 22 Sep 57. RHB, WK. SUSSEX –

uncapped. F-c career: 12 matches; 175 runs (av 19.44); 34 ct, 2 st. HS 31 v Oxford U. (Oxford) 1978.

Reserve wicket-keeper who kept impressively when given the opportunity in the 1st XI. Should prove a good replacement when Long retires.

HEMMINGS, Edward Ernest, b Leamington Spa, Warwicks 20 Feb 49. RHB, RM/OB. NOTTINGHAMSHIRE – uncapped. Played for Warwickshire 1966–78 (cap 1974). F-c career: 200 matches; 4,759 runs (av 21.34); 507 wkts (av 31.49), 1 hat-trick; 96 ct. HS 85 Warwicks v Essex (Birmingham) 1977. BB 7–33 Warwicks v Cambridge U. (Cambridge) 1975.

A rather flat off-break bowler, somewhat lacking in penetration on good pitches. He proved a considerable asset to his new county, being their leading wicket-taker in Championship matches. Also proving an above-average tailender.

HEMSLEY, Edward John Orton, b Norton, Staffs 1 Sep 43. RHB, RM. WORCESTERSHIRE cap 1969. F-c career: 189 matches; 7,979 runs (av 30.57), 8 hundreds; 68 wkts (av 33.89); 147 ct. HS 176* v Lancs (Worcester) 1977. BB 3–5 v Warwicks (Worcester) 1971.

A well-above-average middle-order batsman who, since his retirement from football, has proved himself a valuable asset to Worcestershire.

HENDERSON, Stephen Peter, b Oxford, Oxon 24 Sep 58. LHB, RM. WORCESTERSHIRE – uncapped. F-c career: 12 matches; 237 runs (av 14.81); 6 ct. HS 52 v Northants (Worcester) 1977.

Competent batsman yet to make the grade in first-class cricket.

HENDRICK, Michael, b Darley Dale 22 Oct 48. RHB, RFM. DERBYSHIRE cap 1972. 25 England caps 1974–79, scoring 98 runs (av 5.15), HS 15, and taking 78 wkts (av 22.64), BB 4–28. F-c career: 202 matches; 1,209 runs (av 9.90); 575 wkts (av 20.78); 132 ct. HS 46 v Essex (Chelmsford) 1973. BB 8–45 v Warwicks (Chesterfield) 1973.

Seamer in the true Derbyshire tradition. Tends to move the ball away from the bat and brings the odd one back off the seam. Tall and accurate with a long – dare one say over-long – amble up to the wicket and a high action with plenty of body. Tidy and accurate, he is now considered to be the most dangerous seam bowler in the country, but has been disturbingly injury-prone – as was again illustrated when he was forced to return from Australia last winter. Outstanding fielder close to the wicket.

HERBERT, Reuben, b Cape Town, South Africa 1 Dec 57. RHB. ESSEX – uncapped. F-c career: 3 matches; 33 runs (av 6.60), 2 ct. HS 12 v Cambridge U. (Cambridge) 1977.

Apprentice opening bat who has made a marked advance as an off-spinner.

HIGGS, Kenneth, b Sandyford, Staffs 14 Jan 37. LHB, RFM. LEICESTERSHIRE cap 1972. Captain since 1979. Played for Lancs 1958–69 (cap 1959). 15 England caps 1965–68, scoring 185 runs (av 11.56), HS 63, and taking 71 wkts (av 20.74), BB 6–91. F-c career: 505 matches; 3,628 runs (av 11.26); 1,524 wkts (av 23.56), 3 hat-tricks; 309 ct. HS 98 v Northants (Leicester) 1977 – sharing in record Leicestershire tenth wicket partnership of 228 with R. Illingworth. BB 7–19 Lancs v Leics (Manchester) 1965.

Powerfully-built stock seam bowler who formerly did extremely well both for Lancashire and England. From a short run-up, he hits the deck sufficiently hard to jar a batsman's right hand more than many bowlers who are much quicker through the air. Tempted out of early retirement by Leicestershire he has bowled extremely well for them. A lefthanded tailender, he has used his ability to push forward with a straight bat to considerable effect on a number of occasions.

HIGNELL, Alastair James, b Cambridge, Cambs 4 Sep 55. RHB. GLOUCESTERSHIRE cap 1977. F-c career: 98 matches; 4,142 runs (av 26.89), 7 hundreds; 104 ct. HS 149* v Northants (Bristol) 1979.

Former Cambridge double Blue; also England rugby international. Hard-hitting batsman with a rugged approach and a splendid temperament. Not a stylist, he possesses a good eye. Possesses a very safe pair of hands. Could be a future captain.

HILL, Alan, b Buxworth 29 Jun 50. RHB. DERBYSHIRE cap 1976. F-c career: 144 matches; 6,749 runs (av 28.12), 7 hundreds; 5 wkts (av 25.60); 57 ct. HS 160* v Warwicks (Coventry) 1976. BB 3–5 Orange Free State v Northern Transvaal (Pretoria) 1976–77.

A sound, somewhat conventional acquirer of runs. Good defence, short of strokes.

HILLS, Richard William, b Borough Green 8 Jan 51. RHB, RM. KENT cap 1977. F-c career: 74 matches; 913 runs (av 15.74); 145 wkts (av 27.37); 22 ct. HS 45 v Hants (Canterbury) 1975. BB 6–64 v Glos (Folkestone) 1978.

Useful 'bits and pieces' cricketer who was unable to command a regular place in the 1st XI.

HOADLEY, Simon Peter, b Eridge 16 Aug 56. Younger brother of Stephen J. Hoadley (Sussex). RHB, OB. SUSSEX – uncapped. F-c career: 12 matches; 329 runs (av 17.31), 1 hundred; 5 ct. HS 112 v Glam (Swansea) 1978.

A young opener of considerable potential.

HOBBS, Robin Nicholas Stuart, b Chippenham, Wilts 8 May 42. RHB, LB. GLAMORGAN cap 1979. Captain since 1979. Played for Essex 1961–75. 7 England caps 1967–71 scoring 34 runs (av 6.80), HS 15*, and taking 12 wkts (av 40.08), BB 3–25. F-c career: 418 matches; 4,805 runs (av 12.10), 2 hundreds; 1,056 wkts (av 27.09); 287 ct. HS 100 Essex v Glam (Ilford) 1968, and 100 (in 44 minutes) Essex v Australians (Chelmsford) 1975. BB 8–63 Essex v Glam (Swansea) 1966.

Had a disastrous first season as captain of Glamorgan. Personal injury kept him out of action most of the summer, and he was leading an indifferent side. Good, accurate leg-break bowler; dashing, unorthodox and sometimes spectacular bat with a passion for the cut. Brilliant field.

HOGG, William, b Ulverston 12 Jul 55. RHB, RFM. LANCASHIRE – uncapped. F-c career: 30 matches; 102 runs (av 5.10); 73 wkts (av 26.47); 7 ct. HS 19 v Middx (Lord's) 1978. BB 7–84 v Warwicks (Manchester) 1978.

A most impressive young pace bowler who would have been in serious contention for a place in the England party to tour Australia had he not again broken down through injury.

HOLDER, Vanburn Alonza, b Bridgetown, Barbados 8 Oct 45. RHB, RFM. WORCESTERSHIRE cap 1970. 40 West Indies caps 1969–79, scoring 682 runs (av 14.20). HS 42, and taking 109 wkts (av 33.27), BB 6–28. F-c career: 305 matches; 3,481 runs (av 13.08), 1 hundred; 932 wkts (av 24.40); 94 ct. HS 122 Barbados v Trinidad (Bridgetown) 1973–74. BB 7–40 v Glam (Cardiff) 1974.

With his high action, control, and stamina he is an attacking fast bowler who can also be employed for long, economical spells. His pace, except for the odd ball, is a hostile fast-medium, rather than genuinely fast. A competent tail-end bat with a highly individual technique.

HOLMES, Geoffrey Clark, b Newcastle upon Tyne, Northumberland 16 Sep 58. RHB, RM. GLAMORGAN – uncapped. F-c career: 12 matches; 283 runs (av 21.76), 1 hundred; 7 wkts

Willie Hogg of Lancashire – a fast bowling talent frustrated by fitness problems.

(av 34.57); 2 ct. HS 100* v Glos (Bristol) 1979. BB 4–78 v Sri Lankans (Swansea) 1979.

After starting his first-class season in good style with an undefeated 100, this promising young right-hand bat began to struggle for runs like the majority of his colleagues.

HOPKINS, David Charles, b Birmingham 11 Feb 57. RHB, RM. WARWICKSHIRE – uncapped. F-c career: 23 matches; 159 runs (av 7.22); 37 wkts (av 37.05); 7 ct. HS 34* v Essex (Birmingham) 1979. BB 6–67 v Somerset (Taunton) 1979.

Tall (6ft 6½in) seam bowler who, with his height, could become an above-average seamer. Not helped by playing with an unsuccessful team but made a considerable advance.

HOPKINS, John Anthony, b Maesteg 16 Jun 53. RHB, occ WK. GLAMORGAN cap 1977. F-c career: 115 matches; 5,245 runs (av 27.60), 5 hundreds; 84 ct, 1 st. HS 230 v Worcs (Worcester) 1977.

Has developed into a mature and reliable opener, strong off his legs. Again showed consistency.

HOWARTH, Geoffrey Philip, b Auckland, New Zealand 29 Mar 51. RHB, OB. SURREY cap 1974. 17 New Zealand caps 1975–79, scoring 1,040 runs (av 35.86), with 4 hundreds (HS 123), and taking 2 wkts (av 83.50), BB 1–13. F-c career: 190 matches; 10,187 runs (av 32.65), 19 hundreds; 86 wkts (av 30.08); 124 ct. HS 183 v Hants (Oval) 1979. BB 5–32 Auckland v Central Districts (Auckland) 1973–74.

Attractive and forceful batsman who cuts and pulls effectively. It might be said that he really came of age as a class player for New Zealand during 1978, when he at last fulfilled the promise shown when he first joined Surrey. Last summer he topped his county's batting averages and is now a true international cricketer. Fine field and occasional off-spinner.

HUGHES, David Paul, b Newton-le-Willows 13 May 47. RHB, SLA. LANCASHIRE cap 1970. F-c career: 241 matches; 4,263 runs (av 18.37), 1 hundred; 525 wkts (av 29.15); 151 ct. HS 101 v Cambridge U. (Cambridge) 1975. BB 7–24 v Oxford U. (Oxford) 1970.

Left-arm orthodox bowler with excellent line and length. He is invariably tidy, but does not spin the ball viciously enough to reap the benefits of a bad track. However, he has the knack of picking up vital wickets rather in the same way as he so often scores runs when they are most needed.

HUMPAGE, Geoffrey William, b Birmingham 24 Apr 54. RHB, RM, WK. WARWICKSHIRE cap 1976. F-c career: 95 matches; 4,212 runs (av 33.16), 4 hundreds; 189 ct, 14 st. HS 125* v Sussex (Birmingham) 1976.

Dependable performer behind the stumps,

especially against seam, and a very lively, pugnacious batsman. Midway through last summer he was superseded as 'keeper by Maynard, but retained his place as a batsman and as an occasional seam bowler in limited-overs cricket.

HUMPHRIES, David John, b Alveley, Shropshire 6 Aug 53. LHB, WK. WORCESTERSHIRE cap 1978. Played for Leicestershire 1974–76. F-c career: 73 matches; 1,905 runs (av 22.15), 1 hundred; 130 ct, 22 st. HS 111* v Warwicks (Worcester) 1978.

A highly competent county 'keeper who made very few mistakes. A useful performer in the middle order.

IMRAN KHAN NIAZI, b Lahore, Pakistan 25 Nov 52. RHB, RFM. SUSSEX cap 1978. Played for Worcs 1971–76 (cap 1976). 22 Pakistan caps 1971–79, scoring 760 runs (av 23.75), HS 59, and taking 93 wkts (av 32.53), BB 6–63. F-c career: 184 matches; 8,168 runs (av 31.65), 14 hundreds; 622 wkts (av 24.78), 69 ct. HS 170 Oxford U. v Northants (Oxford) 1974. BB 7–52 v Glos (Bristol) 1978.

Outstanding all-rounder. A lively, fast-medium bowler who moves the ball into the righthander and achieves considerable lift and movement. His batting is rich in promise, with a wealth of strokes and the time to play them. A world-class outfielder, he could well become the finest Pakistan all-rounder.

INCHMORE, John Darling, b Ashington, Northumberland 22 Feb 49. RHB, RFM. WORCESTERSHIRE cap 1976. F-c career: 100 matches; 1,337 runs (av 15.19), 1 hundred; 268 wkts (av 26.91); 37 ct. HS 113 v Essex (Worcester) 1974. BB 8–58 v Yorks (Worcester) 1977.

A useful opening bowler who could do with a little more pace.

INGHAM, Peter Geoffrey, b Sheffield 28 Sep 56. RHB, RM. YORKSHIRE – uncapped. F-c career: 2 matches; 32 runs (av 10.66); 0 ct. HS 17 v Warwicks (Sheffield) 1979.

Sound, correct opening batsman who has scored heavily in 2nd XI cricket but has yet to show he can do likewise in the first-class game.

INTIKHAB ALAM KHAN, b Hoshiarpur, India 28 Dec 41. RHB, LB. SURREY cap 1969. 47 Pakistan caps 1959–77, scoring 1,493 runs (av 22.28), 1 hundred, HS 138, and taking 125 wkts (av 35.93), BB 7–52. Also 5 unofficial Tests for Rest of the World 1970, scoring 240 runs (av 34.28) and taking 14 wkts (av 45.50). F-c career: 460 matches; 13,646 runs (av 22.37), 9 hundreds; 1,469 wkts (av 27.96), 1 hat-trick; 225 ct. HS 182 Karachi Blues v PIA 'B' (Karachi) 1970–71. BB 8–54 Pakistanis v Tasmania (Hobart) 1972–73.

Cheerful cricketer and leg-break bowler. An accurate spinner with a teasing flight, he is usually happier on the fast pitches abroad than at The Oval. Unlike some, he does not wilt under pressure and will simply go on bowling. He hits straight with remarkable power and ferocity and is the ideal person to have coming in down the order when quick runs are the order of the day.

JACKMAN, Robin David, b Simla, India 13 Aug 45. RHB, RFM. SURREY cap 1970. F-c career: 325 matches; 4,391 runs (av 16.63); 1,122 wkts (av 23.15), 3 hat-tricks; 149 ct. HS 92* v Kent (Oval) 1974. BB 8–40 Rhodesia v Natal (Durban) 1972–73.

An ideal county all-rounder especially well suited to the particular needs of limited-overs cricket. An accurate fast-medium bowler who generally moves the ball about; a determined bat who likes to go for his shots, several of which are unconventional and would not be found in any coaching manual; a first-rate field.

JARVIS, Kevin Bertram Sidney, b Dartford 23 Apr 53. RHB, RFM. KENT cap 1977. F-c career: 97 matches; 118 runs (av 3.47); 253 wkts (av 28.19); 27 ct. HS 12* v Cambridge U. (Canterbury) 1977. BB 8–97 v Worcs (Worcester) 1978.

A tall young fast bowler of promise, but he must learn greater control. His line and length frequently left much to be desired.

JAVED MIANDAD KHAN, b Karachi, Pakistan 12 Jun 57. RHB, LB. GLAMORGAN – uncapped. Played for Sussex 1976–79 (cap 1977). 21 Pakistan caps 1976–79, scoring 1,831 runs (av 70.42), with 6 hundreds (including 163 on début), HS 206, and taking 17 wkts (av 32.70), BB 3–74. F-c career: 140 matches; 9,195 runs (av 46.91); 25 hundreds; 153 wkts (av 31.75); 152 ct, 2 st. HS 311 Karachi Whites v National Bank (Karachi) 1974–75. BB 6–93 Sind v Railways (Lahore) 1974–75.

A most accomplished young Pakistan batsman who was hardly able to play for Sussex owing to the restriction on overseas players. Has joined Glamorgan and should make over 1,000 runs for them this season. Also an extremely useful leg-break bowler and close fielder.

JENNINGS, Keith Francis, b Wellington 5 Oct 53. RHB, RM. SOMERSET cap 1978. F-c career: 55 matches; 413 runs (av 9.83); 78 wkts (av 34.79); 33 ct. HS 49 v West Indians (Taunton) 1976. BB 5–18 v Sussex (Hove) 1978.

Typical medium-paced English seamer with an unusual and rather unattractive action.

JESTY, Trevor Edward, b Gosport 2 Jun 48. RHB, RM. HAMPSHIRE cap 1971. F-c career: 247 matches; 9,760 runs (av 28.37), 12 hundreds; 371 wkts (av 28.51); 149 ct, 1 st. HS 159* v Somerset (Bournemouth) 1976. BB 7–75 v Worcs (Southampton) 1976.

Hard-hitting batsman with a most attractive style; has the ability to drive off both front and back foot. With his medium-pace bowling he moves the ball away in the air, and is also a splendid fieldsman.

JOHNSON, Colin, b Pocklington 5 Sep 47. RHB, OB. YORKSHIRE – uncapped. F-c career: 100 matches; 2,960 runs (av 21.44), 2 hundreds; 4 wkts (av 66.25); 49 ct. HS 107 v Somerset (Sheffield) 1973. BB 2–22 v Oxford U. (Oxford) 1971.

Useful middle-order batsman and brilliant field.

JOHNSON, Graham William, b Beckenham 8 Nov 46. RHB, OB. KENT cap 1970. F-c career: 256 matches; 9,612 runs (av 25.56), 10 hundreds; 340 wkts (av 31.45); 205 ct. HS 168 v Surrey (Oval) 1976. BB 6–32 v Surrey (Tunbridge Wells) 1978.

A good county all-rounder who has never made as many runs or taken as many wickets as expected.

JONES, Alan, b Swansea 4 Nov 38. LHB, occ OB. GLAMORGAN cap 1962. Captain 1976–78. Played one unofficial Test v Rest of the World 1970. F-c career: 554 matches; 30,914 runs (av 32.64), 48 hundreds; 3 wkts (av 109.66); 269 ct. HS 187* v Somerset (Glastonbury) 1963. BB 1–24.

Neat, competent opening bat who has given fine service to Glamorgan over the years. His consistency is shown by the fact that in 1979 he passed 1,000 runs for the 19th consecutive season. Many lesser players have represented England in official Tests.

JONES, Alan Lewis, b Alltwen 1 Jun 57. LHB. GLAMORGAN – uncapped. F-c career: 47 matches; 1,485 runs (av 19.03); 20 ct. HS 83 v Worcs (Worcester) 1979.

Like many Glamorgan batsmen he has been unable to translate obvious promise into runs in the quantity required.

JONES, Barry John Richardson, b Shrewsbury, Shropshire 2 Nov 55. LHB, occ RM. WORCESTERSHIRE – uncapped. F-c career: 36 matches; 849 runs (av 13.91); 19 ct. HS 65 v Warwicks (Birmingham) 1977.

Left-handed opener who had few opportunities.

JONES, Eifion Wyn, b Velindre 25 Jun 42. Brother of A. Jones. RHB, WK. GLAMORGAN cap 1967. F-c career: 330 matches; 7,120 runs (av 18.35), 3 hundreds; 690 ct, 76 st. HS 146* v Sussex (Hove) 1968.

Has never really received full recognition for his wicket-keeping, which has been of a

Eifion Jones – sound performances behind the stumps for Glamorgan and a century in 1979.

consistently high standard for many years. A useful person to have in the lower order, especially during a crisis.

KALLICHARRAN, Alvin Isaac, b Port Mourant, Berbice, B.G. 21 Mar 49. LHB, occ LB. WARWICKSHIRE cap 1972. 51 West Indies caps 1971–79 (9 as captain), scoring 3,869 runs (av 49.60), with 11 hundreds, including two in his first two innings, HS 187, and taking 1 wkt (av 82.00), BB 1–7. F-c career: 267 matches; 17,150 runs (av 43.30), 40 hundreds; 28 wkts (av 52.71); 185 ct. HS 197 Guyana v Jamaica (Kingston) 1973–74. BB 4–48 v Derbys (Birmingham) 1978.

A sparkling strokemaker from the Caribbean, he rather resembles a left-handed Kanhai. Relying largely on timing and wristwork for the power in his strokes, he can nevertheless be very quick on his feet against spin and when hooking the bouncer. Was appointed captain of West Indies to India when they went there minus their WSC players.

KEMP, Nicholas John, b Bromley 16 Dec 56. RHB, RFM. KENT – uncapped. F-c career: 7 matches; 36 runs (av 6.00); 5 wkts (av 48.20); 1 ct. HS 14 v Lancs (Tunbridge Wells) 1977. BB 3–83 v Pakistanis (Canterbury) 1978.

Lively opening bowler from Tonbridge school; also an attractive batsman in the lower middle order.

KENNEDY, Andrew, b Blackburn 4 Nov 49. LHB, RM. LANCASHIRE cap 1975. F-c career: 95 matches; 3,818 runs (av 28.28), 4 hundreds; 2 wkts (av 29.50); 61 ct. HS 176* v Leics (Leicester) 1976. BB 2–29 v Cambridge U. (Cambridge) 1978.

A left-handed batsman who appears to have a good technique but has suffered from a number of bad patches, which suggests doubts about his temperament.

KIRSTEN, Peter Noel, b Pietermaritzburg, South Africa 14 May 55. RHB, OB. DERBYSHIRE cap 1978. F-c career: 94 matches; 5,957

runs (av 38.93), 16 hundreds; 42 wkts (av 37.38); 65 ct. HS 206* v Glam (Chesterfield) 1978. BB 4–44 v Middx (Derby) 1979.

Yet another fine South African cricketer: scored over 1,000 runs for his adopted county and also picked up some useful wickets. Like all his fellow countrymen he hits the ball sweetly and is difficult to contain because he has the ability to punish the good, as distinct from the bad, ball. Fine field.

KNIGHT, Roger David Verdon, b Streatham, Surrey 6 Sep 46. LHB, RM. SURREY cap 1978. Captain since 1978. Played for Surrey 1968–70, for Gloucestershire 1971–75 (cap 1971), and for Sussex 1976–77 (cap 1976). F-c career: 268 matches; 13,612 runs (av 31.22), 21 hundreds;

Roger knight, captain of Surrey.

260 wkts (av 35.54); 199 ct. HS 165* Sussex v Middx (Hove) 1976. BB 6–44 Glos v Northants (Northampton) 1974.

A fine all-round cricketer: strong front-foot driver and a useful seam bowler who tends to move the ball into the bat. He led the revitalised Surrey with enthusiasm and considerable success.

KNOTT, Alan Philip Eric, b Belvedere 9 Apr 46. RHB, WK. KENT cap 1965. 89 England caps 1967–77, scoring 4,175 runs (av 33.66), with 5 hundreds, HS 135, and making 252 dismissals – world Test record (233 ct, 19 st). F-c career: 389 matches; 14,243 runs (av 30.49), 16 hundreds; 1 wkt (av 77.00); 943 ct, 105 st. HS 156 MCC v South Zone (Bangalore) 1972–73. BB 1–40.

Follows the tradition of those great Kent wicket-keepers of the past, Leslie Ames and Godfrey Evans. Exceptionally agile and nimble, he has already established himself as one of the great wicket-keepers of all time. His remarkable powers of concentration enable him to be as brilliant in the closing session of a long day as at the start. In addition to his value as a wicket-keeper, he is also a highly proficient, and on occasions dashing, batsman who has many outstanding innings to his credit when runs were really wanted for both Kent and England. Knott is the equivalent of another top-class all-rounder, for he is certainly worth his place in any county side for his batting alone. Did not play for Kent in 1978 because of his contract with WSC and played only half the matches last summer, which was Kent's loss.

LAMB, Allan Joseph, b Langebaanweg, Cape Town, South Africa 20 Jun 54. RHB, occ RM. NORTHAMPTONSHIRE cap 1978. F-c career: 74 matches; 4,666 runs (av 46.19), 10 hundreds; 3 wkts (av 9.33); 57 ct. HS 178 v Leics (Leicester) 1979. BB 1–1 v Derbys (Derby) 1978.

Brilliant little South African batsman with all the shots and a sound technique. Would walk into the current England team as a batsman because his figures for Northants are far superior to those of Larkins and Willey.

LAMB, Hon Timothy Michael, b Hartford, Cheshire 24 Mar 53. RHB, RM. NORTHAMPTONSHIRE cap 1978. Played for Middlesex 1974–77. F-c career: 90 matches; 833 runs (av 12.62); 195 wkts (av 29.57); 23 ct. HS 77 Middx v Notts (Lord's) 1976. BB 6–49 Middx v Surrey (Lord's) 1975.

Former Oxford Blue who, after several seasons with Middlesex, joined Northants for whom he has done well. Great trier but lacks that extra yard or so of pace.

LARKINS, Wayne, b Roston, Beds 22 Nov 53. RHB, occ RM. NORTHAMPTONSHIRE cap 1976. F-c career: 119 matches; 4,922 runs (av 27.19),

11 hundreds; 19 wkts (av 35.31); 63 ct. HS 170* v Worcs (Northampton) 1978. BB 3–34 v Somerset (Northampton) 1976.

A natural strokemaker with a wide range of strokes. He had his best ever season for Northants and was rewarded by being selected to tour Australia. His ability to score quickly is especially useful in limited-overs cricket and in the first innings of county matches, when he frequently provided his county with a large and fast start.

LEE, Peter Granville, b Arthingworth, Northants 27 Aug 45. RHB, RFM. LANCASHIRE cap 1972. Played for Northants 1967–71. F-c career: 179 matches; 715 runs (av 8.61); 554 wkts (av 25.10); 28 ct. HS 26 Northants v Glos (Northampton) 1969. BB 8–53 v Sussex (Hove) 1973.

A very good fast-medium bowler who has twice taken over 100 wickets in a season. Has been troubled by injury and has yet to rediscover his best form.

LE ROUX, Garth Stirling, b Cape Town, South Africa 4 Sep 55. RHB, RF. SUSSEX uncapped. F-c career: 29 matches; 331 runs (av 17.42); 133 wkts (av 20.73); 16 ct. HS 47* Western Province v Transvaal (Cape Town) 1977–78. BB 7–40 Western Province v Eastern Province (Port Elizabeth) 1977–78.

Big, strong, handsome pace bowler who is genuinely fast and obtains an unpleasant amount of lift. Among the quickest in the world, as he showed with WSC in Australia. He is likely to win several matches for his adopted county and should prove a great favourite with Sussex crowds. A decidedly useful striker of the ball in the lower order.

Alan Lilley of Essex.

John Lever of Essex – first bowler to take 100 wickets in 1979.

LEVER, John Kenneth, b Ilford 24 Feb 49. RHB, LFM. ESSEX cap 1970. 15 England caps 1976–79, scoring 229 runs (av 12.72), HS 53 – on début, and taking 51 wkts (av 23.60), BB 7–46 – on début, the best analysis by an England bowler in his first Test innings. F-c career: 311 matches; 1,996 runs (av 10.73); 950 wkts (av 23.17); 128 ct. HS 91 v Glam (Cardiff) 1970. BB 8–49 v Warwicks (Birmingham) 1979.

A well-above-average left-arm opening bowler who had to wait rather a long time before being capped by England and celebrated the event with the best-ever performance by anyone making a Test début for England. Has a good build, pleasing approach, and a splendid body action, which enables him to move the ball in the air. Was first to 100 wickets and played a major part in the success of Essex. A great trier; top-class outfielder. Elected Player of the Year by the biggest-ever majority.

LILLEY, Alan William, b Ilford 8 May 59. RHB, WK. ESSEX – uncapped. F-c career: 5 matches; 198 runs (av 33.00), 1 hundred; 1 ct.

HS 100* v Notts (Nottingham) 1978 – on début.

A natural with plenty of scoring strokes. He did not get many opportunities with Essex and failed to make as many runs as expected, even in club cricket.

LISTER, John Wilton, b Darlington, Co. Durham 1 Apr 59. RHB, occ RM. DERBYSHIRE – uncapped. F-c career: 5 matches; 205 runs (av 20.50); 1 ct. HS 48 v Warwicks (Birmingham) 1978.

Young opening batsman who has yet to establish himself in first-class cricket.

LLEWELLYN, Michael John, b Clydach 27 Nov 53. LHB, OB. GLAMORGAN cap 1977. F-c career: 113 matches; 3,762 runs (av 23.51), 3 hundreds; 23 wkts (av 26.73); 74 ct. HS 129* v Oxford U. (Oxford) 1977. BB 4–35 v Oxford U. (Oxford) 1970 – on début.

A most attractive lefthander who hits the ball exceptionally hard. He might well score more runs if he was less impetuous, too often giving his wicket away when looking set for a three-figure score.

Clive Lloyd – safe if somewhat short of dignity in avoiding being run out.

LLOYD, Barry John, b Neath 6 Sep 53. RHB, OB. GLAMORGAN – uncapped. F-c career: 74 matches; 796 runs (av 11.37); 107 wkts (av 43.55); 45 ct. HS 45* and BB 4–49 v Hants (Portsmouth) 1973.

Captured only 26 wickets with his off-breaks in more than 370 overs, which is too many, and the cost was too high. Showed improved form with the bat.

LLOYD, Clive Hubert, b Georgetown, British Guyana 31 Aug 44. LHB, RM. LANCASHIRE cap 1969. 65 West Indies caps 1966–78 (29 as captain), scoring 4,594 runs (av 43.75) with 11 hundreds, HS 242*, and taking 10 wkts (av 62.10), BB 2–13. Also 5 unofficial Tests for Rest of the World 1970, scoring 400 runs (av 50.00) with 2 hundreds, and taking 6 wkts (av 20.00). F-c career: 342 matches; 22,401 (av 49.89); 60 hundreds; 114 wkts (av 35.99); 247 ct. HS 242* West Indies v India (Bombay) 1974–75. BB 4–48 v Leics (Manchester) 1970.

Superb West Indian strokemaker who has the ability to win matches with his aggressive batting; is especially valuable in limited-overs cricket. Liable to be diffident at the start of an innings, but once established he invariably takes the initiative away from the bowlers. He is a world-class performer and a natural entertainer, the type of batsman spectators love, because he hits the ball so hard and so often. Useful medium-pace change bowler and one of the most exciting, brilliant fieldsmen the game has produced. Captained West Indies until walking out with the other WSC players after a dispute with the West Indies Board in

the 1977–78 Australian series, but has since been reinstated following the peace with Packer.

LLOYD, David, b Accrington 18 Mar 47. LHB, SLA. LANCASHIRE cap 1968. Captain 1973–77. 9 England caps 1974–75, scoring 552 runs (av 42.46) with 1 hundred, HS 214*. F-c career: 334 matches; 15,442 runs (av 32.44), 28 hundreds; 171 wkts (av 28.47); 292 ct. HS 214* England v India (Birmingham) 1974. BB 7–38 v Glos (Lydney) 1966.

A competent, above-average county player with a sound technique and a pleasing stance. He possesses some attractive strokes, especially off the front foot; is not afraid to use his feet against the spinners; and has an admirable temperament. Also useful slow left-arm spinner.

LLOYD, Timothy **Andrew,** b Oswestry, Shropshire 5 Nov 56. LHB, occ RM. WARWICKSHIRE – uncapped. F-c career: 36 matches; 1,421 runs (av 29.60), 1 hundred; 2 wkts (av 46.00); 33 ct. HS 104 v Notts (Birmingham) 1979. BB 1–14.

Recovered from glandular fever to come into the side in mid-June, when he proceeded to bat most impressively and to suggest that he has the ability to become a very good county batsman.

LLOYDS, Jeremy William, b Penang, Malaya 17 Nov 54. LHB, RM. SOMERSET – uncapped. F-c career: 4 matches; 117 runs (av 16.71); 2 ct. HS 43 v Sussex (Hove) 1979.

Useful all-rounder who spent three years on the MCC staff and has coached for two years in South Africa.

LONG, Arnold, b Cheam 18 Dec 40. LHB, WK. SUSSEX cap 1976. Captain since 1978. Played for Surrey 1960–75 (cap 1962). F-c career: 436 matches; 6,636 runs (av 16.75); 892 ct, 112 st. HS 92 Surrey v Leics (Leicester) 1970. Held 11 catches in match Surrey v Sussex (Hove) 1964 to set world f-c record – equalled by R. W. Marsh for Western Australia in 1975–76.

Chirpy little wicket-keeper whose unspectacular but efficient handling of a vital job did not always receive the praise it deserved. Useful lower-order batsman. Has shown himself to be a more than competent captain of his adopted county.

LOVE, James Derek, b Leeds 22 Apr 55. RHB. YORKSHIRE – uncapped. F-c career: 59 matches; 2,388 runs (av 28.09), 4 hundreds; 35 ct. HS 170* v Worcs (Worcester) 1979.

A good young batsman in the best Yorkshire tradition but failed to score enough runs. This may have been due to a lack of confidence, because there is certainly no lack of ability.

LUMB, Richard Graham, b Doncaster 27 Feb 50. RHB. YORKSHIRE cap 1974. F-c career: 166 matches; 8,088 runs (av 31.71), 16 hundreds; 107 ct. HS 159 v Somerset (Harrogate) 1979.

Sound, competent county batsman who enjoyed his best ever season and was first to 1,000 runs.

LYNCH, Monte Alan, b Georgetown, British Guyana 21 May 58. RHB, occ RM/OB. SURREY – uncapped. F-c career: 26 matches; 774 runs (av 17.59), 1 hundred; 2 wkts (av 29.50); 10 ct. HS 101 v Pakistanis (Oval) 1978. BB 1–14.

Young batsman who has yet to establish himself in the 1st XI.

LYON, John, b St Helens 17 May 51. RHB, WK. LANCASHIRE cap 1975. F-c career: 86 matches; 1,016 runs (av 13.91), 1 hundred; 159 ct, 12 st. HS 123 v Warwicks (Manchester) 1979.

Neat little wicket-keeper who impressed some very good judges with his ability. Also a useful member of the lower order.

McEVOY, Michael Stephen Anthony, b Jorhat, India 25 Jan 56. RHB, RM. ESSEX – uncapped. F-c career: 16 matches; 404 runs (av 16.16); 18 ct. HS 67* v Yorks (Middlesbrough) 1977.

Possesses an exceptionally correct technique but did not make as many runs as expected.

McEWAN, Kenneth Scott, b Bedford, South Africa 16 Jul 52. RHB, occ WK. ESSEX cap 1974. F-c career: 189 matches; 11,305 runs (av 38.32) 27 hundreds; 2 wkts (av 43.50); 193 ct, 7

st. HS 218 v Sussex (Chelmsford) 1977. BB 1–0 (with his second ball in f-c cricket).

Has strokes, class and timing so that he inevitably scores heavily and quickly for his adopted county. Rather oddly, his record with the bat in South African cricket is not all that impressive but in England he is clearly an international class. One of the most exciting bats to watch.

McFARLANE, Leslie, b Portland, Jamaica 19 Aug 52. RHB, RMF. NORTHAMPTONSHIRE – uncapped. F-c career: 8 matches; 0 runs; 13 wkts (av 43.76); 3 ct. BB 3–83 v Glos (Northampton) 1979.

Lively quick bowler who has taken many wickets in local club cricket.

MACK, Andrew James, b Aylsham, Norfolk 14 Jan 56. LHB, LFM. GLAMORGAN – uncapped. Played for Surrey 1976–77. F-c career: 23 matches; 85 runs (av 4.47); 37 wkts (av 41.27); 4 ct. HS 18 v Indians (Swansea) 1979. BB 4–28 v Worcs (Worcester) 1978.

This left-arm, former Surrey bowler did not enjoy as much success for his new county as had been hoped.

MACKINTOSH, Kevin Scott, b Surbiton, Surrey 30 Aug 57. RHB, RM. NOTTINGHAMSHIRE – uncapped. F-c career: 15 matches; 140 runs (av 12.72); 16 wkts (av 44.75); 8 ct. HS 23* v Essex (Nottingham) 1978. BB 4–49 v Surrey (Oval) 1978.

Apprentice all-rounder.

McLELLAN, Alan James, b Ashton-under-Lyne, Lancs 2 Sep 58. RHB, WK. DERBYSHIRE – uncapped. F-c career: 26 matches; 99 runs (av 6.18); 41 ct, 2 st. HS 41 v Hants (Basingstoke) 1979.

Reserve wicket-keeper. Played very competently behind the stumps when Taylor was required for international duty.

MALONE, Michael Francis, b Perth, Western Australia 9 Oct 50. RHB, RMF. LANCASHIRE – uncapped. 1 Australia cap 1977, scoring 46 runs (av 46.00), HS 46, and taking 6 wkts (av 12.83), BB 5–63. F-c career: 33 matches; 406 runs (av 17.65); 143 wkts (av 20.16); 16 ct. HS 46 Australia v England (Oval) 1977. BB 7–88 v Notts (Blackpool) 1979.

Fine Australian swing bowler who moves the ball more, and later, than most. Should cause considerable problems for batsmen on the county circuit this summer.

MALONE, Steven John, b Chelmsford 19 Oct 53. RHB, RFM. HAMPSHIRE – uncapped. Played for Essex 1975–78. F-c career: 2 matches; has not batted; 2 wkts (av 50.50); 0 ct. BB 1–28 Essex v Cambridge U. (Cambridge) 1978.

Lively, but somewhat erratic, pace bowler.

MARKS, Victor James, b Middle Chinnock 25 Jun 55. RHB, OB. SOMERSET cap 1979. F-c career: 90 matches; 3,708 runs (av 28.52), 1 hundred; 176 wkts (av 32.11); 38 ct. HS 105 Oxford U. v Worcs (Oxford) 1976. BB 6–33 v Northants (Taunton) 1979.

Played an important part in Somerset's success last summer. His off-break bowling has improved enormously and he is a very competent batsman with a good temperament. Fine field. Considered by some as a potential England all-rounder.

MARSHALL, Malcolm Denzil, b St Michael, Barbados 18 Apr 58. RHB, RFM. HAMPSHIRE – uncapped. 3 West Indies caps 1978–79, scoring 8 runs (av 2.00), HS 5, and taking 3 wkts (av 88.33), BB 1–44. F-c career: 35 matches; 395 runs (av 9.63); 121 wkts (av 19.49); 20 ct. HS 59 West Indians v West Zone (Baroda) 1978–79. BB 6–42 West Indians v Karnataka (Ahmedabad) 1978–79.

Comparatively slightly built fast bowler whom opposing batsmen have found distinctly sharp. In his first season he proved to be a fine replacement for Roberts and was chosen to tour Australia with West Indies. Still improving, he is a real find for Hampshire.

MAYNARD, Christopher, b Haslemere, Surrey 8 Apr 58. RHB, WK. WARWICKSHIRE – uncapped. F-c career: 15 matches; 327 runs (av 29.72); 31 ct, 1 st. HS 85 v Kent (Birmingham) 1979.

Forced his way into the 1st XI as a wicket-keeper and has shown himself to be a useful batsman in the middle order.

MELLOR, Alan John, b Burton upon Trent, Staffs 4 Jul 59. RHB, SLA. DERBYSHIRE – uncapped. F-c career: 12 matches; 26 runs (av 3.71); 17 wkts (av 36.23); 4 ct. HS 10* v Essex (Southend) 1978. BB 5–52 v Kent (Maidstone) 1978 – on début.

Slow left-arm spinner of promise.

MENDIS, Gehan Dixon, b Colombo, Ceylon 24 Apr 55. RHB, WK. SUSSEX – uncapped. F-c career: 61 matches; 2,617 runs (av 27.54), 4 hundreds; 47 ct, 1 st. HS 128 v Essex (Hove) 1978.

Opening batsman with a series of sound and attractive displays, which suggest he is destined for a long and successful career in county cricket. Possesses a very good pair of hands.

MERRY, William Gerald, b Newbury, Berkshire 8 Aug 55. RHB, RMF. MIDDLESEX – uncapped. F-c career: 8 matches; 7 runs (av 3.50); 10 wkts (av 43.10); 1 ct. HS 4*. BB 3–46 v Kent (Tunbridge Wells) 1979.

Medium-pace seamer who has had Minor County experience with Hertfordshire. A surveyor by profession.

MILLER, Geoffrey, b Chesterfield 8 Sep 52. RHB, OB. DERBYSHIRE cap 1976. Captain since 1979. 23 England caps 1976–79, scoring 784 runs (av 29.03), HS 98*, and taking 42 wkts (av 27.00), BB 5–44. F-c career: 153 matches; 4,961 runs (av 25.57); 399 wkts (av 22.91); 87 ct. HS 98* England v Pakistan (Lahore) 1977–78. BB 7–54 v Sussex (Hove) 1977.

Talented all-rounder: off-spinner; correct batsman with a fine defence; excellent field. In performance terms rather fortunate to have already gained so many caps for England, but is clearly destined for a long and successful career in both international and county cricket. Took over as captain of Derbyshire and has the personality and cricket knowledge to do a good job.

MOSELEY, Hallam Reynold, b Christchurch, Barbados 28 May 48. RHB, RFM. SOMERSET cap 1972. F-c career: 158 matches; 1,203 runs (av 12.15); 433 wkts (av 23.55); 58 ct. HS 67 v Leics (Taunton) 1972. BB 6–34 v Derby (Bath) 1975.

Lively West Indian pace bowler who can be quite sharp. A hard, if somewhat erratic, hitter.

MOULDING, Roger Peter, b Enfield 3 Jan 58. RHB, LB. MIDDLESEX – uncapped. F-c career: 17 matches; 448 runs (av 21.33); 9 ct. HS 77* Oxford U. v Worcs (Worcester) 1978.

A useful batsman who is a product of the Middlesex Young Cricketers XI. Has already won a Blue at Oxford, where he is in his second year, and will be available for the county in the long vacation.

NASH, Malcolm Andrew, b Abergavenny, Monmouths 9 May 45. LHB, LM, SLA. GLAMORGAN cap 1969. F-c career: 274 matches; 6,260 runs (av 18.74), 2 hundreds; 806 wkts (av 25.70); 115 ct. HS 130 v Surrey (Oval) 1976 – in 119 minutes before lunch. BB 9–56 v Hants (Basingstoke) 1975.

The value to Glamorgan of this all-rounder is considerable. In addition to being a disconcerting medium-pace bowler who swings the ball very late, he also bowls cutters at a reduced pace. He is a naturally aggressive left-handed bat with enormous enthusiasm for vast sixes. Just the person to swing a match by a fierce assault.

NEALE, Phillip Anthony, b Scunthorpe, Lincs 5 Jun 54. RHB, occ RM. WORCESTERSHIRE cap 1978. F-c career: 80 matches; 4,101 runs (av 32.80), 7 hundreds; 1 wkt (av 66.00); 39 ct. HS 163* v Notts (Worcester) 1979. BB 1–15.

Another outstanding season by this good and ever-improving batsman, who hit four centuries and is a much better player than is generally appreciated outside Worcestershire. A brilliant cover and natural athlete, as one would expect from a professional footballer.

NEEDHAM, Andrew, b Calow, Derbyshire 23 Mar 57. RHB, OB. SURREY – uncapped. F-c career: 13 matches; 83 runs (av 6.91); 9 wkts (av 49.00); 5 ct. HS 21 v Sussex (Hove) 1978. BB 3–25 v Oxford U. (Oxford) 1977.

Young all-rounder yet to establish himself in the county XI.

NICHOLAS, Mark Charles Jefford, b London 29 Sep 57. RHB, occ RFM. HAMPSHIRE – uncapped. F-c career: 7 matches; 210 runs (av 23.33), 1 hundred; 3 ct. HS 105* v Oxford U. (Oxford) 1979.

Promising young batsman.

NICHOLLS, David, b East Dereham, Norfolk 8 Dec 43. LHB, WK, occ LB. KENT cap 1969. F-c career: 202 matches; 7,072 runs (av 22.23), 2 hundreds; 339 dismissals (326 ct, 13 st); 2 wkts (av 11.50). HS 211 v Derbys (Folkestone) 1963. BB 1–0.

Chunky left-hand bat who hits the ball hard and is at his best opening, for he is particularly partial to seam bowling. Cuts well and is strong off the back foot. Useful reserve wicket-keeper, and 2nd XI coach.

OLD, Christopher Middleton, b Middlesbrough 22 Dec 48. LHB, RFM. YORKSHIRE cap 1969. 41 England caps 1972–78, scoring 751 runs (av 14.72), HS 65, and taking 129 wkts (av 27.86), BB 7–50, F-c career: 262 matches; 5,775 runs (av 21.79), 6 hundreds; 761 wkts (av 21.90); 163 ct. Scored 100 in 37 minutes (second-fastest in all f-c cricket) v Warwicks (Birmingham) 1977. HS 116 v Indians (Bradford) 1974. BB 7–20 v Glos (Middlesbrough) 1969.

Tall fast-medium bowler with a straightforward style who bangs the ball down enthusiastically, moving it away in the air. Can extract life from even the deadest of pitches and has outstanding control. One advantage he enjoys over most of his seam bowling rivals for a place in the England side is that, at county level, he comes into the all-rounder category. Is an impressive driver, but has certain difficulty in negotiating the bouncer. Looks sounder going for his strokes, possibly because he appears fallible when playing defensively on the back foot. Fine fielder. Rather injury prone.

OLDHAM, Stephen, b Sheffield 26 Jul 48. RHB, RM. YORKSHIRE – uncapped. F-c career: 49 matches; 119 runs (av 7.00); 108 wkts (av 28.18); 15 ct. HS 50 v Sussex (Hove) 1979. BB 5–40 v Surrey (Oval) 1978.

A sound, dependable seamer with a League background. Gives little away, utilises a

Steve Oldham – one of a number of useful seam bowlers to be found in Yorkshire.

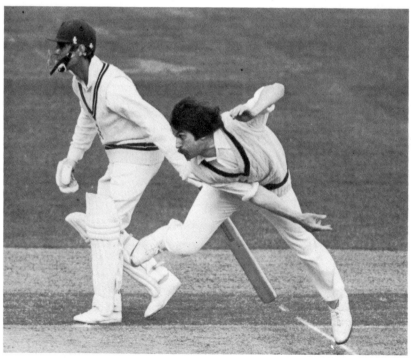

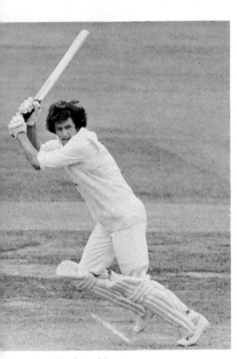

Paul Parker of Sussex.

helpful pitch, but is a shade short of pace for an easy wicket.

OLIVE, Martin, b Watford, Herts 18 Apr 58. RHB, RM. SOMERSET – uncapped. F-c career: 5 matches; 105 runs (av 13.12); 4 ct. HS 39 v Cambridge U. (Bath) 1979.

Young apprentice batsman.

OLIVER, Philip Robert, b West Bromwich, Staffs 9 May 56. RHB, RM. WARWICKSHIRE – uncapped. F-c career: 52 matches; 1,210 runs (av 20.16); 18 wkts (av 89.27); 26 ct. HS 83 v Yorks (Birmingham) 1979. BB 2–28 v Sussex (Birmingham) 1978.

Failed to capitalise on his potential in the three-day game but of value in limited-overs matches.

ONTONG, Rodney Craig, b Johannesburg, South Africa 9 Sep 55. RHB, RFM. GLAMOR-GAN cap 1979. F-c career: 101 matches; 3,903 runs (av 26.19), 6 hundreds; 198 wkts (av 29.75); 44 ct. HS 135* v Warwicks (Birmingham) 1979. BB 7–60 Border v Northern Transvaal (Pretoria) 1975–76.

Hard-hitting, somewhat unconventional batsman; useful lively seam bowler and somewhat erratic off-cutter. A very enthusiastic cricketer and a natural competitor who is proving a considerable asset to Glamorgan.

ORMROD, Joseph **Alan,** b Ramsbottom, Lancs 22 Dec 42. RHB, occ OB. WORCESTER-SHIRE cap 1966. F-c career: 402 matches; 18,230 runs (av 30.48), 24 hundreds; 25 wkts (av 43.56); 352 ct. HS 204* v Kent (Dartford) 1973. BB 5–27 v Glos (Bristol) 1972.

Correct, good-looking batsman with the ability to hit with a straight bat off his back foot. Always appears to have plenty of time to play his shots. A good county player, he enjoyed another successful season.

PARKER, Paul William Giles, b Bulawayo, Rhodesia 15 Jan 56. RHB, RM. SUSSEX cap 1979. F-c career: 83 matches; 4,323 runs (av 34.58), 9 hundreds; 8 wkts (av 52.50); 45 ct. HS 215 Cambridge U. v Essex (Cambridge) 1976 – in his third f-c match. BB 2–23 Cambridge U. v Essex (Cambridge) 1978. Cricket Writers' Club Young Cricketer of the Year 1979.

Neat, correct player with a pleasing style; runs well between the wickets. His temperament is excellent and he is not afraid to use his feet against spin bowling. Magnificent fields-man in the covers and a fine rugby player. A serious candidate for international honours and a possible future captain.

PARSONS, Gordon James, b Slough, Bucks 17 Oct 59. LHB, RFM. LEICESTERSHIRE – uncapped. F-c career: 5 matches; 31 runs (av 6.20); 9 wkts (av 28.55); 0 ct. HS 17 v Worcs (Leicester) 1979. BB 4–43 v Oxford U. (Oxford) 1979.

One for the future. Talented young all-rounder.

PARTRIDGE, Martin David, b Stroud 25 Oct 54. LHB, RM. GLOUCESTERSHIRE – uncapped. F-c career: 35 matches; 916 runs (av 27.75); 30 wkts (av 50.13); 12 ct. HS 90 v Notts (Nottingham) 1979. BB 5–29 v Worcs (Worcester) 1979.

The batting of this young all-rounder improved considerably and he became a 1st XI regular. A useful medium-pace bowler but at the moment lacking real penetration.

PATEL, Dipak Narshibhai, b Nairobi, Kenya 25 Oct 58. RHB, OB. WORCESTERSHIRE cap 1979. F-c career: 75 matches; 2,105 runs (av 21.05), 4 hundreds; 80 wkts (av 36.61); 45 ct. HS 118* v Sri Lankans (Worcester) 1979. BB 5–22 v Sussex (Eastbourne) 1978.

Still young and therefore has the time, as well as the ability, to become an outstanding all-rounder in the next few years. At the moment a vital member of his county team, picking up wickets with his off-breaks and scoring runs, though possibly not quite as many as he should, in the middle order.

PAULINE, Duncan Brian, b Aberdeen, Scot-land 15 Dec 60. RHB, RM. SURREY – uncapped. F-c career: 1 match; did not bat; 1 ct.

Young England batsman with plenty of natural ability, though still rather on-side conscious. Had an average of over 50 in 2nd XI cricket, but will need to tighten up his fielding in the first-class game.

PAYNE, Ian Roger, b Lambeth 9 May 58. RHB, RFM. SURREY – uncapped. F-c career: 12 matches; 96 runs (av 6.85); 3 wkts (av 108.33); 10 ct. HS 29 v Kent (Oval) 1977. BB 2–41 v Cambridge U. (Cambridge) 1978.
Apprentice all-rounder.

PERRY, Neil James, b Sutton, Surrey 27 May 58. RHB, SLA. GLAMORGAN – uncapped. F-c career: 6 matches; 8 runs (av 2.66); 13 wkts (av 43.30); 1 ct. HS 5* and BB 3–51 v Indians (Swansea) 1979.
Useful all-round prospect who might prove to be another of those Surrey let 'get away'.

PERRYMAN, Stephen Peter, b Birmingham 22 Oct 55. RHB, RM. WARWICKSHIRE cap 1977. F-c career: 103 matches; 631 runs (av 10.17); 264 wkts (av 28.36); 36 ct. HS 43 v Somerset (Birmingham) 1977. BB 7–49 v Hants (Bournemouth) 1978.
Good county seam bowler who moves the ball a little either way. Was his county's leading wicket-taker, but the cost was high.

PHILLIP, Norbert, b Bioche, Dominica 12 Jun 48. RHB, RFM. ESSEX cap 1978. 9 West Indies caps 1978–79, scoring 297 runs (av 29.70); HS 47, and taking 26 wkts (av 37.17), BB 4–48. F-c career: 104 matches; 3,440 runs (av 25.67), 1 hundred; 325 wkts (av 23.21); 31 ct. HS 134 v Glos (Gloucester) 1978. BB 6–33 v Pakistanis (Chelmsford) 1978 – on Essex début.
Ideal replacement for Keith Boyce. Another West Indian who bowls fast and hits hard. A match-winner and an entertainer.

PHILLIPSON, Christopher Paul, b Brindaban, India 10 Feb 52. RHB, RM. SUSSEX – uncapped. F-c career: 105 matches; 1,563 runs (av 16.98); 151 wkts (av 33.10); 58 ct. HS 70 v Oxford U. (Oxford) 1978. BB 6–56 v Notts (Hove) 1972.
A 'run of the mill' seamer who has also developed into a useful, somewhat unorthodox batsman in the middle order. His determination compensates for a certain lack of style.

PIGOTT, Anthony Charles Shackleton, b London 4 Jun 58. RHB, RFM. SUSSEX – uncapped. F-c career: 20 matches; 361 runs (av 15.69); 37 wkts (av 33.05), 1 hat-trick; 7 ct. HS 55 v Yorks (Hove) 1979. BB 4–40 v Cambridge U. (Cambridge) 1979.
Sussex are hoping he will develop into a successor to John Snow as a genuine fast bowler. Distinctly sharp and a most exciting prospect. He can also score runs.

Norbert Phillip of Essex.

PILLING, Harry, b Ashton-under-Lyne 23 Feb 43. RHB, occ OB. LANCASHIRE cap 1965. Is the shortest (5ft 3in) current British f-c cricketer. F-c career: 330 matches; 15,199 runs (av 32.40), 25 hundreds; 1 wkt (av 195.00); 88 ct. HS 149* v Glam (Liverpool) 1976. BB 1–42.
Diminutive early-order batsman who, like so many little men, is an extremely effective cutter. Has the ability to improvise, which makes him more valuable in limited-overs cricket than many big hitters.

POCOCK, Nicholas Edward Julian, b Maracaibo, Venezuela 15 Dec 51. RHB, LM. HAMPSHIRE. Captain 1980. F-c career: 27 matches; 838 runs (av 19.95), 1 hundred; 2 wkts (av 49.00); 24 ct. HS 143* v Middx (Portsmouth) 1979. BB 1–4 v Sussex (Bournemouth) 1979.
Scored an impressive hundred against Middlesex to suggest that this coming summer could see him provide some of the runs at present missing from the Hampshire team.

POCOCK, Patrick Ian, b Bangor, Caernarvons 24 Sep 46. RHB, OB. SURREY cap 1967. 17 England caps 1968–76, scoring 165 runs (av 6.60), HS 33, and taking 47 wkts (av 43.04), BB 6–79. F-c career: 410 matches; 4,038 runs (av 11.67); 1,257 wkts (av 25.47), 2 hat-tricks; 140 ct. HS 75* v Notts (Oval) 1968. BB 9–57 v

Glam (Cardiff) 1979. Took 7 wkts in 11 balls (incl. 4 in 4, 5 in 6, and 6 in 9) v Sussex (Eastbourne) 1972.

Fine off-break bowler with a deceptive dipping flight. A thoughtful, attacking bowler who gives the ball a considerable tweak, he is prepared to experiment rather more than the average English off-spinner. A rather awkward-looking tailender, he nonetheless makes some useful scores when he gets his head down.

PONT, Keith Rupert, b Wanstead 16 Jan 53. RHB, occ RM. ESSEX cap 1976. F-c career: 114 matches; 3,670 runs (av 23.67), 5 hundreds; 56 wkts (av 33.51); 62 ct. HS 113 v Warwicks (Birmingham) 1973. BB 4–100 v Middlesex (Southend) 1977.

Useful county all-rounder. A good attacking batsman who has the ability to hit balls off his front foot. Especially valuable in limited-overs cricket. A straight-forward seamer rather lacking in bite on an easy pitch. Fine field.

POPPLEWELL, Nigel Francis Mark, b Chislehurst, Kent, 8 Aug 57. RHB, RM. SOMERSET – uncapped. F-c career: 32 matches; 595 runs (av 18.03) 31 wkts (av 52.35); 7 ct. HS 92 Cambridge U. v Lancs (Cambridge) 1979. BB 3–18 Cambridge U. v Somerset (Bath) 1979.

Typical 'bits and pieces' cricketer whose batting benefited at Cambridge from his promotion up the order.

Mike Procter of Gloucestershire.

PRIDGEON, Alan Paul, b Wall Heath, Staffs 22 Feb 54. RHB, RM. WORCESTERSHIRE – uncapped. F-c career: 76 matches; 277 runs (av 7.10); 140 wkts (av 39.45); 20 ct. HS 32 v Yorks (Middlesbrough) 1978. BB 7–35 v Oxford U. (Oxford) 1976.

A seamer who was unable to find his form of the previous season. Lacks pace and does not do enough with the ball.

PRINGLE, Derek Raymond, b Nairobi, Kenya, 18 Sep 58. Son of Donald Pringle (East Africa). RHB, RM. ESSEX – uncapped. F-c career: 14 matches; 464 runs (av 33.14), 1 hundred; 23 wkts (av 28.69); 8 ct. HS 103* Cambridge U. v Oxford U. (Lord's) 1979. BB 4–43 Cambridge U. v Yorks (Cambridge) 1979.

Tall young all-rounder who did well for Cambridge University and was most unfortunate not to be given any opportunities with Essex. He would clearly have commanded a regular place in the county team.

PROCTER, Michael John, b Durban, South Africa 15 Sep 46. RHB, RF. GLOUCESTERSHIRE cap 1968. Captain since 1977. 7 South African caps 1967–70, scoring 226 runs (av 25.11), HS 48, and taking 41 wkts (av 15.02), BB 6–73. Also 5 unofficial Tests for Rest of the World 1970, scoring 292 runs (av 48.66), HS 62, and taking 15 wkts (av 23.93). F-c career: 339 matches; 19,324 runs (av 37.44), 45 hundreds; 1,231 wkts (av 19.09), 4 hat-tricks; 278 ct. Scored hundreds in six successive innings 1970–71 to equal world record. HS 254 Rhodesia v Western Province (Salisbury) 1970–71. BB 9–71 Rhodesia v Transvaal (Bulawayo) 1972–73.

Still a world-class all-rounder, and appears to have completely recovered from a serious injury which threatened to end his career as a fast bowler. Bowls his very quick inswingers and off-breaks off the wrong foot with a very open-chested action. Just as well no purist coach tried to change him early on! Another wonderful season with both bat and ball shows that he is still one of the finest all-rounders in the world and would walk into most Test teams as either a batsman or a bowler. He captained Gloucestershire splendidly and their lack of success was no reflection on his wholehearted efforts. Twice did the hat-trick last summer, one of them accompanied by a century, and hit the season's fastest hundred.

RADLEY, Clive Thornton, b Hertford, Herts 13 May 44, RHB, occ LB. MIDDLESEX cap 1967. 8 England caps 1978, scoring 481 runs (av 48.10) with 2 hundreds, HS 158. F-c career: 378 matches; 18,304 runs (av 34.53), 30 hundreds; 3 wkts (av 12.33); 383 ct. HS 171 v Cambridge U. (Cambridge) 1976. BB 1–7.

Has always been one of the most consistent run accumulators in the country. Called into international cricket late in his career he continued to score well at this level. Effective, rather than attractive, he uses plenty of right hand, cuts well, and is especially strong off his legs; is suspect against the fast lifting ball. Excellent temperament, natural fighter, and fine field.

RAMAGE, Alan b Guisborough 29 Nov 57. LHB, RFM. YORKSHIRE – uncapped. F-c career: 5 matches; 33 runs (av 16.50); 15 wkts (av 23.20), 0 ct. HS 19 and BB 3 – 24 v Cambridge U. (Cambridge) 1979.

A fine all-round sportsman – he is a professional footballer with Middlesbrough – and a most promising fast bowler. With his height, pace and lift, he could become a class quick bowler if he concentrates on cricket.

RANDALL, Derek William, b Retford 24 Feb 51. RHB, occ RM. NOTTINGHAMSHIRE cap 1973. 25 England caps 1977–79, scoring 1,099 runs (av 29.70), with 2 hundreds. HS 174 in the Centenary Test. F-c career: 198 matches; 10, 714 runs (av 34.33), 16 hundreds; 112 ct. HS 209 v Middx (Nottingham) 1979.

One of the best and most exciting English-born batsmen of the last decade. Although he produced a masterly century in the Centenary Test, it was noticeable that, unlike most of the great players, he was on the move when the ball was about to be delivered; like a cat on hot bricks. This is probably why he has experienced several bad patches. Last summer he found late form with Notts and was rewarded by another tour to Australia, where he has shown a partiality for the faster pitches and the steeper bounce. One of the big attractions of his batting is that he will suddenly produce an impossibly impudent stroke to the surprise of the bowler and the delight of the spectator. But under the clowning there is both a wonderful eye and true ability. His athletic fielding is an enormous asset to any side and it would be no exaggeration to say that he often goes into bat with a bonus of 20 runs to his credit for those saved in the field.

RATCLIFFE, Robert Malcolm, b Accrington 29 Nov 51. RHB, RM. LANCASHIRE cap 1976. F-c career: 78 matches; 984 runs (av 16.67), 1 hundred; 203 wkts (av 25.48); 23 ct. HS 101* v Warwicks (Manchester) 1979. BB 7–58 v Hants (Bournemouth) 1978.

A steady, accurate seamer whose pace is closer to medium than fast. He moves the ball considerably and achieves a surprising amount of lift for his pace.

REIDY, Bernard Wilfrid (*sic*), b Whalley 18 Sep 53. LHB, SLA. LANCASHIRE – uncapped. F-c career: 67 matches; 2,147 runs (av 26.18), 1 hundred; 23 wkts (av 46.60); 33 ct. HS 131* v Derbys (Chesterfield) 1979. BB 5–61 v Worcs (Worcester) 1979.

This former England Young Cricketer showed considerable promise for Lancashire on a number of occasions with both bat and ball and could well replace Hughes in the near future.

RICE, Clive Edward Butler, b Johannesburg, South Africa 23 Jul 49. RHB, RFM. NOTTING-HAMSHIRE cap 1975. Captain since 1979. F-c career: 185 matches; 10,075 runs (av 38.01), 11 hundreds; 461 wkts (av 23.14); 134 ct. HS 246 v Sussex (Hove) 1976. BB 7–62 Transvaal v W. Province (Johannesburg) 1975–76.

Outstanding all-rounder who would walk into any current Test XI. Exciting and prolific scorer of runs. Has all the shots, and there can be few better drivers off the front foot. Lively opening bowler and fine fieldsman. Was appointed captain midway through the season. This year, under his enthusiastic and competitive approach, Notts could well have their best season since the war.

RICE, John Michael, b Chandler's Ford 23 Oct 49. RHB, RM. HAMPSHIRE cap 1975. F-c career: 125 matches; 3,504 runs (av 19.79); 219 wkts (av 31.68); 114 ct. HS 96* v Somerset (Weston-s-Mare) 1975. BB 7–48 v Worcs (Worcester) 1977.

Typical county all-rounder who picks up some useful wickets with his seam bowling and can be relied upon to play some good innings.

RICHARDS, Clifton James (**'Jack'**), b Penzance, Cornwall 10 Aug 58. RHB, WK. SURREY cap 1978. F-c career: 59 matches; 630 runs (av 12.85); 99 ct, 21 st. HS 50 v Notts (Oval) 1978.

Splendid young wicket-keeper who could be destined for top honours. Especially impressive against spin and missed very little.

RICHARDS, Gwyn, b Maesteg 29 Nov 51. RHB, OB. GLAMORGAN cap 1976. F-c career: 107 matches; 3,370 runs (av 22.77), 1 hundred; 48 wkts (av 47.02); 36 ct. HS 102* v Yorks (Middlesbrough) 1976. BB 5–55 v Somerset (Taunton) 1978.

Another Glamorgan batsman who is failing to make the runs he promises. If he could secure more wickets with his off-breaks, he might be able to command a regular place as an all-rounder.

RICHARDS, Isaac Vivian Alexander, b St John's, Antigua 7 Mar 52. RHB, OB. SOMERSET cap 1974. 28 West Indies caps 1974–78, scoring 2,500 runs (av 55.55) with 8 hundreds, HS 291, and taking 4 wkts (av 58.75), BB 2–34. Set world record for most Test runs in a calendar year with 1,710 (av 90.00) in 11 Tests. F-c career 187 matches; 14,108 runs (av 47.34), 38 hundreds; 64 wkts (av 41.04); 174 ct, 1 st. HS 291 West Indies v England (Oval) 1976. BB 3–15 v Surrey (Weston-s-Mare) 1977.

The finest strokemaker in the world. Has

every shot in the book plus several of his own. Equally impressive off front and back foot and against speed and spin. Hits the ball hard and yet possesses a most sound defence. A major innings by Richards is something to treasure and is liable to contain such jewels as a driven six over extra cover from a ball on the leg stump, or a good length fast-medium delivery on the off stump sent scudding to the mid-on boundary off the back foot. Brilliant fielder and useful occasional bowler, seam or off-spin.

Viv Richards of West Indies and Somerset.

ROBINSON, Robert Timothy, b Sutton-in-Ashfield 21 Nov 58. RHB, RM. NOTTINGHAM-SHIRE – uncapped. F-c career: 2 matches; 104 runs (av 34.66); 1 ct. HS 40 v Middx (Nottingham) 1979.
  Apprentice batsman.

ROCK, David John, b Southsea 20 Apr 57. RHB. HAMPSHIRE – uncapped. F-c career: 37 matches; 1,227 runs (av 19.17), 3 hundreds; 19 ct. HS 114 v Leics (Leicester) 1977.
  A local batsman who, after a most encouraging start to his career, has found runs hard to com by. This season might prove to be a make-or-break one for him.

ROEBUCK, Peter Michael, b Oxford, Oxon 6 Mar 56. RHB, LB. SOMERSET cap 1978. F-c career: 92 matches; 4,153 runs (av 32.70), 4 hundreds; 39 wkts (av 45.05); 55 ct. HS 158 Cambridge U. v Oxford U. (Lord's) 1975. BB 6–50 Cambridge U. v Kent (Canterbury) 1977.
  Cultured young batsman, despite a rather ungainly stance. Plays very straight with a pleasing backlift and follow-through; suggests

he would do well overseas. Good temperament and sound defence. Could well be seriously challenging for a place in the England XI in the next few seasons.

ROOPE, Graham Richard James, b Fareham, Hants 12 Jul 46. RHB, RM. SURREY cap 1969. 21 England caps 1973–78, scoring 860 runs (av 30.71), HS 77. F-c career: 344 matches; 16,652 runs (av 37.58), 24 hundreds; 217 wkts (av 37.53); 511 ct, 1st. HS 171 v Yorks (Oval) 1971. BB 5–14 v West Indians (Oval) 1969.
  Fine county batsman who has missed out at the highest level somewhere along the line. He has always been an impressive driver off the front foot and has improved his defensive technique. A typical, rather negative, medium-pace change bowler, more useful in the denial of runs than the gaining of wickets. A top-class fieldsman and superb pair of hands with more than 500 catches to his credit.

ROSE, Brian Charles, b Dartford, Kent 4 June 50. LHB, occ LM. SOMERSET cap 1975. Captain since 1978. 5 England caps 1977–78, scoring 100 runs (av 14.28), HS 27. F-c career: 156 matches; 7,908 runs (av 32.40), 17 hundreds; 6 wkts (av 29.83); 74 ct. HS 205 v Northants (Weston-s-Mare) 1977. BB 3–9 v Glos (Taunton) 1975.
  Good county lefthander who looks a little suspect outside the off stump and round the corner against the new ball. Plays primarily off his front foot and drives handsomely. Led his team with enthusiasm and skill, always setting a splendid example in the field.

Brian Rose, captain of Somerset.

Graham Roope – a solid contribution to Surrey's season, both with the bat and fielding.

ROUSE, Stephen John (**'Mick'**), b Merthyr Tydfil, Glam 20 Jan 49. LHB, LM. WARWICK-SHIRE cap 1974. F-c career: 109 matches; 1,603 runs (av 15.26); 252 wkts (av 28.78); 50 ct. HS 93 v Hants (Bournemouth) 1976. BB 6–34 v Leics (Leicester) 1976.

Useful left-arm seamer who missed most of last summer through injury. A hard-hitting batsman, especially well-suited to the limited-overs game, he should score more runs than he does.

ROWE, Charles James Castell, b Hong Kong 27 Nov 51. RHB, OB. KENT cap 1977. F-c career: 102 matches; 3,545 runs (av 27.48), 4 hundreds; 55 wkts (av 37.81); 33 ct. HS 147* v Sussex (Canterbury) 1979. BB 6–46 v Derbys (Dover) 1976.

Very orthodox county batsman who plays straight. Correct, but rather lacking in flair. A useful off-break bowler but handicapped by lack of opportunities. Splendid field.

RUSSELL, Philip Edgar, b Ilkeston 9 May 44. RHB, RM/OB. DERBYSHIRE cap 1975. F-c career: 167 matches; 2,015 runs (av 12.36); 335 wkts (av 30.17); 124 ct. HS 72 v Glam (Swansea) 1970. BB 7–46 v Yorks (Sheffield) 1976.

Medium-pace bowler who can move the ball rather more than is normally expected and can also deliver a most effective cutter. Now the county's coach.

RUSSOM, Neil, b Finchley, Middx 3 Dec 58. RHB, RM. SOMERSET – uncapped. F-c career: 3 matches (for Cambridge U.); 32 runs (av 16.00); 2 wkts (av 44.00); 0 ct. HS 12 Cambridge U. v Sussex (Cambridge) 1979. BB 1–28.

SADIQ MOHAMMAD, b Junagadh, India 3 May 45. LHB, LB. GLOUCESTERSHIRE cap 1973. 35 Pakistan caps 1969–79, scoring 2,387 runs (av 38.50), with 5 hundreds. HS 166. F-c career: 285 matches; 17,940 runs (av 38.49), 41 hundreds; 200 wkts (av 30.08); 226 ct. Scored four hundreds in successive innings 1976. HS 184* v New Zealanders (Bristol) 1973. BB 7–34 United Bank v Universities (Peshawar) 1978–79.

Diminutive left-handed opening batsman of world-class stature; has always possessed a sound defence, but is now prepared to attack the bowlers when required. Plays a wide range of attractive strokes, including a flashing hook, a delightful pick-up off his toes, and a good cover drive. A useful change spin bowler.

SAINSBURY, Gary Edward, b Wanstead 17 Jan 58. RHB, LMF. ESSEX – uncapped. F-c career: 1 match; did not bat; 1 wkt (av 79.00); 1 ct. BB 1–38 v Northants (Chelmsford) 1979.

Fast bowler whom Essex are hoping will be the eventual replacement for John Lever.

SAM, Alphie, b St Vincent 7 May 53. LHB. WARWICKSHIRE – uncapped. Played in 2 JPL matches 1979 but has yet to make his first-class début.

A West Indian who qualifies for the county by 10 years' residence. A dashing, flashing left-hand batsman, he has made a stack of runs in club and 2nd XI cricket.

SARFRAZ NAWAZ, b Lahore, Pakistan 1 Dec 48. RHB, RFM. NORTHAMPTONSHIRE cap 1975. 34 Pakistan caps 1969–79, scoring 626 runs (av 16.05). HS 53, and taking 120 wkts (av 30.56). BB 9–86. F-c career: 220 matches; 4,311 runs (av 19.07); 802 wkts (av 23.23); 122 ct. HS 86 v Essex (Chelmsford) 1975. BB 9–86 Pakistan v Australia (Melbourne) 1978–79.

A fast bowler with an ugly but powerful and

effective body action. Moves the ball and is capable of producing a genuine bouncer on a placid pitch. Capable of bowling for long spells, but extremely volatile and needs careful handling. A useful striker in the lower order.

SAVAGE, Richard LeQuesne, b London 10 Dec 55. RHB, RM/OB. WARWICKSHIRE – uncapped. F-c career: 44 matches; 196 runs (av 7.25); 127 wkts (av 29.81); 14 ct. HS 22* Oxford U. v Worcs (Oxford) 1977. BB 7–50 v Glam (Nuneaton) 1977.

Intriguing off-spinner of around medium pace who cuts rather than spins the ball. A different and therefore exciting bowler, he might do well, or could just as easily disappear from the first-class scene.

SCHEPENS, Martin, b Barrow upon Soar 12 Aug 55. RHB, LB. LEICESTERSHIRE – uncapped. F-c career: 18 matches; 399 runs (av 19.00); 12 ct. HS 57 v Glam (Leicester) 1979.

Another of Leicestershire's good young prospects. Extremely promising batsman.

SCOTT, Christopher John, b Swinton 16 Sep 59. LHB, WK. LANCASHIRE – uncapped F-c career: 8 matches; 49 runs (av 7.00); 16 ct, 3 st. HS 16 v Cambridge U. (Cambridge) 1979. Youngest player to keep wicket for Lancashire in f-c matches (17 years 251 days).

Highly rated reserve wicket-keeper. He has the ability and the time to develop into an exceptionally good 'keeper.

SELVEY, Michael Walter William, b Chiswick 25 Apr 48. RHB, RFM. MIDDLESEX cap 1973. Played for Surrey 1968–71. 3 England caps 1976–77, scoring 15 runs (av 7.50), HS 5*, and taking 6 wkts (av 57.16); F-c career: 187 matches; 1,175 runs (av 9.95); 582 wkts (av 24.85); 52 ct. HS 45 v Essex (Colchester) 1979. BB 7–20 v Glos (Gloucester) 1976.

Fine opening bowler who swings the ball in the air and maintains a full length. Rather unfortunate that the wealth of seam bowling talent in the country has limited his international chances.

SHANTRY, Brian Keith, b Bristol 26 May 55. LHB, LFM. GLOUCESTERSHIRE – uncapped. F-c career: 3 matches; did not bat; 3 wkts (av 55.66); 0 ct. BB 2–63 v Somerset (Bristol) 1978 – on début.

Left-arm seamer.

SHARP, George, b West Hartlepool, Co Durham 12 Mar 50. RHB, WK. NORTHAMPTONSHIRE cap 1973. F-c career: 192 matches; 3,932 runs (av 18.54); 361 ct, 68 st. HS 85 v Warwicks (Birmingham) 1976.

Probably the most under-rated 'keeper on the circuit. A quiet and efficient performer. A useful batsman.

Mike Selvey of Middlesex.

SHARP,Kevin, b Leeds 6 Apr 59. LHB, OB. YORKSHIRE – uncapped, F-c career: 44 matches; 1,585 runs (av 25.56); 11 ct. HS 91 v Middx (Bradford) 1978.

A potentially outstanding prospect as a free-flowing left-hand batsman, but he had a disastrous first full season with Yorkshire. He seemed to lose confidence, played too much across the line, and was the victim of some poor decisions.

SHEPHERD, JOHN Neil, b St Andrew, Barbados 9 Nov 43. RHB, RM. KENT cap 1967. 5 West Indies caps 1969–71, scoring 77 runs (av 9.62). HS 32, 19 wkts (av 25.21), BB 5–104. F-c career: 317 matches; 10,116 runs (av 25.87), 7 hundreds; 881 wkts (av 26.42); 236 ct. HS 170 v Northants (Folkestone) 1968. BB 8–40 West Indians v Glos (Bristol) 1969.

Fine, natural, all-round cricketer who bowls just above medium pace with a whippy action. Moves the ball a little bit off the seam either way, is accurate, and can keep going for extremely long spells. His batting has probably suffered from his representing a county with so much talent in this department. A brilliant all-purpose fieldsman and just the type of player, and person, any captain would like to have.

SHUTTLEWORTH, Kenneth, b St Helens 13 Nov 44. RHB, RFM. LEICESTERSHIRE cap 1977. Played for Lancashire 1964–76 (cap 1968). 5 England caps 1970–71, scoring 46 runs (av

7.66), HS 21, and taking 12 wkts (av 35.58). BB 5–47. F-c career: 236 matches; 2,583 runs (av 16.77); 622 wkts (av 24.32), 1 hat-trick; 127 ct. HS 71 Lancs v Glos (Cheltenham) 1967. BB 7–41 Lancs v Essex (Leyton) 1968.

At his best, an above-average, destructive fast bowler with an action reminiscent of Fred Trueman's.

SIDEBOTTOM, Arnold, b Barnsley 1 Apr 54. RHB, RM. YORKSHIRE – uncapped. F-c career: 48 matches; 830 runs (av 17.65), 1 hundred; 76 wkts (av 29.86); 15 ct. HS 124 v Glam (Cardiff) 1977. BB 4–47 v Derbys (Chesterfield) 1975.

Like so many in English county cricket he is not quite good enough to rate singly as either a batsman or as a bowler.

SIMMONS, Jack, b Clayton-le-Moors 28 Mar 41. RHB, OB. LANCASHIRE cap 1971. F-c career: 265 matches; 4,962 runs (av 21.76), 3 hundreds; 587 wkts (av 27.07), 1 hat-trick; 205 ct. HS 112 v Sussex (Hove) 1970. BB 7–59 Tasmania v Queensland (Brisbane) 1978–9.

Burly off-spinner with excellent control and a very flat trajectory. He has proved a great success in limited-overs cricket when he fires in full length deliveries at the batsman. Competent batsman who can defend or attack according to the situation.

SLACK, Wilfred Norris, b Troumaca, St Vincent 12 Dec 54. LHB, RM. MIDDLESEX – uncapped. F-c career: 19 matches; 569 runs (av 17.78); 9 ct. HS 66 v Notts (Nottingham) 1979.

Young lefthander yet to establish himself in first-class cricket. Likes to play plenty of strokes.

SLOCOMBE, Philip Anthony, b Weston-s-Mare 6 Sep 54. RHB. SOMERSET cap 1978. F-c career: 98 matches; 4,408 runs (av 29.98), 6 hundreds; 48 ct. HS 132 v Notts (Taunton) 1975. First Somerset player to score 1,000 runs in season of f-c |début.

A batsman inclined towards the front foot and a reliable accumulator who plays straight. Happier in three-day, rather than one-day, cricket. Fine fielder.

SMITH, Christopher Lyall, b Durban, South Africa 15 Oct 58. RHB, occasional OB. HAMPSHIRE – uncapped. Played 1 match for Glamorgan 1979. F-c career: 2 matches; 82 runs (av 27.33); 2 ct. HS 67 Glam v Sri Lankans (Swansea) 1979.

Played for Glamorgan 2nd XI last summer and has been offered a year's contract with Hampshire as a replacement for Greenidge, who will be on tour with the West Indies. Should top 1,000 runs for the county.

SMITH, David Mark, b Balham 9 Jan 56. LHB, RM. SURREY – uncapped. F-c career: 75 matches; 1,952 runs (av 24.40), 2 hundreds; 21 wkts (av 55.23); 36 ct. HS 115 v Hants (Portsmouth) 1978. BB 3–40 v Sussex (Oval) 1976.

Essex 'keeper Neil Smith – Yorkshire's contribution to the Championship team.

SMITH, Kenneth **David**, b Jesmond, Northumberland 9 Jul 56. RHB.WARWICKSHIRE cap 1978. F-c career: 83 matches; 3,747 runs (av 28.60), 5 hundreds; 25 ct. HS 135 v Lancs (Manchester) 1977.

Lefthander who continued to improve and played a number of very good innings when the runs were really wanted.

An accomplished county batsman who experienced a disappointing 1979: failed to make a hundred, despite Edgbaston being his home ground, and averaged only 22.

SMITH, Michael John, b Enfield 4 Jan 42. RHB, SLA. MIDDLESEX cap 1967. F-c career: 417 matches; 19,731 runs (av 31.82), 40 hundreds; 57 wkts (av 32.73); 216 ct. HS 181 v Lancs (Manchester) 1967. BB 4–13 v Glos (Lord's) 1961.

Tall, effective very experienced opener, though his on-the-move, onside technique must make him suspect against top-class bowling. Many find him difficult to bowl at, and he is a particularly good pacer of an innings in limited-overs cricket.

SMITH, Neil, b Dewsbury, Yorks 1 Apr 49. RHB, WK. ESSEX cap 1975. Played for Yorks 1970–72. F-c career: 156 matches; 2,855 runs (av 18.06), 2 hundreds; 334 ct, 45 st. HS 126 v Somerset (Leyton) 1976.

Has proved to be a highly efficient performer behind the stumps. Also batted with considerable skill and determination when runs were needed.

SOUTHERN, John William, b King's Cross, Middx 2 Sep 52. RHB, SLA. HAMPSHIRE cap 1978. F-c career: 95 matches; 694 runs (av 11.37); 259 wkts (av 29.03); 27 ct. HS 61* v Yorks (Bradford) 1979. BB 6–46 v Glos (Bournemouth) 1975.

Tall, accurate slow left-arm bowler; not a big spinner. Useful lower-order batsman.

SPELMAN, Guy Dennis, b Westminster, Middx 18 Oct 58. LHB, RM. KENT – uncapped. Played in 3 JPL matches 1978 (taking 3–39 v Derbys) but has yet to make his first-class début.

Promising seamer whose University studies restricted his cricket to 2nd XI level.

SPENCER, John, b Brighton 6 Oct 49. RHB, RM. SUSSEX cap 1973. F-c career: 207 matches; 2,721 runs (av 13.53); 540 wkts (av 26.08); 72 ct. HS 79 v Hants (Southampton) 1975. BB 6–19 v Glos (Gloucester) 1974.

Ideal stock bowler; an accurate seamer who depends on movement rather than pace for his wickets.

STEELE, David Stanley, b Bradeley, Staffs 29 Sep 41. Brother of J. F. Steele (Leics). RHB, SLA. DERBYSHIRE cap 1979. Captain 1979. Played for Northants 1963–78 (cap 1965). 8 England caps 1975–76, scoring 673 runs (av 42.06), with one hundred (106), and taking 2 wkts (av 19.50), BB 1–1. F-c career: 381 matches; 18,565 runs (av 33.45), 29 hundreds; 320 wkts (av 24.33); 429 ct. HS 140* Northants v Worcs (Worcester) 1971. BB 8–29 Northants v Lancs (Northampton) 1966.

Has gradually developed from an average county batsman into one of the more consistent and dependable players. Dogged and determined, he should provide Derbyshire with stability and backbone. These characteristics were at last recognised by the selectors against Ian Chappell's Australians and the 1976 West Indians, but his brief, valuable international career would now appear to be over. A very useful, very slow left-arm bowler.

STEELE, John Frederick, b Brown Edge, Staffs 23 Jul 46. Brother of D. S. Steele (Derbys). RHB, SLA. LEICESTERSHIRE cap 1971. F-c career: 246 matches; 11,047 runs (av 30.26), 17 hundreds; 337 wkts (av 26.45); 275 ct. HS 195 v Derbys (Leicester) 1971. BB 7–29 Natal B v Griqualand West (Umzinto) 1973–74.

Dedication and enthusiasm have made this talented all-rounder an integral part of the Leicestershire side. Originally a grafting bat, he is now more eager to play his strokes. His trajectory when bowling is inclined to be too flat but he is difficult to score runs against, hence his success in limited-overs cricket.

STEPHENSON, George **Robert**, b Derby, Derbys 19 Nov 42. RHB, WK. HAMPSHIRE cap 1969. Captain in 1979. Played for Derbys 1967–68. F-c career: 255 matches; 4,477 runs (av 16.39), 1 hundred; 565 ct, 76 st. HS 100* v Somerset (Taunton) 1976.

A neat, diminutive wicket-keeper who has secured a large haul of dismissals in the past seasons. Useful batsman with an unusually upright stance. Took over the captaincy at a difficult period of adjustment for the county.

STEVENSON, **Graham** Barry, b Ackworth 16 Dec 55. RHB, RM. YORKSHIRE cap 1978. F-c career: 80 matches; 1,754 runs (av 21.65); 205 wkts (av 28.02); 38 ct. HS 83 v Derbys (Chesterfield) 1976. BB 8–65 v Lancs (Leeds) 1978. Bouncy young all-rounder who looks to have the ability, confidence, and that little extra fire which make all the difference. Lively seamer, batsman with a keen eye, and a dashing field. Chosen as a replacement for Hendrick in Australia on potential and past performances, rather than his form with bat and ball for Yorkshire last summer, when he failed to do himself full justice.

STEVENSON, **Keith**, b Derby 6 Oct 50. RHB, RM. HAMPSHIRE cap 1979. Played for Derbys 1974–77. F-c career: 91 matches; 581 runs (av

8.18); 223 wkts (av 28.11). HS 33 Derbys v Northants (Chesterfield) 1974; 29 ct. BB 7–22 v Oxford U. (Oxford) 1979.

A seamer with a pleasing body action; bowled well for Hampshire last season and was their leading wicket-taker.

STOVOLD, Andrew Willis-, b Bristol 19 Mar 53. RHB, WK. GLOUCESTERSHIRE cap 1976. F-c career: 135 matches; 6,862 runs (av 29.70), 6 hundreds; 2 wkts (av 31.00); 143 ct, 25 st. HS 196 v Notts (Nottingham) 1977. BB 1–0.

Has developed into a most attractive, fast-scoring opener with a wide range of attacking strokes. He has the ability to hit boundaries off his back foot with straight-bat strokes on both sides of the wicket. As one would expect from a former wicket-keeper, possesses a fine pair of hands.

STOVOLD, Martin Willis-, b Bristol 28 Dec 55. Younger brother of Andrew. LHB. GLOUCESTERSHIRE – uncapped. F-c career: 7 matches; 84 runs (av 9.33); 1 ct. HS 27 v Worcs (Worcester) 1979.

Aggressive, if somewhat impetuous, middle-order batsman and good fielder.

STUCHBURY, Stephen, b Sheffield 22 Jun 54. LHB, LFM. YORKSHIRE – uncapped. F-c career: 1 match; did not bat; 2 wkts (av 30.00); BB 2–39 v New Zealanders (Leeds) 1978.

Left-arm fast-medium bowler.

SURRIDGE, Stuart Spicer, b Westminster, Middx 28 Oct 51. Son of W. S. Surridge. RHB, WK. SURREY – uncapped. F-c career: 1 match; 2 runs; 1 ct, 0 st. HS 2*.

Reserve wicket-keeper.

TAVARÉ, Christopher James, b Orpington 27 Oct 54. RHB, occ RM. KENT cap 1978. F-c career: 99 matches; 5,147 runs (av 36.24), 8 hundreds; 2 wkts (av 43.50); 114 ct. HS 150* v Essex (Tunbridge Wells) 1979.

A graceful, correct batsman who topped the Kent averages and batted more impressively than Woolmer, which is an indication of his potential. Very much on the present England short-list and could well be in the side against West Indies this summer. Outstanding close-to-the-wicket fielder.

TAYLOR, Leslie Brian, b Earl Shilton 25 Oct 53. RHB, RFM. LEICESTERSHIRE – uncapped. F-c career: 29 matches; 54 runs (av 6.00); 87 wkts (av 24.57); 7 ct. HS 15 v Kent (Canterbury) 1978. BB 6–61 v Essex (Chelmsford) 1979.

Powerfully built fast bowler who turned in several good performances and was even talked about as a potential England opener. However, he lacks that extra yard or so of pace.

TAYLOR, Derek John Somerset, b Amersham, Bucks 12 Nov 42. Twin brother of M. N. S. Taylor (Notts and Hants). RHB, WK. SOMERSET cap 1971. Played for Surrey 1966–69 (cap 1969). F-c career: 241 matches; 5,957 runs (av 22.39), 4 hundreds; 492 ct, 70 st. HS 179 v Glam (Swansea) 1974.

Highly competent wicket-keeper and extremely useful batsman with a fine defence.

TAYLOR, Michael Norman Somerset, b Amersham, Bucks 12 Nov 42. Twin brother of D. J. S. Taylor (Somerset). RHB, RM. HAMPSHIRE cap 1973. Played for Notts 1964–72 (cap 1967). F-c career: 365 matches; 7,752 runs (av 19.92), 3 hundreds; 821 wkts (av 26.49), 1 hat-trick; 211 ct. HS 105 Notts v Lancs (Nottingham) 1967. BB 7–23 v Notts (Basingstoke) 1977.

Typical modern all-rounder – accurate medium-pace seamer; pleasant-looking, attacking bat; fine outfielder.

TAYLOR, Neil, b Orpington 21 July 59. RHB, OB. KENT – uncapped. F-c career: 1 match; 121 runs (av 60.50), 1 hundred; 0 ct. HS 110 v Sri Lankans (Canterbury) 1979 – on début.

Opening batsman who, after his impressive début against the Sri Lankans, found runs more difficult to come by in the 2nd XI later in the season.

TAYLOR, Robert William, b Stoke, Staffs 17 Jul 41. RHB, WK. DERBYSHIRE cap 1962. Captain 1975–76. 22 England caps 1971–79, scoring 475 runs (av 20.65), HS 97, and making 64 dismissals (59 ct, 5 st). F-c career: 503 matches; 9,822 runs (av 17.08); 1,173 ct, 143 st. HS 97 International Wanderers v South African Invitation XI (Johannesburg) 1975–76, and 97 England v Australia (Adelaide) 1978–79.

Extremely efficient, undemonstrative wicket-keeper of Test calibre who maintains the highest standard day after day. A competent tailender with plenty of determination and a penchant for the cut. Only the presence of Alan Knott prevented him from gaining numerous caps for England, and following the defection of the Kent 'keeper to Packerland his selection for England was automatic and highly successful.

TERRY, Vivian Paul, b Osnabruck, West Germany 14 Jan 59. RHB, RM. HAMPSHIRE – uncapped. F-c career: 7 matches; 102 runs (av 10.20); 4 ct. HS 21 v Warwicks (Nuneaton) 1979.

Young batsman still attempting to establish himself in the 1st XI.

THOMAS, David James, b Solihull, Warwicks 30 Jun 59. LHB, LFM. SURREY – uncapped. F-c career: 23 matches; 132 runs (av 6.28); 34 wkts (av 46.47); 7 ct. HS 15* v Worcs (Guildford)

1979. BB 6–84 v Derbys (Oval) 1979.

Young fast bowler whose chances were restricted by the number of quickies on the Surrey staff.

THOMAS, Gary Philip, b Birmingham 8 Nov 58. RHB, occ RM. WARWICKSHIRE – uncapped. F-c career: 2 matches; 14 runs (av 4.66); 0 ct. HS 9.

Apprentice batsman.

THOMAS, John Gregory, b Garnswllt 12 Aug 60. RHB, RMF. GLAMORGAN – uncapped. F-c career: 1 match; 34 runs (av 34.00); 1 wkt (av 132.00); 0 ct. HS 34 and BB 1–65 v Sri Lankans (Swansea) 1979.

Tall young fast bowler with the potential to develop even more pace. Also a useful bat.

TINDALL, Robert Michael b Harrow, Middx 16 June 59. Son of Mark Tindall (Middlesex 1933–38) LHB, SLA. NORTHAMPTONSHIRE – uncapped. Played in 1 JPL match 1979 but has yet to make his first-class début.

Graceful, attractive left-hander with a flowing style. His fielding could stand improvement.

TODD, Paul Adrian, b Morton 12 Mar 53. RHB. NOTTINGHAMSHIRE cap 1977, F-c career: 104 matches; 4,934 runs (av 28.03), 5 hundreds; 77 ct. HS 178 v Glos (Nottingham) 1975.

Firmly established as a correct, competent opening bat with a good defence and an equable temperament. Particularly impressive off his back foot.

TOLCHARD, Roger William, b Torquay, Devon 15 Jun 46. RHB, WK. LEICESTERSHIRE cap 1966. 4 England caps 1976–77, scoring 129 runs (av 25.80), HS 67 on début. F-c career: 390 matches; 12,022 runs (av 31.30), 10 hundreds; 1 wkt (av 20.00); 757 ct, 100 st. HS 126* v Cambridge U. (Cambridge) 1970. BB 1–4.

Lively, aggressive, agile 'keeper, he is also a pugnacious fast-scoring batsman and an outstanding runner between the wickets. He is especially valuable when runs are needed quickly and is not afraid to hook fast bowling.

TOMLINS, Keith Patrick, b Kingston upon Thames, Surrey 23 Oct 57. RHB RM. MIDDLESEX – uncapped. F-c career: 15 matches; 300 runs (av 16.66); 10 ct. HS 94 v Worcs (Worcester) 1978.

Young all-rounder who was formerly a member of the Middlesex Young Cricketers.

TREMLETT, Timothy Maurice, b Wellington, Somerset 26 Jul 56. Son of M. F. Tremlett. RHB, RM. HAMPSHIRE – uncapped. F-c career: 14 matches; 254 runs (av 13.36); 17 wkts (av 30.17); 5 ct. HS 50 v Glos (Basingstoke) 1978.

Glenn Turner – Worcestershire's run machine.

BB 2–9 v Surrey (Oval) 1979.
Promising young seamer.

TRIM, Geoffrey Edward, b Openshaw 6 Apr
56. RHB, occ LB. LANCASHIRE – uncapped. F-c
career: 10 matches; 294 runs (av 17.29); 9 ct.
HS 91 v Derbys (Chesterfield) 1979.
A diminutive batsman whom his county
hope will prove to be another Pilling.

TUNNICLIFFE, Colin John, b Derby 11 Aug
51. RHB, LFM. DERBYSHIRE cap 1977. F-c
career: 76 matches; 848 runs (av 13.46); 154
wkts (av 31.64); 31 ct. HS 82* and BB 4–22 v
Middx (Ilkeston) 1977.
Dependable opening bowler; has good line
and length and moves the ball off the seam.
Useful late-order batsman.

TUNNICLIFFE, Howard Trevor, b Derby,
Derbyshire 4 Mar 50. RHB, RM. NOTTINGHAM-
SHIRE – uncapped. F-c career: 55 matches;
1,820 runs (av 26.37); 33 wkts (av 42.84); 30 ct.
HS 97 v Glam (Nottingham) 1979. BB 4–30 v
Sri Lankans (Nottingham) 1979.
Enjoyed his best season to date and played
some good innings. However, he has yet to hit
a century and he will be 30 this summer.
Occasional seam bowler.

TURNER, David Roy, b Chippenham, Wilt-
shire 5 Feb 49. LHB, occ RM. HAMPSHIRE cap
1970. F-c career: 263 matches; 11,384 runs (av
28.10),18 hundreds; 5 wkts (av 40.20); 145 ct.
HS 181* v Surrey (Oval) 1969. BB 1–1.
Small, neat lefthander who is very quick on
his feet and a good county batsman, having at
one time promised rather more. A fine fielder.

TURNER, Glenn Maitland, b Dunedin, New
Zealand 26 May 47. RHB, occ RM/OB. WOR-
CESTERSHIRE cap 1968. 39 New Zealand caps
1969–77 (10 as captain), scoring 2,920 runs (av
45.62) with 7 hundreds. HS 259. F-c career: 391
matches; 28,797 runs (av 48.72), 81 hundreds; 5
wkts (av 37.80); 352 ct. HS 259 New Zealand v
West Indies (Georgetown) 1971–72 and 259
New Zealanders v Guyana (Georgetown)
1971–72. BB 3–18 v Pakistanis (Worcester)
1967.
World-class opening batsman from New
Zealand with the pedigree one expects from an
outstanding player. Was playing Test cricket
and making runs in his early 20s, and in 1973
scored a thousand runs before the end of May.
He plays straight, and with this and a sound
defensive technique as the vital base, he has
blossomed forth so that he can adjust his tempo
to suit the requirements. Possesses a temperament and singleness of purpose that have given
him an insatiable appetite for records and runs.
Last season became the first player to score a
century against each of the 17 first-class
counties, having scored 143 against his own
county for the 1973 New Zealanders.

TURNER, Stuart, b Chester, Cheshire 18 Jul 43.
RHB, RM. ESSEX cap 1970. F-c career: 266
matches; 6,764 runs (av 21.67), 4 hundreds; 641
wkts (av 25.00), 1 hat-trick; 178 ct. HS 121 v
Somerset (Taunton) 1970. BB 6–26 v Northants
(Northampton) 1977.
Good county all-rounder and a natural for
limited-overs cricket. He is an accurate fast-
medium bowler – a shade nippier than he looks
– an attacking batsman, and a splendid
fieldsman.

UNDERWOOD, Derek Leslie, b Bromley 8
June 45. RHB, LM. KENT cap 1964. 74 England
caps 1966–77, scoring 824 runs (av 11.94), HS
45* and taking 265 wkts (av 24.90), BB 8–51. F-c
career: 470 matches; 3,476 runs (av 9.24); 1,840
wkts (av 19.28), 1 hat-trick; 208 ct. HS 80 v
Lancs (Manchester) 1969. BB 9–28 v Sussex
(Hastings) 1964.
A world-class bowler; on a pitch giving any
assistance at all, he is most devastating. His
pace is close to medium, so he gives batsmen few
opportunities to use their feet. On perfect
pitches he can be employed as a stock bowler
because his accuracy always makes him difficult to score against, and he has an outstanding
record in limited-overs games when the denial
of runs is all-important. It is noticeable that he is
less effective against lefthanders, and he could
do with a well-disguised slower ball that turns as
much as his normal delivery. He can bat with
great tenacity when the situation demands. As a
result of his WSC contract he was not
considered by the England selectors until they
picked the side for Australia. In the interim he
took 100 wickets in two successive seasons for
Kent, a reminder that he is easily the best spin
bowler in the land, and probably the world.

WALLER, Christopher Edward, b Guildford,
Surrey 3 Oct 48. RHB, SLA. SUSSEX cap 1976.
Played for Surrey 1967–73 (cap 1972). F-c
career: 142 matches; 880 runs (av 8.80); 362 wkts
(av 27.69); 77 ct. HS 47 Surrey v Pakistanis
(Oval) 1971. BB 7–64 Surrey v Sussex (Oval)
1971.
A slow left-armer who gives the ball air, can
run it in with his arm, and imparts sufficient
spin. Not really flat enough for limited-overs
cricket, especially on a small ground.

WALTERS, John, b Brampton, Yorks 7 Aug 49.
LHB, RFM. DERBYSHIRE – uncapped. F-c
career: 41 matches; 836 runs (av 19.44); 46 wkts
(av 39.23) 10 ct. HS 90 v Hants (Bournemouth)
1978. BB 4–100 v Worcs (Derby) 1979.
Has yet to establish himself in first-class
cricket after three years on the staff.

WATSON, Gregory George, b Gulgong, NSW,
Australia 29 Jan 55. RHB, RFM. WORCESTER-
SHIRE – uncapped. F-c career: 44 matches; 552
runs (av 12.83); 100 wkts (av 36.97); 11 ct. HS 38
v Somerset (Taunton) 1978. BB 6–45 v Sussex
(Eastbourne) 1978.

Australian fast bowler who is not quite quick enough and inclined to be erratic.

WATSON, William Kenneth, b Port Elizabeth, South Africa 21 May 55. RHB, RFM. NOTTING-HAMSHIRE – uncapped. F-c career: 51 matches; 432 runs (av 12.34); 164 wkts (av 25.23); 19ct. HS 28* v Cambridge U. (Cambridge) 1978. BB 6–51 v Derbys (Nottingham) 1979.

A reasonable, but not exceptional, South African quickie who could play only when Hadlee or Rice was absent.

WATTS, Patrick James, b Henlow, Beds 16 Jun 40. LHB, RM. NORTHAMPTONSHIRE cap 1962. Captain 1971–74 and since 1978. F-c career: 361 matches; 14,229 runs (av 28.17), 10 hundreds; 333 wkts (av 25.99); 266 ct. HS 145 v Hants (Bournemouth) 1962. BB 6–18 v Somerset (Taunton) 1965.

A dependable lefthander with a marked preference for the front foot, he plays straight, has a fluent off-drive, and is difficult to remove. Bowls a steady and accurate medium pace. Captained Northants quietly and effectively.

WELLS, Colin Mark, b Newhaven 3 Mar 60. RHB, RM. SUSSEX – uncapped. F-c career: 5 matches; 60 runs (av 12.00); 10 wkts (av 13.70); 1 ct. HS 29 v Hants (Bournemouth) 1979. BB 4–23 v Oxford U. (Pagham) 1979.

Aggressive, hard-hitting batsman and seamer who hits the deck in an attacking manner. Has the right competitive temperament to go far; a name to watch.

WESSELS, Kepler Christoffel, b Bloemfontein, South Africa 14 Sep 57. LHB, OB. SUSSEX cap 1977. F-c career: 65 matches; 4,525 runs (av 45.25), 10 hundreds; 3 wkts (av 27.66); 48 ct. HS 187 v Kent (Eastbourne) 1979. BB 1–4.

Brilliant young South African batsman, currently one of the most effective players in the world. Debarred from Test cricket because of his nationality, he is hoping to qualify to play for Australia, who could certainly do with his services.

WESTON, Martin John, b Worcester 8 Apr 59. RHB, RM. WORCESTERSHIRE – uncapped. F-c career: 1 match; 59 runs (av 29.50); 0 ct. HS 43 v Sri Lankans (Worcester) 1979.

Taken on a month's trial last summer, he scored nearly 1,000 runs for the 2nd XI, and a series of impressive performances led to his being retained. Could be a useful find.

WHITEHOUSE, John, b Nuneaton 8 Apr 49. RHB, occ OB. WARWICKSHIRE cap 1973. Captain 1978–79. F-c career: 170 matches; 7,968 runs (av 30.64), 14 hundreds; 6 wkts (av 76.50); 117 ct. HS 173 v Oxford U. (Oxford) 1971–on début. BB 2–55 v Yorks (Birmingham) 1977.

Right-handed bat with an open stance and a

tendency to play across the line, but he times the ball well and has a good eye. His appointment as skipper of an unsuccessful side proved to have a disastrous effect on his own form. Relieved of this appointment, he should start scoring heavily in 1980.

WHITELEY, John Peter, b Otley 28 Feb 55. RHB, OB. YORKSHIRE – uncapped. F-c career: 21 matches; 60 runs (av 8.57); 32 wkts (av 31.90); 9 ct. HS 20 v Northants (Northampton) 1979. BB 4–14 v Notts (Scarborough) 1978.

An off-spinner who promised so much in 1978, but for some inexplicable reason met with no success last summer.

WILKINS, Alan Haydn, b Cardiff 22 Aug 53. RHB, LFM. GLAMORGAN – uncapped. F-c career: 51 matches; 317 runs (av 8.12); 123 wkts (av 27.51); 16 ct. HS 70 v Notts (Worksop) 1977. BB 6–79 v Hants (Southampton) 1979.

Left-arm seamer who still needs to learn to move the ball into the righthander. Found wickets hard to obtain and too expensive, but finished at the top of the Glamorgan averages.

WILLEY, Peter, b Sedgefield, Co Durham 6 Dec 49. RHB, RM. NORTHAMPTONSHIRE cap 1971. 3 England caps 1976–79, scoring 198 runs (av 33.00), HS 52, and taking 2 wkts (av 60.50), BB 2–96. F-c career: 263 matches; 9,693 runs (av 26.62), 12 hundreds; 375 wkts (av 28.26); 112 ct. HS 227 v Somerset (Northampton) 1976. BB 7–37 v Oxford U. (Oxford) 1975.

One of the best home-born strokemakers. His striking of the ball off his back foot is especially impressive and he always has enough time to give himself room to play his shots. Although very open when playing, he drives well through the covers, but is slightly suspect against the ball leaving him sharply. Has become an efficient off-break bowler and was chosen to tour Australia as an all-rounder.

WILLIAMS, Richard Grenville, b Bangor, Caernarvons 10 Aug 57. RHB, OB. NORTHAMP-TONSHIRE cap 1979. F-c career: 63 matches; 2,023 runs (av 23.52), 4 hundreds; 50 wkts (av 35.42); 25 ct. HS 151* v Warwicks (Northampton) 1979. BB 5–57 v Sussex (Northampton) 1979.

Chunky little batsman with the ability to hit the ball off his back foot. He really came into his own last summer, making his maiden hundred and then following it up with three more in easily the most impressive season of his career. If he continues to improve like this, his future must be very bright. Useful change bowler.

WILLIS, Robert George Dylan, b Sunderland, Co Durham 30 May 49. RHB, RF. WARWICK-SHIRE cap 1972. Captain 1980. Played for Surrey 1969–71. 50 England caps 1971–79, scoring 430 runs (av 13.03), HS 24*, and taking 181 wkts (av 24.37), BB 7–78. F-c career: 1,626 runs (av 14.64); 627 wkts (av 23.48), 2 hat-tricks; 92 ct. HS 43 v Middx (Birmingham) 1976. BB 8–32 v Glos (Bristol) 1977.

Tall, rather open-chested fast bowler. Hits the deck and achieves lift even on a placid pitch. Does not move the ball much, either in the air or off the wicket, but makes batting uncomfortable and is the main strike bowler in the England XI. Is prepared to keep going for long periods. Occasionally inaccurate, owing to an action which is not smoothly grooved. His speed is the result of sheer effort. Useful tailender who does not reckon to play back more than once a season. Fine field. Forceful personality who should make a good county captain.

WILSON, Peter **Hugh** L'Estrange, b Guildford 17 Aug 58. RHB, RFM. SURREY – uncapped. F-c career: 26 matches; 57 runs (av 14.25); 41 wkts (av 29.65); 4 ct. HS 15 v Worcs (Guildford) 1979.

Exceptionally promising pace bowler; distinctly sharp and achieves considerable lift.

WINCER, Robert Colin, b Southsea, Hants 2 Apr 52. LHB, RFM. DERBYSHIRE – uncapped. F-c career: 21 matches; 131 runs (av 10.07); 43 wkts (av 35.90); 8 ct. HS 26 v Kent (Chesterfield) 1979. BB 4–42 v Leics (Derby) 1978 – on début.

Useful all-rounder in one-day games.

WOOD, Barry, b Ossett, Yorks 26 Dec 42. RHB, RM. LANCASHIRE cap 1968. Played for Yorkshire 1964. 12 England caps 1972–78, scoring 454 runs (av 21.61), HS 90. F-c career: 294 matches; 14,261 runs (av 33.79), 24 hundreds; 261 wkts (av 27.65); 226 ct. HS 198 v Glam (Liverpool) 1976. BB 7–52 v Middx (Manchester) 1968.

Tough, gutsy little opener with a penchant for fast bowling. A good cutter and hooker, he is also prepared to take on a sheet-anchor role. Certain deficiencies in technique can lead to his downfall against top-class spin, as was seen in India. A more than useful county medium-pace seam bowler who wobbles the ball about. Brilliant field and born competitor.

WOOLMER, Robert Andrew, b Kanpur, India 14 May 48. RHB, RFM. KENT cap 1970. 15 England caps 1975–77, scoring 920 runs (av 36.80) with 3 hundreds, HS 149, and taking 4 wkts (av 74.75), BB 1–8. F-c career: 268 matches; 11,410 runs (av 33.55), 23 hundreds; 388 wkts (av 26.12), 1 hat-trick; 183 ct. HS 169 v Yorks (Canterbury) 1979. BB 7–47 v Sussex (Canterbury) 1969.

For several years with Kent he was regarded as a steady seam bowler and handy number 8 batsman but has now blossomed forth into primarily a batsman. He has an impressive repertoire of strokes and plenty of time to make them, as he has shown for both Kent and England. Has a fine pair of hands and is a useful

bowler on a green wicket or in limited-overs cricket. Joined WSC and has not played for England since; but his subsequent performances for Kent suggest that he could well be in the running for a recall against West Indies.

WRIGHT, John Geoffrey, b Darfield, New Zealand 5 Jul 54. LHB. DERBYSHIRE cap 1977. 8 New Zealand caps 1978–79, scoring 401 runs (av 26.73), HS 88. F-c career: 92 matches; 5,369 runs (av 34.86), 10 hundreds; 59 ct. HS 164 v Pakistanis (Chesterfield) 1978.

Has developed into a true international opening bat with plenty of patience and an excellent temperament. He hit five centuries for his adopted county and comfortably headed their batting averages.

YARDLEY, Thomas **James,** b Chaddesley Corbett, Worcs 27 Oct 46. LHB, occ WK. NORTHAMPTONSHIRE cap 1978. Played for Worcestershire 1967–75 (cap 1972). F-c career: 209 matches; 6,688 runs (av 25.52), 4 hundreds; 184 ct, 2 st. HS 135 Worcs v Notts (Worcester) 1973.

Solid lefthander with a rather limited range of strokes.

YOUNIS AHMED, Mohammad, b Jullundur, India 20 Oct 47. Step-brother of Saeed Ahmed. LHB, SLA/LM. WORCESTERSHIRE cap 1979. Played for Surrey 1965–78. 2 Pakistan caps 1969, scoring 89 runs (av 22.25), HS 62. F-c career: 329 matches; 17,806 runs (av 37.32), 27 hundreds; 35 wkts (av 37.51); 179 ct. HS 221* v Notts (Nottingham) 1979. BB 4–10 Surrey v Cambridge U. (Cambridge) 1975.

Dashing lefthander who, after some inhibited years at The Oval, gave full vent to his large repertoire of strokes in his first season with Worcestershire. Only Boycott headed him in the national averages. At his happiest and most effective going after the bowling. A memorable season was climaxed by a return to favour with the Pakistan authorities, who rescinded an earlier ban imposed because he toured South Africa.

ZAHEER ABBAS, Syed, b Sialkot, Pakistan 24 Jul 47. RHB, occ OB. GLOUCESTERSHIRE cap 1975. 33 Pakistan caps 1969–79, scoring 2,460 runs (av 43.92), with 6 hundreds, HS 274. F-c career: 291 matches; 22,339 runs (av 50.31), 68 hundreds; 20 wkts (av 34.10); 212 ct. HS 274 Pakistan v England (Birmingham) 1971. BB 5–15 Dawood Club v Railways (Lahore) 1975–76. Only batsman to score a double-century and a century in a match on three occasions – all six innings were not out.

A strokemaker of very high class. His graceful style, combined with his ability to hit the ball on the rise along the ground, make him a delight to watch and a menace to bowl against. Although he has a wide variety of off-side strokes he is especially devastating to leg.

WISDEN CRICKETERS' ALMANACK 1980

117th Edition
Edited by Norman Preston

The 'bible' of cricket makes its appearance once more. Its pages contain complete details of the 1979 season in England and as usual there are the five cricketers of the year and full coverage of overseas cricket, including winter tours.
1110pp   illustrated   £6.75 (cloth)   £5.75 (limp)

RAY ILLINGWORTH
An Autobiography

Ray Illingworth, the distinguished Yorkshire, Leicestershire and England cricketer, tells his *own* story for the first time. He recalls the controversies, as well as the triumphs which have marked his illustrious career and also looks at his greatest challenge yet – his return to Yorkshire CC as their first-ever cricket manager.
192pp   illustrated   May 1980   £5.95

Available from booksellers or in case of difficulty write to QAP Direct Sales, 9 Partridge Drive, Orpington, Kent, England, enclosing cheque/PO payable to Macdonald & Jane's Publishing Group + 10% for postage & packing (UK only). Allow up to 28 days for delivery, subject to availability.

M&J **Queen Anne Press**

FIXTURES 1980

West Indian Tour

All matches 3 days unless otherwise stated
*Includes play on Sunday
†Holt Products Trophy Match

MAY

Thursday	8	ARUNDEL – Lavinia, Duchess of Norfolk's XI (1 day)
Saturday	10	†*WORCESTER – Worcestershire
Wednesday	14	†LEICESTER – Leicestershire
Saturday	17	†*MILTON KEYNES – Northamptonshire
Tuesday	20	LORD'S – Middlesex (1 day)
Wednesday	21	LORD'S – Middlesex (1 day)
Thursday	22	CHELMSFORD – Essex (1 day)
Friday	23	CHELMSFORD – Essex (1 day)
Saturday	24	*CHESTERFIELD – Derbyshire
Wednesday	28	LEEDS – England (Prudential Trophy – 1 day)
Friday	30	LORD'S – England (Prudential Trophy – 1 day)
Saturday	31	†*CANTERBURY – Kent

JUNE

Thursday	5	NOTTINGHAM – ENGLAND 1st Cornhill Test (5 days)
Thursday	12	CAMBRIDGE – Cambridge & Oxford Us. (2 days)
Saturday	14	†*HOVE – Sussex
Thursday	19	LORD'S – ENGLAND 2nd Cornhill Test (5 days)
Wednesday	25	DUBLIN – Ireland (1 day)
Thursday	26	DUBLIN – Ireland (1 day)
Saturday	28	†SWANSEA – Glamorgan
Sunday	29	SWANSEA – Glamorgan (1 day)

JULY

Wednesday	2	†BRISTOL – Gloucestershire
Saturday	5	†*TAUNTON – Somerset
Thursday	10	MANCHESTER – ENGLAND 3rd Cornhill Test (5 days)
Thursday	17	BROUGHTY FERRY – Scotland (2 days)
Saturday	19	†*LEEDS/MANCHESTER – Yorkshire/Lancashire (*depending upon Benson & Hedges finalists*)
Thursday	24	THE OVAL – ENGLAND 4th Cornhill Test (5 days)
Thursday	31	NEWCASTLE UPON TYNE – Minor Counties (2 days)

AUGUST

Saturday	2	†*BIRMINGHAM – Warwickshire
Thursday	7	LEEDS – ENGLAND 5th Cornhill Test (5 days)

Australian Tour

All matches 3 days unless otherwise stated
*Includes play on Sunday
†Holt Products Trophy Match

AUGUST

Wednesday	6	Venue undecided – Hampshire (1 day)
Thursday	7	Venue undecided – Hampshire (1 day)
Saturday	9	†*THE OVAL – Surrey
Wednesday	13	Venue undecided – YOUNG ENGLAND
Saturday	16	†*MANCHESTER/LEEDS – Lancashire/Yorkshire (*depending on which county played the West Indians on 19 July*)
Wednesday	20	THE OVAL – England (Prudential Trophy – 1 day)
Friday	22	BIRMINGHAM – England (Prudential Trophy – 1 day)
Saturday	23	†*NOTTINGHAM – Nottinghamshire
Thursday	28	LORD'S – ENGLAND Cornhill Centenary Test (5 days)

Schweppes County Championship

Wednesday 30 April

SWANSEA – Glamorgan v Essex
CANTERBURY – Kent v Northamptonshire
MANCHESTER – Lancashire v Derbyshire
LEICESTER – Leicestershire v Yorkshire
NOTTINGHAM – Nottinghamshire v Middlesex
TAUNTON – Somerset v Sussex
THE OVAL – Surrey v Hampshire
WORCESTER – Worcestershire v Gloucestershire

Saturday 3 May

ILFORD – Essex v Somerset
BRISTOL – Gloucestershire v Northamptonshire
SOUTHAMPTON – Hampshire v Warwickshire
LORD'S – Middlesex v Lancashire
HOVE – Sussex v Leicestershire

Wednesday 7 May

DERBY – Derbyshire v Northamptonshire
ILFORD – Essex v Kent
BRISTOL – Gloucestershire v Glamorgan
MANCHESTER – Lancashire v Worcestershire
NOTTINGHAM – Nottinghamshire v Yorkshire
THE OVAL – Surrey v Sussex
BIRMINGHAM – Warwickshire v Somerset

Saturday 24 May
CHELMSFORD – Essex v Surrey
SWANSEA – Glamorgan v Nottinghamshire
BOURNEMOUTH – Hampshire v Kent
LORD'S – Middlesex v Sussex
NORTHAMPTON – Northamptonshire v Leicestershire
TAUNTON – Somerset v Gloucestershire
WORCESTER – Worcestershire v Warwickshire
LEEDS – Yorkshire v Lancashire

Wednesday 28 May
CHESTERFIELD – Derbyshire v Hampshire
MANCHESTER – Lancashire v Glamorgan
LEICESTER – Leicestershire v Gloucestershire
NORTHAMPTON – Northamptonshire v Yorkshire
NOTTINGHAM – Nottinghamshire v Warwickshire
THE OVAL – Surrey v Somerset
HOVE – Sussex v Kent
WORCESTER – Worcestershire v Middlesex

Saturday 31 May
CARDIFF – Glamorgan v Northamptonshire
GLOUCESTER – Gloucestershire v Essex
LIVERPOOL – Lancashire v Warwickshire
LEICESTER – Leicestershire v Derbyshire
TAUNTON – Somerset v Middlesex
THE OVAL – Surrey v Nottinghamshire
MIDDLESBROUGH – Yorkshire v Sussex

Wednesday 4 June
SOUTHAMPTON – Hampshire v Sussex
LEICESTER – Leicestershire v Nottinghamshire
LORD'S – Middlesex v Surrey
BIRMINGHAM – Warwickshire v Derbyshire
WORCESTER – Worcestershire v Somerset
SHEFFIELD – Yorkshire v Kent

Saturday 7 June
DERBY – Derbyshire v Glamorgan
MANCHESTER – Lancashire v Nottinghamshire
LORD'S – Middlesex v Yorkshire
NORTHAMPTON – Northamptonshire v
    Gloucestershire
THE OVAL – Surrey v Essex
HOVE – Sussex v Worcestershire

Saturday 14 June
SOUTHEND-ON-SEA – Essex v Warwickshire
SWANSEA – Glamorgan v Worcestershire
BRISTOL – Gloucestershire v Derbyshire
TUNBRIDGE WELLS – Kent v Hampshire
NORTHAMPTON – Northamptonshire v
    Nottinghamshire
BATH – Somerset v Lancashire
THE OVAL – Surrey v Middlesex

Wednesday 18 June
SOUTHEND-ON-SEA – Essex v Middlesex
CARDIFF – Glamorgan v Warwickshire
BRISTOL – Gloucestershire v Lancashire
TUNBRIDGE WELLS – Kent v Sussex
LEICESTER – Leicestershire v Surrey
NORTHAMPTON – Northamptonshire v Derbyshire
BATH – Somerset v Hampshire
BRADFORD – Yorkshire v Worcestershire

Saturday 21 June
CHESTERFIELD – Derbyshire v Essex
BOURNEMOUTH – Hampshire v Gloucestershire
MANCHESTER – Lancashire v Kent
CARDIFF – Glamorgan v Somerset
NUNEATON – Warwickshire v Northamptonshire
WORCESTER – Worcestershire v Leicestershire
HARROGATE – Yorkshire v Nottinghamshire

Wednesday 25 June
MANCHESTER – Lancashire v Surrey (*will be played
    on 27 August if either county in Benson & Hedges
    semi-finals*)

Saturday 28 June
SOUTHAMPTON – Hampshire v Yorkshire
DARTFORD – Kent v Derbyshire
LEICESTER – Leicestershire v Lancashire
NORTHAMPTON – Northamptonshire v
    Worcestershire
NOTTINGHAM – Nottinghamshire v Essex
GUILDFORD – Surrey v Gloucestershire
HOVE – Sussex v Somerset
BIRMINGHAM – Warwickshire v Middlesex

Wednesday 2 July
BURTON UPON TRENT – Derbyshire v Leicestershire
BASINGSTOKE – Hampshire v Glamorgan

Saturday 5 July
BRISTOL – Gloucestershire v Nottinghamshire
MAIDSTONE – Kent v Leicestershire
LORD'S – Middlesex v Northamptonshire
HOVE – Sussex v Hampshire
BIRMINGHAM – Warwickshire v Lancashire
WORCESTER – Worcestershire v Surrey
BRADFORD – Yorkshire v Glamorgan

Wednesday 9 July
CHELMSFORD – Essex v Yorkshire
SWANSEA – Glamorgan v Sussex
MAIDSTONE – Kent v Surrey
LORD'S – Middlesex v Hampshire
NORTHAMPTON – Northamptonshire v Warwickshire
NOTTINGHAM – Nottinghamshire v Somerset

Saturday 12 July
CHESTERFIELD – Derbyshire v Somerset
CHELMSFORD – Essex v Leicestershire
CARDIFF – Glamorgan v Hampshire
BRISTOL – Gloucestershire v Sussex
NOTTINGHAM – Nottinghamshire v Kent
THE OVAL – Surrey v Yorkshire
STOURPORT-ON-SEVERN – Worcestershire v
    Lancashire

Saturday 19 July
LEICESTER – Leicestershire v Glamorgan (*will be
    played on 20 August if either county in Benson &
    Hedges final*)

Wednesday 23 July
PORTSMOUTH – Hampshire v Surrey
SOUTHPORT – Lancashire v Northamptonshire
LEICESTER – Leicestershire v Essex

WORKSOP – Nottinghamshire v Derbyshire
TAUNTON – Somerset v Kent
BIRMINGHAM – Warwickshire v Worcestershire
SCARBOROUGH – Yorkshire v Middlesex

Saturday 26 July
CARDIFF – Glamorgan v Leicestershire
PORTSMOUTH – Hampshire v Lancashire
LORD'S – Middlesex v Kent
HOVE – Sussex v Essex
BIRMINGHAM – Warwickshire v Surrey
WORCESTER – Worcestershire v Derbyshire
SHEFFIELD – Yorkshire v Gloucestershire

Saturday 2 August
CHESTERFIELD – Derbyshire v Yorkshire
CHELTENHAM – Gloucestershire v Hampshire
CANTERBURY – Kent v Glamorgan
MANCHESTER – Lancashire v Sussex
LORD'S – Middlesex v Essex
NORTHAMPTON – Northamptonshire v Surrey
NOTTINGHAM – Nottinghamshire v Leicestershire
WESTON-SUPER-MARE – Somerset v Worcestershire

Wednesday 6 August
CHELTENHAM – Gloucestershire v Worcestershire
CANTERBURY – Kent v Warwickshire
LORD'S – Middlesex v Leicestershire
NOTTINGHAM – Nottinghamshire v Lancashire
WESTON-SUPER-MARE – Somerset v Yorkshire
THE OVAL – Surrey v Glamorgan
EASTBOURNE – Sussex v Northamptonshire

Saturday 9 August
BUXTON – Derbyshire v Lancashire
CHELMSFORD – Essex v Hampshire
CHELTENHAM – Gloucestershire v Middlesex
LEICESTER – Leicestershire v Kent
NORTHAMPTON – Northamptonshire v Somerset
EASTBOURNE – Sussex v Nottinghamshire
BIRMINGHAM – Warwickshire v Yorkshire
WORCESTER – Worcestershire v Glamorgan

Saturday 16 August
DERBY – Derbyshire v Surrey
SWANSEA – Glamorgan v Gloucestershire
FOLKESTONE – Kent v Essex
LORD'S – Middlesex v Nottinghamshire
WELLINGBOROUGH – Northamptonshire v
   Hampshire
TAUNTON – Somerset v Leicestershire
BIRMINGHAM – Warwickshire v Sussex

Wednesday 20 August
BOURNEMOUTH – Hampshire v Somerset
FOLKESTONE – Kent v Gloucestershire
LEICESTER – Leicestershire v Glamorgan (*if not
   played on 19 July*)
LORD'S – Middlesex v Derbyshire
NORTHAMPTON – Northamptonshire v Essex
CLEETHORPES – Nottinghamshire v Worcestershire
HOVE – Sussex v Surrey
BRADFORD – Yorkshire v Warwickshire

Saturday 23 August
COLCHESTER – Essex v Derbyshire
BRISTOL – Gloucestershire v Somerset
BOURNEMOUTH – Hampshire v Worcestershire
MANCHESTER – Lancashire v Yorkshire
LEICESTER – Leicestershire v Northamptonshire
THE OVAL – Surrey v Kent
HOVE – Sussex v Middlesex
BIRMINGHAM – Warwickshire v Glamorgan

Wednesday 27 August
ILKESTON – Derbyshire v Nottinghamshire
COLCHESTER – Essex v Worcestershire
MANCHESTER – Lancashire v Surrey (*if not played on
   25 June*)
TAUNTON – Somerset v Glamorgan
BIRMINGHAM – Warwickshire v Gloucestershire

Saturday 30 August
DERBY – Derbyshire v Sussex
CARDIFF – Glamorgan v Middlesex
BLACKPOOL – Lancashire v Essex
LEICESTER – Leicestershire v Warwickshire
NOTTINGHAM – Nottinghamshire v Hampshire
WORCESTER – Worcestershire v Kent
LEEDS – Yorkshire v Northamptonshire

Wednesday 3 September
CHELMSFORD – Essex v Northamptonshire
SOUTHAMPTON – Hampshire v Leicestershire
CANTERBURY – Kent v Middlesex
TAUNTON – Somerset v Warwickshire
THE OVAL – Surrey v Lancashire
HOVE – Sussex v Gloucestershire
WORCESTER – Worcestershire v Nottinghamshire
SCARBOROUGH – Yorkshire v Derbyshire

Other First-Class Matches

*Includes play on Sunday
Wednesday 23 April
LORD'S – MCC v Essex
CAMBRIDGE – Cambridge U. v Leicestershire
OXFORD – Oxford U. v Gloucestershire

Saturday 26 April
CAMBRIDGE – Cambridge U. v Essex
OXFORD – Oxford U. v Somerset

Wednesday 30 April
OXFORD – Oxford U. v Warwickshire

Saturday 3 May
CAMBRIDGE – Cambridge U. v Surrey
OXFORD – Oxford U. v Yorkshire

Wednesday 7 May
CAMBRIDGE – Cambridge U. v Middlesex
OXFORD – Oxford U. v Hampshire

Saturday 31 May
OXFORD – Oxford U. v Worcestershire

Wednesday 4 June
CAMBRIDGE – Cambridge U. v Northamptonshire
OXFORD – Oxford U. v Lancashire

Saturday 7 June
CAMBRIDGE – Cambridge U. v Warwickshire

Saturday 14 June
OXFORD – Oxford U. v Leicestershire

Wednesday 18 June
CAMBRIDGE – Cambridge U. v Nottinghamshire

Saturday 21 June
HASTINGS – Sussex v Cambridge U.

Saturday 28 June
LORD'S – Cambridge U. v Oxford U.

Saturday 16 August
*PERTH – Scotland v Ireland

John Player League

Sunday 4 May
DERBY – Derbyshire v Surrey
ILFORD – Essex v Somerset
BRISTOL – Gloucestershire v Northamptonshire
SOUTHAMPTON – Hampshire v Warwickshire
LORD'S – Middlesex v Lancashire
NOTTINGHAM – Nottinghamshire v Kent
HOVE – Sussex v Leicestershire
BRADFORD – Yorkshire v Worcestershire

Sunday 11 May
CANTERBURY – Kent v Somerset
MANCHESTER – Lancashire v Glamorgan
NORTHAMPTON – Northamptonshire v Sussex
HUDDERSFIELD – Yorkshire v Warwickshire

Sunday 18 May
SWANSEA – Glamorgan v Essex
LEICESTER – Leicestershire v Gloucestershire
NOTTINGHAM – Nottinghamshire v Derbyshire
TAUNTON – Somerset v Yorkshire
THE OVAL – Surrey v Hampshire
BIRMINGHAM – Warwickshire v Sussex
WORCESTER – Worcestershire v Middlesex

Sunday 25 May
CHELMSFORD – Essex v Surrey
SWANSEA – Glamorgan v Nottinghamshire
BOURNEMOUTH – Hampshire v Kent
MANCHESTER – Lancashire v Gloucestershire
LORD'S – Middlesex v Northamptonshire

Sunday 1 June
CARDIFF – Glamorgan v Northamptonshire
GLOUCESTER – Gloucestershire v Essex
PORTSMOUTH – Hampshire v Worcestershire
LIVERPOOL – Lancashire v Warwickshire
LEICESTER – Leicestershire v Derbyshire
TAUNTON – Somerset v Middlesex
THE OVAL – Surrey v Nottinghamshire
MIDDLESBROUGH – Yorkshire v Sussex

Sunday 8 June
DERBY – Derbyshire v Glamorgan
CANTERBURY – Kent v Gloucestershire
LEICESTER – Leicestershire v Hampshire

LORD'S – Middlesex v Yorkshire
TRING – Northamptonshire v Lancashire
HORSHAM – Sussex v Worcestershire
BIRMINGHAM – Warwickshire v Surrey

Sunday 15 June
SOUTHEND-ON-SEA – Essex v Warwickshire
SWANSEA – Glamorgan v Yorkshire
BRISTOL – Gloucestershire v Worcestershire
LORD'S – Middlesex v Surrey
NOTTINGHAM – Nottinghamshire v
    Northamptonshire
BATH – Somerset v Lancashire

Sunday 22 June
CHESTERFIELD – Derbyshire v Essex
MANCHESTER – Lancashire v Kent
BATH – Somerset v Glamorgan
THE OVAL – Surrey v Sussex
NUNEATON – Warwickshire v Northamptonshire
WORCESTER – Worcestershire v Leicestershire
SCARBOROUGH – Yorkshire v Nottinghamshire

Sunday 29 June
CHELMSFORD – Essex v Nottinghamshire
BASINGSTOKE – Hampshire v Yorkshire
CANTERBURY – Kent v Derbyshire
LEICESTER – Leicestershire v Lancashire
NORTHAMPTON – Northamptonshire v
    Worcestershire
GUILDFORD – Surrey v Gloucestershire
HOVE – Sussex v Somerset
BIRMINGHAM – Warwickshire v Middlesex

Sunday 6 July
BRISTOL – Gloucestershire v Nottinghamshire
MAIDSTONE – Kent v Leicestershire
MANCHESTER – Lancashire v Surrey
LORD'S – Middlesex v Derbyshire
HOVE – Sussex v Hampshire
WORCESTER – Worcestershire v Warwickshire
LEEDS – Yorkshire v Essex

Sunday 13 July
CHESTERFIELD – Derbyshire v Somerset
CHELMSFORD – Essex v Leicestershire
CARDIFF – Glamorgan v Hampshire
MORETON-IN-MARSH – Gloucestershire v Sussex
LUTON – Northamptonshire v Kent
NOTTINGHAM – Nottinghamshire v
    Warwickshire
THE OVAL – Surrey v Yorkshire
WORCESTER – Worcestershire v Lancashire

Sunday 20 July
PORTSMOUTH – Hampshire v Somerset
MAIDSTONE – Kent v Sussex
LEICESTER – Leicestershire v Middlesex
NORTHAMPTON – Northamptonshire v Derbyshire
NOTTINGHAM – Nottinghamshire v Worcestershire
THE OVAL – Surrey v Glamorgan
BIRMINGHAM – Warwickshire v Gloucestershire

Sunday 27 July
DERBY – Derbyshire v Warwickshire

EBBW VALE – Glamorgan v Leicestershire
SOUTHAMPTON – Hampshire v Lancashire
LORD'S – Middlesex v Kent
TAUNTON – Somerset v Nottinghamshire
HASTINGS – Sussex v Essex
WORCESTER – Worcestershire v Surrey
HULL – Yorkshire v Gloucestershire

Sunday 3 August
CHELTENHAM – Gloucestershire v Hampshire
CANTERBURY – Kent v Glamorgan
MANCHESTER – Lancashire v Sussex
LORD'S – Middlesex v Essex
NORTHAMPTON – Northamptonshire v Surrey
NOTTINGHAM – Nottinghamshire v
    Leicestershire
WESTON-SUPER-MARE – Somerset v Worcestershire
LEEDS – Yorkshire v Derbyshire

Sunday 10 August
BUXTON – Derbyshire v Lancashire
CHELMSFORD – Essex v Hampshire
CHELTENHAM – Gloucestershire v Middlesex
LEICESTER – Leicestershire v Yorkshire
NORTHAMPTON – Northamptonshire v Somerset
EASTBOURNE – Sussex v Nottinghamshire
BIRMINGHAM – Warwickshire v Kent
WORCESTER – Worcestershire v Glamorgan

Sunday 17 August
SWANSEA – Glamorgan v Gloucestershire
FOLKESTONE – Kent v Essex
LORD'S – Middlesex v Nottinghamshire
WELLINGBOROUGH – Northamptonshire v
    Hampshire
TAUNTON – Somerset v Leicestershire
WORCESTER – Worcestershire v Derbyshire

Sunday 24 August
COLCHESTER – Essex v Worcestershire
BRISTOL – Gloucestershire v Somerset
SOUTHAMPTON – Hampshire v Derbyshire
MANCHESTER – Lancashire v Yorkshire
LEICESTER – Leicestershire v Northamptonshire
THE OVAL – Surrey v Kent
HOVE – Sussex v Middlesex
BIRMINGHAM – Warwickshire v Glamorgan

Sunday 31 August
DERBY – Derbyshire v Sussex
CARDIFF – Glamorgan v Middlesex
MANCHESTER – Lancashire v Essex
LEICESTER – Leicestershire v Warwickshire
NOTTINGHAM – Nottinghamshire v Hampshire
TAUNTON – Somerset v Surrey
WORCESTER – Worcestershire v Kent
SCARBOROUGH – Yorkshire v Northamptonshire

Sunday 7 September
CHESTERFIELD – Derbyshire v Gloucestershire
CHELMSFORD – Essex v Northamptonshire
BOURNEMOUTH – Hampshire v Middlesex
CANTERBURY – Kent v Yorkshire
NOTTINGHAM – Nottinghamshire v Lancashire
THE OVAL – Surrey v Leicestershire

HOVE – Sussex v Glamorgan
BIRMINGHAM – Warwickshire v Somerset

Benson and Hedges Cup

Saturday 10 May
CHELMSFORD – Essex v Sussex
BRISTOL – Gloucestershire v Glamorgan
CANTERBURY – Kent v Somerset
LORD'S – Middlesex v Surrey
NORTHAMPTON – Northamptonshire v Combined Us
NOTTINGHAM – Nottinghamshire v Derbyshire
LEEDS – Yorkshire v Warwickshire
GLASGOW – Scotland v Leicestershire

Wednesday 14 May
SOUTHAMPTON – Hampshire v Middlesex
MANCHESTER – Lancashire v Nottinghamshire
THE OVAL – Surrey v Kent
HOVE – Sussex v Gloucestershire
BIRMINGHAM – Warwickshire v Northamptonshire
WATFORD – Minor Counties v Essex
CAMBRIDGE – Combined Us v Worcestershire
GLASGOW – Scotland v Derbyshire

Saturday 17 May
CHESTERFIELD – Derbyshire v Lancashire
SWANSEA – Glamorgan v Minor Counties
BRISTOL – Gloucestershire v Essex
LEICESTER – Leicestershire v Nottinghamshire
TAUNTON – Somerset v Middlesex
THE OVAL – Surrey v Hampshire
BIRMINGHAM – Warwickshire v Combined Us
WORCESTER – Worcestershire v Yorkshire

Tuesday 20 May
CHELMSFORD – Essex v Glamorgan
CANTERBURY – Kent v Hampshire
LEICESTER – Leicestershire v Lancashire
NORTHAMPTON – Northamptonshire v
    Worcestershire
NOTTINGHAM – Nottinghamshire v Scotland
TAUNTON – Somerset v Surrey
HOVE – Sussex v Minor Counties
OXFORD – Combined Us v Yorkshire

Thursday 22 May
DERBY – Derbyshire v Leicestershire
CARDIFF – Glamorgan v Sussex
BOURNEMOUTH – Hampshire v Somerset
MANCHESTER – Lancashire v Scotland
LORD'S – Middlesex v Kent
WORCESTER – Worcestershire v Warwickshire
BRADFORD – Yorkshire v Northamptonshire
CHIPPENHAM – Minor Counties v Gloucestershire

Wednesday 11 June – Quarter-Finals
Wednesday 25 June – Semi-Finals
Saturday 19 July – Final (LORD'S)

Gillette Cup

Wednesday 2 July – First Round
EXETER – Devon v Cornwall
LORD'S – Middlesex v Ireland
NOTTINGHAM – Nottinghamshire v Durham
TAUNTON – Somerset v Worcestershire
THE OVAL – Surrey v Northamptonshire
HOVE – Sussex v Suffolk
BIRMINGHAM – Warwickshire v Oxfordshire

Wednesday 16 July – Second Round
DERBY – Derbyshire v Hampshire
LEICESTER – Leicestershire v Essex
NOTTINGHAM/CHESTER-LE-STREET –
   Nottinghamshire/Durham v Middlesex/Ireland
TAUNTON/WORCESTER – Somerset/Worcestershire
   v Lancashire
THE OVAL/NORTHAMPTON – Surrey/
   Northamptonshire v Gloucestershire
HOVE/MILDENHALL – Sussex/Suffolk v Glamorgan
BIRMINGHAM/OXFORD – Warwickshire/
   Oxfordshire v Devon/Cornwall
LEEDS – Yorkshire v Kent

Wednesday 30 July – Quarter-Finals
Wednesday 13 August – Semi-Finals
Saturday 6 September – Final (LORD'S)

Tilcon Trophy

Played at HARROGATE
Wednesday 25 June –
Thursday 26 June –
Friday 27 June – Final

Fenner Trophy

Played at SCARBOROUGH
Wednesday 27 August – Yorkshire v Hampshire
Thursday 28 August – Leicestershire v Sussex
Friday 29 August – Final

Warwick Under-25 Competition

Sunday 17 (or 24) August – Semi-Finals
Sunday 31 August – Final (BIRMINGHAM)

Courage Challenge Cup

International Batsman of the Year
Played at THE OVAL
Saturday 13 September (2 days)

PRUDENTIAL TROPHY RECORDS 1972–78   *Not out/unbroken

Highest Total	278–5	England v New Zealand	Manchester	1978
Lowest Total	70	Australia v England	Birmingham	1977
Highest Aggregate	531	India (265) v England (266–6)	Leeds	1974
Biggest Victories	8 wkts	West Indies beat England	The Oval	1973
	8 wkts	Pakistan beat England	Birmingham	1974
	132 runs	England beat Pakistan	Manchester	1978
Narrowest Victory	1 wkt	England beat West Indies	Leeds	1973
Highest Score	125*	G. S. Chappell: Australia v England	The Oval	1977
Fastest Hundred	88 balls	Majid Khan: Pakistan v England	Nottingham	1974
Highest Partnership for each Wicket				
1st	161	D. L. Amiss and J. M. Brearley: England v Australia	The Oval	1977
2nd	148	R. D. Robinson and G. S. Chappell: Australia v England	The Oval	1977
3rd	105	C. T. Radley and D. I. Gower: England v New Zealand	Manchester	1978
4th	105	D. I. Gower and G. R. J. Roope: England v Pakistan	The Oval	1978
5th	64	G. D. Barlow and G. A. Gooch: England v West Indies	Scarborough	1976
6th	42	A. W. Greig and A. P. E. Knott: England v India	Leeds	1974
7th	77	A. W. Greig and A. P. E. Knott: England v Australia	Lord's	1972
8th	68	B. E. Congdon and B. L. Cairns: New Zealand v England	Scarborough	1978
9th	40	R. W. Taylor and D. L. Underwood: England v Pakistan	Birmingham	1974
10th	24	Sikander Bakht and Liaquat Ali: Pakistan v England	Manchester	1978
Best Bowling	5–18	G. J. Cosier: A v E	Birmingham	1977
Most Economical Bowling	11–4–12–1	L. R. Gibbs: W I v E	The Oval	1973
Most Expensive Bowling	11–0–84–0	B. L. Cairns: N Z v E	Manchester	1978
Wicket-Keeping – Most Dismissals				
4 (all ct)		R. W. Marsh: Australia v England	Birmingham	1972
4 (all ct)		A. P. E. Knott: England v New Zealand	Swansea	1973
4 (all ct)		R. W. Marsh: Australia v England	Birmingham	1977
4 (3ct, 1st)		R. D. Robinson: Australia v England	The Oval	1977
Fielding – Most Catches				
3		A. W. Greig: England v West Indies	Leeds	1973
3		B. S. Bedi: India v England	Leeds	1974

CRICKETERS IN THE MAKING
Trevor Bailey

A coaching book written especially for all young cricketers by one of the foremost authorities on the game.

Using schoolboys aged 10 to 13 to depict all aspects of batting, bowling, fielding and tactics, Trevor Bailey emphasises that young players should be coached according to their physical development rather than by imitation of established cricketers.

Illustrated throughout with specially commissioned photographs by Patrick Eagar.
128pp   June 1980   £5.95

CRICKET CONTEST 1979/80
The Post-Packer Test Matches in Australia
Christopher Martin-Jenkins

All the drama and excitement of this winter's triangular tournament involving the top players from England, Australia and the West Indies captured by the BBC's cricket correspondent, Christopher Martin-Jenkins.
192pp   photographs   June 1980   £6.50

Available from booksellers, or in case of difficulty write to QAP Direct Sales, 9 Partridge Drive, Orpington, Kent, England, enclosing cheque/PO payable to Macdonald & Jane's Publishing Group + 10% for postage & packing (UK only). Allow up to 28 days for delivery from publication.

M&J Queen Anne Press